# Wellington's Military Machine

### Philip J Haythornthwaite

Guild Publishing
London

# Wellington's Military Machine

## Philip J Haythornthwaite

**In the Spellmount Military list:**

*The Territorial Battalions – A pictorial history*
*The Yeomanry Regiments – A pictorial history*
*Over the Rhine – The Last Days of War in Europe*
*History of the Cambridge University OTC*
*Yeoman Service*
*The Fighting Troops of the Austro-Hungarian Army*
*Sea of Memories*
*Intelligence Officer in the Peninsula*
*The Scottish Regiments – A pictorial history*
*The Royal Marines – A pictorial history*
*The Royal Tank Regiment – A pictorial history*
*The Irish Regiments – A pictorial history*
*British Sieges of the Peninsular War*
*Victoria's Victories*
*Heaven and Hell – German paratroop war diary*
*Rorke's Drift*

**In the Military Machine list:**

*Napoleon's Military Machine*
*Falkland's Military Machine*
*Wellington's Military Machine*

**In the Nautical list:**

*Sea of Memories*
*Evolution of Engineering in the Royal Navy Vol 1*
*1827-1939*

**In the Aviation list:**

*Diary of a Bomb Aimer*

---

This edition published in 1989 by
Book Club Associates
by arrangement with
Spellmount Ltd
12 Dene Way, Speldhurst,
Tunbridge Wells, Kent TN3 0NX

CN 3209

© Ravelin Limited 1989

Design by Ravelin Ltd, Braceborough, Lincs./Gareth Jones Design Associates, Langtoft, Lincs.
Figure artworks by Richard Scollins.
Typesetting by Vitaset, Paddock Wood, Kent.
Printed in Great Britain by W.S. Cowell Ltd, Ipswich, Suffolk.

# Wellington's Military Machine

# Introduction

Approximately 107 days before Letizia Buonaparte gave birth to her son Napoleone, at Ajaccio in Corsica on 15 August 1769, a fourth son was born to Garrett Wesley, 1st Earl of Mornington, probably in Dublin (both place and date of birth are not certain). One of these children was destined to become Emperor of half Europe; the other, his nemesis; and both among the greatest soldiers in history.

Arthur Wesley (the name was later changed to Wellesley) was not regarded by his family as capable of any other occupation than that of a soldier, so after Eton, was sent to a French military academy, his only apparent talent being the violin, and totally overshadowed by his brilliant elder brother Richard, later the diplomat and politician Marquess Wellesley. The Morningtons were not among the first rank of the British aristocracy, yet possessed sufficient influence and funds to push on Arthur in his new profession: commissioned at age 18, he rose through an array of regiments until he arrived at the command of the 33rd Foot in 1793 at age 24, having served in addition as ADC to the Lord-Lieutenant of Ireland and as Member of Parliament for Trim. Despite the beneficial influence of his brother Richard, the succeeding steps up the ladder of promotion were negotiated as a result of his own ability, which from the outset of his active military career was prodigious.

Wellesley commanded the 33rd Foot in the unsuccessful Netherlands campaign of 1794, when the deficiencies of the British Army became apparent; as he wrote later, 'There was a fellow called Hammerstein, who was considered the chief authority in the army for tactics, but was quite an imposter; in fact, no one knew anything of the management of an army, though many of the regiments were excellent.' As JF Neville (who served in the same campaign) remarked, 'It would be fulsome flattery to give the name of "AN ARMY" to an unwieldy concourse of men, necessarily ill-disciplined, from the fatal circumstance of their being ill-officered.' From this time, Arthur Wellesley began to study his profession seriously, and won

his reputation in India, having been granted his first independent command by his brother, the new Governor-General. India was the scene of his most important military education, where he learned not only the management of forces larger than a battalion, but how to organise and administer the supporting services of an army, a vital factor in his subsequent successes. Returning home to marry in 1805 (not a felicitous match: Catherine Pakenham, his fiancée of pre-Indian days, was somewhat below his intellectual plane and caused him much unintended annoyance), he became a Member of Parliament and Chief Secretary for Ireland, until his active military career resumed with the expeditions to Denmark and Portugal. From his return to Portugal in 1809, he enjoyed independent command in the field, and by 1814 was the foremost soldier in Europe. His meeting and defeat of Napoleon in the following year confirmed his position as Britain's greatest soldier since Marlborough, and arguably among the greatest two or three of all time.

It is difficult to encapsulate the characteristics or abilities which led to this position of prominence, and it is futile to compare him directly with Napoleon in the wider context. Napoleon was his own political master, and enjoyed 'unity of command': in matters military and political the policy was his own and his word was law. Wellington, though commanding his immediate forces without interference (by virtue of holding rank in allied armies as well as in his own), was not even free to select or reject his own subordinates, but had to bow to the will of the Ministry and those who controlled military and diplomatic policy. (He admitted to Robert Craufurd in 1810, 'Adverting to the number of General officers senior to you in the army, it has not been an easy task to keep you in your command.') The knowledge that the Peninsular army was virtually the only one which Britain possessed put many strictures upon his freedom of actions; as he recalled to Stanhope, 'I knew that in my early years in the Peninsula if I were to lose 500 men without the clearest necessity, I should be recalled, and

brought upon my knees to the bar of the House of Commons.'

Fear of recall was not the only reason why he was always unwilling to risk the lives of his army without necessity, and this was one of the sharpest contrasts with Napoleon; for not even the latter's most partisan supporters could claim him as a model of moral rectitude. Wellington, conversely, carried the concept of duty to king and country to its ultimate, coupled with scrupulous honesty (to the point of rudeness in correspondence). A child of the time and background from which he had risen, Wellington was no dissembler or placator of bruised feelings; the image of the austere, unfeeling and superior being who looked down his long nose at all those below him was a facade borne of necessity and the need to appear the self-confident master of every aspect of military affairs. That he *was* such a master is obvious, but its cause was not totally the result of innate genius but the product of assiduous study, ever-increasing experience and a capacity for unremitting toil.

Having a staff so small that it would have been insufficient for a French Corps commander, Wellington undertook the greater part of his work personally, partly because there were few of his subordinates whom he could trust to do their duty without supervision (though it may have impaired the development of capable generals like Hill). An iron constitution was a great asset which allowed him to ride for days on end, and an abhorrence of idleness and the inflexible rule to 'do the business of the day, in the day', were vital factors, but even so the volume of his work is quite staggering. Throughout the Peninsular War he devoted his time to the job in hand and lived frugally (his dinners were notoriously bad, though his staff found them convivial when he was in a good mood, and unbearable when out of humour).

*The Duke: the magnificent portrait by Sir Thomas Lawrence shows Wellington c1815 wearing the uniform of the general staff, with the sash of the Order of the Garter and the decorations of the GCB and the Spanish Order of the Golden Fleece.*

Nothing was too small to escape his notice, from the great affairs of state to the fact that he had noticed an incorrect medal-ribbon being worn; though in matters of uniform and equipment, he cared not how his men were dressed providing they had 60 rounds of ball-cartridge and adequate rations. His dispatches illustrate his energy; an indefatigable correspondent, he wrote most personally, at great speed. For example, on 20 October 1809 he drafted the instructions which put in motion the construction of the Lines of Torres Vedras, an immense and meticulous document; yet on the same day he sent three separate dispatches to Castlereagh concerning the Portuguese army, wrote to his enemy General Kellerman regarding the exchange of prisoners, wrote a cartel of exchange for the same purpose and even wrote personally to the French subaltern involved, Véron de Farincourt. The very volume of his correspondence is perhaps one reason for the curt and uncompromising language in which many letters were composed.

Although the hard mask concealed a compassionate heart (being moved to tears at the sight of casualty-returns), Wellington gave the appearance of a stern disciplinarian. In action a cooler head nor clearer brain can never have existed, and allied to his masterful eye for terrain and abilities in the handling of troops on the battlefield was a quite reckless disregard of danger which several times put him in perilous situations. Every where the fire was hottest, the fact that he suffered no more injury than bruising from spent balls is little short of miraculous and after Waterloo moved him to say that the finger of God must have been upon him. His constant presence in circumstances of greatest hazard was responsible to a considerable degree for the respect which he was accorded by the ordinary soldiers. None would say they loved him in the sense that Napoleon was worshipped by his followers, nor could the ordinary troops

ever have called him affectionate nicknames like Marlborough's 'Corporal John'; instead they referred to him by his aquiline nose, 'Beaky' or 'Hooky'. But they trusted him implicitly, that he would do his utmost to ensure their rations arrived, that he would not risk their lives unnecessarily and that under him they were completely confident of victory. As Kincaid of the 95th noted, 'We would rather see his long nose in a fight than a reinforcement of ten thousand men any day.' Fusilier Horsefield of the 7th spoke for the army as he advanced into the storm of shot at Albuera (from which carnage Wellington was absent): 'Whore's ar Arthur? Aw wish he wor here.'

Wellington's generals ranged between the extremely competent (like Hill), the brave but not always willing to follow orders (like Picton or Craufurd) to the totally incompetent, lazy or even deranged; and it was a considerable trial to Wellington that he had the greatest dif-

ficulty ridding himself of the latter. The army's regimental officers followed a similar mixture, though it was easier to be rid of the small number of rogues and cowards who found their way into the commissioned ranks. Although all officers had to be literate, military education was extremely limited. In the early years of the Revolutionary Wars, the officer corps was very bad in parts: JF Neville probably exaggerated when he wrote that commissions were thrown away on 'boys at school . . . the brother or relative of a *pretty prostitute* . . . the son of a low but opulent *mechanic*, by the means of a bribe, saw himself at the head of a troop of horse, which he had neither the courage nor the abilities to lead', but though a tiny minority, some shocking characters did find their way into high command; even a colonel of the Foot Guards was suspended after being prosecuted 58 times for debt in five years and for a criminal charge of gross indecency.

A young man might apply for a com-

mission if he could provide a recommendation and afford to purchase his rank (an ensigncy in a regiment of foot cost £400, for example). This led to an iniquitous practice of children being bought commissions by their family; before 1802, 20 per cent of new officers were under 15 years. William Howe DeLancey, head of the Quartermaster-General's Department at Waterloo, was apparently first commissioned at age 11, and Joseph Logan, who succeeded to the command of the 2/95th at Waterloo, was a lieutenant at age 12. The practice was ended by regulations which stated 'no person is considered eligible for a commission until he has attained the age of sixteen years', but even after 1802 half the new appointments were under 18. Promotion was largely by seniority, though additional 'steps' could be purchased (a lieutenancy £550, a captaincy £1,500, a lieutenant-colonelcy £3,500 in the line, for example; in more exalted regiments the price of the latter rank rose to £5,200 in the Life Guards). Though 'purchase' represented only a minority of promotions – less than 20 per cent in the line during the Peninsular War – it was extemely difficult for an officer to live on his pay of 5/3d per diem for an ensign, 10/6d for a captain, etc; in 1804 Sir John Moore remarked that a private income of £50 to £100 p.a. was really necessary. Even basic equipment was expensive: the regimental sabre of the 52nd (at four guineas) represented 16 days' pay for an ensign, and whilst an impoverished officer might buy his kit for under £60, he would feel very inferior to peacocks like Capt Hobkirk of the 43rd who was reputed to spend almost £1,000 p.a. on his uniform alone.

Promotion by seniority could be very slow, as 'brevet' promotions for valour did not normally count as regimental 'steps'. New commissions could be attained by enlisting a certain number of recruits (such as 40 militiamen; ultimately almost 20 per cent of commissions came this way), and a further 4½ per

cent were from 'volunteers', young gentlemen who were allowed by a battalion commander to serve in the ranks (but live with the officers) until death created a vacancy. Only after 1809 was the 'purchase' system regulated to prevent incompetents buying their way to high command; but whatever the ills of the system, it worked remarkably well and allowed those of genuine talent (such as Wellington himself) to make a flying start to a career and thus achieve high command at an early age.

Though officers were predominantly gentry and middle-class, promotion from the ranks was not impossible, and (excluding the Veteran Battalions, whose officers were almost all ex-NCOs) more than 5 per cent rose in this manner, though they were usually confined to the more unfashionable regiments. The two most notable exceptions were Sir John Elley of the Royal Horse Guards and James I Hamilton of the 2nd Dragoons, rising to command from being the humble offspring of an eating-house keeper and a sergeant-major respectively. (Wellington did not approve of such promotions: he claimed such men could never resist drink, when 'their low origin then came out, and you could never perfectly trust them'!) Such officers were not popular with the rank-and-file either; as Rifleman Harris remarked, respect required 'one who has authority in his face . . . command does not suit ignorant and coarse-minded men'.

Wellington's most misunderstood

comment is his reference to his men as 'the scum of the earth'; actually he added, 'it is really wonderful that we should have made them the fine fellows they are.' His meaning was that the rank-and-file were drawn from the lowest members of society: as one veteran admitted, 'whoever "listed for a soldier" was at once set down among a catalogue of persons who had turned out ill'. Unlike many armies, enlistment was entirely voluntary, despite Wellington's plea that 'we must compose our army of soldiers drawn from all classes of the population; from the good and middling, as well in rank as in education, as from the bad . . . ' As it was, conditions were so bad that only the impoverished or desperate would enlist willingly, plus a few actuated by what Wellington called 'fine military feeling', but most, he thought, enrolled from 'having got bastard children', or fleeing justice, or 'many more for drink'. To a degree the army was a refuge for the criminal (one officer estimated that every regiment contained from 50 to 100 incorrigibles), but simple poverty was the motivation for many enlistments. Men received a 'bounty' on enlisting (£7 12s 6d in 1803 rising to £23 17s 6d in 1812 for those enlisting for life, and five guineas less for a seven year enlistment; the vast majority enlisted for life). This bounty was often consumed by purchase of 'necessaries' and the buying of drinks for the recruiting-party, but remained a great temptation to a man existing at subsistence level (in 1787 a man was hanged for taking 49 bounties, deserting each time!); and deception by the recruiting-sergeants also played a sad part, each man bringing the recruiting-officer 16/-, the recruiting-party 15/6d and the 'bringer of the recruit' (often a publican) £2 12s 6d, thus making it worth their while to entrap a drunk or delude a yokel with tales of rapid promotion and the glories of military life.

Such glories were few; the 1/- per day wage was consumed by stoppages (4d per week for laundry etc), food to supplement the meagre ration, and the perpetual scourge of alcohol to bring temporary relief. Discipline was savage, with execution or transfer to penal corps being one method of punishment, but the lash was the commonest. Tied to a 'triangle' of sergeants' spontoons, the miscreant would be flogged across the back by a 'cat', and though the maximum of 1,200 lashes was rarely inflicted, 1,000 was not uncommon and 3-700 commonplace. The injury it caused was appalling, but even the rank-and-file accepted it as a necessary way of controlling the worst elements; one admitted that a flogging saved him from a life of evil, Harris of the 95th stated that 'I detest the sight of the lash, but I am convinced the British army can never go on without it', and Cooper of the 7th agreed that it was the only way of controlling an army 'composed of the lowest orders. Many, if not most of them, were ignorant, idle and drunken'. Throughout the period, only one officer was convicted of using the lash unjustly (Col Archdall of the 1/40th in 1813, and that perhaps unfairly), though the general belief that the most floggings occurred in units with the worst commanders seems borne out by the hideous catalogue of punishments imposed by Quentin of the 10th Hussars.

The general impression is of the British Army being composed of somewhat patient men, determined and brave in a stolid manner, fighting as a duty rather than from resentment (though many would doubtless have agreed with Neville who remarked, as he saw the Princesse de Lamballe's head carried past on a pike, 'How grateful should I not be to the Almighty, for not having made me a Frenchman'!) They regarded fighting as a matter of fact; an English lady who spoke to men immediately after Waterloo found them not the slightest

*Grenadier sergeant, 2nd (Coldstream) Guards, 1792. The uniform is typical of that worn by the infantry prior to the adoption of the closed jacket, but the cap is that peculiar to the regiment. (print after Edward Dayes)*

bit proud of what they had done but regarding the victory as 'quite a matter of course'. Unlike the French, the British were not susceptible to theatrical exhortations of the kind Napoleon used to encourage his men, and would have regarded such as nonsense. Bell of the 34th recorded the speech of Col Brown of the 28th at St Pierre: 'There they come boys; if you don't kill them, they'll kill you; fire away.' Bell added: 'This was the longest address he ever made to his men. He never had but one book, and that was the Army List.' This was altogether typical.

But they were no unfeeling lumps, as George Napier was at pains to point out, quoting the case of an Irish private in his company, John Dunn. After both Napier and his brother were wounded, Pte Dunn came to enquire after their health, walking seven miles from his bivouac: 'I'm come to see how you and your brother is after the wounds. Didn't I see you knocked over by the bloody Frenchmen's shot? And sure I thought you was kilt. But myself knew you wouldn't be plaised if I didn't folly on after the villains, so I was afeard to go pick you up

when ye was kilt, long life to you! But I pursued the inimy as long as I was able, and sure I couldn't do more; and now I'm come to see your honour.' Napier saw that Dunn was bandaged: 'Why sure it's nothing, only me arrum was cut off a few hours ago below the elbow joint, and I couldn't come till the anguish was over a bit. But now I'm here, and thank God your honour's arrum is not cut off, for it's mighty cruel work; by Jasus, I'd rather be shot twinty times.' Napier then enquired of Dunn's brother: 'I seed him shot through the heart alongside wid me just as I got shot myself . . . but, captain, he died like a soldier, as your honour would wish him to die, and sure that's enough. He had your favour whilst he lived, God be with him, he's gone now.'

Dunn was a reprobate and a drunkard but, wrote Napier, to walk seven miles after amputation, without food or drink and in the midst of bereavement just to see if he could help his officer was, he said, typical; and exhorted his sons 'whenever you see a poor lame soldier, recollect John Dunn, and never . . . pass him coldly by.' Thus is the refutation of the term 'scum of the earth'.

The Napoleonic Wars were the most memorable – even traumatic – events which their participants experienced, and the careers of Wellington's men after 1815 were as diverse as their backgrounds. Some rose to high office: Fitzroy Somerset, who lost an arm at Waterloo, died in command of the British forces in the Crimea, and William Elphinstone, who commanded the 33rd at Waterloo, led a British army to destruction in Afghanistan in 1842. Those who survived had great physical resilience: Thomas Noel Harris, who also lost an arm at Waterloo, swam one-armed for two miles after his yacht sank off Portsmouth, whilst in advanced old age John Bush, ex-1st Guards, emerged unscathed after falling down a 60ft well. Some went on to serve in foreign armies: Lt Anthony Bacon of the 10th Hussars, who lay wounded all night on the field of Waterloo, became a Portuguese general; John Cross, a gunner at Trafalgar, was murdered by the Mexicans at Goliad whilst fighting for the independence of Texas in 1836. John Wilson was so impoverished after his discharge from HMS *Namur* in 1814 that he was arrested for stealing a pair of boots; Lt-Col James Poole of the 2nd Dragoons suffered

derangement from a head wound at Waterloo and killed himself with an opium overdose in 1817, aged 31. George Gleig of the 85th took holy orders and wrote military history; Enoch Hall, who had fought through the Pyrenees and later guarded the captive Napoleon, returned home to become village schoolmaster at Elslack in the West Riding, forebearing to use his cane only on the anniversary of Napoleon's arrival at St Helena. Sir George Grey, a Peninsular veteran by virtue of being born in Lisbon eight days after the death of his father (Lt-Col of the 30th) at Badajoz, became premier of New Zealand; the last British eye-witness of Waterloo, Elizabeth Gale (a soldier's child who recalled cutting up dressings at age 5) was still alive in 1903. John Spencer Cooper, veteran of 21 actions with the 7th Fuzileers, received a pension of 1/- per diem, not granted until 50 years after his discharge, a typical example of neglect. Marine William Corfield was indicted for throwing a prostitute from a second-floor window under suspicion of

*One of the most famous incidents of Waterloo was the apprehension of the French general Cambronne by Col Hew Halkett who commanded the 3rd Hanoverian Brigade, who seized the general's aiguillette as he tried to escape capture.*

stealing his money; Lt J Pierie RN was executed for piracy in 1817; Capt EB Balguy of the York Chasseurs, a man with a heroic combat record, was cashiered for getting drunk to celebrate the Peninsular victory. Artillery Driver Edmund Law (alias 'Owd Bogy'), who had used the spoke of a wheel as a club at Waterloo, became a street-sweeper in Rochdale and asked to be buried standing, so that (like a good soldier) 'when the trumpet sounds, Bogy should like to be off'. Roderick Murchison, who carried the Colours of the 36th at Vimeiro, became Britain's leading geologist and postulator of the Silurian system. Humphrey Allen (alias 'Long Tom of Lincoln') was one of the smartest men in the 95th and renowned for the 'crime' of shooting a French sentry because 'I arn't had

nought to eat these two days, and thought as how I might find summat in the Frencher's knapsack'; he ended his days scavenging for bones in Knightsbridge.

Wellington himself lived a long and distinguished life, loaded with honours, attaining every high office of state, and surviving a brief period of unpopularity as a fearless Prime Minister became the mentor and idol of the young Queen Victoria. When at the end of Waterloo an aide cautioned him for exposing himself to the French fire, Wellington remarked, 'The battle's won; my life is of no consequence now', and the same attitude he carried into political life. When as Prime Minister a mob broke the windows of his London house he simply erected iron shutters and continued the policies he believed right; and hence the nickname 'the Iron Duke'. When he died at Walmer Castle in 1852 (when *The Times* described his career as 'one unclouded longest day') he was, simply, the greatest Britisher of his generation. No one deserved the appelation more: the Great Duke.

11

# Chapter One: THE CAVALRY

Compared to the vast mounted corps employed by other armies, British cavalry forces were small in number. Until the middle of the Peninsular War large numbers of cavalry were not required, as until the British Army progressed into Spain the terrain was not suitable for the deployment of large mounted forces. Wellington was even inclined to refuse the opportunity of acquiring more, though by late summer 1811 he was writing to Lord Liverpool that he believed he could not have too many. In May 1809 there were only 3,134 British cavalrymen in Portugal (13.5 per cent of the whole); 2,969 at Talavera; and 1,854 at Fuentes de Oñoro (representing 4.9 per cent of the entire army). Latterly the numbers rose, but the percentage of the whole remained small; there were 3,543 at Salamanca, plus 482 Portuguese, representing 8.2 per cent; and for the Vittoria campaign, in May 1813 there were 8,317 Anglo-Portuguese cavalry, which was 10.2 per cent of the army.

There were three types of cavalry in British service, though the distinction was blurred. Senior were the Household regiments, two of Life Guards and the Royal Horse Guards (the Blues); the remaining regiments were all styled 'Dragoons', though the original function of dragoons as mounted infantry who rode into action and fought on foot was totally lost. Senior of the 'line' cavalry were the seven regiments of Dragoon Guards, which with the six regiments of Dragoons formed the army's heavy cavalry. The light regiments, numbered in succession after the Dragoons, were styled Light Dragoons. Theoretically, the heavy regiments were intended for use as 'shock' troops, utilising the impetus of the charge; the light regiments were equally adept at this action, and also trained for 'outpost' duty, i.e. scouting, skirmishing and forming the chain of vedettes which preceded the army on campaign and protected lines of communication. The whole cavalry force was organised as a Division of a number of brigades of two regiments each; occasionally brigades might consist of three or even one regiment. The heavy and light regiments

were usually kept separate, the latter being intended for 'outpost' duties; but in practice, the heavy regiments were also sometimes used in this role. Such was the lack of practical training that most were quite unprepared for the duties expected of them, and had to learn the necessary skills once they had embarked on campaign, rendering newly-arrived regiments of only very limited value for a period. (A notable exception were the regiments of the King's German Legion, recognised as the best 'outpost' troops from the beginning.) Unfortunately, the process of learning on campaign not infrequently involved sharp reverses.

At the outbreak of war the small establishments of line cavalry regiments (about 220 of all ranks) was increased to about 530 organised in nine troops, though in the 1794 campaign all except one regiment still had the pre-war six-troop establishment, of which two were always left at home as a depot squadron; so that all except the 1st Dragoon Guards (six troops) had only four troops on active service, organised in two squadrons. In 1800 the establishment of line regiments was increased to ten troops of around 90 rank-and-file each; two formed the depot, so for active service most regiments had eight troops in four squadrons. Actual strength varied with circumstance, and in 1811 it was ordered that regimental strength be reduced to six 'service' troops. In September 1813 light regiments, which had previously had 10 troops, were ordered to increase their establishment to 12 (usually lettered A to M), still of squadrons of two troops each, and still keeping two troops at home to form the depot. Each troop was usually commanded by a captain (prior to 1803 field officers also commanded troops; extra captains were added at that date to relieve the field ranks of such duties) and included one or more lieutenants and a cornet (2nd lieutenant), NCOs, a trumpeter and a number of troopers; in 1793 a typical establishment of 'other ranks' was 3 sergeants, 3 corporals, 1 trumpeter and 47 'private men'.

On active service, regiments were usually well below the established

strength, and often averaged less than 400. Average regimental strength in the Peninsula in May 1809 (before the attrition of campaign) was 614; at Fuentes de Oñoro 385; at Albuera 386; at Salamanca 354; at the start of the Vittoria campaign, 412 (376 when the Portuguese are included). (These statistics generally refer only to British cavalry; when Portuguese regiments are included, the average strength is reduced due to the Portuguese being very weak.)

A factor allied to the cavalry's ignorance of proper training was leadership; few regimental commanders were really bad, but throughout the entire period Britain produced only two really proficient cavalry generals, Lord Paget (later Marquess of Anglesey) who was distinguished in the Corunna campaign but saw no extensive service from then until Waterloo, due in part to a family quarrel with Wellington (Paget having eloped with Wellington's sister-in-law); and JG Le Marchant, who was killed in his first major command, at Salamanca. Of the remainder, Stapleton Cotton (later Lord Combermere) was reliable and competent; poor Sir William Erskine was generally believed to be a madman, was probably certifiable and committed suicide in 1813; 'Jack' Slade was thought of as a coward and was unfit, Wellington believed, to command even a depot squadron; the Hanoverian Baron von Bock was so short-sighted that he had to be pointed in the general direction of the enemy, even in his triumph at Garcia Hernandez; and RB Long, though a worthy man, was an incompetent who only half(?) in jest wrote that he should have planted cabbages rather than commanded cavalry!

*The 1st Life Guards, 1814. The uniform is that worn at Waterloo, including the 1814 helmet with black over red crest, and scarlet jacket with blue facings; on campaign grey overalls were used. The trumpeter wears ceremonial 'state dress'. (Print after CH Smith.)*

FIRST REGIMENT of LIFE GUARDS.

13

# The Heavy Cavalry

The senior of the heavy cavalry regiments were those accorded the distinction of being 'Household' cavalry, i.e. originally the bodyguard of the sovereign. As a result of this unique position, the Household regiments traditionally only took the field if the sovereign were present in person. The two regiments of Life Guards (formed in 1788 by the reorganisation of the previous independent troops) thus saw no active service between the battle of Fontenoy (1745) and 1812. The third 'Household' regiment (though that status was not perfectly defined at the time) was the Royal Horse Guards (The Blues), formed in 1661 and still occasionally referred to as the 'Oxford Blues', an appellation introduced in the reign of King William III to distinguish the regiment from the king's own Dutch 'Blue Horse Guards'. The regiment last served abroad in 1761, but unlike the Life Guards contributed four troops to the Netherlands campaign of 1793-94, and remained in Hanover until 1796. During this campaign the unit distinguished itself at Le Cateau in 1794, and became the only British cavalry unit to wear cuirasses, albeit briefly, on active service during the period. At the same time it is believed that they were issued with iron skull-caps, like the 'secretes' of the 17th century, to wear inside their hats, but it is doubtful whether they were ever actually used.

In 1812 it was decided to send to the Peninsula two squadrons of each of the three Household regiments, almost half the total strength, which troops participated in the latter stages of the Peninsular War, through which they served with considerable reputation despite contrasting markedly with the appearance of the weather-beaten veterans of the other regiments: Leach of the 95th referred to the Life Guards as 'fair and beautiful as lilies'! Well though they behaved, their officers were generally inexperienced and not as efficient as their more tested comrades of the line

*A trooper of the 1st (Royal) Dragoons (centre) wearing the heavy cavalry uniform pre-dating the 1812 regulations. Left: a grenadier of the 4th Foot; right: a Highland NCO (Print from Goddard & Booth's Military Costume of Europe, 1812).*

regiments; the lieutenant-colonel of the 2nd Life Guards was reported to Wellington on arriving in the Peninsula as not only lacking enthusiasm but ignorant of even the basics of regimental duty. In spite of the elevated social position of the Household Cavalry, the officers who went on active service do not seem to have been unusually aristocratic; of those who served in the Waterloo campaign, in which the 1st and 2nd Life Guards each contributed two squadrons and the RHG a full complement, only four were the sons or heirs of peers, three the sons of baronets and one a knight (excluding Wellington himself the regimental colonel of the Blues). The knight, Sir John Elley, had risen by his own merit from the ranks, the son of an eating-house keeper, whose career proves that 'influence' or patronage were not absolute necessities for success in even the most fashionable regiments.

An example of how many years of home service could undermine the calibre of officer is provided in the scurrilous humorous poem *The Blueviad*

written in 1805 by an RHG subaltern, Edward Goulburn. Therein, officers were accorded pseudonyms like 'Pomposo', 'Silenus', 'Tom Slang', 'Numscull', 'Slipslop' and 'Macsycophant', all of which are fairly descriptive of their alleged character, and one of the most distinguished officers of the era was styled 'Lothario': 'Wife Maid or Virgin, are to him the same/And each at his desire, must yield their fame'; whilst others are accused of drunkenness, selling unsound horses, foul language and even indecent exposure. Three of the 25 named officers sued Goulburn for libel, and though they won the case the fine imposed on Goulburn was very small, the judge according the prosecutors as much censure as he did the author. Nevertheless, despite the unfortunate effects of such lack of campaign experience, the Household regiments did all that could be expected of them in battle and were especially distinguished at Waterloo.

An unusual feature of the Life Guards' organisation was their original formation in five troops, each of which comprised three companies of 50 men, instead of the more usual organisation in

14

squadrons of two troops each; the term 'squadron' was used later in the more usual sense to prevent confusion. A sixth troop was added to each regiment of Life Guards in 1799 but appears to have been of short duration.

There was no intrinsic difference between the remaining heavy cavalry regiments, despite the appellations 'Dragoon Guards' and 'Dragoons', the different titles simply arising from the conversion to Dragoon Guards of the original Regiments of Horse in 1746. The senior regiment was the 1st (King's) Dragoon Guards, raised 1685, which saw no active service between 1762 and the Netherlands campaign of 1793. After returning from the continent in 1796 the regiment was stationed at home until 1815, when it served with the Household Cavalry in the Waterloo campaign with great distinction. The 2nd (Queen's) Dragoon Guards, also known by the title adopted officially only in 1872 as the 'Queen's Bays', similarly

*Officer, Life Guards, 1813, in the uniform worn in the later Peninsular War. The 1812-regulation uniform included the unpopular 'classical' leather helmet with horsehair mane; for the Household Cavalry the mane was replaced by a blue and red woollen crest in 1814. Both regiments of Life Guards wore blue facings and yellow lace (gold for officers). Overalls were more practical than the breeches and long boots and were worn at Waterloo.*

served in the Netherlands in 1793-95, but next went abroad in 1815 after the battle of Waterloo. The 3rd (Prince of Wales') Dragoon Guards served in the Netherlands and throughout the Peninsular War, joining the army in 1809 and fighting at Talavera, Albuera and Vittoria; like the 2nd, it only joined the army in Belgium after Waterloo.

The 4th (Royal Irish) Dragoon Guards served in the Peninsula from 1811, without participating in any major action. The 5th Dragoon Guards (titled 'Princess Charlotte of Wales's' from 1804) served in the Netherlands in 1793-95, and was present in Ireland during the '98' rebellion. It served in the Peninsula, at Salamanca, Vittoria and Toulouse. The 6th Dragoon Guards (Carabiniers) (whose title did *not* arise from any special form of carbine carried by the unit) served in the Netherlands and Germany in 1793-96, and was employed in a dismounted role in the South American expedition of 1807. It saw no further active service until the Crimean War. The 7th (Princess Royal's) Dragoon Guards, unique among its fellows, saw no overseas service at all throughout the period; its 'home' posting (much of which time was spent in Ireland) lasted from 1762 until 1842.

The remaining six regiments of heavy cavalry were all styled 'Dragoons' and ranked inferior to the Dragoon Guards. Senior was the 1st (Royal) Dragoons, a unit which saw much service: in the Netherlands and Germany 1793-95 and in the Peninsula from 1809, including the campaigns of Vittoria and Toulouse; and was greatly distinguished at Waterloo as part of the 'Union' Brigade (so named from its component regiments from England, Scotland and Ireland representing the union of kingdoms within Great Britain). The 2nd (Royal North British) Dragoons was better known as the Royal Scots Greys, a title of great antiquity but not officially accorded to the regiment until 1877. The only regiment of regular cavalry which was truly Scottish in composition, it served in the Netherlands and Germany in 1793-95, but saw no more active service until Waterloo, when it became especially famous as part of the 'Union Brigade' in the action in which it captured the 'Eagle' of the French 45th Line. The 3rd (King's Own) Dragoons was stationed at home throughout the Revolutionary Wars, but participated in the Walcheren expedition of 1809, went to the Peninsula in 1811 and fought at Salamanca, Vittoria and Toulouse. The 4th (Queen's Own) Dragoons went to the Peninsula in 1809, and served at Talavera, Busaco, Albuera, Salamanca, Vittoria, the Pyrenees and at Toulouse.

The 5th (Royal Irish) Dragoons occupied a unique place in the Army List of the Napoleonic Wars, in that its number was the only one in either cavalry or infantry lists which was vacant. The unit had served in Ireland almost from the end of Marlborough's campaigns, a period of garrison duty which appears gradually to have worn down the regiment's efficiency; generally it served in small detachments on semi-police, semi-excise duties and assembled as a regiment only for the annual inspection. Its state was not unusual for regiments in such situations, and its 1797 inspection reported it as entirely unfit for active service, but when the 1798 rebellion broke out it

served with honour. Unfortunately it enlisted a number of recruits who were rebels in disguise, and who schemed a massacre of the officers and loyal soldiers. The plot was discovered before it could be enacted, but the regiment was disbanded at Chatham in April 1799, its officers and men being transferred to other corps. As a mark of official disapproval for what was seen as the evidence of disloyalty within the regiment (albeit restricted only to a portion of the whole), the number '5' remained unoccupied until 1858 when a new 5th Dragoons was formed.

The 6th (Inniskilling) Dragoons, another Irish regiment, served in the Netherlands and Germany in 1793-95, and then, like its Scottish companion in the 'Union Brigade' at Waterloo, saw no further active service until 1815.

The equipment of the heavy cavalry was generally of a standard pattern for all regiments, with only minor variations in

insignia, colour of facings and design of officers' lace. All wore red coats save the Royal Horse Guards, who retained the traditional blue uniforms with scarlet facings which had given rise to their sobriquet 'The Blues'. Head-dress was the bicorn hat which had evolved from the tricorn of the 18th century, not a very practical item which tended to collapse in wet weather; 'watering caps' officially reserved for undress uniform, resembling shakos, were a preferred alternative. The bicorn continued in use, units in the Peninsula improvising hats from surplus Portuguese head-dress to replace their own worn-out headgear; until the introduction in 1812 of peaked leather helmets with a brass comb from which fell a horsehair mane, worn with a new single-breasted jacket which dispensed with the colourful lace loops which had decorated the breast of the previous pattern. This new uniform, French in style, was introduced despite the protests of those in the Peninsula; Wellington complained that changing the army's appearance in 1812 could only lead to confusion, when at a distance the shape of the head-dress, rather than the colour of uniform, was the most useful aid to recognition. The French-style uniform was worn in the later stages of the Peninsular War and at Waterloo, despite continuing protests such as that in the *Royal Military Chronicle* of January 1813 that the heavy cavalry 'who had one of the handsomest uniforms in any service, are now a sort of modern antique without a similarity, unless, indeed, in the older wardrobes of some of the theatres'. In 1814 the horsehair names on the helmets of the Life Guards and Royal Horse Guards were replaced by woollen combs. The only regiment to escape the French-style helmet was the 2nd Dragoons, who throughout the period continued to wear their traditional fur grenadier caps.

The cavalry began the Revolutionary Wars armed with the 1788-pattern sabre, not an ideal weapon for either the thrust or the cut, and compared unfavourably with the equipment of the Austrian

*This trooper of Dragoons is taken from* Picturesque Representation of the Dress and Manners of the English (*London 1814) and provides a very reasonable general impression of the heavy cavalry's 1812 uniform.*

*Trooper, 1st (Royal) Dragoons, 1810, in Peninsular campaign dress. The Royals wore the standard red jacket with blue facings and yellow lace, and long boots and breeches instead of the overalls adopted in 1811. The regiment was so famously ragged by 1811 – having received no new hats for three years – that when new clothing was received it was distributed bit by bit so that the army would not mistake them for another unit!*

cavalry with which some British regiments were brigaded in the Netherlands in 1793-94 (when it was found, in the opinion of JG Le Marchant, the intelligent cavalry leader killed at Salamanca, that the Austrians were as superior in training and experience to the British cavalry as the British regulars were to the London militia). Le Marchant, then a troop officer of the Queen's Bays, was responsible for the 1796 manual which reformed cavalry training and weapon-handling, *Rules & Regulations for the Sword Exercise of Cavalry*. Many European experts believed that the thrust was the most effective mode of using the sabre; Le Marchant's manual stated the opposite, that once parried the thrust was incapable of swift recovery, instead urging the cut or slash as the preferred stroke, and contrary to the practice of the French heavy cavalry, the cut was the blow adopted by the British cavalry from that date. New sabres were designed in 1796, that of the heavy regiments being a heavy, unbalanced, cleaver-like weapon which often had a deliberately-blunted point ensuring that the cut had to be used (before the Waterloo campaign many regiments ground their sabres to a point, to enable the thrust to be executed). Styled on the sabre of the Austrian heavy cavalry, the British 1796 sword had a pierced 'disc' guard and a single knuckle-bow, providing only mediocre protection for the hand; yet it remained in use throughout the period. One critic writing anonymously in the *United Service Journal* in 1831 condemned it as a 'lumbering, clumsy, ill-contrived machine. It is too heavy, too short, too broad, too much like the sort of weapon which we have seen Grimaldi cut off the heads of a line of urchins on the stage'. In combat it caused hideous injury; though as one British dragoon noted, though it delivered a fearful chop, it caused far fewer fatalities than did the thrust of the French cavalry sabre.

Cavalry regiments were equipped with firearms, though their use was negligible, especially in the heavy regiments. There existed a wide variety of carbines or cavalry muskets; the initial cavalry musket, as carried by the 'heavies', was reported as inefficient and cumbersome in 1796, when it was recommended that the weapon be cut down in length and instead of being carried in a 'bucket' at the side of the saddle, for a swivel bar to be added allowing for its suspension from the shoulder-belt in the manner of a true carbine. Typical of the redundancy of the carbine in the heavy regiments was Stapleton Cotton's withdrawing of all but six per troop from the Household Cavalry in 1813, as they were troops never called upon to skirmish.

All cavalry were also armed with pistols, of no use in combat; as the *United Service Journal* critic noted, 'We never saw a pistol made use of except to shoot a glandered horse'. Nevertheless, a large variety existed: lack of standardised bores meant that two sets of ammunition often had to be carried, for carbine and pistol. Attempts were made unofficially to adapt the former's cartridge for the pistol by shaking out half the powder, but any confusion would lead to the recoil blowing the pistol from the hand. The 1796 pistol had the ramrod carried in the holster, not a practical method which led to the re-introduction of the previous style and the adoption of swivels which prevented the ramrod from being lost.

# The Light Dragoons

Light Dragoons originated in the late 1750s and early '60s, when the value of 'light horse' became appreciated: regiments which theoretically maintained the 'shock' ability of the charge but in addition were capable of acting as the mounted equivalent of light infantry: as scouts, skirmishers and the army's 'outposts' or vedettes. Thus, the dragoon regiments numbered 7 and upwards were styled 'light dragoons', though it is debatable whether in practice their training was any different from that of the heavy regiments. As numerous contemporary writers testify, the training accorded them in England sent them on campaign quite unfitted for the role expected of them; as Tomkinson of the 16th Light Dragoons complained, 'to attempt to give men or officers any idea of outpost duties was considered absurd', and Ludlow Beamish of the King's German Legion wrote in 1827 that the domestic drill consisted of elaborate parade-ground manoeuvres of negligible use on campaign, 'which, like Chinese puzzles, only engross time and labour to the unprofitable end of forming useless combinations'. Consequently, regiments had to learn their duties actually on campaign, and hence the frequent comments from Wellington and others that newly-arrived regiments were not half so reliable as those which had been with the army some time.

Nevertheless, despite the lack of training (and officers capable of instructing), once regiments had experienced some active service they did perform their duties with distinction; though it was acknowledged universally in the Peninsular army that none were so proficient as the light dragoons of the King's German Legion in 'outpost' duties, these being commanded in general by experienced German officers. Despite the realisation that instruction in skirmishing and 'outpost' duties was necessary, even towards the end of the Peninsular War newly-arrived regiments gave cause for concern in this and in their general proficiency; most of the more glaring examples of lack of control or experience in combat befell units whose campaign service was limited. Set against this was the high standard of the experienced corps; perhaps the most

outstanding example of an 'outpost' action was the capture of an enemy patrol by Corporal William Hanley of the 14th Light Dragoons at Blascho Sancho in July 1811, his regiment significantly having served continuously in the Peninsula since 1808.

Four regiments of Light Dragoons were converted to Hussars (7th, 10th, 15th and 18th) and are thus covered on pp. 20-21; the other light regiments were as follows:

The 8th (King's Royal Irish) Light Dragoons singularly distinguished itself in the Netherlands in 1793-94, was at the Cape in 1796 and sent a detachment to Egypt in 1801-02, but for the remainder of the Napoleonic Wars served in India. The 9th Light Dragoons served in Ireland during the ''98' rebellion, its arrival in England in 1803 ending 86 years of service in Ireland; it went on the South American expedition in 1806 (and was wrecked off Cornwall upon its return), served at Walcheren, and from 1811 was with the Peninsular army, without ever being engaged in a major action.

The 11th Light Dragoons was split into two sections in the mid-1790s, two squadrons serving in the West Indies (at Martinique and Guadeloupe) and the remainder in the Netherlands and Germany in 1793-95, less a detachment which formed part of the escort to Lord Macartney's embassy to China. The regiment served in north Holland in 1799, part in Egypt, and in the 1805 expedition to Hanover; in the Peninsular War it served in 1811-12 (including at Salamanca) and at Waterloo. The 12th (Prince of Wales') Light Dragoons began its active service in the Revolutionary Wars in a most singular manner for cavalrymen, serving dismounted (virtually as marines) with Lord Hood's fleet at Toulon and in Corsica. From 1797 to 1800 it was in Portugal, in Egypt in 1801 and at Walcheren in 1809; in the Peninsula from 1811 and at Waterloo. The 13th Light Dragoons went to the West Indies in 1796 (Barbados, San Domingo and Jamaica) from where it returned in 1798 'a complete skeleton . . . consisting of not more than thirty-five worn out Non-Commissioned Officers', ravaged by sickness. Reconstructed in England, in 1810 the regiment

*Officer, 13th Light Dragoons, 1810. The braided jacket or dolman with coloured facings (pale buff for the 13th) was worn until the adoption of the 1812-pattern uniform, which was generally so slow in being introduced that it was probably not universal until 1813 or 1814. The fur-crested, leather 'Tarleton' helmet originally had a fabric turban of the facing-colour, but from the late 1790s this was usually black; at the same time the facing-coloured plume changed to the national colour of white over red.*

*At Campo Mayor (25 March 1811) a successful cavalry charge failed due to the inability to rally. In a celebrated single combat, Corporal Logan of the 13th Light Dragoons killed Col Chamorin of the French 26th Dragoons; in this print after Denis Dighton Logan erroneously wears the 1812 uniform instead of the 'Tarleton' and braided dolman actually in use.*

went to the Peninsula, serving at Albuera, Vittoria, Orthez and Toulouse, and at Waterloo.

The 14th Light Dragoons (Duchess of York's Own from 1798) provided two squadrons for the Netherlands in 1794, and went to the West Indies in 1796, serving at San Domingo; in 1808 it went to the Peninsula and served throughout the war, at Talavera, Fuentes de Oñoro, Salamanca, Vittoria and Orthez, with great distinction; upon conclusion of peace it went to Jamaica, from where two squadrons served dismounted at New Orleans. The 16th (Queen's) Light Dragoons served in the West Indies in 1794, and then in the Netherlands and Germany until 1796. From 1809 it was in the Peninsula, at Talavera, Fuentes de Oñoro, Salamanca, Vittoria and Nive, and at Waterloo. The 17th Light Dragoons served in the West Indies in the 1790s, two troops serving as marines; a detachment was in the Ostend expedition of 1798. The regiment went to South America in 1806-07, thence to the Cape and spent the remainder of the period in India.

The 19th Light Dragoons served in India from 1782 to 1807, the unit's only

other active service being the two squadrons employed on the Niagara frontier in the War of 1812. The 20th Light Dragoons (titled 'Jamaica' until 1802) was raised in 1791 for service in that island. Part of the regiment served at the Cape in 1806 and then in South America, and was sent to the Peninsula where they suffered severely at Vimeiro; the remainder served in Naples in 1805, Sicily 1806 and one troop at Maida. For the remainder of the war the regiment served in the Mediterranean, in Egypt in 1807, Sicily 1808-12, in eastern Spain 1812-13 and at Genoa in 1814.

The 21st Light Dragoons (raised 1794) served in the West Indies 1795-98, at the Cape in 1806 and in South America; part of the regiment served in Madeira and another part in South Africa until

1817. The 22nd Light Dragoons was raised in 1794, served in Ireland and Egypt and was disbanded in 1802, when the 25th Light Dragoons was re-numbered 22nd; the latter was formed in 1794, had served at the Cape in 1795, and then until disbandment in 1819 in India (including at Assaye). The 23rd Light Dragoons (raised 1794) was disbanded in 1802, and the 26th (also raised 1794) re-numbered 23rd; the latter had served in the West Indies 1796-97, in Portugal until 1800, in Egypt, and after re-numbering in the Peninsular War and at Waterloo. The 24th Light Dragoons (raised 1794) was disbanded in 1802, when the 27th (raised 1795) was re-numbered as the 24th; it had served in the West Indies, the Cape and in India, where it remained until disbandment in 1818. The 25th Light Dragoons was re-created in 1802 when the old 29th was re-numbered, which had been formed in 1794; it served in the West Indies and at the Cape, and afterwards in India. The remaining regiments included the 28th (Duke of York's) Light Dragoons (raised 1796, served in the West Indies and at the Cape, disbanded 1802) and the 30th-33rd, all raised and disbanded 1794-96.

19

# The Hussars

Cavalry regiments were organised in squadrons of two troops each; theoretically two troops formed the depot squadron, and eight more the four 'service' squadrons. Theoretical establishment in 1795 was 3 officers and 55 other ranks per troop; in 1815 this was 1 captain, 1 lieutenant, 1 cornet, 1 sergeant-major, 3 sergeants, 4 corporals, 1 trumpeter, 1 farrier and 63 troopers.

Britain was comparatively late in following the European practice of creating regiments of Hussars, light horsemen dressed and equipped in a style which had evolved from the original Hungarian hussars. In 1806 the first conversions were made, beginning with the 10th Light Dragoons and shortly after the 7th, 15th and 18th; but the only difference between them and the ordinary light dragoons was in their uniform and perhaps the *esprit de corps* it fostered, as all four regiments remained officially titled 'Light Dragoons' throughout.

The ordinary light dragoons all wore blue uniforms with differently-coloured facings, a braided dolman (waist-length jacket) and the handsome, fur-crested leather helmet named after Banastre Tarleton, leader of the British Legion in the American War of Independence. (French-grey uniforms were worn by units serving in tropical climates, and the 20th Jamaica Regt. had a distinctive 'tin helmet' to repel the heat). In 1812 this distinctive uniform was replaced by a Polish-style jacket and French-style shako, easily confused with French uniforms and generally reviled; as a writer in the *Royal Military Chronicle* noted, the Light Dragoons were thus 'absolutely metamorphosed . . . to Frenchmen . . . I presume they have been altered and altered till no English alteration remained, and it was therefore necessary to adopt French ones . . .' Items of hussar uniform, such as the fur-trimmed jacket or pelisse, had been adopted unofficially by some light dragoon regiments as early the 1790s (the 25th Light Dragoons had been known as 'Gwyn's Hussars', for example), but only from 1806 were such items introduced officially. Although hussar uniform was decorative, the tall fur caps were impractical (and replaced by shakos in the later Peninsular War) and the whole ensemble was denounced by the *Public Ledger* in March 1813 as 'the tiddy dol appearance . . . rendering the appearance of our brave fellows ridiculous instead of promoting their health and comfort and security . . . the fribbling ornaments with which they are attired would better become an equestrian performer on one of our inferior stages, than a hardy veteran, when equipped for the field . . .'

Light Dragoons were armed with carbines, necessary for their 'outpost' duties; the most common pattern was the 'Paget' with a 16-inch barrel and swivel ramrod (made even more portable

*Thomas Noel Harris (1783-1860) of the 18th Hussars, who lost an arm serving as Brigade-Major to Vivian's Hussar Brigade at Waterloo. He wears a hussar-style uniform of an ADC to a hussar general, including a typical hussar's fur busby, mocked by the popular name of 'muff-cap'.*

for the 16th Light Dragoons whose carbines had folding butts), but many other varieties existed, including rifled weapons, most of limited use and very short range; Leach of the 95th called them 'pop-guns' which were always out-shot by the French cavalry carbines. The 1796 Light Dragoon sabre was slightly better designed than the equivalent heavy cavalry weapon, but was restricted even more to the slash, having a wide, curved blade and single-bar knuckle-bow. The *United Service Journal* critic remarked that 'we can answer for its utility in making billets for the fire', but it was sufficiently practical to be copied by the Prussian army for their 1811-pattern sabre.

The hussars suffered like all the other regiments in having no practical education of outpost duty or battlefield control before they actually went on campaign. In September 1798 the *Morning Chronicle* described a typical training-camp of 'six veteran Regiments,

*A sergeant of the 18th Hussars capturing two French officers at Albuera. Although the incident depicted presumably never occurred (the 18th was not at the battle) the print shows the later hussar uniform with reasonable accuracy, including the shako which replaced the fur busby. (Print by M Dubourg after W Heath.)*

*Trooper, 10th Hussars, 1815, in the uniform worn at Waterloo, the blue dolman having yellow lace and blue facings, replacing the red facings worn 1811-14. The 10th's grey overalls with yellow stripe were universally worn on campaign, officers having bright blue overalls with gold stripe. Pelisse-fur was black (white or grey for officers). The distinctive scarlet shako was apparently received by the regiment in Lisbon in March 1813. The regimental carbine shown was a 'Baker' rifled weapon with a distinctive 'pistol-grip' stock.*

every one of which had served three campaigns upon the Continent', in which the only manoeuvres practised appear to have been uncontrolled charges at top speed. 'No fatal accident, however, happened till the 27th August, when a private of the 7th Light Dragoons fell, with his horse, and died the next day. On the other days five or six falls generally occurred, but the mischief was confined to the destruction of horses . . . nobody shewed a greater alacrity in falling than General David Dundas. He was once overturned in a *buggy*, and twice he fell from his horse in the middle of the field, and in the presence of his Majesty. The complete revolutions he made in his way from the saddle to the ground entitled him to the praise of an excellent *tumbler*, and give him new claims to the *sobriquet* of *Pivot* Dundas, which he acquired by the introduction of a new manoevure . . . A defect, however, with which our horse is often reproached by foreigners still exists. They are not well broke to fire. When *feux de joye* were fired . . . a great number of horses were so scared by the report of the pistols, as to run out of the ranks, in spite of all the efforts of their riders.'

Horses were almost always supplied from Britain; those which could be acquired on campaign, especially in the Peninsula, were generally found to be unsatisfactory. Although the provision of remounts was a problem, as was the acquisition of regular and suitable forage, the quality of British cavalry horses was generally very good, though even the best regiments never exceeded the German Legion in the care and attention devoted to their mounts. On occasion the mounts were very bad, however, such as the draft received by the 14th Light Dragoons in 1809 which had been rejected as cart-horses by the Irish Commissariat Corps!

The senior hussar regiment was the 7th (Queen's Own) Light Dragoons, which served in the Netherlands and Germany in 1793-95, and in north Holland in 1799. In 1808 it went to the Peninsula and took part in the Corunna campaign, losing 56 men drowned on the return home; it rejoined the Peninsular army in 1813, serving at Orthez and Toulouse. In the Waterloo campaign it was severely handled at Genappe, in the action in which the Life Guards broke the French lancers upon whom the Hussars had foundered.

The 10th (Prince of Wales' Own) Light Dragoons was the most favoured of regiments, having the Prince of Wales as Colonel from 1796, and the title 'Royal' from 1811. It fought at Sahagun and Benevente, but was then employed on domestic and 'court' duties until it rejoined the Peninsular army in 1813, serving in the 'Hussar Brigade' at Vittoria, the Pyrenees, Orthez and Toulouse. After this campaign the unit had the unfortunate distinction of having its commanding officer court-martialled after complaints from many of his officers ranging from failing to lead the regiment in combat to a draconian disciplinary regime (between February and June 1813, *on campaign*, 136 regimental court-martials were held, 38,900 lashes awarded and no less than 21,555 actually inflicted). Clearly something was amiss in the regiment, but Lt-Col George Quentin, who had previously served in the Hanoverian Garde du Corps and presumably had high and royal influence, was acquitted, and almost the entire officer corps was replaced. When the 10th fought at Waterloo (with distinction) only the Major, Paymaster,' Surgeon and Veterinary Officer had been with the unit more than seven months.

The 15th (King's) Light Dragoons had a happier record, and was especially distinguished in the Netherlands in 1794, when at Villiers-en-Cauchies in concert with two Austrian hussar squadrons the regiment made a celebrated and successful charge, for which eight officers of the 15th received a specially-minted gold medal from the Emperor Francis. The regiment served in north Holland in 1799, and in the Peninsula in 1808-09 was especially distinguished at Sahagun. It returned to Spain in 1813, was present at Vittoria, Nivelle, Orthez and Toulouse, and fought at Waterloo.

The 18th Light Dragoons ('King's' from 1807) went to the West Indies in 1795, but was so ravaged by sickness in Jamaica and especially San Domingo that it returned home in 1798 under command of its surgeon! In 1799 it served in north Holland, and in the Corunna campaign was engaged at Benevente. Like the other hussar regiments it returned to the Peninsula in 1813, serving at Vittoria, Nive, Orthez and Toulouse, and fought at Waterloo.

# The Yeomanry Cavalry

There were two categories of 'auxiliary' cavalry: Fencibles and Yeomanry. The term 'fencible' was derived from 'defensible', describing regiments of both infantry and cavalry, basically regular units which according to their terms of enlistment could not be sent abroad without the acquiescence of all members (excepting Skinner's Fencibles, recruited in 1795 for service in Newfoundland and Canada). 34 such regiments of cavalry

were raised, ranging in strength from 6 troops (12 regiments) to corps of only a single troop (Sussex, Cambridgeshire and Linlithgow regiments); two such units may never actually have been formed, St Leger's and Buccleuch's, and there were in addition two Irish regiments. By March 1800 the greater number had been disbanded, though some lasted until 1802.

The Fencibles were organised and equipped as light dragoons, and their military value was in freeing regulars for overseas service; they were most valuable in guarding against civil unrest, though predictably the Opposition in Parliament was critical: Lord John Russell quoted a troop being sent to Odiham to quell a riot which did not exist, but instead 'threw the whole town into consternation'; Pitt

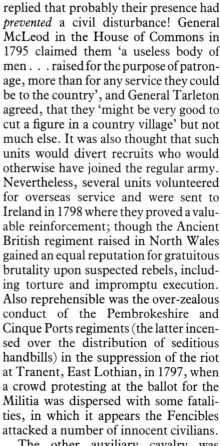

replied that probably their presence had *prevented* a civil disturbance! General McLeod in the House of Commons in 1795 claimed them 'a useless body of men . . . raised for the purpose of patronage, more than for any service they could be to the country', and General Tarleton agreed, that they 'might be very good to cut a figure in a country village' but not much else. It was also thought that such units would divert recruits who would otherwise have joined the regular army. Nevertheless, several units volunteered for overseas service and were sent to Ireland in 1798 where they proved a valuable reinforcement; though the Ancient British regiment raised in North Wales gained an equal reputation for gratuitous brutality upon suspected rebels, including torture and impromptu execution. Also reprehensible was the over-zealous conduct of the Pembrokeshire and Cinque Ports regiments (the latter incensed over the distribution of seditious handbills) in the suppression of the riot at Tranent, East Lothian, in 1797, when a crowd protesting at the ballot for the Militia was dispersed with some fatalities, in which it appears the Fencibles attacked a number of innocent civilians.

The other auxiliary cavalry was the Yeomanry. These units were formed throughout the land with a variety of titles such as 'Gentlemen and Yeomanry Cavalry' or 'Volunteer Cavalry'; they were, in effect, part-time 'home guards' who assembled for training for an hour once or twice a week, and were intended to fulfil a dual duty: to guard their localities against invasion, and to be available at short notice and at the call of the local magistrates to assemble 'in aid of civil power' in suppression of civil unrest. Prior to 1802 the majority of these units were composed of local gentry and their outdoor servants; by January 1801 the nominal strength of Yeomanry in Britain (including Ireland) stood at almost 24,000. There were in addition a number of 'Loyal Associations' or 'Armed Associations' which were mostly urban rather

*Officer of the Parham troop, c1798, one of eight troops of Sussex Yeomanry formed under the direction of the 3rd Earl of Egremont in 1794-95. This officer is based upon a portrait of the troop-commander Sir Cecil Bisshopp Bt, who raised the Parham Yeomanry (about 80 strong) in 1795.*

The Warwickshire Yeomanry was originally raised as a number of independent troops from 1794, formed into a regiment under the Earl of Aylesford in 1798. The unit was active in anti-riot duty in Birmingham, especially after a three-day outbreak in September 1800. This trooper is taken from a print by E Rudge (1801), showing a typical uniform, basically of light dragoon style but with a rather long-skirted tail-less jacket in the attractive regimental colouring of pale blue-grey with green (or blue?) facings.

than rural, which included cavalry troops but whose service was generally limited to the boundaries of their own parish.

Most of the Yeomanry and volunteer cavalry was disbanded upon the conclusion of the Peace of Amiens, but when war broke out again in 1803 vast numbers of corps were raised, generally with greater supervision than before and almost all receiving financial assistance from the government (whereas before most were either self-financing or supported by public subscriptions). The 1803 Volunteer Force was raised in part under the threat of a 'levy en masse' (forcible training of all able-bodied men if insufficient volunteered their services), which resulted in units being recruited from a wider social spectrum, but in the case of the Yeomanry the basis remained the gentry, middle-class and rural agricultural employees. By the end of 1803, when the Volunteer Force reached its peak, no less than 604 troops were enrolled involving 33,992 men. These ranged from the single troop of 40 men existing in Clackmannanshire to Devon's 1,873 cavalrymen in 33 troops. The Yeomanry attracted much derision for being either unmilitary or by being regarded by the radical political elements as the tools of repression; in both cases the criticism is unfair. Certainly a few corps were not proficient and attracted satirical notices such as the 'scurvy set/as ever met' about which a poem was written concerning the Wymondham Cavalry (Norfolk) in 1813; but against that was the alacrity with which the Yeomanry responded when false invasion-alarms were given, or when the French actually landed in Pembrokeshire and were rounded up by the Castlemartin Yeomanry. Equally, though the Yeomanry served as peacekeepers and police on countless occasions, use of force was often kept to the very minimum; one Castleford Yeoman was almost drowned in the River Aire in 1796 when he refused to use his sword to arrest the notorious malcontent Michael Sidebottom.

Civil unrest was especially bad in the mid-1790s and in the Luddite troubles around 1812, occasioned largely by shortages of food and employment. Typical of the more serious incident in which the Yeomanry served as peacekeepers was the following description published by the *London Chronicle* in August 1795, concerning Barrow upon

*Typical of the urban volunteer cavalry, the Clerkenwell Cavalry was the mounted wing of the Clerkenwell Association, formed 1797, 'composed of respectable tradesmen and honest workmen' and commanded by Capt Marmaduke Sellon, original commander of the Clerkenwell Infantry. (Print after Thomas Rowlandson)*

Soar, Leicestershire:

'Thursday evening a waggon loaded with corn, purchased by a person in Leicester, passing through the town, was stopped, and conveyed by the populace to the church. Information was immediately transmitted to the Mayor, who, with the Rev T Burnaby (one of the Magistrates of the county) and the Leicester troop of cavalry, proceeded to the place of their destination. On their arrival they found a vast assemblage of people in the church-yard, who refused to part with the corn. The Magistrates remonstrated with them for a considerable time, and promised to accommodate them with a part if they would disperse, but this they absolutely refused. The Riot Act was then read. Unwilling still to proceed to extremities, it was proposed that eight quarters of corn should be left, which was agreed to, and the remainder was put into the waggon. On their going off, however, the cavalry (who before had been insulted) were assailed with brick bats, and some shots fired upon them from the adjacent houses, one of which wounded Mr Stringer in the knee. The cavalry fired in return, and eleven victims fell; three were shot dead on the spot, and eight dangerously wounded.'

# Chapter Two: THE INFANTRY

Writing of the Battle of Albuera, Sir William Napier, referred in undisguised admiration to the fact that nothing could stop 'that astonishing infantry'. Though not an unbiased observer, Napier was correct in his assessment; the successes of the British Army during the Napoleonic Wars were founded upon the stalwart conduct and indomitable spirit of its Regiments of Foot. They had many imperfections and could be as troublesome to the provost service as to the enemy, but in combat there was no more reliable or heroic body in Europe, though the heroism was more concerned with dogged determination than any French-style élan. Their worth was fully appreciated at the time, especially by Wellington himself, as an anecdote on the eve of the Waterloo campaign demonstrates. Taking the air in a Brussels park, Thomas Creevey questioned the Duke about the coming campaign and how it would be resolved. Wellington pointed to a British infantry private who was wandering through the park and bemusedly staring at the statues; 'It all depends upon that article whether we do the business or not,' said the Duke. 'Give me enough of it, and I am sure.' His confidence was not misplaced.

The regular infantry of the British Army consisted of a series of numbered regiments, in 1815 104 strong (as many as 135 numbered regiments had existed in the 1790s, most of the higher-numbered ones of short duration). There were in addition the three regiments of Foot Guards, but they were not 'line infantry' per se. From 1782 most regiments had been assigned a territorial designation, a county with which the unit was affiliated; the 41st, 89th, 98th, 102nd and 103rd had no such designation, and others had titles which did not reflect such connections, such as the 7th Royal Fuzileers, 60th Royal Americans, 97th Queen's Germans, etc. In some cases these titles reflected their favoured recruiting-grounds, but others were arbitrary choices, and in most cases did not represent the internal composition of the regiment. Exceptions were the Highland and Irish regiments, which drew their recruits mostly from those areas, but the

remainder accepted men from any source, and sent their recruiting-parties far and wide. After the change in regulations allowed militiamen to volunteer into the regular army in 1805 regiments received batches of recruits from county militias which did tend to concentrate men from a small number of counties within a regiment, but rarely did these drafts have any bearing whatever on the regimental affiliation. For example, before going to the Peninsula in 1808 the 77th (East Middlesex) Regiment brought its numbers up to strength (having recently returned from India) by recruiting from five militia regiments; but not one man came from the Middlesex Militia, the units in question being the North and South Mayo, 1st West Riding, South Lincoln and Northampton; similar examples are endless. Even corps which officially had marked national or territorial affiliations often contained a majority of men from other areas; for example, that most Welsh of regiments, the 23rd (Royal Welch) Fuzileers at Waterloo contained (of those men whose origin is recorded) 405 English, 62 Irish, 7 Scots, 1 Dutchman, 1 Canadian, 1 Italian and only 191 Welshmen. In 1809 34 per cent of the 57th (West Middlesex) Regiment was Irish, and in 1811 37 per cent of the 29th (Worcestershire) Regiment. Acknowledgement that territorial designations had little relevance was made officially in 1809 when the 71st, 72nd, 73rd, 74th, 75th and 91st Highland Regiments were de-kilted, adopting ordinary infantry uniform instead.

Organisation of the infantry regiments was standard, though in practice varied with circumstances, and no fully-regulated 'establishment' could ever be described especially on campaign when the number of men available fluctuated greatly. The basic administrative unit was the battalion, a self-contained entity belonging to the regiment but operating independently; only by the wildest of coincidences did two battalions of the same line regiment serve alongside each other (the 7th Fuzileers and 48th Northamptonshire's two battalions at Albuera is a conspicuous example), the link between the battalions being no more than a

transfer of personnel from one to the other when required. At the commencement of the Peninsular War there were 103 regiments of the line (the 104th New Brunswick Fencibles was taken into the line only in 1810), of which 61 regiments had the usual two battalions; 37 regiments had but a single battalion, the 1st (Royal Scots) had four, and the 14th and 27th had three each. The remaining two were the rifle corps, which were different cases, the 60th (Royal Americans – not all riflemen at this period) having seven battalions and the 95th Rifles three battalions. Subsequently, seven of the single-battalion corps raised a second battalion, and the 56th a third. The Foot Guards were organised similarly, the 1st with three battalions and the other two regiments with two battalions each.

Internally, the battalion organisation was standard for all, comprising a small headquarters (basically administrative personnel) and ten companies, eight of which were termed 'battalion' or 'centre' companies (from their position when the battalion was assembled in line), and two 'flank' companies, one of which, the right-flank company (theoretically the biggest and most stalwart members of the battalion) consisted of grenadiers, and the other, the left-flank company (supposedly the smallest and most nimble men) of light infantry. There were few exceptions to this organisation, chiefly in the light infantry and rifle regiments where all companies were alike, having no grenadiers. The three regiments styled 'Fuzileers' (7th Royal, 21st Royal North British and 23rd Royal Welch) owed their titles to their ancient past, when they were armed with light muskets or 'fusils'; at this period their only difference from the ordinary regiments was in the minutiae of their uniform, and the fur caps worn in full dress.

*Privates of the 23rd (Royal Welch Fuzileers) (left) and 6th (1st Warwickshire) Regts in the 1812 uniform, including the grey service-dress overalls but the fusilier cap normally reserved for dress occasions; facings were blue and deep yellow respectively.*
*(Print after CH Smith)*

# The Foot Guards

Together with the three regiments of Household Cavalry, the three regiments of Foot Guards were the elite of the army, at least in the general opinion. Although these regiments were much stronger in numbers when on active service, their organisation, equipment and tactical role was like that of the ordinary infantry, as described in the appropriate section.

In status and *esprit de corps*, however, the Foot Guards were unique, forming the sovereign's official household infantry and undertaking most of the ceremonial duties in the capital (units of Foot Guards always being stationed in or around London). Their uniform resembled that of whichever style was currently worn by the line infantry, with the blue facings which invariably distinguished 'royal' regiments (i.e. those with a 'royal' title or named after a royal personage), with plain white lace for the rank-and-file, gold for sergeants, and broad gold lace edging to the facings of officers' uniforms. For ceremonial occasions, the grenadiers of the Foot Guard regiments retained their fur caps throughout, whereas the grenadiers of most line regiments put their caps into store for years on end and wore instead the ordinary head-dress even on parade.

In the matter of recruitment, the Foot Guards enlisted their rank-and-file in the usual manner, without any official territorial designations or specific recruiting-grounds. In commissioned ranks, however, there was a great difference between the Foot Guards and the line regiments, not only the fact that Guards officers possessed a 'double' rank, regimental and 'army'. Through the army, it was possible for a company officer ranking as (say) a captain in his regiment to hold a brevet or 'army' rank of (say) major, brevet rank often being an award for meritorious service bestowed upon deserving individuals despite there being no immediate vacancy for promotion; but in the Foot Guards *all* officers possessed such a 'double' rank, so that (for example) a Guards lieutenant would be equal in rank to a line captain, hence the use of confusing titles such as 'lieutenant and captain'. Although Guards officers received a higher rate of pay than those of the line, expenses were such that it was quite impossible for a Guards officer to subsist without a very considerable private income. (A Foot Guards major, for example, received £1.4s.6d. per diem, a captain 16/6d, and a lieutenant 7/10d in 1815, as against equivalent line pay of 16/-, 10/6d and 6/6d per diem respectively.) The purchase-fees for commissions in the Foot Guards were enormous. Even though not all commissions, even in the Guards, were obtained by purchase, the scale of fees when compared to those of the line equivalents is staggering: in 1815, for example, a Guards lieutenant-colonelcy cost £6,700, a majority £6,300, a captaincy £3,500 and a lieutenancy £1,500, as against £3,500, £2,600, £1,500 and £550 respectively. Thus, only the affluent or well-connected could ever hope to achieve high rank in the Foot Guards, and the majority of Guards officers were either from the very highest echelon of society or were the offspring of distinguished military officers. The social exclusivity of the Guards can be seen in an assessment of those regimental officers who fought at Waterloo (in both regimental capacity and in various staff appointments); they included at least seven peers (or those with the right to call themselves 'Lord' as heirs to high-ranking peerages), 25 sons or heirs of peers (including one 'natural' son, i.e. an illegitimate), 5 knights (mostly honoured for their own previous services), 9 sons or heirs of baronets, 1 son of a knight and even a son of a Count of the Holy Roman Empire! (CAF Bentinck of the 2nd Foot Guards).

Despite this social status and the ceremonial duties undertaken by the Foot Guards, they remained among the finest combat troops of the army, renowned for the maintenance of high discipline even under the most difficult circumstances; for example, Sir John Moore is said to have remarked on the appearance of the Guards on the retreat to Corunna, standing out among the army by still marching in immaculate ranks, as if on the barrack-square, with the drum-major at the head. Wellington might have complained at Bayonne of

*Colour-sergeant, light company, 2nd Coldstream Guards, 1815, in the campaign uniform worn at Waterloo, including the 1812-pattern shako with a waterproof cover and grey 'service' overalls. The rank of colour-sergeant was instituted in July 1813 as a reward for the most deserving NCOs. The colour-sergeant of this company at Waterloo was John Biddle, a 27-year-old ex-labourer from Little Shelsey, Worcestershire, who was wounded in the action around Hougoumont and who left the regiment with an impeccable record in 1825 after 19 years' service.*

*Foot Guards ensign with Colour, 1814, wearing the long-tailed 'state' coatee and long white gaiters reserved for full dress. In the background are regimental musicians, including an orientally-costumed Negro percussionist. (Aquatint after CH Smith)*

*Foot Guards, 1807, left to right: light company, Coldstream; grenadier, Scots; battalion company. Note the bunch of ribbon at the rear of the light infantryman's 'clubbed' hairstyle; his pouch-badge identifies the regiment. (Print after JA Atkinson)*

officers making themselves appear ridiculous in combat by protecting themselves from the rain by holding umbrellas, but fully recognised the value of the Guards as members of the army; although, as he admitted, their sergeants mostly got drunk every night, they made sure that their duties were completed first!

The services of the three regiments of Foot Guards during the Napoleonic Wars bear testimony to the value and hard campaigning of these superb units, the 1st Foot Guards having three battalions and the other two regiments – 2nd or Coldstream and 3rd or Scots – two each. The first battalions of all three regiments were brigaded together for the Netherlands expedition, being the first troops to embark for the continent, serving at Famars, Valenciennes, and with especial distinction at Lincelles, and through to 1795.

Of the 1st Foot Guards, the 3rd Battalion served in north Holland in 1799; and the 1st and 3rd in Sicily in 1806-07, in the retreat to Corunna and at Walcheren. Part of the 2nd Bn was with Sir Thomas Graham at Cadiz and Barossa, and was relieved by the 3rd Bn from Britain, which later joined Wellington's army in Spain and figured in the retreat from Burgos, as at Corunna being outstanding among the horrors of the retreat. The 3rd Bn was later joined by the 1st Bn, the two being brigaded together, but prevented from joining the army immediately due to exhaustion and fever; they participated in the latter stages of the Peninsular War, at San Sebastian, Nive, Nivelle and Bayonne. The 2nd Bn meanwhile served with Graham again in Holland, including the attack on Bergen-op-Zoom. The regiment was represented at Waterloo by the 2nd and 3rd Bns, which formed the 1st (Guards) Brigade, their light companies assisting in the defence of Hougoumont and, at the culmination of the French attacks, claiming the credit for repelling the attack of the Imperial Guard. For the latter service the 1st Foot Guards was awarded the distinction of becoming an entire regiment of grenadiers (the only one in the army), with the title 'Grenadier Guards'. The 1st Foot Guards was the senior infantry regiment of the British Army, its generally-accepted date of formation being 23 November 1660, following the restoration of King Charles II, but a case could be made for its origin arising even earlier, in the regiment of Guards maintained by Charles II in exile, from at least 1656.

The 2nd or Coldstream regiment was of even greater antiquity, being originally Monck's regiment of foot, formed in 1650, uniquely maintaining an unbroken lineage from Commonwealth to Restoration; and though junior in precedence to the 1st Foot Guards never regarded themselves as such, as evidenced from the name of the officers' dining society formed in 1783, the *Nulli Secundus* Club! The services of the regiment's two battalions in the Napoleonic Wars were extensive; after the Netherlands expedition they participated in the Ostend débâcle in 1798, and served in north Holland in 1799. The 1st Bn served at Ferrol and Vigo, and moved to the Mediterranean where they fought at Aboukir and Alexandria. They served in the Hanover expedition of 1805, at Copenhagen in 1807, and landed in the Peninsula in 1809, serving at Talavera, Fuentes de Oñoro, Ciudad Rodrigo, Badajos, Salamanca, Vittoria, Nive, Nivelle and Bayonne. The regiment's 2nd Bn served at Walcheren (flank companies only) and other companies at Barossa; six companies served in Holland in 1814. Reinforced by four companies from home, the 2nd Bn fought at Waterloo, where Capt and Lt-Col James Macdonell of Glengarry, styled the 'bravest man in the army', won immortal fame in closing the gates of Hougoumont when the French almost succeeded in breaking in. (This sobriquet Macdonell of Glengarry insisted on sharing with Sgt Graham of the Coldstream light company, another hero of Hougoumont.)

The 3rd or Scots regiment, as its name suggests, originated with a few companies formed in Scotland in 1660, and throughout seems to have drawn a large number of its recruits from Scotland. The 1st Bn's services were similar to those of the 1/Coldstream, in the Netherlands in 1793-95, north Holland in 1799, Egypt 1801, Hanover 1805, Copenhagen 1807 and in the Peninsula from 1809 to 1814. Elements of the 2nd Bn served at Walcheren, Barossa and at Bergen-op-Zoom, and represented the regiment in the 2nd (Guards) Brigade at Waterloo.

# The Line Regiments

The organisation of most line regiments into units of two battalions of 10 companies each was a deliberate policy aimed at providing a ready supply of reinforcements, it being intended that one battalion of each regiment should be available for active service and one to remain in garrison. Though no definitive rules were drawn up, it was intended that at full strength a 'service' battalion should include about 1,000 rank-and-file (i.e. 100 men per company), which when officers, NCOs and musicians were added would bring the battalion strength to 1,100. Every battalion possessed a number of men rated as 'inefficient' (infirm, headquarters personnel, men 'worn-out' but not yet discharged, etc.), so that when a battalion was ordered abroad it was customary to transfer its 'ineffectives' to the regiment's 2nd battalion, making the numbers up to a notional 1,100 by taking effectives from the 2nd battalion. In those cases where a 2nd battalion was ordered on active service, it thus contained not only its own complement of ineffectives but also those of the regiment's 1st battalion, which meant that of the (say) 900 men left in the 2nd battalion, probably around 200 would have to be left behind in Britain, to form the regimental depot. Thus, even before the attritional losses of campaigning began to reduce the numbers, 2nd battalions were almost invariably much weaker than 1st battalions. Single-battalion corps fared little better, as even if they were completely at full strength before being ordered abroad (a rare occurrence: few regiments were ever totally up to 'establishment'), having no 2nd battalion upon which to draw fit men, and with the need to leave a regimental depot in Britain, such battalions might be fortunate if they embarked on active service with much in excess of 750 men. No definitive 'establishment' of a typical infantry battalion can thus be formulated; in 1809, for example, the total numbers of officers and men in a regiment ranged from the 1st Foot's 4,926 (in four battalions) down to the 16th Foot's 406 men (one battalion, then in the West Indies).

On campaign, battalion strengths could deteriorate to the extent that battalions might be incapable of operating as independent tactical units. Leaving aside the Foot Guard battalions (which invariably were stronger than line battalions, rarely falling below 1,000 rank-and-file), statistics for the end of the 1811 campaign in the Peninsula are typical. 46 battalions were then with Wellington's army; the average strength of each battalion was but 550 men, ranging from the 1st Bn, 43rd Light Infantry (expressed hereafter as 1/43rd) with 1,005 men, to the 2/38th with only 263. Only nine battalions had more than 700 of all ranks present; ten had between 400 and 500, and no less than eleven battalions had less than 400 men. Of the army at Salamanca (before the losses sustained in the battle) the average strength of a battalion was only 557 of all ranks (calculating both British and KGL infantry but not including detached rifle companies or the provisional battalion formed from the 2/95th and 3/95th Rifles in the Light Division, which at 392 all ranks was stronger than a number of complete battalions.) Of the 44 battalions involved, only three numbered in excess of 900 (as expected including the 1/2nd and 1/3rd Foot Guards; of the line regiments only the 1/42nd Highlanders with 1,039 men exceeded this figure), whilst twelve battalions had less than 400 men, the weakest being the 2/44th with only 231 rank-and-file.

Reinforcements on campaign were obtained by two methods: either entire new battalions would be despatched from home, or drafts of men would be sent from the regimental depot (or recovered wounded or sick men could rejoin their battalions from local hospital). Only rarely were battalions so reduced in numbers that they had to be withdrawn from the army completely; in these cases they might be assigned to duties at the rear of the army (if ill-disciplined or otherwise not combat-effective, very rare occurrences), or might be sent home to recruit or be completely reconstructed, in which case it was not unusual for only the cadre of officers, NCOs and headquarters personnel to return home, the remaining fit rank-and-file remaining behind to be distributed among other units. (This was frequently the case with battalions returning from tropical postings, especi-

*Private, battalion company, 33rd (1st West Riding) Regiment, 1794. This member of Wellesley's own regiment (in 1853 the title was changed to the Duke of Wellington's Regiment) wears a typical 'campaign' uniform of the early Revolutionary Wars, the coat having open lapels revealing the waistcoat; from 1796 it was closed to the waist. The regiment was almost unique (with the 53rd and 76th) in having red facings, and was one of many to adopt upright collars prior to these being made regulation.*

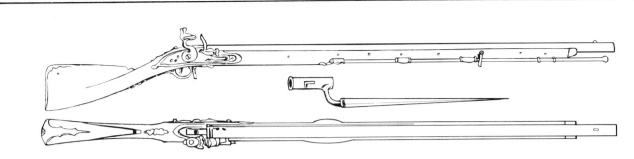

*Brown Bess was an affectionate nickname for the British infantry musket from the early 18th century; it was more correctly termed the Land Pattern (in various forms known as Long and Short), and latterly the Indian Pattern.*

ally from the West Indies, when so few men might have survived that it was not worthwhile sending home what remained.) Generally, however, a battalion would soldier on through a campaign, gradually becoming weaker every year and relying upon drafts from home to keep the unit operational. Even when the strength dwindled so far that the unit was too small to operate on its own – if there were, for example, too few men left to make the formation of a square a practical battlefield proposition – it might have to struggle on as a 'provisional battalion', an *ad hoc* formation in which two shattered battalions would be combined to form one tactical unit. In January 1814, for example, the Peninsular army had no less than four such provisional battalions, the 1st composed of the 2/31st and 2/66th Foot, the 2nd of the 2nd and 2/53rd Foot, the 3rd of the 2/24th and 2/58th Foot, and the 4th of the 2/30th and 2/44th Foot. It is significant that these Provisional Battalions were drawn from one single-battalion corps (2nd) and seven 2nd battalions, exemplifying the comparative weakness of such formations. Similar units could be formed *in extremis* from recovered invalids and stragglers if the situation were critical, such as the 'Battalions of Detachments' drawn from many units which fought at Talavera.

A further method of creating new units of 'specialist' personnel was by detaching the flank companies of a number of battalions and assembling the personnel into a 'flank battalion', a way of providing a light infantry unit for a small force which did not possess such a specialist corps; though the practice was not widespread in larger forces which usually had an adequate provision of such troops.

A battalion was normally commanded by a lieutenant-colonel; the regimental colonel was a purely administrative appointment granted to a distinguished officer or royal personage. Although in the previous century colonels had been virtually the 'proprietors' of their regiments, they no longer had any actual power and never commanded the regiment in person. In addition to the lieutenant-colonel, each battalion had two other 'field officers', ranking as regimental majors (because of the system of brevet rank they might hold 'army' commissions one grade higher). The basic subdivision was the company, commanded by a captain (thus there were 10 captains per battalion), though in the

*The infantry shoulder-belt plate (known at the time as a 'breastplate') invariably bore the unit's distinctive badges or number; this officers' pattern of the 20th (East Devonshire) Regt dates from the later Napoleonic Wars.*

earlier years it was usual for the battalion-commander also to be in nominal control of a company; actual command of the lieutenant-colonel's company was vested in the regimental 'captain-lieutenant', generally the senior subaltern. This practice arose from the old fashion of the company-captain being virtually the 'proprietor' of the company, responsible for its accounts, pay and administrative matters. By the late 18th century these were the responsibility of the colonel, who was given a financial grant by the government to cover the unit's upkeep, and frequently managed to make a profit on such items as the provision of uniform and accoutrements, a system of financial abuse which attracted some criticism. (In 1798 it was estimated that a colonel might expect between £400 and £800 profit per annum on the clothing of his regiment.)

Below the company-captain came two subalterns, either lieutenants or ensigns. The latter rank dated from the period in which each company had its own Colour, and thus required an ensign to carry it; by the period in question there were only two Colours per battalion, but the rank of ensign persisted. In fusilier and light regiments it was usual for the two grades of subaltern to be 1st and 2nd lieutenant; light infantry battalions, needing more control for operating in 'open order', had two lieutenant-colonels per battalion and an extra subaltern per company. The company was composed of a number of NCOs (sergeants), corporals (regarded as members of the rank-and-file rather than NCOs), two drummers (buglers in light regiments) and a fluctuating number of privates. Battalion headquarters included the adjutant (a subaltern, sometimes also a company officer), the field officers, paymaster, medical staff, and bandsmen. The latter were often professional musicians, many of them foreigners, and rarely exceeded eight in number; battalions wishing to field larger bands 'hid' the additional members in the company rolls. The company drummers, originally used to transmit orders by beat of drum in action, were regarded as members of their company rather than bandsmen. A good band was of great value to a regiment, both in attracting recruits at home and maintaining morale in action; there are numerous examples of bands playing during battle, though in very desperate circumstances the musicians themselves might be required to fight, as did the

48th's at Talavera. The battalion's pioneer section, normally ten strong plus a corporal, might march together at the head of the regiment but were normally distributed among the companies for administrative purposes, one pioneer per company plus the corporal in the grenadier company, so were not classified as headquarters personnel.

In 1797 a sergeant-major was first officially included in a battalion's establishment, but prior to that date it had not been uncommon for a senior sergeant to occupy this position. The rank of colour-sergeant was instituted as a mark of distinction for deserving men in July 1813, to occupy a position which might be described as company sergeant-major (in the Royal Artillery this rank was officially designated as 'Company Sergeant'), and though the arm-badge of this rank featured a representation of the regimental Colours, colour-sergeants were not intended as Colour-escorts. Each battalion possessed two flags, a King's Colour (basically the Union Flag with battalion identification) and a Regimental Colour, normally of the regimental facing-colour with a Union in the upper canton nearest the staff and similar devices. In the Foot Guards the appellation was reversed so that the King's Colour was crimson and the Regimental Colour of the Union pattern. Symbolising the battalion's honour and devotion to its sovereign, reinforced by the religious consecration of each new pair, the Colours were the focal point of the battalion and a rallying-point in battle. The greatest disgrace which could befall a unit was the loss of its Colours, and thus the most desperate struggles raged around them, giving rise to epics of heroism unequalled in any military history, such as the defence of the Colours of the 3rd (Buffs) at Albuera, in which action Lt Matthew Latham suffered appallingly disfiguring wounds and had an arm severed rather than relinquish hold of his Colour, and finally fell upon it beneath the hooves of the French cavalry rather than let the precious flag fall into enemy hands.

*Grenadier corporal, 45th (Nottinghamshire) Regt, in the uniform of Talavera, wearing the 'stovepipe' shako used throughout the Peninsular War; with the white plume and 'wings' of grenadier companies. Facings were deep green and the lace 'bastion' shape with a green stripe.*

*George Morland's painting 'The Billeted Soldier's Departure' shows the infantry uniform of the early 1790s; in the background is a drummer in the 'reversed colours' worn by most musicians before 1812, coats of the facing-colour with red facings. (Engraving by Graham)*

Casualties were often most severe among the NCOs who provided the small escort for the Colours, so that (as one veteran observed) it was not regarded as an honour to be ordered to the Colours as much as a possible sentence of death.

A battalion could be sub-divided into other units; confusingly, for tactical purposes each company could be styled a platoon, within which were two sub-divisions each of two sections; when a battalion dwindled in numbers each company might be divided into three sections instead of four. The eight 'battalion' companies could form four 'grand divisions' (each of two companies), with the flank companies as a separate 5th 'grand division'; the battalion could also be divided into right and left wings, officially of five companies each, though both the terms 'division' and 'wing' were sufficiently loose to imply subdivisions of undefined size. As the company was the basic administrative unit and the platoon the tactical unit, it was theoretically possible for a very strong company to form two platoons, though in general the term 'platoon' always referred to a company in its tactical role.

Many regiments of the British Army

*Privates of the 23rd (Royal Welch Fuzileers) and 6th (1st Warwickshire) Regt, in the 1812-pattern uniform characterised by the false-fronted 'Belgic' shako. The 23rd man wears the fur fusilier cap reserved for full dress. (Aquatint by IC Stadler after CH Smith)*

were of great antiquity, some having enjoyed continuous existence at least from the Restoration of Charles II if not before, but most of those numbered 78 onwards were formed from the Revolutionary Wars when an urgent expansion of the army was required. Not all the higher-numbered units were newly-formed; the 94th 'Scotch Brigade' had links (somewhat tenuous) with the Scottish regiments in Dutch service whose history extended back into the 17th century. When a new regiment was required, the nominated Colonel was issued a 'letter of service' giving royal assent to the raising of the regiment; officers might be recommended by the Colonel (giving an element of 'patronage') but all commissions were approved by the government and signed by the king or his representative (such as the Prince Regent during George III's incapacity). Not all regiments thus authorised were even intended to operate as individual entities; myriad units formed in the 1790s were never even issued with a number, but were formed simply as 'recruiting regiments', i.e. a temporary depot for recruits who were almost immediately drafted to other corps. These units bore the name of the colonel,

as did some of those which were issued with numbers but soon disbanded and their personnel transferred elsewhere. This system produced a number of exotically-named units such as Leatherband's 123rd, the Jedburgh Burghs Regiment or the 129th Gentlemen of Coventry, but the process must have been regarded as an inferior way of raising men and was not copied after 1798. Raising regiments from scratch resulted in no established regimental framework or *esprit de corps*, which was probably the reason for the 'mutiny' of DJ Cameron's Loyal Sheffield Regiment in June 1795, which refused to dismiss as the men's enlistment-bounties had not been paid; the Sheffield Volunteers were assembled to oppose them and two civilians were killed when they opened fire in an attempt to impose order. (This incident was not isolated; in the previous month the Loyal Irish Fencibles mutinied at Bristol and were only quietened by a charge of the 10th Light Dragoons!)

The training of the infantry revolved around the army's firearm, the smoothbore flintlock musket known by the generic term 'Brown Bess'. In actual fact, many different patterns were covered by this affectionate nickname (derived probably from browned or dulled barrels plus 'Bess', the latter either a term of endearment or a corruption of the German *Büsche* = gun). The standard arm at the beginning of the Revolutionary Wars was the 'Land pattern' musket (to distinguish it from the similar 'Sea Service' musket), known from the length of barrel as either the 'Long Land Pattern' or 'Short Land Pattern', a shortening of the length from 46 to 42ins making the weapon more easily handled. Upon the outbreak of war the Board of Ordnance was faced with a huge inadequacy of muskets – in 1794 with 110,000 muskets for 250,000 men – so tried to acquire a sufficient number from abroad, many of very inferior quality. A better method of supply was found when the East India Company was persuaded by the government to transfer its

*Ensign, 3/14th (Buckinghamshire) Regt, in the 1812-pattern uniform, as worn at Waterloo, carrying the battalion's Regimental Colour. Ensign Hon George T Keppel who carried the battalion's Colour celebrated his sixteenth birthday five days before the battle.*

arsenal, intended for use by the Company's troops in India, to the Ordnance, immediately providing the government with over 30,000 longarms and 2,600 pistols. So good was the East India musket that from 1797 Ordnance gunsmiths were ordered to produce only 'India pattern' muskets; it had simplified 'furniture' (fittings) and a 39in barrel, and though quicker to produce was slightly inferior in quality to the Short Land Pattern. It remained the standard weapon of the infantry throughout the Napoleonic Wars, the only modification being the introduction of a reinforced cock in 1809. Between 1804 and 1815 some 1,603,711 India Pattern muskets were manufactured (many being sent to Allied nations abroad: Prussia alone received 113,000), the other subsequent patterns (the New Land Service with 42in barrel, and the same with 39in barrel and backsight for light infantry) having only limited use.

The musket fired a spherical lead ball of an ounce in weight, capable of inflicting horrendous injury; but from the viewpoint of range and accuracy, the musket was wildly impractical. This inaccuracy was not because technology was limited, for a superb mass-produced musket, known as the 'Duke of Richmond's' pattern, was designed by the gunsmith Henry Nock, incorporating his patent 'screwless lock', with all the working parts on the interior. This would have been the finest musket ever produced, but as Nock was unable to supply them sufficiently quickly the project was abandoned in 1798. In fact, in the context of Napoleonic warfare, it was not

necessary for a musket to be any more accurate than to be able to register a hit anywhere upon a large mass of troops. The very inaccuracy of the musket had helped formulate the tactics which involved the manoeuvre of compact blocks of troops, but tactics would probably not have changed even had a more accurate firearm been widely available.

Probably the best judgement on the ordinary musket was that given by Col George Hanger, a somewhat eccentric but experienced officer and himself an expert marksman; he wrote in *To All Sportsmen* (1814) that

'A soldier's musket, if not exceedingly ill-bored (as many are), will strike the figure of a man at 80 yards; it may even at a hundred; but a soldier must be very unfortunate indeed who shall be wounded by a common musket at 150 yards, provided his antagonist aims at him; and as to firing at a man at 200 yards with a common musket, you may as well fire at the moon and have the same hope of hitting your object. I do maintain and will prove . . . that no man was ever killed at 200 yards, by a common musket, by the person who aimed at him.'

In Hanger's *Reflections on the Menaced Invasion* he claimed that under combat conditions, one hit per 200 shots might be registered, so bad were the muskets made or 'bent in soldering the loops on'. This tends to be supported by such statistics as are available. Tests with the 'Brown Bess' in 1841 hit a target twice as high and twice as broad as a man three times out of four at 150 yards; at any greater range not one hit was registered. The author of *Elements of the Science of*

*War*, Müller, estimated that about 50 per cent of shots at 100 yards would hit a target representing a line of cavalry; at 300 yards the striking-rate could drop to under 20 per cent. Given the conditions of combat (when the target would be moving and partially obscured by smoke) rather than controlled test, and including the misfire-rate (calculated at one in 6½ under test conditions in 1834), an effectiveness rate of around 5 per cent might be expected at around 100 yards, dropping to 2 or 3 per cent at greater distance. R Henegan, head of the field train department in the Peninsular War, calculated that at Vittoria *excluding* any casualties caused by the 6,800 artillery rounds fired, the British inflicted one

*Private, 5th (Northumberland) Regt, in a print published by Genty of Paris in 1815. The regiment wore 'gosling green' facings; the large feather plume was a regimental peculiarity, green denoting the light company.*

### Organisation of a typical infantry division: H Campbell's 1st Division at Salamanca

| | | officers | other ranks |
|---|---|---|---|
| Fermor's Bde.: | 1/2nd Foot Guards | 26 | 928 |
| | 1/3rd Foot Guards | 23 | 938 |
| | Rifle coy 60th (R. Americans) | 1 | 56 |
| Wheatley's Bde: | 2/24th (2nd Warwickshire) | 23 | 398 |
| | 1/42nd (R. Highlanders) | 40 | 1,039 |
| | 2/58th (Rutlandshire)* | 31 | 369 |
| | 1/79th (Cameron Highlanders) | 40 | 634 |
| | Rifle coy 60th (R. Americans) | 1 | 53 |
| Löwe's Bde: | 1st Line Bn KGL | 26 | 615 |
| | 2nd Line Bn KGL | 26 | 601 |
| | 5th Line Bn KGL | 30 | 525 |

*2/58th temporarily attached from 5th Division

casualty per 459 rounds fired; and that this casualty-rate was almost universal throughout the Peninsular War. The fact that in a dense press of men a casualty might be hit by more than one ball probably explains in part the difference between the calculations of theoretical and actual performance.

Other weapons carried by the infantry included triangular-sectioned socket-bayonets used by all who carried a musket, straight-bladed swords carried by officers and sergeants, short swords by musicians and curved sabres by officers of flank companies (and others who preferred the sabre to the regulation pattern; providing their own equipment, officers were permitted a degree of laxity, especially on campaign). Sergeants of all except light infantry carried a half-pike or 'spontoon', which replaced their earlier halberds in 1792. Officers of fusilier regiments initially carried light muskets, and occasionally other officers carried muskets on campaign.

Ammunition was provided in the form of a greased paper cartridge, each containing a musket-ball and sufficient powder for one shot; to load the musket, the soldier bit off the end of the cartridge, poured a little of the gunpowder into the 'pan' of his musket-lock, which was then closed, poured the remainder down the barrel, spat the ball after it and finally inserted the paper tube, all of which he rammed down with the iron ramrod carried beneath the musket-barrel. The weapon was discharged when the trigger was depressed, causing a wedge-shaped lump of flint held in the jaws of the 'cock' to strike sparks upon the steel of the pan-cover, igniting the powder in the pan which was communicated to the propellant charge via a 'touch-hole' in the barrel, whereupon the musket discharged with a loud bang, clouds of dense smoke and a vicious recoil. The normal provision of ball-cartridge was 60 rounds per man, carried in a leather cartridge-box suspended on a belt over the right shoulder. A similar belt over the left shoulder supported the bayonet-scabbard, and further straps around the armpits and across the chest supported the knapsack, originally a soft canvas or hide pack but latterly a box-type structure reinforced by wood, hideously uncomfortable to carry and giving rise to a condition known as 'pack palsy'. A wooden water-canteen, a haversack and a rolled blanket or greatcoat ('watch-coat') carried atop the knapsack completed the basic equipment, though additional ammunition could be accommodated in an extra 'magazine'. The whole ensemble was both impractical and uncomfortable but was inflicted upon the infantryman throughout the period, with little concern for the immense burden he had to carry. John Spencer Cooper, a sergeant of the 7th Fuzileers, calculated the total weight which had to be carried (with weight in lbs in parentheses): musket and bayonet (14), pouch and ammunition (6), canteen and belt (1), mess-tin (1), knapsack and belts (3), blanket (4), greatcoat (4), dress jacket (3), fatigue jacket (½), 2 shirts (2½), 2 pairs shoes (3), trousers (2), gaiters (¼), 2 pairs stockings (1), cleaning equipment (3), shoulder-belts (1), pipe-clay (1), 2 tent pegs (½), three days' provisions (5), water in canteen (3), plus an additional ¼lb of pen, ink and paper (for an NCO), giving a total (without personal impedimenta) of 59lbs. Well might Cooper note that 'The government should also have sent us new backbones to bear the extra weight'!

The infantry uniform consisted of the traditional brick-red coat, initially with long tails and lapels but from 1800 single-breasted and short-tailed, with regimentally-coloured facings and lace. Breeches and gaiters were the usual wear on home service, but one-piece 'mosquito trousers' or gaiter-trousers were used abroad, and latterly loose overalls, regulated as grey in 1812. The head-dress was initially the bicorn hat, and from 1800 a cylindrical shako termed a 'stove-pipe', replaced in 1812 by a false-fronted cap known as the 'Belgic' pattern, though its introduction was generally delayed until *c.* 1814. The whole ensemble was described by Cooper as more resembling 'a child's doll in a toyshop', and 'nothing could be contrived worse for real service', but great latitude was allowed on campaign obviating the worst features of the uniform, and the powdered 'queue' or pigtail was removed in 1808 to the unrelieved joy of the entire army.

*Officer, light company, 82nd Regt (Prince of Wales' Volunteers), 1808. Light infantry officers wore shakos and short jackets even before these were introduced for all in 1812; the facings here are yellow, with silver buttons and dark green shako-cords and plume.*

# The Scottish Regiments

Scotland was a fertile ground for recruiting-parties, so that many regiments not officially 'Scottish' numbered Scotsmen in their ranks. There were also a considerable number of line regiments which were officially Scottish (though the kingdoms of Scotland and England no longer had separate military establishments as in the past), including some styled 'Highland' regiments, which wore the military tailors' idea of what traditional Highland dress comprised, principally a kilt and feathered bonnet. The ornateness of this uniform and the singular appearance of the regiments so dressed doubtless attracted more attention than did the plainer English and Irish regiments, and some English writers suggested that the Scots gained undue credit in the eyes of the civilian population as a result. Whatever truth there may be in this opinion, there is no doubt that the Scottish regiments contributed very greatly to British successes during the Revolutionary and Napoleonic Wars, and were renowned not only for reliability and courage but (the Highland regiments in particular) for excellent behaviour off the field of battle.

A number of ordinary line regiments were recruited in Scotland, or were Scottish by designation; though most 'Scottish' regiments included a proportion of English or Irishmen in the same way that 'English' regiments included Scotsmen. Even ostensible 'Highland' regiments contained non-Scots; though the state of the 79th in the late 1790's (needing to recruit after a spell in the West Indies and finding the potential 'Highland' areas well-scoured by recruiters from other regiments) was exceptional, temporarily having only 38 per cent Scots. The Scottish non-Highland regiments – which might be termed 'Lowland' though this term was not in use at the time – included a number of the briefly-formed regiments of the 1790's, such as Montgomerie's (un-numbered) Glasgow Regiment, but more significantly comprised a number of the most celebrated line regiments. These included the 1st (Royal Scots), 21st (Royal North British Fuzileers), 25th (Sussex Regt until 1805; thereafter the King's Own Borderers), 26th (Cameronians), 70th (Surrey until 1812; thereafter

Glasgow Lowland), 90th (Perthshire Volunteers), 94th (Scotch Brigade, whose unusual title was a relic of their service in the Dutch army) and the 'de-kilted' ex-Highland regiments mentioned previously. Although these regiments preserved an element of 'Scottishness' in such minor details as the use of Scottish symbols in their insignia (thistle motifs or the star of the Order of the Thistle) and similar minor features, they were to

all intents like the ordinary line regiments in matters of recruiting and service.

The Highland regiments, however, preserved a character of their own, reinforced by their unique costume. The earliest Highland regiment to be taken into the British line was the 42nd (Royal Highlanders), traditionally known by their rather dubious nickname, 'Black Watch', though not until 1861 was this title granted officially. Taken into the line as the 43rd Foot (soon renumbered) when the previous 'independent companies' were regimented in 1739, its excellent service set the trend for the formation of an increasing number of Highland regiments which served in the later 18th century. The lineage of such regiments is confused by frequent disbandings and the subsequent raising of different regiments with the same num-

ber, and later by re-numbering of regiments, so that, for example, the 100th Highland Regt was re-numbered as the 92nd in 1799, bearing no relation to the previous units with that number: the Donegal Light Infantry of 1760-63, the

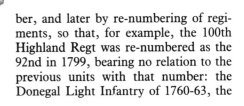

*Private, battalion company, 92nd Highlanders, 1815, in typical campaign uniform, wearing the regimental 'Gordon' tartan, created by adding a yellow overstripe to the 'Government' (Black Watch) sett. The feathered bonnet by this period had attained the now-familiar shape; though regimental orders for the 92nd forbade the use of the detachable peak used by most Highland regiments, contemporary illustrations show it in use in the Waterloo period. The plume at the left of the bonnet was coloured as for the line regiments (white-over-red for battalion companies, white for grenadiers and green for light infantry). The sporran was rarely, if ever, worn on campaign.*

92nd of 1779-83, raised at Bedford, or the Irish 92nd of 1794-95.

At the beginning of the Revolutionary Wars the Highland regiments comprised the 42nd and five comparatively newly-formed regiments numbered 71 to 75. Among the regiments formed in the rapid expansion of the army in the 1790s were those which became the 78th (Ross-shire Buffs), raised 1793; 79th (Cameronian Volunteers, from 1804 Cameron Highlanders), raised 1793; 91st (Argyllshire Highlanders), numbered as the 98th from 1794-98; 92nd, known as the Gordon Highlanders, a title adopted officially in 1861, raised as the 100th in 1798; 93rd Highlanders, raised 1800; 97th (Inverness-shire Highlanders), a corps of brief duration whose number was eventually occupied by the Queen's Germans; the 109th (Aberdeen-shire), 116th (Perthshire Highlanders) and the 132nd and 133rd, corps of similarly ephemeral duration.

It has been stated that in some cases, the new Highland regiments were formed as a result of the last vestige of the 'clan system' which had been suppressed after the Jacobite Rebellion of 1745-46, by officers enrolling the members of their own clan under an almost feudal system of loyalty accorded the clan or sept chieftain. Whilst this would appear to be a simplistic interpretation of the mode of recruiting in the Highlands, there would appear to be some validity to it. By the system of awarding commissions in new regiments to those candidate officers who brought in a number of recruits, family ties do appear to have had some considerable influence in the early 1790s, before the traditional

recruiting-grounds had been saturated with recruiting-parties from many regiments. As an example, it is noteworthy that in the Grant or Strathspey Fencibles authorised in 1793 and formed by Sir James Grant Bt, the initial intake of men included 41 named Fraser, 94 named McDonald (or variants of that name) and 79 named Grant; of the officers who served during the unit's existence (disbanded 1799), 3 were named Fraser, 6 McDonald and 35 plus the chaplain named Grant. The fact that so many were related to the family or clan of their officers must have engendered a 'family' feeling within the regiment, but produced a clerical problem common to all Highland regiments within the period, that of confusing men of the same name. Within the rank-and-file of the Strath-speys, for example, there were 20 men named John Grant, so each was assigned a number, to differentiate between (say) John Grant (5), a 40-year-old ex-labourer from Abernethy, and John Grant (8), a 22-year-old dancing-master from Kirk-michael. A further relic of old Highland custom was evident in the presence in some regiments of the foster-brothers of officers, who served as private soldiers (chieftains following the old practice of adopting foster-children); thus when the famous John Cameron of Fassiefern, commander of the 92nd, was killed at Quatre Bras, he was buried by his foster-brother Private Ewen McMillan. (This unit was singularly unlucky in its commanding officers; in addition to Cameron of Fassiefern, Col Erskine of Cardross was killed in Egypt and Col Napier of

*An officer of the 79th Highlanders as depicted in Goddard and Booth's* Military Costume of Europe, 1812. *Though officers usually wore overalls on campaign, they used the kilt for full dress; note also the distinctive shoulder-sash restricted to Highland regiments, instead of the waist-sash of the remainder, and the traditional Highland 'broadsword'.*

Blackstone at Corunna.) A further distinction enjoyed almost exclusively by Scottish regiments was the presence of bagpipes, important for maintaining morale, though not officially sanctioned at this period.

In other ways, recruiting for Highland regiments followed the normal course, as the purchase of 66 gallons of whisky (£12.8.3d) in 1793 by a recruiting-party probably at Fort William testifies! Another inducement was apparently offered by the beautiful Duchess of Gordon, who assisted her young son, the Marquess of Huntly, in raising his 100th (later 92nd) in 1798; according to legend, she placed the traditionial 'king's shilling' recruiting-bounty between her lips, so that each recruit almost kissed her as he took it in his own mouth. Whether apocryphal or not, like many other stories it entered the folklore surrounding the Highland regiments.

In addition to the regular regiments, Scotland provided the bulk of the Fencible corps, many of whose members ultimately transferred to regular service. Between 1794 and 1798 at least 37 of the battalions formed were Scottish, and the bulk of these were Highland corps. Being virtually regular regiments but for the proviso that they were not to be sent abroad except at their own behest, they had to compete for recruits with the regular regiments, but as Scotland had no Militia until 1797 adequate numbers were found. The understanding that they were not to serve 'abroad' (i.e. not outside the country in which they were raised) caused much concern and led to a number of 'mutinies' ('protests' might be a better description) among units which were ordered to go to England, most notably probably the revolt of the Strathspeys at Dumfries in 1795. The cause was a mixture of ignorance, perhaps some radical agitation from the local civilian population, and equally the unfeeling attitude of the central government which could not appreciate the fears of the ordinary men that once aboard ship they would be drafted into other regiments or sent to the disease-ridden West Indies, they having enlisted specifically for service in their own country and with their kinsmen; probably the fact that some spoke only Gaelic widened the gulf between the men and the government. Such mutinies were suppressed by the arrest and trial of perceived ring-

*'Big Sam' MacDonald of the Sutherland Fencibles, who stood 6ft 10in tall and who was allowed an extra 2/6d per diem for sustenance! His feats of strength became legendary, though he died aged only 35. Regimental facings were yellow and the tartan of 'Government' sett.*
*(Print after John Kay, 1796)*

leaders, some of whom were executed; in the case of the Strathspeys, five were condemned and two actually shot. A number of similar outbreaks afflicted regiments in Scotland in the mid-1790s, though few were prepared to rest the blame where it was deserved. Among these was Col Hay of the 109th (Aberdeenshire) Regt, who was a Member of Parliament and declaimed in the House of Commons that the unrest was due to the government not having kept to the terms of enlistment under which the men had enrolled. The Secretary at War replied, not surprisingly, that the trouble was due to the fact that in recruiting, 'it was always necessary to employ men of a very low description'!

Nevertheless, by 1798 the situation had cleared so much that a number of Fencible regiments volunteered to serve abroad if required, and some greatly distinguished themselves in Ireland during the "98" rebellion, especially the Breadal-

bane and Reay regiments; and when the Fencibles were disbanded, large numbers of men entered regular service. Col Wemyss of Wemyss, commander of the Sutherland Fencibles, for example, appears to have recruited many of his ex-Fencible men when forming his 93rd Highlanders in 1800.

Throughout the Peninsular War and Waterloo campaign, the Scottish regiments continued to distinguish themselves in action and, especially the Highland regiments, remained comparatively free of crime and punishment; several contemporary writers record how popular they were in occupied territory from their fair dealing with the civilians, and it was said that in the 93rd's light company not a man had to be punished within a 19-year period. The Highlanders appear to have been extremely resourceful, whether in the improvisation of 'bothies' made from brushwood and turf as bivouacs, or in the manufacture of 'brogues' from rawhide during the Peninsular War (to replace worn-out shoes). A different type of resourcefulness was displayed by one John Fisher, a native of Berwick, who was probably unique in surviving the two most terrible retreats of the age, to Corunna and from Moscow. Captured at the former, he was one of very few British soldiers to escape from their unpleasant prison-camps by enlisting in the French army, with whom he made the 1812 campaign and survived the horrors of the crossing of the Beresina, thereafter refusing to carry arms against his own countrymen. On his discharge from British service, which he rejoined after the war, he became a detective and was partly responsible for the arrest of Burke and Hare.

The equipment of the Highland regiments resembled that of the ordinary line infantry, except that the officers and some NCOs carried 'broadswords' instead of the infantry pattern swords, though some officers of flank companies had curved sabres like those of the line. Their uniform was distinctive, with the kilt which existed in two styles, the traditional 'belted plaid' (*breacan-an-feile*) giving way to the *philabeg* or 'little kilt' with which a shoulder-plaid was not worn. 'Clan' tartans had not evolved at this period in the accepted sense, and a number of the military designs produced for regiments at this period were the origin of the later 'clan' patterns, such as the 92nd's 'Gordon' tartan, basically the traditional dark 'government' sett worn by the 42nd with a yellow overstripe, or the 'Cameron of Erracht' designed for the 79th. The kilt being regarded detrimental to the recruiting of non-Highlanders led to the de-kilting of the regiments previously mentioned in 1809. Officers usually wore overalls rather than the kilt on campaign, and certain regiments wore overalls at times, in tropical climates; the 71st wore tartan *truibhs* (trews) on their return from South America, prior to their conversion to light infantry. Trews were an alternative 'Highland' dress of some antiquity; indeed, Sir John Sinclair of Ulbster Bn, commander of the Rothsay and Caithness Fencibles, attempted to prove that trews rather than the kilt was the original Highland dress, and costumed his regiment accordingly. The 'feather bonnet' evolved from the traditional blue cloth cap to which feathers were added during this period, often at the expense of the individual, so that a regiment embarking for foreign service put its privately-purchased feathers into store to be reclaimed on its return.

The service of the regiments which remained 'Highland' throughout were extremely distinguished. The 42nd served in the Netherlands and the West Indies, and then in the Mediterranean from 1798, winning especial fame in Egypt. An incident at Alexandria perhaps indicates the especial attention paid to the Scottish regiments at the expense of the less-glamorous but no less worthy ordinary line regiments, when the standard of what became known in Britain as Bonaparte's 'Invincible Legion' (actually the 21st *Demi-Brigade Légère*) was supposedly captured by a sergeant of the 42nd. Much publicity was accorded the deed, and the Highland Society of London struck commemorative medals to be awarded to each man; but it appears that though the 42nd man may have been involved in the action, the flag was actually captured by a Swiss, Anton Lutz of the Minorca Regiment (later 97th Foot). William Cobbett, the political radical, gave much publicity to the case in his newspaper, which resulted in Lutz being accorded his due and the medal-issue apparently cancelled. (Cobbett was later imprisoned for his protests over the issue of flogging in the army.) Both battalions of the 42nd ser-

ved in the Peninsular War, and following the disbanding of the 2nd Bn, the remaining one fought with great distinction at Quatre Bras and Waterloo.

The 78th also served in the Netherlands, and both its battalions went to the Cape in 1795, where they were amalgamated, and thence to India. A new 2nd Bn served in the Mediterranean (including at Maida) before sending the bulk of its personnel to reinforce the battalion in India; re-recruited, the 2nd Bn served with Graham in the Netherlands in 1813-14. The 1st Bn came home only in 1817.

The 79th was re-formed on its return from the West Indies, and served in north Holland in 1799, and then in the Mediterranean, including Egypt. Its 2nd Bn remained at home, but the 1st went to Copenhagen in 1807 and the Peninsula in 1808 (and to Walcheren), fighting with distinction at Fuentes de Oñoro (where its commanding officer was killed), Salamanca, Nivelle, Nive and Toulouse; originally destined for America, it was diverted to Flanders and served with distinction at Quatre Bras and Waterloo.

The 92nd served in north Holland in 1799 and in Egypt in 1802; at Copenhagen and in the Peninsula, at Corunna, to Walcheren, and back to the Peninsula where it fought at Fuentes de Oñoro, Vittoria, Nive and Orthez, and with particular distinction in the Pyrenees. It served at Quatre Bras and Waterloo with equal distinction; during this period the 2nd Bn (raised 1803) remained at home as a source of manpower for the 1st. Typical of the 'mythology' which has tended to surround the Scottish regiments is the famous story concerning the 92nd at Waterloo, of their charging with the 2nd Dragoons (Royal Scots Greys), the infantry hanging onto the cavalrymen's stirrup-leathers, sweeping away the French in a frenzy of Celtic ardour; though the subject of many later and generally very inaccurate battle-paintings, and featuring in numerous non-contemporary accounts, the incident almost certainly never occurred, but probably arose from some detached members of the 92nd becoming entangled in the charge of the Union Brigade.

The 93rd served at the Cape from 1806 to 1814, its hardest service coming at New Orleans in 1815, where it lost heavily. The 2nd Bn was raised only in 1814, for service in Newfoundland.

# The Irish Regiments

Ireland was a most fertile recruiting-ground for the whole army, not just those regiments bearing Irish titles; but it also provided the scene for the only widespread conflict within the British Isles during the period. Political and religious grievances had troubled Ireland for years, and in the early 1790s the Society of United Irishmen led the agitation which resulted in some relaxation of the strictures upon Roman Catholics. Both the United Irishmen and the Catholic association of 'Defenders' entered into negotiation with France, the more radical elements believing that a French invasion would cure all ills; and France, recognising that rebellion in Ireland would occupy Britain's military resources, promised aid. In the event, French rhetoric was greater than their ability to mount an invasion, an attempt under General Hoche to land at Bantry Bay in 1796-97 ending in utter failure.

The threat of invasion, however, accelerated the polarization of views in Ireland; the United Irishmen assembled an underground military organisation, and as a safeguard against invasion or insurrection a force of Yeomanry was established in opposition, encouraged by the Orange Society, a vehemently Protestant and loyalist organisation. The United Irishmen's hope of a front embracing all Irish people was dashed; instead, the stage was set for what was virtually a civil war. The British troops in Ireland were comparatively few in number and dispersed widely, with the Irish militia regiments often ill-officered and infiltrated by United Irishmen. The government did little to remedy the situation and the general commanding in Ireland, the worthy Sir Ralph Abercromby, resigned after issuing a General Order which expressed his lack of confidence in the forces in Ireland. Shortly afterwards the rebellion of 1798 broke out, a spasmodic rising of the United Irishmen (the arrest of whose leader, Lord Edward Fitzgerald, confounded their plans), which only in Wexford assumed a very dangerous aspect.

The ''98' was a catalogue of horror, with massacre and atrocity perpetrated by both sides, each avenging long-held hatreds. The rebels, though ill-armed and ill-organised, fought at times with considerable bravery and inflicted some reverses upon the government forces, especially upon the Irish militia of which some units were good, but many justified the complaint of the lord-lieutenant and commander during the rebellion, Marquess Cornwallis, who condemned them as 'totally without discipline, contemptible before the enemy when any serious resistance is made to them, but ferocious and cruel in the extreme when any poor wretches with or without arms come within their power'. The major rebel force had been defeated totally at Vinegar Hill in Wexford in June 1798 before the French assistance arrived, a small expedition under General Humbert which landed at Killala Bay, County Mayo, in August. He put to

*One of the most celebrated Peninsular exploits was the capture of the 'Eagle' of the French 8th Line Regt at Barrosa by Sgt Patrick Masterson of the 87th. In this print by Clark & Dubourg, Masterson wrests the 'Eagle' from its bearer, Sous-Lieutenant Edmé Guillemin.*

flight a force of militia, Fencibles and a few regulars at Castlebar, but received little popular support, and after a most valiant fight had been put up against the French by the Limerick Militia at Coloony, who behaved magnificently against great odds, Humbert surrendered his surviving 800 men at Ballinamuck on 8 September. The ''98' rebellion was thus crushed, but reprisals continued, a sad chapter in British history.

Despite the suppression of the rebellion, resources had been severely tested, to the extent that it was necessary for the government to accept the offer of English militia regiments to serve in Ireland (indeed, militiamen served there as late as 1811), perhaps indicative of the defects in the organisation of the garrison in Ireland. Nevertheless, Ireland continued to provide a flood of recruits, apparently unaffected by the events of the rebellion (save for the emigration of a few men who joined Napoleon's 'Irish Legion'). Contemporary writers caricature the Irish troops as generally good-humoured ruffians with a penchant for alcohol (conceivably an unjust stereotyping), and perhaps a higher punishment-rate than that of English and Scots, but an indomitable fighting spirit resulting in some of the Irish regiments enjoying a fearsome reputation.

Senior of the Irish regiments was the 18th (Royal Irish), an ancient and distinguished corps which served in the Mediterranean in the early Revolutionary Wars (a detachment as marines at Cape St Vincent), and in Egypt. With a newly-raised 2nd Bn, both went to the West Indies and wasted away; when the 1st Bn came home in 1817 it was said to have lost over 3,000 men in twelve years to disease.

The 27th (Enniskillen) served in the Netherlands and in the West Indies (greatly distinguished at St Lucia), and then in the Mediterranean and Egypt. The 1st and 2nd Bns remained in the Mediterranean theatre whilst the 3rd Bn (raised 1805) served in the Peninsula, including Badajos, Salamanca and Vittoria. The 1st and 3rd then went to north America, the former returning for the 1815 campaign where it won its greatest distinction, suffering appalling losses and memorably described as 'lying dead in a square' at Waterloo.

The 86th (Leinster; from 1812, Royal County Down) was raised in Shropshire,

Lancashire and Yorkshire, but in 1809 was given the Irish appellation; most of its service was in India. The 89th (Prince of Wales' Irish) was captured in the Netherlands in 1795 and re-formed, the 1st Bn serving in the West Indies, the Cape and Mauritius. The 2nd Bn won great fame in the Peninsula, at Barrosa, Tarifa and Vittoria.

The 88th (Connaught Rangers) was perhaps the most renowned of all, a unit second to none in its fighting record in the Peninsula, where both battalions served, in addition to service in India, South America and the Cape, and in the War of 1812. As a tribute to its magnificent Peninsular record, a regimental 'Order of Merit' was established in 1819, many of its members receiving a 'first-class'

*Sergeant, battalion company, 88th Foot, 1812. The Connaught Rangers were perhaps the most audacious unit of the Peninsular army, with a combat record surpassed by none. One of their officers, William Grattan, wrote especially of the 'desperate calm' which 'had descended on the ranks of tattered, tanned soldiers waiting in their open-necked shirts and trousers rolled up' at Badajos. All 'line' sergeants carried the spontoon (half-pike) and wore white lace.*

award for service in 12 or more battles.

The 99th (Tipperary) Regt was formed in 1805, succeeding an earlier 99th which had wasted away in Demarara; it served in Bermuda and the West Indies. The 100th (County of Dublin) Regt was raised in 1905 and took the number vacated by the Gordon Highlanders; half its number died by shipwreck off Newfoundland in October 1805, and the remainder spent the war in north America. The 101st (Duke of York's Irish) was formed in 1806, replacing another Irish 101st 'drafted' in 1794-95; it served in the West Indies and Canada. Many of the ephemeral 1790's regiments were Irish, with titles like the 121st County Clare and 134th Loyal Limerick, but were of short duration.

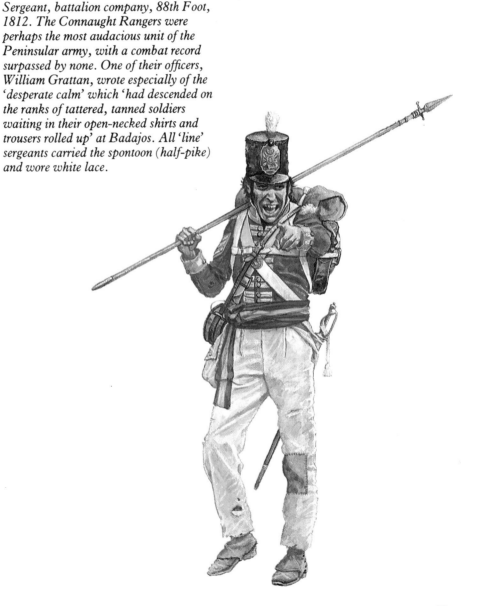

# The Light Infantry

The concept of light infantry had evolved in the latter half of the 18th century as a reaction and contrast to the formalised lines-of-battle of the ordinary infantry: fast-moving troops skilled in skirmishing, scouting and operating in 'open order', covering the flanks, rear and van of an army. The British Army had become very adept at light infantry tactics as a result of the campaigns in North America, but following the end of the War of American Independence these skills had, to a considerable extent, been lost. Each regiment might have its light company, but their proficiency declined remarkably.

Much criticism has been levelled, for this and other reasons, at Sir David Dundas, a Scottish officer whose 1788 publication entitled *Principles of Military Movements* was re-issued in amended form with official sanction in 1792 as *Rules and Regulations for the Movements of His Majesty's Infantry*. This codification of the infantry movements into 'Eighteen Manoeuvres' had two main disadvantages: it recommended a line of three men deep as the ideal formation (which was soon abandoned in practice for a two-deep line) and did not give sufficient emphasis to light infantry tactics (devoting 9 out of 458 pages to it!). These criticisms were justified, but in other ways Dundas' book was of the greatest benefit to the army, regulating the infantry manoeuvres which had previously been influenced by regimental practice (as late as 1798 H Dickinson's commentary on the 'Eighteen Manoeuvres' noted that some 'Deviations . . . are permitted in most Regiments'). But beneficial though Dundas' work may have been – it earned the nickname 'Old Pivot' for its author! – it made little difference to the state of light infantry drill or the accompanying requisite of accurate muskets and aiming-drill; for line regiments only thirty rounds of ball ammunition and seventy blank (the latter for volley-firing practice) were allocated per man per annum, and even for light infantry the number was only fifty and sixty respectively.

Consequently, the army was at a great disadvantage when it met the French, whose swarms of *tirailleurs* (sharpshooters) preceded every advance, and

initially the defect had to be remedied by the hiring of foreign regiments, generally Germans trained in light infantry duties. The need was recognised, however, and a process of creating adequate light infantry was begun. Most of the credit for the evolution of the light infantry arm is traditionally accorded to Sir John Moore, who perfected the system of training at his camp at Shorncliffe; though he first wrote about and practised light infantry drill as early as 1798-99, in Ireland. Moore was not the creator of the light infantry, but deserves much of the credit for improving and

putting into practice the theories of earlier writers. Probably the first light infantry school in the period was that established by General Grey in the West Indies (with the purpose not of originating skills but restoring those learned in the American War), but though Moore probably learned of it, it is more likely that a greater influence was the book on rifle-tactics written by Francis de Rottenburg, commander of the 5th Bn 60th Royal Americans, under Moore's command in Ireland. By extracting the best of de Rottenburg's theories and combining them with elements of Dundas, Moore perfected the light infantry training so that the resulting units were equally adept at fighting in a conventional manner *and* in open order, which had not always been the case with continental light troops, some of whom were incapable of fighting according to the more traditional methods.

Perhaps the most significant development was the formation of entire regiments of light infantry, instead of relying simply upon the regimental light companies of line regiments or rather *ad hoc*

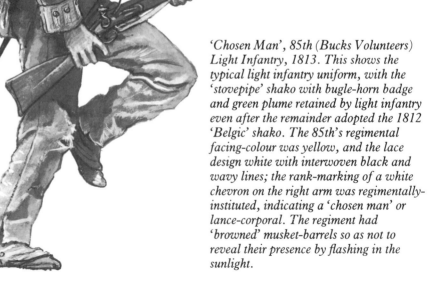

*'Chosen Man', 85th (Bucks Volunteers) Light Infantry, 1813. This shows the typical light infantry uniform, with the 'stovepipe' shako with bugle-horn badge and green plume retained by light infantry even after the remainder adopted the 1812 'Belgic' shako. The 85th's regimental facing-colour was yellow, and the lace design white with interwoven black and wavy lines; the rank-marking of a white chevron on the right arm was regimentally-instituted, indicating a 'chosen man' or lance-corporal. The regiment had 'browned' musket-barrels so as not to reveal their presence by flashing in the sunlight.*

*Major William Napier, 43rd Light Infantry, 1816, depicting the scarlet jacket with white facings and silver epaulettes atop wings (field officers' distinction), and the scarlet pelisse with grey fur adopted unofficially by the 43rd in imitation of that of the 95th.*

temporary training of whole regiments. The first complete regular light infantry regiment (though not so titled until 1815) was the 90th Perthshire Volunteers, raised in 1794 by the francophobe Sir Thomas Graham of Balgowan, whose hatred of the French was aroused by the desecration of his wife's coffin. His regiment served in the Mediterranean and under Rowland (later Lord) Hill in Egypt, and from 1805 to 1814 was in the West Indies, when it transferred to Canada. The 2nd Bn (raised 1804) remained at home throughout.

Next to be converted officially was the 43rd (Monmouthshire) Regt, 1803, which was trained with the 52nd at Shorncliffe, having spent 1794 to 1801 in the West Indies. Its 2nd Bn (raised at Worcester in 1804) served in the Corunna campaign and at Walcheren, and thereafter remained at home as a depot for the 1st Bn, which served throughout the Peninsular War, from Vimeiro and Corunna to the end, and then went to north America. This splendid battalion, which served in the Light Brigade, later Division, exemplified the excellence of this formation, which was regarded as the élite of the Peninsular army.

The 51st (2nd West Riding) served in the Mediterranean, Ceylon, India and in the Corunna campaign before it was converted to light infantry in 1809. After the Walcheren expedition it joined the Peninsular army in 1811, serving throughout the remainder of the war, and was present at Waterloo. The 52nd (Oxfordshire) served in India and Ceylon until returning home in 1798. Although it was made into light infantry in 1803, the title was not conferred officially until 1809. Both battalions served at Vimeiro and with Moore, and the 2nd at Walcheren, after which it remained at home save for Graham's expedition to Holland in 1813-14. The 1st Bn served in the Light Division from 1809, winning a splendid reputation and, under its commander John Colborne, played a most decisive part in the defeat of the last French attack at Waterloo.

The 68th (Durham), converted in 1808, spent much of the period in the West Indies, but served at Walcheren and in the Peninsula from 1811, including Salamanca, Vittoria, Nivelle, Nive and Orthez. The 71st Highlanders were converted to the Highland Light Infantry (initially 'Glasgow Highland') in 1809 after its return from South America, having earlier served in India, Ceylon and the Cape. After service at Walcheren it was transferred to Portugal, serving throughout the Peninsular War from 1810, and was in Adam's brigade with the 1/52nd and 2/ and 3/95th at Quatre Bras and Waterloo. The 85th (Bucks Volunteers) was converted to light infantry in 1808, having served as a newly-raised regiment in the Netherlands, at Gibraltar and in north Holland in 1799, and from 1803 to 1808 in Jamaica. It fought at Walcheren and in 1810-11 in the Peninsular War, but was sent home in the latter year. Considerable unrest among the officers caused the whole body to be removed (less 2 captains, 1 lieutenant and the surgeons) and the unit re-officered, which transformed a mediocre regiment into a very fine one. It rejoined the Peninsular army in 1813 and at the end of the war went to north America, where it fought at Bladensburg and New Orleans.

In addition to these light infantry regiments, the line regiments retained their light companies so that each battalion was capable of throwing forward a screen of trained skirmishers, and for a short period some battalions trained

*Officer and private of the 52nd Light Infantry, from CH Smith's* Costume of the Army of the British Empire *(1814). This depicts the classic light infantry uniform, characterised by the green plume, and shoulder-wings. The 52nd wore buff facings, including turnbacks.*

additional men, termed 'flankers', to supplement their light company, but though these were employed at Maida the practice was not widespread, and was rendered largely unnecessary by the later practice of attaching companies of riflemen to each Division, so that each semi-independent formation possessed its light infantry capabilities.

In uniform and weaponry the light infantry resembled the line, with minor variations. Most significant was the issue of slightly shorter 'light infantry'-pattern muskets, some equipped with backsights to facilitate aiming. Their uniform was like that of the line, except for the whole wearing the shoulder-'wings' normally indicative of line 'flank' companies, and green plumes; the light regiments retained the 'stovepipe' shako throughout, which was also worn by officers, unlike officers of the line who never adopted the 'stovepipe' cap. The two Scottish regiments had unique features of uniform, the 71st having Scottish bonnets blocked into shako-shape and retaining their bagpipers, whilst the 90th wore a crested leather helmet of light dragoon style. Officers of the 43rd aped light cavalry styles to such an extent that they even adopted pelisses.

# The Rifle Corps

Although some continental armies, notably in Germany, had made use of riflemen for a considerable time, Britain possessed no such native unit until 1800, save Ferguson's ephemeral formation of the American War. The great accuracy attainable with these firearms enabled them to do great damage to the enemy ranks, and out-shoot the French skirmishers who habitually preceded their advances. A level of intelligence and initiative was required from the ordinary riflemen, to take advantage of available cover, qualities which the more mechanical drill-movements of the line did not encourage. Some believed that a whole regiment armed with rifles, due to their slower rate of fire, could not stand against conventional troops armed with the musket, so that the preference was for individual companies armed with rifles which could be distributed throughout the army, much as the few foreign units had been in the early 1790s.

*Marksmen of the 5/60th (left) and 95th Rifles, the former distinguished by the regimental red facings and blue breeches. The 95th is shown in green overalls, though grey would be equally common on campaign. (Print by I C Stadler after C H Smith, 1813.)*

As Commander-in-Chief the Duke of York was responsible for many of the improvements to the British Army around the turn of the century – his worth has not always been recognised – and it was he who ordered the formation of an 'Experimental Corps of Riflemen' in 1800, to be composed of officers and men selected from fourteen line regiments, who were to be trained in rifle-shooting and then returned to their units, as the first stage in providing each battalion with a rifle detachment. Commanded by Lt-Col Hon William Stewart (67th) and Col Coote Manningham (41st), the detachments assembled in 1800, but after training were employed as a body in the operation against Ferrol; after which, reinforced by drafts from 26 Fencible regiments, they remained as a unit and were numbered as the 95th Foot.

About forty types of rifle, including German and American weapons, were tested, and the choice made for the pattern submitted by the London gunsmith Ezekiel Baker, probably the finest mass-produced weapon of its era, its 30-inch barrel especially suited to skirmish duties, and equipped with a wide-bladed sword-bayonet for use in close combat. It fired the standard ball (though Baker's calibre varied slightly), the great accuracy being imparted by the grooved rifling on the inside of the barrel, which demanded a tightly-fitting projectile: to force the ball down the barrel, mallets were provided for use in conjunction with the ramrod! It was a most formidable weapon; Baker himself fired at a man-sized target at 100 and 200 yards range with 34 and 24 shots respectively, every one hitting the target. In battle, similar feats were recorded on innumerable occasions: at Waterloo, John Kincaid silenced two French guns before their crews could discharge a second shot, and George Simmons performed a similar feat at Badajos. Unlike the musket, the rifle could be loaded and fired in the prone position, enabling marksmen to take advantage of small cover or to gain additional accuracy by bracing their elbows against their knees, or even to fire whilst lying on the back. The effect of this ability to hit a specific target at long range enabled the skirmish-

*Private, 95th Rifles, 1808, a typical appearance of the retreat to Corunna. The magnificent 95th retained its readiness to fight despite appalling privations; Harry Smith recorded, 'Oh, the filthy state we were all in! . . . literally covered and almost eaten up with vermin, most of us suffering from ague and dysentery, every man a living still active skeleton', whilst rifleman Harris described their appearance as resembling the makings of hell: 'feet swathed in bloody rags, clothing that hardly covered their nakedness, accoutrements in shreds, beards covering their faces, eyes dimmed with toil.'*

screens of riflemen to single out enemy officers and NCOs, and so thoroughly disorder their opponents.

Along with these singular skills came reinforced *esprit de corps* and the highest morale, so that the 95th developed into a corps unsurpassed in the army. A 2nd Bn was raised in 1805 and a 3rd in 1809, all three of which served in the Peninsular War with such distinction that after Waterloo they were taken out of the line and established as an independent corps, the Rifle Brigade. In addition, detachments served as marines at Copenhagen, in South America and at Walcheren. Their distinctive uniform (dark or 'rifle' green with black equipment and facings) served not only to increase regimental prestige (and gave rise to the nickname 'The Sweeps') and be a major aid to recruiting, but also acted as a rudimentary camouflage.

The 95th was not the first or only rifle corps, for in 1797 a 5th battalion was added to the 60th (Royal American) Regt, the first green-coated regular battalion in the army (the North York Militia's rifle company predated them by a short time), and further battalions were raised subsequently, though not until 1814 was the entire regiment ordered to be clothed in green. The unit was originally formed in America and throughout was used as a receptacle for foreigners wishing to serve in the British Army, its red-coated 'line' battalions generally serving in north America and the West Indies. The 5th Bn was armed with rifles and utilised the service of many Germans who had previously served in the emigrant corps, and were thus already trained in the use and tactics of the weapon. Serving with great distinction throughout the Peninsular War, the extent to which the regiment remained 'foreign' is evident from the fact that after the 5th Bn was disbanded at the end of hostilities and a draft sent to the 2nd Bn at Quebec, only 11 English names were present in the 426 men. At the end of the Peninsular War, something approaching half the regiment was German in composition and in 1814, of 299 officers ranking as major or below, 40 bore German names, 24 French, 5 Italian, 1 Dutch and 1 Spanish, with others whose names may be anglicizations of foreign ones. Orders were read in German and their nickname 'Jaggers' is an anglicization of the German *Jäger*, = riflemen.

Among several other corps equipped as riflemen or which included rifle companies were the two light battalions of the King's German Legion, dressed in green and armed with rifles; whilst the 8th Bn of the German Legion complained in 1807 that they had been supplied with rifles of three different

*Capt Edward Kent, 95th Rifles, in a typical Peninsular War campaign uniform which though in 'rifle' colouring is styled like that of the light cavalry which the light infantry aped, including a cap with folding peak resembling a hussar 'mirliton' and furred pelisse. (Reconstruction by PW Reynolds after a contemporary portrait.)*

calibres, and among the other rifle companies, the 22nd (Cheshire) Regt provided men for a rifle corps in South Africa. In the Peninsular War, much of the army's 'rifle' capacity was provided by the Portuguese Caçadores, and a large proportion of the domestic volunteers were armed and trained as riflemen. On active service, in order to provide each of the major Divisons with a 'rifle' capacity, it was common practice to distribute companies of riflemen individually throughout the army, though battalion-sized formations were also employed, as in the matchless Light Brigade, later Division.

---

## Organisation of a typical 95th Rifles company c. 1809:

**Headquarters:**
  1 Captain, 1 or 2 lieutenants,⋆
  1 sergeant-major, 1 armourer.

**Two platoons each of two squads plus headquarters:**
  Platoon headquarters: 1 lieutenant or 2nd lieutenant, 1 bugler.
  Each squad: 1 sergeant, 1 corporal,
  25 riflemen.

**Total strength:**
  1 captain, 3 or 4 lieutenants,
  1 sergeant-major, 4 sergeants,
  4 corporals, 2 buglers, 1 armourer,
  100 riflemen.

(⋆) it was usual to have one extra subaltern per two companies, presumably to ensure a sufficiency of officers for detached duties. (The corporals were often counted *with* the riflemen, giving a theoretical company-establishment of 112 or 113 of all ranks.)

# Militia, Fencibles and Volunteers

There existed a number of different categories of what might be termed 'auxiliary' infantry. The Fencibles mentioned previously, though in most respects they resembled regular regiments, and though the majority were Scottish a number were raised in England. Of the 41 battalions still existing in 1801, only 23 were Scottish, two Manx, and one each from Newfoundland, Wales, Ireland and Scillonian. A number did volunteer to serve 'abroad' – 12 regiments in 1799 offered to go to Europe – and performed useful service in Ireland; the Cambrian Fencibles apparently went to Portugal in 1800 and the Ancient Irish served in Egypt. Only the Manx corps was re-formed after the renewal of the war in 1803, and existed until 1811.

The statutory home-defence force was the Militia, a series of infantry battalions formed upon a county basis. Originating in the 17th century, it was usual for the Militia to be formed ('embodied') only in time of war, though the mechanism for its assembly remained in place throughout, and unlike every other military force it involved a degree of 'conscription'. Each county was allotted a 'quota' of men to be raised in wartime, according to the population of the county; thus small counties might form very small battalions, whilst Yorkshire had several full-strength battalions. These men were recruited in two ways: by voluntary enlistment upon the payment of a bounty, as in the regular army, and if sufficient men were not forthcoming the balance was selected by ballot from among the able-bodied inhabitants of the county, less a wide range of exempted categories ranging from apprentices to dissenters. It was not a true conscription, however, as those selected might elect to pay for a 'substitute' to serve in their place, often a considerable expense but one which could be reduced by joining an insurance club, which for an annual subscription guaranteed to provide a substitute. Once a militia battalion had been formed in wartime, it resembled a regular unit in that it was employed in permanent garrison duty throughout Great Britain, but could not be sent abroad and was never left in its own area, to prevent any conflict of loyalty arising from anti-riot duty, which could have been compromised if the men were in their own home area. There were several advantages to joining the militia rather than the regular army, in that the dangers of battle were avoided and militiamen's families were financially supported by their own parish, dependants of regular soldiers receiving no such support; thus the very existence of the militia was detrimental to recruiting for the regular army. From 1805 the difficulty was recognised and militiamen permitted, in fact earnestly encouraged, to volunteer into the line, with a ten-guinea bounty (later £14 for life and £11 for limited service), from which time almost half the army's recruits came from the militia. This had a marked effect in improving the overall calibre of the regular army, for not only did the militia recruits bring in a slightly wider social base than previous recruits, but also entered the army already having a knowledge of arms and drill, and experience of discipline. In the first four years of the Peninsular War, 55,000 militiamen joined the regular army.

In their domestic duties the militia was of great value in releasing regular troops from garrison-duty, but in the mid-1790s in particular they were not always well-disciplined: in June 1795 some of the Oxford Militia were shot and more flogged for participating in riots, and in that December the Huntingdon and South Lincoln rioted and broke up their barracks at Great Yarmouth, but such incidents were unfortunate exceptions. Some units volunteered for service overseas (the Cornwall went to Ireland as late as 1811) and at the end of the Peninsular War three 'provisional battalions' were sent to Spain, but arrived too late to be engaged. Exceptions were the Scottish Militia, in that they were formed only in 1797; the London in that they were not sent from their home locality; and the Channel Isles regiments in that *all* able-bodied men were trained and used only for protection of the islands.

The other main auxiliary force were the Volunteers, the infantry equivalent of the yeomanry, part-time 'home guards' who drilled for a few hours a week and whose duties were to defend their locality in case of invasion, or to assist the magistrates in time of riot. Prior to 1803

*Left: The volunteer forces awarded many regimental medals, some of the superb workmanship illustrated; this example was awarded to Charles Doubble by Capt Samuel Edwards of the St Clement Danes Volunteers, a London corps of two light infantry companies.*
*Right: Grenadier of the Bank of England Volunteers, a unit formed from Bank employees in 1798 specifically to protect the Bank; its uniform was red with green facings.*
*(Print by John Wallis, published 1804.)*

*Volunteer corps wore uniforms of regular army style, blue coats being very popular before 1802; from 1803 infantry wore red, artillery blue and rifle corps green. This typical uniform shows an officer of the Roxwell Volunteers, 1804, an Essex light infantry company 68 strong and commanded by Capt George Cheveley. The single-breasted scarlet jacket has yellow facings, gold lace and ornaments; green plume and white or blue breeches.*

the volunteer forces were mostly self-supporting and middle-class in composition, but a great deal more order was imposed when the force was re-formed in 1803 when the danger of invasion was very real. Those corps which accepted governmental assistance (finances and weaponry) were obliged to do more than defend their own villages; under the so-called 'June Allowances' system they were paid for 85 days' training per year, and required to serve within their own Military District. In July 1803 the Levy en Masse Act was passed enabling the government to drill every able-bodied man if necessary, which would be enacted if insufficient volunteers came forward. Under this degree of compulsion (the 'August Allowances' by which units were paid for 20 days' training per year and compelled to agree to 'march to any part of Great Britain for the defence thereof' upon the appearance of an invasion-force or for suppression of insurrection arising from such invasion), an immense force was formed, covering the entire country. By December 1803 some 380,193 men were enrolled, units ranging in size from the South Regt of Devon Volunteers (two cavalry troops, 36 infantry companies) at 2,483 rank-and-file, to the Norfolk Mounted Rifles with 24 men. The strongest units composed of infantry alone were the Loyal Birmingham and Shropshire Regiments, each with 1,800 rank-and-file. County-strengths ranged from Devon with 15,212 men and the three Yorkshire Ridings with 22,580, to Bute's 90 men. Despite the regulations, 'terms of service' of the myriad corps varied wildly, some offering to serve *anywhere* required, down to Westminster's Somerset Place Infantry, 'Solely for the Defence of Somerset House'. Partly as an attempt to remedy these varied conditions of service, from 1808 the volunteers were largely absorbed by a new Local Militia, battalions formed on county lines to replace the small independent units; (in 1803 there were 604 cavalry troops, 3,976 infantry and 102 artillery companies, 742 units consisting only of single companies); but some volunteer units existed until the peace of 1814.

The military value of the volunteers is debatable; regular inspections eliminated the worst, and some officers considered the discipline of some equal to that of the regulars, and certainly they responded

*An officer's silver shoulder-belt plate of the 1st Bn Cinque Ports Volunteers, 1804, a three-battalion corps formed on the Kent-Sussex coast, which was commanded by none other than William Pitt, in his capacity as Lord Warden of the Cinque Ports.*

with enthusiasm to any false invasion-alarms. The most famous of these was caused in 1804 when a bonfire in Northumberland was mistaken as the ignition of the chain of warning-beacons which studded the coast; the whole of the border-country turned out, volunteers marching to their assembly-points, the Liddesdale men to the old Border tune of '*Wha daur meddle wi' me*'! Secretary of State Windham might call the volunteers 'painted cherries' which only simple birds would mistake for real fruit, but they fulfilled a valuable role in society, suppressing disorder when it occurred and, perhaps, raising public confidence in the security of the country. Volunteer service itself involved some hazards; civil unrest was rife in the 1790's and volunteers were frequently called upon to aid the local magistrates; an especially unpleasant event occurred in Rochdale in 1795, for example, when the local volunteers opened fire over the heads of a mob but accidently killed two spectators, whilst in the same year the unpopularity of the volunteers with the lower classes was shown by the beating to death of Thomas Purvis for no other reason than his wearing the Newcastle Volunteers' uniform.

# Chapter Three: THE ARTILLERY

The artillery might be divided into three basic categories: field, siege and garrison, with the field artillery being subdivided into 'foot' and horse artillery. These categories existed only with regard to the type of gun employed; they were manned by personnel of the same corps, though the mounted branch was to a degree separate (even having their own distinctive uniform), and the garrison artillery was frequently manned by so-called 'invalid companies', personnel fit to operate the guns but not to serve in the open field. All were part of the the the Royal Artillery, which in the strictest sense was not part of the army; instead of being controlled by the 'Horse Guards' (the term signifying the headquarters of the Commander-in-Chief), like most engineer services the Royal Artillery was controlled by the Board of Ordnance, headed by the Master-General of the Ordnance. The result was a distinct organisation, with all clerical duties run from the corps headquarters at Woolwich by the Deputy Adjutant-General, Royal Artillery, with a tiny staff of one assistant and five clerks, and in general a very close-knit, almost family feeling existed among the officers of the corps.

Throughout the period, the British artillery arm was small, at least when compared to the enormous numbers of guns fielded by the major continental armies. Despite the expansion of the artillery during the Napoleonic Wars (there were 274 artillery officers in 1791, increasing to 727 in 1814), a limitation both of resources but mainly of trained personnel precluded the deployment by the British of anything akin to the 'massed batteries' which could be assembled by continental armies. But although the Royal Artillery might be small in numbers, the excellence of training received by officers resulted in the lower ranks at least being highly proficient in their duties. All artillery officers had to undergo both theoretical and practical training before they were commissioned, and unlike the remainder of the army their promotion depended upon seniority within the corps, and could not be short-cut by the purchase of commissions as in the remainder of the army. Most of this train-ing was given at the corps' own instructional centre at Woolwich, though candidates could also train at other establishments. The training, though thorough, limited the rate at which the corps could be expanded; whereas virtually any young gentleman of reasonable education and someone to recommend him might be able to gain a line commission, even without purchase, only a limited number of artillerymen could graduate in any one year, as there was no auxiliary artillery upon which to draw; there was, for example, no artillery militia, and in general volunteer artillery companies were limited to the manning of shore-batteries, the government not being willing to risk field-pieces in the hands of part-time soldiers lest these be captured easily in the event of French invasion. (Certain inland volunteer units *did* possess artillery – notably the Honourable Artillery Company of London, the Bradford Volunteers and the Bedfordshire Horse Artillery (the only mounted unit), but these almost always used field-pieces which they had bought themselves or had presented privately).

Thus, although the resources were available to produce a large number of guns, the problem of finding trained gunners limited the number which could ever be employed in the field; though the comparative size of British armies, compared with the enormous numbers of men which comprised continental armies, meant that although more guns could have been used, the 'shortages' of guns were usually not very severe. In continental terms, however, the army's artillery was often minute in scale; in August 1808 Wellesley apportioned his artillery to six line brigades and a reserve, each having only three guns (six in the reserve), a total of but 24 pieces; and in April 1809 the army had 34 officers and 949 other ranks (plus 3 officers, 103 Waggon Train men and 224 civilians to drive the reserve ammunition), and a total of 19 6pdrs, 6 3pdrs and 5 howitzers, a force which would have been regarded as negligible in the terms of Napoleon's *Grande Armée* or those of his main continental opponents. Both number and quality of artillery increased as the Peninsular War progressed (and the army increased in size), but remained small in comparison with those employed in the great campaigns of central Europe.

Though the calibre of officer was generally very high, central direction was often a problem. Wellington was dissatisfied with a number of his artillery commanders in the Peninsula, though as usual found it difficult to have them replaced; he considered that he would be lucky if one, Howarth, 'does not get me into a scrape' (his own brigade-major thought he had confidence neither in himself nor anyone else), and another, Borthwick, Wellington recommended to go home as he wanted an 'active officer' to fill the important position of artillery chief. In 1813 Wellington at last found the competent commander he needed, Alexander Dickson, and appointed him to command the army's artillery on the strength of his Portuguese commission (there were seven RA officers with the army who were his regimental seniors); to avoid giving them offence, Dickson habitually wore his Portuguese uniform!

The shortage of trained artillery led to the retention of the so-called 'battalion guns', an outmoded system by which each infantry battalion was equipped with two light field-pieces, intended to provide immediate fire-support whenever they went into action. These were crewed by an officer and 34 men drawn from the battalion (an officer and 18 men to manage the mobile 'galloper' guns of the cavalry), but in practice were more of an encumbrance than an asset, and the system was virtually extinct by 1799. Perhaps the last unit to keep their 'battalion guns' was the Buckinghamshire Militia (their two brass 6pdrs being purchased by public subscription in 1794), which they took to Ireland in 1798 and were even deployed on anti-riot duty in 1811/12.

*Members of the Royal Foot Artillery, 1807, wearing the uniform used throughout most of the Peninsular War, with the 'queue' and hair-powder abandoned in 1808. The corporal's blue breeches are perhaps a battalion individuality or an 'undress' item. (Print after JA Atkinson)*

# Field Artillery

Two basic varieties of fieldpiece were used by the British Army: smoothbore cannon (usually termed 'guns') and howitzers. The cannon was the ordinary artillery-piece which normally had a flat trajectory (making the firing over the heads of friendly troops virtually impossible unless the guns were sited at a higher level than the troops); the howitzer was a short-barrelled piece normally with a high trajectory, used to lob shells in an arc and thus drop the projectiles on top of the enemy or over obstructions. As the two varieties of artillery were complementary, it was usual (where possible) to combine both within the same artillery unit.

Cannon were classified into 'natures' or types, depending upon their weight of projectile; thus a '9-pounder' was a cannon firing a solid 'roundshot' weighing 9lbs. Howitzers (pieces with a barrel-length of between five and ten calibres, i.e. 5 to 10 bore-diameters in length) were normally classified by that calibre, e.g. '5½in', rather than from the weight of shot. All field artillery was constructed in the same basic manner: a cast tube of iron or 'Gun Metal' (known as 'brass': an alloy of copper and tin, sometimes with zinc added) with the centre bored out, into which the propellant charge and projectile were inserted. At the closed end of the barrel was a 'touch-hole' connecting the outside with the interior of the barrel, through which the ignition-spark was passed to explode the propellant charge. Cast on to each side of the barrel was a cylindrical projection or 'trunnion', which fitted into semi-circular depressions in the gun's carriage, secured by iron brackets or 'capsquares' which held the barrel in place. The carriage was a wooden framework supporting the barrel, beneath which was an axle for the two large wheels. Two varieties of carriage existed, a 'double bracket' or oblong framework, and the 'block trail' in which the barrel-support was made from a single baulk of timber, widening towards the trunnions, moving forward the gun's centre of gravity and thus making traversing easier by decreasing the weight at the end of the carriage furthest from the barrel. The 'double bracket' was commonly used throughout continental Europe, but Congreve's 'block

trail' was first introduced for the British horse artillery in 1793 and was a significant improvement, though the 'double bracket' was retained for howitzers and heavier guns. Woodwork was usually painted in the 'common colour', a greenish-grey, with metalwork painted black with a little red paint added.

Three basic types of projectile were used by artillery, roundshot, canister

*The three basic methods of moving guns. Top: artillery pulled by teams of horses between the limber-shafts, with a hired civilian driver running alongside. Centre: the crew of apparently a 'battalion gun', with team attached by a prolonge, with which the horses dragged the gun directly, not requiring the limber, hastening movement on the battlefield. Bottom: advance by bricole, in which the crew dragged the gun with ropes. Note the 'handspikes' inserted in the bracket trails. (Print after WH Pyne, 1802)*

48

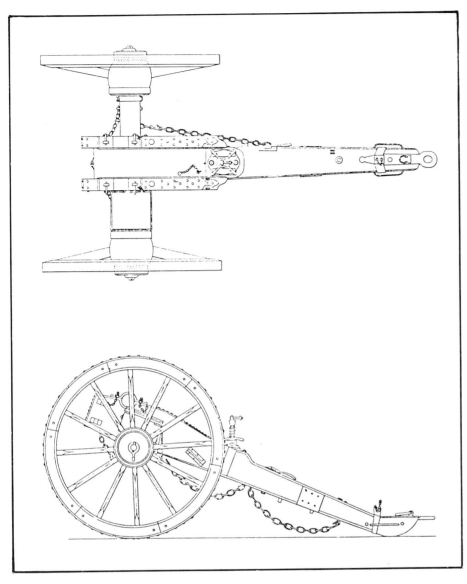

Congreve's 'block trail' artillery carriage was introduced originally for horse artillery in 1793, but later was used for all field-ordnance excluding siege-guns and howitzers, being much superior to the alternative 'double bracket' trail, especially in ease of traversing. The wheels for both 6 and 9pdr guns were 5 feet in diameter; the screw-elevator was positioned in the centre of the trail, with the handspike-socket at the end.

and shell. Roundshot was simply an iron sphere, representing the largest proportion of ammunition, used to strike down men and demolish obstacles. Although muzzle-velocities of all cannon were similar, the heavier the shot the greater its velocity when it struck the target, so that heavy roundshot was considerably more effective than light; the artillery writer Müller calculated that a 6lb shot was 50 per cent more effective than a 3lb shot. When fired, a roundshot fell steadily to earth until it touched ground, when (unless it hit mud or swamp) it bounced up from this 'first graze', a ricochet which carried it to its 'second graze', whereupon most bounced up again. Anything in its path would be struck down; whole files could be carried away, and even rolling along the ground like a cricket-ball the roundshot would strike off a limb in its path. Due to the low trajectory, virtually anything between the gun's muzzle and the final resting-place of the shot would be struck.

Ranges of artillery were dependent largely upon the amount of gunpowder used as propellant (each type had its regulated weight of powder) and the elevation at which it was fired, though naturally accuracy decreased with longer range. Tests in 1793 with 'brass' guns gave the distances to 'first graze' with a light 24pdr as 162yds with 0° elevation, 364yds with 1°, 606yds with 2° and 1,390yds with 5°. With a light 12pdr the range to 'first graze' was 601yds at 1°, 816yds at 2° and 1,063 at 3°. Elevation was generally by screw, an iron rod which raised or lowered the barrel, and the direction of shot determined by 'traversing', moving the trail by brute force, generally with the use of 'hand-spikes', iron bars inserted into brackets on the trail to swing the gun around. To compensate for the fall of shot in flight, the senior gunner then used the 'tangent sight', a notched crossbar at the closed end of the barrel, which was aligned with the foresight at the muzzle and the target. The screw-elevator and the tangent sight, both perfected by c1780, turned the haphazard aiming by guesswork into a science, gunnery officers having printed tables of statistics to which to refer as an aid to aiming.

To load the cannon, it was usual to use 'fixed ammunition' in which the projectile and propellant were fastened together, usually with a wooden 'sabot' or plug attached, which greatly speeded the process of firing. After each shot, the barrel would be swabbed out with a 'sponge', a fleece nailed onto a rammer and soaked in water to prevent any smouldering powder from the previous shot causing premature ignition. To prevent such powder blowing-back at the 'spongeman', at this moment one of the guncrew, the 'ventsman', put his thumb (in a leather stall) over the touch-hole to prevent ingress of air. The fourth crewman (the first being the aimer) then inserted the 'fixed ammunition' into the muzzle, whereupon the 'spongeman' reversed his sponge and rammed it down with the solid end of his rammer. The propellant charge affixed to the projectile was contained in a paper or canvas bag, which the 'ventsman' punctured by inserting a 'pricker' down the touch-hole, which he then filled either with a quill or paper tube of gunpowder or (before about 1800) a length of 'quick-match', strands of cotton soaked in salt-petre and spirits of wine; or finely-ground priming-powder could be poured directly from a flask into the touch-hole. The fifth member of the gun-crew then ignited the charge in the touch-hole by applying a

*Senior of the London volunteer corps was the Honourable Artillery Company (existing in 1537 if not before), comprising companies of infantry (above) and artillery in a similar uniform in blue faced red. (Print after E Walker, 1803)*

*Artillery on the march: a heavy gun with a team from the Corps of Drivers, the crew following on foot. The company officer (mounted, right) converses with an officer of the RHA. (Print after J A Atkinson, 1807)*

lighted 'portfire', a holder for a piece of smouldering 'slow-match'. The ignition of the powder in the touch-hole communicated with the charge in the barrel, which shot out the projectile with a loud report, a cloud of thick smoke and a fierce recoil (necessitating the re-positioning and aiming of the gun after every shot). Additional 'packing' for the charge in the barrel might be provided by a 'wad', a bundle of hay or straw, or lumps of turf cut by the regulation 'punch for sod wad'.

Among other factors affecting accuracy was the 'windage', the space between the ball and the barrel, a tighter-fitting ball travelling with greater accuracy than a loose one; thus rusty roundshot with flakes coming off were not as accurate, best of all being those rusty balls which had been repaired with molten lead, making the tightest fit.

At short range, artillery would fire 'canister' or case-shot, metal cans filled with small balls which turned the guns into giant shotguns. Two varieties were used, 'light case' (which for a 6pdr contained 85 1½oz bullets) and 'heavy case' (41 3½oz). They were not normally discharged at over 350yds, being reserved as the last resort for repelling a charge, though 'heavy case' would hit at up to 600yds. 'Grapeshot' is often mentioned in contemporary sources, though proper grape (a number of larger iron balls arranged around a metal rod, covered

with printed canvas) was used only at sea; the grapeshot referred to on land was 'heavy case'. Tests in 1802 with a 6pdr firing canister of 34 3oz balls against a target 8ft by 90ft at 1° elevation scored 9 hits at 300yds range and 8 at 400yds; at 0° elevation the proportion was distinctly higher. (Müller's statistics show greater effectiveness: 41 per cent at 400yds and 23 per cent at 600.)

The third variety of projectile was 'common shell', the main ammunition for howitzers, iron spheres filled with combustible material, sealed with a wooden plug through which a fuse or wick was inserted; the explosion of the propellant ignited the fuse, which had to be trimmed by the gunner to sufficient length so that it burst among the enemy. 'Shrapnel' was used only by the British; the invention of a British gunner, Henry Shrapnel, it was as near to a 'secret weapon' as existed, and was first used in 1804. It resembled common shell but had a thinner casing and was filled with gunpowder and musket-balls, which with careful fuse-trimming could be timed to burst over the heads of the enemy, when it rained down like canister shot; hence its official name 'spherical case'. It depended greatly on the accuracy of timing, imperfect fusing causing Wellington to doubt its efficacy after Busaco, when he noted that the wounds caused were not severe, the French

*A gunner of the Royal Foot Artillery c1808, in the Peninsular campaign uniform worn before the adoption of overalls. The uniform was in the traditional RA colouring; equipment was of infantry style, but the cartridge-box was white leather with a brass badge, and the scarlet cord along the shoulder-belt supported a powder-horn; a 'pricker' and small hammer were carried on the front of the belt.*

general Simon having pieces picked out of his face like duck-shot; but when correctly timed, shrapnel was both effective and demoralising to the enemy. It represented up to 15 per cent of gun-ammunition, and up to 50 per cent of howitzer ammunition.

For transportation, each gun was equipped with a limber, a two-wheeled cart with shafts for the attachment of the team-horses, and a 'pintle' upon which the gun-trail was affixed, dragging the gun after the limber. Apart from transportation, the limber served as a receptacle for each gun's initial supply of ammunition, carried in chests or 'limber-boxes'; in 1802, for example, each light 6pdr had 36 roundshot and 16 canister in its limber-boxes, a heavy 6pdr 36 and 14 respectively, and a medium 12pdr 6 roundshot and 6 canister. Reserve ammunition was carried in ammunition-waggons.

Artillery was organised in 'brigades' or companies; the term 'battery', which usually describes an artillery unit, was used at the time to describe a gun-emplacement. Each 'brigade' or company was a semi-independent unit, including all the vehicles, supplies, teams and personnel needed to sustain the unit in the field. The Royal Artillery was composed of a number of 10-company battalions, 8 in 1803, with a 9th formed in 1806 and a 10th in 1808. Battalions did not serve as complete units but as individual companies, each with its detachment of drivers, each company or 'brigade' normally being identified by the name of its captain, e.g. 'Sandham's Company'. Prior to 1802 guns were grouped for administrative purposes into 'brigades' of about 12 pieces, but later it was usual for each company to consist of 6 pieces, normally 5 guns and 1 howitzer, though all-gun and occasionally all-howitzer 'brigades' were not unknown. In addition to the six guns and their limbers, each 'brigade' possessed its own vehicles, eight ammunition-waggons, three baggage-waggons, a spare-wheel waggon and a mobile forge, with 200 draught animals. For the ordinary field batteries (known as 'Foot Artillery') the waggon in the later period normally carried 72 rounds for a 12pdr, 156 for a light 6pdr or 72 for a 5½in howitzer, for example. (Older waggons, still in use in 1802, carried slightly less.) Establishment of a Foot 'brigade' in 1808 was 2

captains, 2 1st lieutenants, 1 2nd lieutenant, 4 sergeants, 4 corporals, 9 bombardiers, 3 drummers and 116 gunners.

The number of different patterns of gun in use was vast; Adye's *Bombardier & Pocket Gunner* (2nd edn 1802), the gunner's most valuable pocket reference, lists 64 distinct varieties of British ordance, including mortars, but of these only about ten were commonly used in the field. The terminology of these is confusing in the extreme; there was, for example, no such thing as simply a '6pdr'; Adye lists two iron 6pdrs, 8 and 6ft long, and in brass the following varieties: Heavy, Desagulier's Medium, New Medium, Reduced Medium, General Belford's and Common Light! This great variety was gradually standardised, though not until Waterloo was the ideal equipment achieved. Initially the 'foot' brigades were armed with the light 6pdr and 5½in howitzer (after failing in the Peninsula the original 8 and 10in howitzers were withdrawn and replaced by the 5½in and 4⅖in). Even in the early part of the Peninsular War, the hitting-power of the British artillery was very inferior to that of the equivalent French units; in May 1809, for example, the army's artillery consisted of three batteries ('brigades') of light 6pdrs and three of 3pdrs, the latter having very limited effect. As the 6pdr was greatly inferior to the French 8pdr (the latter having even greater impact due to the French 'pound' weighing more than the British), as soon as practicable the British 9pdr was introduced, so that by 1813 the Peninsular army could field seven 'brigades' of 9pdrs to six of 6pdrs, and by Waterloo all the Foot 'brigades' had five 9pdrs and one 5½in howitzer.

Shortages of guns resulted in 'brigades' being split between units; Wellesley's artillery in August 1808, for example, had to be arrayed in eight 'half-brigades', four of two 6pdrs and a howitzer, two of three 6pdrs, one of three 9pdrs and one of two 9pdrs and a howitzer, together representing three 6pdr brigades and one 9pdr. Despite the need for every available gun at the time, it is worth noting that a brigade sent from Gibraltar with light 3pdrs was condemned as 'totally inapplicable' for the Peninsula, having old carriages of single-horse draught, each team requiring 6 horses, 8 for a 'long 6pdr' and 10 horses for a 12pdr.

# The Horse Artillery

Horse Artillery was created in the British Army in 1793, to provide fast-moving fire-support for cavalry, with all gunners either mounted or riding upon the limbers and battery vehicles. By 1801 there were seven 'horse brigades' (which were more commonly referred to by the cavalry term 'troop'), rising to 12 by 1806. These might be considered the élite of the artillery (they regarded themselves as such!), and reinforced their association with the cavalry by their uniform and equipment; whereas the Foot Artillery wore infantry-style uniform in the Royal Artillery's distinctive colouring of blue faced red, the Royal Horse artillery wore cavalry-style dolmans in the same colours with yellow braid and 'Tarleton' light dragoon helmets, and carried the 1796-pattern light cavalry sabre.

The Horse Artillery was armed initially with the 6pdr, though a number of 9pdrs were introduced latterly. Troops were commonly identified by letters (e.g. 'A Troop') and as in the Foot Artillery ideally contained five guns and one howitzer each. Even by 1815 9pdrs were not universal, so that the Troops present at Waterloo included three with 9pdrs (A, E and G), three with light 6pdrs (D,

F and H), one with exclusively 5½in howitzers (I), and one with light 6pdrs and rockets. As with the Foot brigades, Horse troops were normally distributed throughout the army; at Waterloo all were attached to the cavalry, save A and D with the artillery reserve. (Foot companies were normally attached partly at divisional or brigade level, with a smaller number as the reserve.)

Each Horse Artillery troop was divided into three two-gun 'divisions' of two 'subdivisions' each; each subdivision comprised a gun and its attendant ammunition-waggon and gun-crew; there was an extra ammuntion-waggon per 'division', and the attendant battery vehicles were regarded as part of the troop 'headquarters'. In Mercer's G Troop at Waterloo, in addition to five 9pdrs and a 5½in howitzer (8 horses each), 9 ammunition-waggons (6 horses each) and gun-crews, the troop included a forge, baggage-waggon and curricle-cart (4 horses each), a spare-wheel cart (6 horses), 6 officers' baggage-mules, 17 officers' horses, 30 spare horses and his 'headquarters' personnel, a surgeon, 2 staff-sergeants, collar-maker, farrier and 5 horses. Each 'division' was commanded by a lieutenant, each right subdivision

by a sergeant and each left subdivision by a corporal. When divided into 'half-brigades' of three guns each, one was commanded by the captain and one by the 2nd captain. The practice of guns operating in 'divisions' (i.e. pairs) was common, theoretically so that one could fire whilst the other was re-loading.

Associated with the Royal Horse Artillery was the Mounted Rocket Corps, a unique formation of two troops armed with Congreve's explosive rockets. Designed by Sir William Congreve and first used in action in 1805, the rocket consisted of an explosive head of various types and a stick, the longer ones made in sections joined by iron fittings, which were launched from a tripod, ignited by a portfire. Three varieties of rocket included 'heavies' used as incendiaries at up to 2,500yds, 'medium' (42, 32 and 24pdrs) and 'light' (18, 12, 9 and 6pdrs), the 32pdr being the heaviest 'field' rocket and the lightest 'bombardment' rocket. The medium pattern could carry round-shot or shell, and the 24pdr canister to air-burst over the target. Congreve proposed 'rocket infantry' with missiles

*A troop of horse artillery. Although this illustration post-dates the period by a century, it portrays the speed at which horse artillery could move into action. (Painting by WB Wollen.)*

*Officer, Royal Horse Artillery, campaign uniform, 1815. The light cavalry-style uniform in blue with red facings and gold lace retained the 'Tarleton' helmet even after its discarding by the light dragoons; the pelisse (unusually shown draped over both shoulders in a portrait of Alexander Frazer) and moustaches which were popular with officers reinforced the 'hussar' aspect of the costume. The overalls were grey with red stripes.*

---

**Establishment of a troop of horse artillery, 1808:**
1 captain, 1 2nd captain, 3 subalterns, 2 staff sergeants, 3 sergeants, 3 corporals, 6 bombardiers, 80 gunners, 60 drivers, 1 farrier, 1 carriage-smith, 2 shoeing-smiths, 2 collar-makers, 1 wheelwright, 1 trumpeter; 56 saddle-horses, 108 draught horses.
(Establishments fluctuated; in Mercer's troop at Waterloo, for example, there were 84 drivers and a surgeon in addition, with 120 draught and 100 saddle-horses and 6 mules.)

---

launched from 'cars' (2 wheeled carts), but in the event rockets were only used by the Horse Artillery, missiles being carried in saddle-panniers and bundles of sticks carried like lances. Though easily-portable (172 men could carry 840 rockets) they were greatly erratic and highly unpopular with Wellington, who accepted a rocket troop after the corps had been established as a separate entity in January 1813 simply as a way of obtaining the horses; as for the rockets, he said, as he had no wish to set fire to a town he had no use for them! Erratic though their flight was (rockets might even double-back upon the firers), some 40,000 were fired at Copenhagen in 1807 and were employed in Spain, at Leipzig and Waterloo, and though their hitting-power was not great their effect on enemy morale was profound. 'The devil's own artillery' as the Russian general Wittgenstein called them could throw into panic any troops upon which they fell, their very erratic behaviour making it impossible to know where they would land; Gleig of the 85th, who saw them in the Peninsula, wrote that 'the confusion created in the ranks of the enemy beggars all description.' Nevertheless, Wellington insisted that Capt Whinyates' troop at Waterloo be equipped with guns as well as rockets.

The artillery transport was a separate service, the Corps of Drivers (alias 'Wee Gees'), which like the RHA was the creation of the Duke of Richmond. Prior to the foundation of this corps, artillery vehicles had been driven by teams and teamsters hired from civilian contractors before the opening of a campaign. As they remained civilians and were thus outside military discipline, the system was a total failure, exemplified by Fontenoy when the hired Flemish drivers fled, leaving the guns without means of evacuation, but it took 49 years for the system to be altered and the Corps of Drivers formed in 1794. By 1808 the

corps comprised 8 troops, each of five sections of 90 drivers plus craftsmen, totalling 554 men, 945 draught and 75 saddle horses, commanded by a captain; ultimately there were 11 troops. These troops did not serve as units, however, but were divided up among the artillery companies (both Foot and Horse), each company's drivers coming under control of the battery-commander. Thus, they were not supervised by their own officers, who in many cases were negligent; the result was that the Corps of Drivers became renowned for bad discipline and poor morale. The earnest Dickson thought the Corps of Drivers an 'Augean stable', whilst Swabey, an RHA officer of much Peninsular experience, described the corps as 'that nest of infamy'. He records the practice of stealing Royal Artillery ammunition and selling it to the Portuguese! A solution to the ills of the Corps of Drivers, given that they were broken-up in small detachments precluding supervision by their own officers, would have been a complete integration with the gunners, but this was not achieved until after the war. The gunners themselves tended to look down upon the drivers and there was considerable friction at times between the two services.

An innovation achieved in 1813, when the Peninsular campaigning had reached the Pyrenees, was the formation of a 'mountain battery' equipped with 3pdr guns which could be dismantled and carried on mule-back, one mule to carry the gun-barrel and two the carriage. Other, more bizarre forms of mobile artillery were devised but never employed in action: a somewhat eccentric inventor, James Sadler, devised a two-gun 'war chariot' with which he equipped his London volunteer unit, Sadler's Sharpshooters, and General Money proposed the deployment of 'land frigates' on the coast to guard against invasion, basically farm-carts mounted with guns.

# Siege and Garrison Artillery

Heavier guns than those used by the field artillery were employed in siege and garrison duty. The fortifications used to protect Britain's coasts and bases were never tested; during the whole Revolutionary and Napoleonic Wars, there was nothing to compare with the great siege of Gibraltar. The design of the heavier garrison guns (up to 42pdrs, immense pieces up to 10 feet long and weighing 65 to 67cwt) was similar to that of the lighter ordnance, but of a larger scale; but the design of carriage was often different, more resembling naval patterns, occasionally made of iron but usually wood, with small, iron 'truck' wheels (wooden 'trucks' were usually restricted to sea service). The heavier ordnance usually employed 'quoin' elevation in place of the modern screw-elevators of the lighter pieces, because of the greater weight of barrel; the quoin was a wooden chock inserted between the closed end of the barrel and the carriage, the gun being raised by being levered up by handspikes, the barrel pivoting on its trunnions to allow the quoin to be inserted further or withdrawn. For both siege and garrison work, artillery was ideally sited upon wooden platforms (to prevent the guns sinking), and for garrison duty 'traversing platforms' might be used, upon which the gun was secured firmly, the entire wooden platform traversing to facilitate aiming. To reduce recoil a wooden block might replace the two rear trucks on the carriage, forming a 'rear chock carriage'; or the trucks could be removed completely, forming a 'sliding carriage' which limited recoil. Full-size artillery wheels could also be used for garrison guns, with the recoil directed by wooden rails mounted on the platform.

Siege warfare similarly required heavy guns, sufficient to batter in the walls of a besieged fortress, which although this could be achieved quite satisfactorily there were a number of drawbacks. Primarily, the very weight of metal needed to equip a siege-train (or 'battering-train') resulted in their being able to move only at very slow speed, and an immense train of supply-waggons was required in addition to transport the equipment, ammunition and powder expended in even a small-scale opera-

tion. In larger sieges, the expenditure of ammunition was staggering; the breaching-batteries at Badajoz, for example, used 2,523 barrels of gunpowder at 90lbs per barrel, 18,832 24pdr roundshot and 13,029 18pdr roundshot, together weighing over 900,000lbs or over 400 tons, 5,000 mule-loads; and this does not include shell or canister. At San Sebastian, 70,563 shots or shells were fired, using 5,579 barrels of powder or over half a million pounds. Rates of fire were much less than those commonly achieved by field artillery; it was reckoned that at the commencement of a siege, five rounds per gun per day was sufficient, rising to ten rounds per gun and, in the final stages of breaching the walls, 60 rounds per day. The 23 rounds per hour for 15½ hours a day maintained against San Sebastian was regarded as a most singular feat.

The 9pdr was the heaviest gun normally used for field service, but many other 'natures' existed, from 12pdrs upwards, to 18, 24, 32 and 42pdrs, of which a wide variety existed. The usual siege-guns were the 18 and 24pdrs (the immense weight of the larger pieces making their transport even more difficult), the 24pdr being universally preferred due to its comparative striking-power being vastly superior to the 18pdr. In the earlier stages of the Peninsular War, however, the army's battering-train was wretched in the extreme, relying to a large extent upon an antiquated collection of Spanish and Portuguese ordnance dating back to the early 17th century, without a stand-

ard calibre or ammunition and in a poor state of repair. Eventually the siege-train received better guns, though as late as the second siege of Badajoz Wellington was sent Russian 18pdrs which his ammunition did not fit! Where the situation allowed, naval ordnance could be landed from the fleet to provide an augmentation of heavy guns, and such were used (with naval gun-crews) at San Sebastian, for example. Both iron and 'brass' ordnance was used for siege-work, the two metals having differing imperfections: iron guns could rust and scales fall off both inside and outside (an ingenious machine known as the 'Desaguliers instrument' was employed to detect fissures within a barrel, an arrangement of geared rods to 'search' or probe any cracks), and after repeated firing might burst or crack. Brass guns after repeated firing could suffer 'muzzle droop' (distortion of the barrel) or could develop widened touch-holes or vents, these requiring re-bushing before the gun could resume its service. In the Peninsular War, it was usual for the siege-train to be hauled by teams of oxen, which plodded at the most ponderous of paces, with ammunition-carts similarly hauled by ox-teams and conducted by hired Portuguese muleteers.

Among the siege-pieces was the mortar, a very short-barrelled weapon intended exclusively for high-angle fire with 'mortar-bombs' or shells, explosive projectiles lobbed high into the air to drop almost vertically upon the besieged garrison. These weapons had no wheels, but

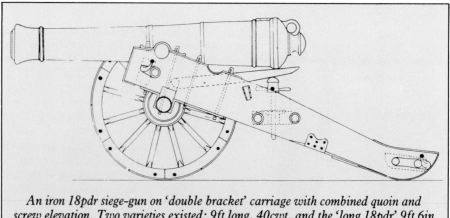

*An iron 18pdr siege-gun on 'double bracket' carriage with combined quoin and screw elevation. Two varieties existed: 9ft long, 40cwt, and the 'long 18pdr' 9ft 6in long, 42cwt.*

gun-barrel would be slung. To move a gun from such a vehicle, or to position a mortar, a three-legged 'triangle gin' (or 'gyn') was used, a sixteen-feet high tripod from which a block-and-tackle was suspended.

Mortar-bombs were similar to 'common shell', but with a thicker base to ensure that they landed fuse-uppermost, and could have devastating effect when dropping almost vertically (such as that which blew up the Almeida magazine); and in addition other projectiles existed which were used only in siege-work. Chief among these were 'carcasses' or incendiary shells, tarred canvas bags or later cast-iron cases, filled with combustible material which once alight was almost impossible to extinguish (the 213lb carcass, fired from a 13in mortar, burned for 11 minutes). The filling varied in composition but was usually a mixture of saltpetre, sulphur, antimony and pitch. A similar mixture containing gunpowder and linseed oil could be made into 'light balls', iron frames covered with painted cloth and used as illumination-flares.

Carronades (short, wide-bore cannon) were normally restricted to naval service, but could be used mounted on iron 'garrison carriages' for static defensive roles, or *in extremis* could even be used in the field, as in the War of 1812.

When a fortification was invested, it was usual for the siege-batteries to be pushed closer to the walls as the operation progressed and as the 'parallels' (trenches) drew nearer. Great care was taken in the siting of the first batteries, for as Adye commented, 'If these first batteries be favourably situated, the artillery may be continued in them nearly the whole of the siege,' and only re-positioned when the trenches had reached the glacis of the fortification. The batteries were constructed with the protection of gabions (earth-filled wicker baskets) to absorb enemy fire, and where possible with wooden plank flooring to prevent the guns sinking into the ground.

were affixed securely to solid wooden 'beds', as ordinary carriages would have been demolished by the absorbed recoil from the discharge. The barrels of such mortars were immensely heavy; the British iron 13in 'Land Service' mortar was 3ft 7½in in length but weighed over 36cwt. Elevation was by a wooden quoin inserted between the barrel and the 'bed', but in practice it was easier to position the barrel permanently (at 45°) and vary the range by the amount of powder used; for example, a British 13in mortar at 45° threw its bomb 318yds with 1lb of gunpowder, and 2,706yds with 8lbs; in the latter case its flight was no less than 25 seconds. The commonest mortars were the 13in and 10in varieties, but brass 5½in and 4⅖in also existed, the latter only 13½in long, weighing 3qtrs 11lbs and sufficiently portable to be carried by two men. It was commonly termed a 'Coehoorn' or 'Coehorn', after its Dutch inventor. A variety of specially-built vehicles were used for the transportation of mortars and heavy guns, including a 'devil carriage' in which the barrel was slung below the rear axle, a flat-bed 'platform carriage' on which both the gun and gun-carriage rested, or a 'sling-cart', basically a two-wheeled, shafted framework below which the

# Chapter Four: THE SUPPORTING ARMS

Wellington conducted the Peninsular campaign in the knowledge that his was the only field army which Britain could deploy in Europe, and thus a major defeat could effectively wreck the chances of continuing to oppose France on land. But the danger was more than purely military, for a severe reverse would have had serious political consequences. Unlike the other great British commander, Marlborough, Wellington enjoyed the complete support of the Ministry throughout the Peninsular War (even though government departments often disregarded his advice on purely military matters, and prohibited him from selecting the subordinates he wanted), but the parliamentary opposition was vociferous if often ill-informed about the conduct of the war, and, principally, of the expense. After the very early stage of the French Revolution, few politicians were prepared to condone the actions of successive French governments, but many members of parliament, especially those regarded as 'radicals', criticized the Ministry's handling of the war and even agitated for a negotiated peace. (Due to British subsidies financing the war-efforts of a number of states opposed to Napoleon, a British withdrawal from the war might have resulted in Napoleon keeping his Empire). William Cobbett, the earnest radical, wrote in his *Weekly Political Register* in November 1811 that as the Spanish armies were frequently beaten by the French, it proved that the Spanish nation was not really desirous of expelling the French; thus the Peninsular War was 'nothing but a drain on this country, without the smallest chance of any ultimate benefit . . . there exist not the means of final success; and, therefore, the sooner we abandon the undertaking the better.' (He even preferred to believe Soult's despatches to British ones!) Two months later, when the House of Commons was asked to grant a £2,000 annuity to Wellington in gratitude for his services, Sir Francis Burdett objected, saying that Wellington did not deserve it, as it was 'impossible to conceive that less should have been done when the means were so ample', which

even though Burdett 'professed himself to be uninformed on military matters' demonstrates quite astounding ignorance. On Ciudad Rodrigo, he said that 'if such useless operations as this were to be thus recompensed out of the pockets of the people, the sooner the war was at an end the better.' Canning replied with such vigour that Burdett was in a minority of one when the vote was taken.

As far as it is possible to determine, there was little popular support for Burdett's radical viewpoint, especially after the political associations of the 1790s had dwindled. Civil unrest, including violent riots, were not uncommon throughout the period, especially in the mid-1790s and around 1811-12, but the reasons behind these ugly incidents were many. Prices of food were a major cause in the 1790s, high bread-prices threatening widespread starvation, and the unemployment caused by technological change triggered the later 'Luddite' disturbance, but riots arose from many other causes, even to the 'No Program' anti-nonconformist trouble in Suffolk in 1811. Violence directed against the military, whether protesting at the militia-ballot or press-gang, preventing the apprehension of deserters or attacking volunteers, were caused by other reasons than a protest against the war and the military establishment *per se*.

The civilian population throughout the period was bombarded with anti-French, later anti-Bonaparte, propaganda, whether in the form of cartoons, hand-bills or even sermons (in 1799 a clergyman in Skipton declared he wished of Bonaparte that 'if he is not assassinated, he may be devoured by the Crocodiles of the Nile'!) Pamphlets of incredible vituperation poured out, such as *The Atrocities of the Corsican Daemon* of 1803 ('Do but observe the face of Villainy/How different from the brow of Innocence!'), or *Bonaparte* ('this Consular frog') about 'this raw-head and bloody-bon'd chief, Bonaparte.' Whether influenced by such or not, the overwhelming popular opinion, especially in the period of danger of invasion, appears to have been definitely anti-French and in support of the war.

This seems to have been reflected in the army, which remained very unpolitical. In the early 1790s copies of Paine's *Rights of Man* circulated in soldiers' hands, but with little if any effect; a political club in the 2nd Dragoons was suppressed in 1792, but its aim seems to have been directed towards higher pay than any unpatriotic sentiments. Indeed, the rank-and-file of several regiments subscribed for rewards for information leading to the apprehension of circulators of seditious pamphlets, and the general reaction to such seems exemplified by some Guardsmen in October 1798 who made citizens' arrests on John Glass, a journeyman currier, for damning the king and the Duke of York in the Craven Head Inn, Drury Lane, whilst hopelessly drunk, and on J Blachford, shoemaker, for making 'seditious and disloyal expressions' in St James' Park!

Given the vicissitudes of the war and the enormous drain it imposed upon British resources, the government remained remarkably steadfast throughout several changes of Ministry; the Tories ruled from 1783 to 1830, less the brief period of Grenville's coalition government. William Pitt the Younger led the government from 1783 to 1801, and from 1804 until his death in 1806, presiding over the commencement of the war and its renewal after the collapse of the Peace of Amiens. Addington led the Ministry from 1801 to 1804; and after Grenville (1806-07) the prime ministers were Portland (1807-09), Spencer Perceval (1809 until his assassination in 1812) and from 1812 to 1827, Lord Liverpool. Despite some ill-advised moves, especially concerning the deployment of Britain's limited military resources, the government fulfilled Pitt's last great speech of 9 November 1805: 'England has saved herself by her exertions; and will, I trust, save Europe by her example.'

*Royal Military Artificers, 1802, wearing infantry-style uniform in the 'Ordnance' colouring of blue with black facings and yellow lace, and the 'stovepipe' shako adopted in 1802. The sergeant (right) wears a crimson sash and carries a spontoon. (Print after GB Campion)*

57

# The Commissariat

The basic element of the commissariat organisation was the ordinary soldier's daily ration, which was provided by the government. Unlike the French army, which was fed to a large extent by 'living off the land' or forcibly requisitioning sustenance, in British service any form of plundering or illegal foraging was strictly prohibited, and though it occurred it carried heavy punishment. Anything taken from the countryside by a British army was supposed to be paid for, either in cash or by a ticket, and in the overwhelming majority of cases this was done; only 'private' scavenging by individuals was unpaid. Subsistence-farming in the Peninsula produced little surplus and the civilians could not, they said, eat money; but in general they were well recompensed for what was taken and could complain to have any wrongs redressed.

The soldier's daily ration varied with circumstances and availability (as below), and was often of poor quality, the biscuit provided in iron-hard lumps which had to be soaked or pounded to pieces before it could be eaten, always presuming that it was not honeycombed by weevils or full of maggots. Cooking was the responsibility of the individual, so that 'messes' of several men would pool their 'prog' (food) and produce their meals, commonly 'stirabout', a stock-pot into which everything was tipped. (The weight of meat issued included the bone, so that boiling was the most practical way of extracting the goodness, providing a pint of broth per man per day.) Contemporary accounts suggest that meals were frequently quite revolting (to modern eyes), especially when men were billeted on innkeepers who tended to cheat them of their rations and provide only greasy pea soup with scum floating top, and stale bread.

On campaign, the problems of providing an army with its food were immense; for a division of 7,000 men, for example, 10,500lbs of bread, 7,000lbs of meat and 7,000 pints of wine (in the Peninsula) would be required every day. The alcohol consumption was equally large, a quart of beer per man per day being the usual issue, though at sea the daily rate was four gallons between six men; and rather than spend what little money they had on supplementing their two meals a day (breakfast and dinner), many men consumed vast amounts of additional alcohol. In the Peninsula the usual daily ration was 1lb of biscuit, 1lb of meat and a pint of wine or 1/3 pint of rum, which in itself, as Cooper of the 7th remarked, was reason that when a man enlisted 'he should have parted with half his stomach'! Very often, inadequate rations arrived, or no rations at all; Cooper records periods of half-rations, or sheaves of wheat and potatoes out of the fields. George Wood of the 82nd records his regiment living four days in the Peninsula with nothing to eat but the leaves of trees, 'which we chewed as we passed along', after which the arrival of beef, biscuit and rum left them 'wallowing in luxury, which gave us such spirits that, woe to the enemy who dare oppose us.' After Vittoria, when a regiment had nothing to eat but sheaves of unground cereal, it was said an Irishman volun-

*Officer, Royal Waggon Train, 1815. The unit wore a distinctive uniform based on the pre-1812 light dragoon style, but in their colouring of red with blue facings and silver lace. The officers' original bicorn hats were replaced by shakos of the 1812 light dragoon pattern, which were worn by all light cavalry except hussars from the later Peninsular War. The sabre is the 1796 light dragoon pattern.*

---

### Complete daily ration of a soldier:

| | |
|---|---|
| **Flour or bread:** | 1½lbs (or 1lb biscuit) |
| **Beef:** | 1lb (or ½lb pork) |
| **Peas:** | ¼ pint |
| **Butter or cheese:** | 1oz |
| **Rice:** | 1oz |

If some of these commodities were unavailable, a daily ration might be just 1½lbs of bread and 1½lbs of beef; or 3lbs of beef; or 2lbs cheese.

| | |
|---|---|
| Ration for a horse on home service: | 14lbs hay, 10lbs oats, 4lbs straw per day. |

teered for a job because 'a'nt we all as strong as horses, for you know we got a good feed of corn this morning!'

As the commissariat was run by the Treasury, the commissaries were civilians and thus not subject to military control; totally untrained, many were inefficient and corrupt, hardly surprising when their home-service pay of 15/- dropped to 5/- on campaign! Appointments were rife with 'patronage' by Treasury officials, and not until 1810 were any qualifications required, and even then commissaries had only to be 16 years old with a year's clerking experience. Assistant-commissaries, Deputies and clerks were attached to each infantry brigade and cavalry regiment, and were superintended by the Commissary-General and his Assistant and Deputies, many of whom were no more efficient than their subordinates; in 1809 Wellington had to reprimand General Sherbrooke for abusing one commissariat officer (though he totally agreed with the general's disgust at the incompetence), and the cautionary story that Picton threatened to hang a commissary if rations were late may not be an exaggeration. Many commissaries, however, tried to do a good job under near impossible conditions, beset by countless clerical regulations and assailed by officers like Sir

*An officer, waggon and team of the Royal Waggon Train. Several varieties of waggon existed, according to the intended use; for example, ammunition-waggons had fireproof 'tilts' (covers). (Print after Charles Hamilton Smith's* Costume of the Army of the British Empire, *1812.)*

William Payne Bt, who in the Talavera campaign told his commissaries that none were doing their duty, as anyone who did his duty properly, 'could not possibly remain alive. He would be forced to die. Of all my commissaries, not one has yet sacrificed his life; consequently they are not doing their duty'; to which the German commissary Schaumann noted that most high-borne Englishmen in hot climates 'are a little mad'!

An attempt was made to form a military transport-service in 1794, but the 'corps of Royal Waggoners' was a miserable failure; as Commissary-General Havilland LeMesurier wrote, 'it failed completely in every part, and the only trace remaining of it is a heavy charge on the half-pay list'. The Treasury reverted to the practice of hiring civilian carters, teams and waggons as and when required, a totally unsatisfactory system but one which continued in use, to some extent, right throughout the period. In the

Peninsular War this involved hiring thousands of Portuguese pack-mules, primitive ox-carts with ungreased axles which screeched and wailed at the most ponderous of paces, and often-rascally muleteers like the wretch who sold British troops 'pork slices' cut from a dead Frenchman. The result was that the inefficiencies of the commissariat only became worse; Wellington wrote in exasperation of empty waggons on a good road moving at five miles per day! In August 1799 another military transport unit was formed, the Royal Waggon Train, initially for service in Holland; from five troops of 72 men each it increased by 1814 to 14 troops with 1,903 other ranks. Equipped with its own teams, controlled by the army and possessing its own waggons of various types, it could do no more than solve a fraction of the commissariat problems. Even then, its reputation was not good; Schaumann referred to its commander, Digby Hamilton, as 'Fat general Hamilton . . . with his useless wagon corps', and their nickname was 'Newgate Blues', after the London goal of that name! Nevertheless, in exploits like the bold re-supply of ammunition to Hougoumont at the battle of Waterloo, the Waggon Train performed many valuable services.

# The Medical Services

Like the army's commissariat, the medical services suffered from lack of organisation, and were rendered worse by the general ignorance of medical science, though the latter could hardly have been cured due to the general level of understanding of hygiene; the majority of military surgeons struggled manfully with a situation which was to a modern viewpoint quite out of control.

The army's medical service was superintended by the Medical Board, comprising the Surgeon General, the Physician General and the Inspector General of Hospitals, who being civilian doctors with private practices were unable or unwilling to superintend the army's medicine as they ought. Each was responsible for his own department, though the purchase of medical supplies was the responsibility of the Apothecary General, and non-medical supplies for use in hospitals that of the Purveyor General; the level of professional competence in the appointment of the former official may be gauged by the fact that it was a hereditary office and had been since 1747! When the Physician General was asked to investigate 'Walcheren fever' he declined on the grounds that he was unacquainted with the diseases of soldiers' camps.

With such lack of direction from above, the army's medical services devolved upon the officers belonging to each regiment; each battalion had a surgeon (ranking as captain) and two assistant-surgeons (ranking as lieutenants) who were appointed to the battalion or cavalry regiment direct, not seconded from a central medical corps, which did not exist. Shortages of personnel resulted in half-trained surgeons, apothecaries and even apprentice druggists being appointed, to the detriment of all concerned; but for every useless man there were several who conscientiously tried their best. There were no trained medical orderlies or ambulance personnel; regimental musicians often helped to carry stretchers, but there was no regulated system of casualty-evacuation, so that wounded men might lie on the field of battle for hours or even days before the over-burdened surgeons attended to them. Surgeons purchased their own medical equipment, and had no assistance unless they themselves taught rudimentary first-aid to their soldier-servant or orderly.

In battle, a battalion surgeon and his deputies might establish a battalion 'aid post' at a suitable location in the rear, but if the unit moved during the action the medical staff might have to keep up as best they could. Wounded men who could move were expected to make their own way to the rear generally without assistance, so as not to weaken the unit by having fit men leave the ranks to help the injured. Otherwise, the wounded would have to remain where they were until someone came to them. After receiving what might be termed battlefield first-aid (including arrest of bleeding and amputation of limbs), survivors could be conveyed to a 'hospital' (which might simply be any commandeered building) in carts; there were no purpose-built ambulances and the jolting in unsprung vehicles for many miles not only caused excruciating agony for the wounded, but many recorded cases of fatal haemorrages occasioned by the shaking.

Improvised hospitals of this nature depended for quality upon the type of building commandeered; but the permanently-established hospitals were probably even worse. Sgt Cooper of the 7th spent time in five Peninsular hospitals and recorded his impressions of them: the hospital at Villa Viciosa was in a convent, the patients laid in four corridors, with small windows and little ventilation, open tubs standing for sewage purposes, with fires burning in each corner of the building to drive away infection, producing blinding smoke which compounded the foul stench. The Elvas hospital had no ventilation whatever save the door and chimney, being a 'long bomb proof room' containing 20 patients (18 of whom died during Cooper's stay), with all others laid on the pavements outside. At Celorica the hospital comprised two rooms crowded with delirious patients, with no 'chamber utensils' or ventilation; those at Guarda and Olivenza just as miserable. It is

*The appearance of a battlefield after the conflict (as in this detail from a print of Waterloo by Dubourg after Clark) was horrific beyond description; as one veteran remarked of such scenes, 'May God in his goodness preserve England from the horrors of a Campaign . . .'*

Colonel Gordon mortally Wounded

amazing that in such insanitary conditions anyone survived.

Surgery was primitive, conducted without anaesthetic and with amputation the standard practice for badly-damaged limbs; when George Napier was hit by grapeshot in the elbow at Ciudad Rodrigo, his arm was removed by blunted instruments ('from the number of amputations he had already performed . . . so it was a long time before the thing was finished'), after which he was sent on his way and after stumbling around for an hour found a fire by which he could sit for the remainder of the night! In such cirumstances it was expected that patients bore the pain with silence and stoicism; but as Napier remarked, he was ashamed to admit that 'I did not bear the amputation of my arm as well as I ought to have done, for I made noise enough when the knife cut through my skin and flesh. It is no joke I assure you, but still it was a shame to say a word, and is of no use.' Contrasting to Napier's behaviour (he thanked the surgeon 'for his kindness, having sworn at him like a trooper while he was at it, to his great amusement'); some showed un-

believable *sang-froid*; when Thomas Noel Harris' arm was amputated at Waterloo, he called for it to be brought back so he might shake the amputated hand! Bullets were extracted if possible (entry-holes being probed by the surgeon's finger), but often it was considered safer to leave the bullet in rather than risk extraction; shot in 1799, the Marquess of Huntly found a musket-ball working out of his body four inches from the wound, seven years later! Medical treatment remained primitive and unhygenic, but a marked improvement occurred from 1811 when the great humanitarian Dr James McGrigor was appointed Inspector General of Hospitals in the Peninsula. His establishment of portable, prefabricated hospitals which could accompany the army was a major advance, avoiding the agonising transportation of casualties in unsprung Portuguese carts.

More than wounds and infections and gangrene which set in after, disease was the greatest killer or crippler of soldiers. In 1794–97 80,000 men died or were ruined by sickness in the West Indies; and of almost 23,000 men lost in 1811

(the year of the carnage of Albuera), about 20,000 were killed or crippled by ailments other than enemy action. Medical knowledge had no conception of the causes of epidemics like 'Walcheren fever', 'Guadiana fever' (both malarial) or the sicknesses endemic in the West Indies, and thus had no effective cure. (Over 4,000 died at Walcheren, barely 100 of enemy action). Jonathan Leach wrote of his 70th Foot in Antigua being ravaged by fever, which in five years had killed 2,400 men and 68 officers of the 68th Foot, the only 'cure' which saved him being the drinking of a whole jug of boiling Madeira. Neither certain cure nor prevention was known, one group of 21 newly-arrived Europeans, it was reported, deciding that some should drink only wine and others only water, to determine which practice was most conducive to health. The ten water-drinkers all died; as did ten of the wine-drinkers! Some ailments were recognised as being most prevalent in certain areas; 'trench fever', so-called, was an accepted hazard to the besiegers of fortifications, probably arising from stagnant water, and opthalmia, an inflammation of the eyes which could cause blindness but from which many recovered, was a major affliction of troops serving in Egypt. For 'putrid fever' it was recommended that people washed in 'Marseilles vinegar' (a concoction of herbs, wormwood, camphor and vinegar) and wore camphor in a bag on the stomach; another military 'cure' for this was 'free air' and dosing with sulphuric acid and snakeroot! Sickness was not restricted to the most infamous areas, however; in October 1811 over 14,000 men were in hospital in the Peninsula, largely with fever and ague, and with regimental statistics like that of the 51st Foot (246 sick, 251 fit) one can appreciate Wellington's plea that no more Walcheren regiments be sent him, as the recurring fever would surely decimate them. Rates of sickness in the Peninsula varied, up to 30 per cent of the army at any one time.

# The Corps of Royal Engineers

All engineering duties were the responsibility of the Corps of Royal Engineers which, like the artillery, came under the authority of the Board of Ordnance. It was a unit composed exclusively of officers, and throughout the period remained very much smaller than the number required; in 1792 there were only 73 members, and as late as 1814 numbered only 218, 38 of whom were field officers, most of whom would be unlikely to serve in the field. Like the artillery, commissions were only granted to those with a thorough technical training (the corps had its own school at Woolwich), and promotion depended upon seniority rather than purchase. They were unique in that their pay was increased when serving abroad, and the amount of work required of them was prodigious. Regarded very much as 'specialists', they tended to be consulted only for major undertakings such as a siege, surveying or bridge-building, temporary field-works usually being erected by the infantry. The senior ranks were long-serving and somewhat inactive ('inherent pomp and acquired gravity' like the Board of Ordnance according to

Blakeney!), so that much of the work was thrown upon the junior officers, whose casualty-rates were appalling. Ever in the most exposed position in the conducting of sieges, so many became casualties that Wellington commented that no matter how badly they were required, he could hardly wish for any more in case the same fate befell them. 25 of the 102 engineer officers who served in the Peninsula died (24 in action, one from fatigue), and equally hard-hit were the 'assistant engineers', officers from line regiments who temporarily took on engineer duties, as the only way of remedying the shortage of *bona fide* engineers. It is not correct to regard all these assistants as necessarily unskilled in specialist engineer duties; for example, Capt John Blakiston of the 17th Portuguese Regt, a volunteer 'assistant' at the siege of San Sebastian, had originally trained with the Madras Engineers and was the officer responsible for blowing down the fortress-gate at Vellore, allowing the suppression of the mutiny there. (At San Sebastian, 11 engineers out of 18 engaged became casualties.)

Excellent though the calibre of most

of the engineer officers was, they operated with almost no support for almost the entire period; the result being that, as Napier wrote, 'the sieges carried on by the British in Spain were a succession of butcheries.' Not even the capable Richard Fletcher, perhaps the greatest military engineer of his day, commander of the engineers in the Peninsula until killed at San Sebastian and designer of the Lines of Torres Vedras, could overcome the fact that for the manual labour involved, the engineers had to rely almost exclusively upon detachments of infantrymen totally unskilled in any engineering duties. The rank-and-file of the engineer service was provided by the Royal Military Artificers and Labourers (Royal Military Artificers from 1798), a unit which consisted of twelve companies of 'tradesmen', each commanded by a sub-lieutenant (always an ex-NCO) plus a staff-sergeant seconded from the Royal Artillery. These men were not, however,

*Sergeant and private of the Royal Sappers and Miners, 1813, in working dress, including a short-tailed jacket without turnbacks, grey-blue reinforced overalls and a peakless leather cap bearing the brass letters 'RS&M' on the front. (Print after GB Campion.)*

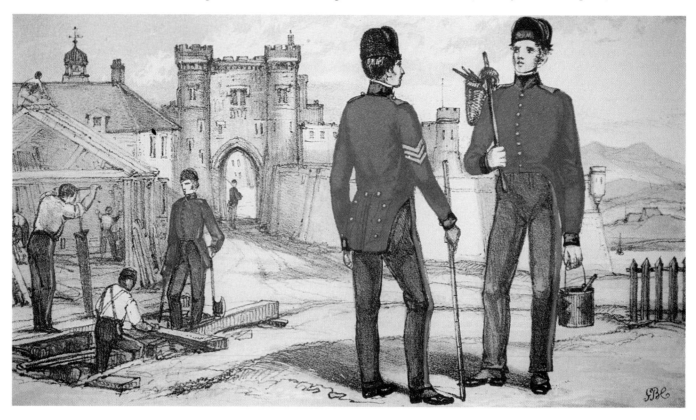

practical 'field' engineers, but rather carpenters, builders, etc. who maintained fortresses. Eight companies were stationed in Britain, two (originally semi-autonomous) in Gibraltar, one in Nova Scotia and one in the West Indies. They remained in these stations 'in a state of vegetation', in some cases for their entire service, so that the corps' most experienced men had never made a day's march or seen a field-works constructed. For campaigns, tiny detachments were sent from these companies to the field army, and it was usual practice for company-commanders to keep their best men and send on service only the most ignorant and useless; hence the description of them as a set of 'undisciplined vagabonds' by one engineer officer, and the fact that in the Mediterranean theatre, newly-formed companies of Maltese and Sicilian pioneers were found more effective. The detachments sent to the Peninsula were so small as to be almost useless; in late 1809 the total strength was 19 effectives, plus four infirm and two 'missing'. At Ciudad Rodrigo 18 artificers were present, and at Burgos only 8.

The slaughter of Badajos finally compelled the overhaul of the organisation, and Wellington's pleas to be heeded. In April 1812 a new corps was formed, the Royal Military Artificers or Sappers and Miners (Royal Sappers and Miners from the following year), consisting of 2,800 rank-and-file, with companies commanded by officers of the Royal Engineers. The men were trained in their field duties at Chatham, and by 1813 300 were present with the Peninsular army; at San Sebastian their services were valuable, and at Bergen-op-Zoom they actually led the assault.

A further unit was formed in 1798 to provide an engineer corps which would take its orders from the Horse Guards, rather than from the Board of Ordnance, the Royal Staff Corps. Initially consisting of a headquarters and four companies, it attained battalion size in 1809, though its companies and especially officers were employed on detached duty. The rank-and-file, though trained in engineer tasks, were also trained as infantry, their intended duty being as overseers of the parties of impressed infantrymen who did most of the manual labour. Their ranks, uniquely, were divided into 1st, 2nd and 3rd-class privates; even the latter were paid more than ordinary

*Officer, Royal Engineers, c.1809, in typical campaign dress of the Peninsular War. The original blue uniform with black facings was easily confused with French uniforms, so was altered to scarlet with facings of 'Garter blue', a lighter shade than the usual dark blue of 'royal' regiments, with gold lace in full dress; though the change was not universally popular. Casualties among engineer officers in sieges were so high due to their constant presence in front-line trenches, and their usually accompanying storming-parties.*

infantrymen. The Staff Corps officers were employed on duties which overlapped with those of the Royal Engineers and Quartermaster-General's department, as engineers, surveyors, and even as guides; for example, their enterprising Col Sturgeon was responsible for the repair of the Alcantara bridge in 1812, and the construction of the bridge of boats over the Adour in the following year.

Initially, the engineer service had *no* transport whatever, but was dependent upon whatever vehicles and teams could be spared by the artillery. With the overhaul of the system towards the end of the Napoleonic Wars, however, they at last became self-sufficient; in 1815, for example, each Division included an engineer 'brigade', each consisting of a Sapper and Miner company, transport and entrenching-tools to equip 500 infantrymen. The total with the field army comprised 800 Sappers and Miners, 41 Royal Engineer officers, 160 waggons and over 1,000 horses, plus 550 drivers, the latter an unsatisfactory mixture of men recruited partly from the Royal Artillery Drivers and partly from unreliable Belgian civilians.

The Royal Engineers initially wore blue uniforms and black facings (blue coats being the standard Board of Ordnance colour), but these caused confusion in the field when they were mistaken for the French (for example, at Badajos a British sentry confused Capt Patten RE for a Frenchman); the uniform was thus changed in 1812 to scarlet with blue facings, as worn by the Sappers and Miners. The Artificers (who also wore blue, faced black) were armed in part with muskets, but pikes and blunderbusses are mentioned for Peninsular detachments, and a frequent cause of complaint (made by Wellington himself who declared it shameful) was that the tools with which they were equipped were very inferior to those of the French, so that captured French implements were used whenever they were available.

The personnel required to besiege and capture a fortification was enormous; the Peninsular engineer Lt-Col John T Jones calculated that for a fortress garrisoned by 5,000 men, the attackers required three shifts per day of 3,750 men to guard the trenches, four shifts of 2,000 men to construct the trenches, and four shifts for support totalling 7,700, a grand total of 26,950 men.

# The Staff and Intelligence

Compared with the vast and often sophisticated staff organisation of many continental armies, the 'headquarters' establishment of the British Army was tiny, and virtually totally untrained. Excluding 'general officers' (i.e. generals) and the commanders of garrisons and bases abroad, there were but ten full-time staff officers in the whole British Army, the Permanent Assistants of the Quartermaster-General's Department. All other staff officers had to be detached from regimental duty (they remained on the regimental rolls during such detachment) and were generally taken from units serving in the campaign in question. (This was not universally true: hence the presence at Waterloo of members of the 1st, 4th and 5th West India Regts and the 1st Ceylon Regt.) No regiment was expected to have to detach more than four officers for staff duty, but at Waterloo, for example, the 1st Foot Guards had 17 officers in staff situations. Although the Royal Military College existed to train officers (the 'Senior Department' as a kind of ṣtaff college), few who occupied staff situations had trained there.

Staff duties were divided between the departments of the Adjutant-General and Quartermaster-General, whose functions were clearly defined: the Quarter-General's department for marches, quarters, conveyance of troops, and the Adjutant-General's for equipment and discipline; but for many other vital duties (such as the gathering and evaluation of intelligence) there was no established system. Wellington tended to favour the Quartermaster-General's department, largely because its head in the Peninsula was George Murray, more capable than the Adjutant General's departmental head, William Stewart; but in practice Wellington kept both departments under his own personal supervision. The Adjutant-General's department claimed responsibility for intelligence (prisoners-of-war coming under their duties), but in the Peninsula the department was eclipsed by the Quartermaster-General's, which eventually took on all the important duties. The Adjutant- and Quartermaster-General were assisted by officers detached from their regiments as Assistants (AAGs and AQMGs) and Deputy Assistants (DAAGs and DAQMGs); in

the Waterloo campaign, for example, the Adjutant-General's department of 22 officers was drawn from 16 regiments, plus one on the 'unattached list' and one on half-pay, six from line regiments not present with the army (6th, 7th, 46th, 55th, 60th and 90th), two from the German Legion and one from the 7th Veteran Bn.

In addition to these departments, headquarters might be expected to include the commanders of the Royal Artillery and Royal Engineers, the Commissary-General and staff, the Deputy Paymaster-General, head of the

*Trooper, Cavalry Staff Corps, 1814. This unit was formed in 1813 as a provost corps for Peninsular service; two troops were raised there, one in Britain and one in Ireland, formed from selected cavalry troopers of the highest character. They were also used as couriers, guides and orderlies, and wore a red jacket faced blue and the 1812 light dragoon shako with white lace. They were also known as 'Staff Dragoons', the letters 'SD' appearing on their valises.*

campaign's medical department, the Judge-Advocate, the liaison officers of any Allied nations.

Each general maintained a personal staff, colloquially known as his 'household'. At least one aide-de-camp was authorised for every general, two for a lieutenant-general, and the commander of the forces three; for each the general was allowed 9/6d per diem for subsistence, any additional ADCs having to be fed out of the general's personal supplies. The appointment was purely personal, so generals often took their relatives or sons of their friends for ADCs. Their duties were to link the general with the units under his command, and thus demanded capabilities of hard riding and nerve; when Harry Smith was appointed ADC he joked that the only abilities required were to ride and to eat (just as well, as he was then limping with a shot ankle), but their role was much more vital, the most important link in the chain of communication. The job was hazardous in the extreme; Wellington had eight ADCs at Waterloo (about the number he usually kept), of whom two were killed, whilst all three of Picton's regular ADCs became casualties in the same action. In addition, each commanding general had a Military Secretary, who dealt with the general's correspondence; Wellington's was Lord Fitzroy Somerset (later Lord Raglan) who lost his arm at Waterloo in this post.

An examination of the staff present at Waterloo demonstrates how the British system operated with only a fraction of the personnel employed by Napoleon in staff duties; and it is interesting to note that of all his subordinates, only with his personal 'household' was Wellington able to select those officers he wanted without government interference, because he personally paid for the subsistence of his aides. As late as 1815, when the Duke was undisputedly the leading figure in British military affairs, the Horse Guards denied him even officers he stated were indispensable, a quite incredible state of affairs. The height of absurdity was reached when an experienced officer Wellington needed badly for the 1815 campaign was forbidden by the Horse Guards, the officer in question having to brief the head of the Adjutant-General's department (Sir Edward Barnes) with details of the 'Peninsular' system, before quitting the army with which the Horse

Guards would not let him remain!

Wellington's personal staff at Waterloo was a typical collection of the highest echelon of the aristocracy; for example, Somerset was the son of the Duke of Beaufort. Only the senior ADC, Lt-Col Fremantle, was not a member of the aristocracy, and he was an old ADC of the Peninsular campaign.

At brigade level were the 'brigade majors', officers detached from regimental duty, who were responsible for the communication of orders and the day-to-day staff duties concerning the brigade.

Intelligence was a vital function, but one without a recognised staff post. At its most basic level were reports from the 'outposts', the light cavalry screen and scouts which preceded an army, with the 'observing officers' who rode ahead of the army to report on the enemy movements and sometimes penetrate great distances behind enemy lines. Their reports were collated by members of the commander's staff (in Wellington's case, often by the commander himself). Four of these 'observing officers' were especially valuable in the Peninsula: Waters of the Portuguese Staff, Cocks of the 16th Light Dragoons, Leith Hay of the 29th and above all Colquhoun Grant of the 11th Foot. The latter was an intelligence officer of incredible resourcefulness; when he was captured Wellington said he was worth a brigade, but even in captivity (from which he escaped in less than four months) his network of agents was such that he still got messages back to headquarters. By any standards, he was one of the most remarkable agents of all time. Another duty of the 'observing officers' (or any employed on scouting) was to make sketch-maps of the terrain, as what maps existed for reference varied from wretched to misleading; Murray's 'sketching officers' gradually produced maps of parts of the Peninsula, but in the early part of the war the situation was so bad that Moore's advance into Spain was seriously impaired by his lack of knowledge of the roads.

Information was collated from many other sources; in the Peninsula, captured French despatches were especially valuable, passed to the headquarters by guerrilla chieftains. Most of these were written in code, but the Quartermaster-General's department possessed a genius code-breaker in Major George Scovell, who even cracked the 'Great Paris

*One of Wellington's most valuable staff officers was the American-born Col Sir William Howe De Lancey, who was wounded by a roundshot as DQMG at Waterloo. Despite the nursing of his young bride the wound was mortal and he died, mourned by the whole army.*

Cypher', so that much of the French planning was in Wellington's hands as soon as in those of the intended recipients. Information came directly from Spanish guerrillas, or from the network of 'correspondents' who reported secretly to Wellington, such as Dr Patrick Curtis, rector of the Irish College in Salamanca, who supplied much valuable material about the French, with whom he was on good terms. Deserters from the French army brought more information; Benjamin d'Urban records in 1810 a typical defection of an officer who fled to the British after killing his captain in a duel. Most unusual of all were the true spies, almost professional agents who operated behind enemy lines. Some, like the enigmatic 'Baron Kolli', supposedly a Piedmontese, were of little value; others were of vital importance, like James Robertson, alias the Benedictine monk 'Brother Gallus', who almost single-handedly was responsible for the operation which brought La Romana's Spanish army from the Baltic to Spain, deserting Napoleon and being transported in British ships. It is often forgotten that the officer most responsible for recruiting this master-spy Robertson and sending him to Germany was none other than Sir Arthur Wellesley.

# Chapter Five: BRITAIN'S ALLIES

Britain's Allied troops during the Revolutionary and Napoleonic Wars may conveniently be divided into three basic categories: foreign nationals who formed an integral part of the British Army, foreign troops in British pay or under British command, and the forces of states which were allied to Britain out of a mutual opposition to France.

Britain's most important physical military contribution to the effort against France was in the Peninsular War; the other theatres in which British troops were engaged, from the Netherlands and the Mediterranean in 1794, to Egypt and through to the operations in Holland in 1813-14 and the small contingent which fought in the German theatre in the same years, were comparatively minor. In other aspects, however, Britain's role was vital, as the only nation which remained opposed to France virtually from the outbreak of the Revolutionary Wars to Napoleon's final defeat in the 'Hundred Days', with only the brief Peace of Amiens to interrupt hostilities. The presence of the Royal Navy imposed a stranglehold upon Napoleon's commerce, but equally important was the diplomatic and material assistance which Britain afforded to the other states at war with France. Britain's participation in all the Coalitions organised against France (indeed, Britain was instrumental in the creation of these) went much further than diplomatic support and the distraction of French resources. There is some justification in regarding Britain as the paymaster of the anti-French alliance, for in the manner of subsidies to Allied nations, Britain encouraged and enabled many states to continue the fight.

An examination of British Treasury statistics makes apparent the continual drain that such subsidies and loans made upon British resources. In 1800, for example, total government revenue amounted to £39,512,000 (of which £5,300,000 came from the new Income Tax and £18,500,000 by a loan); total expenditure (excluding the Civil List and interest on public debt) amounted to £37,920,000. Of this figure, the largest single expenditure was on the Royal Navy, £12,619,000, and on the army

£11,370,000; next after that came £3,000,000 in 'subsidies to Germans and Russians', including a grant of £2,500,000 to the Emperor of Austria. Thus, the subsidy represented more than one-quarter of the amount expended on Britain's own military forces. In 1813, the total public revenue amounted to £108,991,071 (£35,050,534 of which was in loans); expenditure amounted to £114,263,673. Of this, the army and ordnance took up £40,763,741, of which £11,294,416 was expended in advances to other countries, giving the British Army expense £29,469,325; whilst the navy took £21,996,623. Loans to Allied nations to finance the war amounted to £11,335,412 (i.e. more than half that spent on the navy), of which Portugal took £2,000,000 and Spain, Russia, Prussia and Sweden all more than £1,500,000. In the following year the loans and subsidies amounted to £10,024,618, of which Russia received £2,555,473, Portugal £1,500,000, Austria £1,475,632 and Prussia £1,330,171, down to a grant of £10,007 to Oldenburg. When such sums are multiplied by the number of years over which the war was fought, the support afforded by the British Treasury can be seen to have been crucial in maintaining the resistance to France.

Vast quantities of arms, equipment and supplies were conveyed from Britain to the Allied nations; this might be expected to states like Portugal, whose army was ultimately under British direction and integrated with the British troops in the Peninsular War, but the *matériel* supplied to other nations was also prodigious. Lord Londonderry recorded that for the 1813 campaign, British supplies to the Russian, Prussian and Swedish forces included 218 fieldpieces and all necessary supplies, 124,119 muskets and over 18 million rounds of ammunition, 150,000 complete uniforms, 100,000 head-dress, almost 176,000 pairs of boots, shirts, gaiters, blankets in proportion, 34,443 swords, 90,000 sets of equipment, 63,457 knapsacks, almost 15,000 complete sets of horse-furniture, vast quantities of cloth, over 700,000lbs of biscuit and flour, almost the same amount of meat, and almost 29,000 gal-

lons of brandy and rum. Thus, not only were many of the Allied troops armed with excellent British muskets (generally superior to their home-produced ones: in the Russian army British muskets were distributed as rewards to deserving soldiers), but were even dressed in uniforms made in Britain; hence several of the Prussian 'reserve' regiments of 1813-14 wearing Portuguese costume, their original destination having been changed to support the war in northern Europe.

Throughout the war, Britain maintained a keen interest in the events occurring in other theatres of war, an interest extending much further than the departments of government. The *Royal Military Chronicle* recorded gloomily on Borodino, 'the calamity of our northern allies. It is unmanly to deceive ourselves with false hopes . . .', as a result of which, on news of the fall of Moscow, the British 95th – then heavily engaged in the Peninsula – voluntarily subscribed a day's pay from every man to assist the Russians in their fight. British assistance even extended to the supply of officers to Allied nations; this would be expected in the Portuguese Army, given its virtual British control, but British officers served in several other armies as well; serving as a Russian colonel in 1812 was Captain Nesbit Willoughby, RN, who being on British half-pay decided his time could be spent more profitably fighting the French under a different flag! (This noted character was described by Blakiston of the Portuguese service as 'a man who thrust his head into every gun, and ran it against every stone wall, he could find from Cape Comorin to Moscow. When I knew him, his face was cut and hacked in all directions . . .'). On balance, for all its Victorian nationalism, the title of Fitchett's history of the Napoleonic Wars, *How England Saved Europe*, may not be so exaggerated.

*Left to right: grenadier of a Line Bn, private of a Light Bn, and trooper of the 3rd Hussars of the King's German Legion, the finest of all Britain's Allied troops, though an integral part of the British Army.*

*(Print after Charles Hamilton Smith.)*

# The Spanish

Although Spain had opposed France in the early part of the war in Europe, it was as an ally of the French that Britain first came into major contact with the Spanish, and against the Spanish navy that most British efforts were directed, with conspicuous success. At the start of the Peninsular War the majority of the Spanish nation changed sides upon the imposition of Joseph Bonaparte as the new king; though a minority of Spaniards supported the Bonapartist faction, their military value was negligible.

The Spanish army in 1808 was in a wretched condition, having suffered many years of neglect, maladministration and corruption. The inept King Charles IV had not been the dominant power in the country; that had resided in the hands of the Queen's 'favourite', Manuel Godoy (1767-1851), a man totally corrupt and who had led Spain (against his will) in the 1793-95 war against France, which had virtually bankrupted the country. Under Godoy's rule, the Spanish army had declined to a state of almost total inefficiency, and in 1807 the only decent units had been sent to serve as French allies in northern Europe, under perhaps the only capable Spanish general, the Marquis of La Romana (1761-1811). What remained in Spain was in little condition to oppose the French occupation.

The army in 1808 comprised a Royal Guard of two cavalry regiments, six infantry battalions and a ceremonial company of halbardiers, and a large number of line regiments which on paper represented a strong army. In fact, most units were appallingly under-strength and ill-equipped. The 35 line regiments each had an establishment of three battalions of four companies each, totalling 2,186 men; in practice, the average strength was but 1,325, with only two regiments having more than 2,000 men (Asturias and Guadalajara, both in Denmark), and eleven with less than

1,000 men. The twelve light infantry battalions, each of six companies, totalling 1,200, were generally up to strength (only two with less than 1,000). The cavalry comprised twelve heavy regiments, and six of hussars and six of chasseurs, each of five squadrons and about 700 men; the average strength was 600, but they were so short of horses that barely two-thirds of these could be mounted. The 51 militia battalions were reasonably up to strength. Probably the best of the army were the foreign regiments, 12 Swiss battalions, one Italian and 9 Irish; in fact the Spanish army had many second- or third-generation Irish officers (hence Spanish generals with names like O'Donnell, Blake, Lacy and O'Neill), who were at least eager to fight (unlike many native-born Spanish generals), even if they possessed no great skill.

(Three of the Guard battalions were officially 'Walloons', though the Belgians in their ranks by this date were no longer in the majority; they included many Germans as well as many Spanish.) The army was formed by voluntary enlistment, plus a selective conscription called the 'Quinta' (so-called from originally taking every fifth man) which ensured that only the lowest and worst-educated of the population were selected; but the worst element of the army was probably the officer corps, one-third of whom were promoted NCOs (seldom allowed to rise above captain) and of the remainder many were place-seekers or appointed by influence or patronage controlled by the corrupt Ministry. In general they were uninterested, untrained and, in Surtees' words, 'the most contemptible creatures that I ever beheld . . . utterly unfit and unable to command their men.' Perhaps the best part of the army was the artillery, which though very under-

*Spanish line infantry c1808, in the traditional white or off-white uniform with coloured facings, worn until the adoption of different uniforms by the Junta forces. The man at right wears undress uniform, including stocking-cap and sandals. (Print published by J Booth)*

strength generally fought well, suffering enormous losses in many actions vainly attempting to defend their guns after the remainder had fled; hence the capture of large numbers of Spanish cannon in almost every battle.

The quality of the troops in Spain was improved by the escape (in British ships) of the majority of La Romana's troops in Denmark and north Germany, which returned to Spain; but the overall standard remained poor, and Spanish armies were almost always beaten with some ease by the French (excepting the capture of Dupont's force at Baylen). Once the war had broken out, practical government devolved upon a number of local administrations or *Juntas*, which raised their own units. The cavalry remained universally wretched, and the infantry prone to panic (they fled at Talavera apparently frightened by their own musketry) so that the Anglo-Portuguese staff officer Warre could comment that what was most to be regretted was the loss of muskets, 'which the fools throw away in their flight'. On occasion, though, they fought heroically, for example the stout defence of Zayas' brigade at Albuera (though it is interesting to note that the troops involved in this stand included both Walloon and Spanish Guards and the Irish regiment 'Irlanda'). The resulting opinion of the Spanish troops in the eyes of the British was very low; bugler Green of the 95th voiced the feelings of the rest when he termed them 'bad-plucked ones; they would rather run than fight'. Surtees of the 95th, claimed that even 'in their best days are more like an armed mob then regularly organised soldiers.' Although most of the Spanish war effort was directed towards opposing the French independently, considerable numbers served under Wellington's command; when these were in receipt of 'regular pay and food, and good care and clothing' as Wellington described, with competent leaders, they could fight well, for example Morillo's Division in the Pyrenees. The general impression, though, was that quoted by Wellington – that they were children in the art of war, who did only one thing properly: 'running away and assembling again in a state of nature'. At Toulouse, when the Spanish attacks failed (to the taunts of the Portuguese, who as Blakiston noted 'were not sorry to have a wipe at their neighbours'), Wellington is said to have

*In the later Peninsular War considerable numbers of Spaniards served under Wellington's direct command: over 46,000 in General Giron's '4th Army' and the Conde de Abispal's 'Army of Reserve of Andalusia', for example. The line infantry was uniformed in British style, in blue jackets with scarlet facings and piping, with light blue or grey overalls and 'stovepipe' shakos, here with the brass grenade-badge and red ornaments of grenadiers; fusiliers had white decorations and* cazadores *(chasseurs) green.*

remarked with resignation, 'There they go, off to Spain, by God!'

With good reason, many British observers doubted the good faith of many Spanish governmental and military leaders; a lack of willingness to co-operate led in good measure to the Corunna retreat, and Wellington was unsupported and unsupplied after Talavera. Chief culprit in British eyes was General Gregorio de la Cuesta (1740-1812), Captain-General of Old Castile; D'Urban at first noted him at Medellin acting 'with the fire of five-and-twenty' until ridden-over when his cavalry fled; yet shortly after was wondering whether the Spanish were suffering from panic or treachery. Costello of the 95th described him as 'that deformed-looking lump of pride, ignorance and treachery, General Cuesta. He was the most murderous-looking old man I ever saw.'

Very different, however, was the attitude of the overwhelming majority of the Spanish population. Their resistance to the French and adherence to the exiled King Ferdinand was uncompromising, and led to great epics of sacrifice and devotion, none more famous than the siege of Saragossa, in which only 20,000 of the 54,000 Spaniards killed were soldiers. Characters like 'the Maid of Saragossa' (who crewed a cannon after her family had been slain) entered the folk-myth of the country and served as inspiration to the remainder. The most significant contribution to French defeat in the Peninsular War made by the Spanish was that of the quasi-military guerrilla groups, ranging in number from a handful to 'armies' thousands strong, which proved a continual drain upon French resources, incessant warfare which wore down French resolve and killed thousands of soldiers. The guerrilla war, which made Spain a living hell for the occupiers, was conducted by chieftains ranging from ex-regular officers to bandits and maniac killers, with revolting cruelty and atrocity on both sides. Guerrilla leaders like 'El Empecinado' (Juan Martin Diaz, who later entered politics and died on the gallows), Fransisco Espoz y Mina and Don Julian Sanchez, whose cavalry served in Wellington's Spanish contingent contributed more to the French defeat than the regular troops, and kept alive the honour of their country. 'Guerrilla' also coined a new word in military vocabulary.

# The Portuguese

'The fighting-cocks of the army' was how Wellington described his Portuguese troops, and in the Peninsular War they represented an invaluable part of his forces, both in quality and numbers. At Salamanca, for example, there were 18,017 Portuguese to 30,562 British (more Portuguese were killed than British in this battle); in May 1813, when all but one Division and the cavalry were integrated into the British divisional system, there were 28,792 Portuguese to 52,484 British; at Nivelle, 24,240 Portuguese to 36,678 British. The contribution was such that it would have been very difficult for the British Army to have won the Peninsular War unaided; yet at the start of the war, the Portuguese army was in little better condition than that of Spain.

From 1792 Portugal had been controlled by the heir-apparent, Don John, his mother Queen Maria I having become insane. In 1801 Portugal declared war on Spain, was invaded by a Franco-Spanish army and knocked out of the war. In 1807 the French invaded to force Portugal to accept the Continental System, the embargo on British goods; Don John and the royal family fled to the Portuguese colony of Brazil, leaving the government in the hands of a Council of Regency, headed by the Bishop of Oporto, who appealed to Britain for help, thus precipitating the Peninsular War.

The quality of the army in 1807 was poor, badly-equipped and ill-led. Officers were held in low esteem; one-third were ex-sergeants and the remainder exclusively the nobility. There was no centralised training and promotion prospects were wretched, 60-year-old subalterns being not uncommon. The rank-and-file were recruited by a selective conscription for 10 years' service which took only the poorest and least skilled, and were appallingly paid. The Council of War (established 1643) which nominally ran the army had minimal powers; morale was low, and discipline generally lax, though it was enforced by beatings, hanging and shooting. Administratively, the army was divided into three 'Grand Divisions', numbered 1st-3rd, covering the South, Centre and North of the country respectively.

After Junot's invasion in 1807 the Portuguese army was largely disbanded, and re-assembled in a very poor state. Although the army retained its original framework of regiments, it was reconstructed totally under William Carr Beresford (1764-1854), an Irish officer of the British Army appointed as Marshal of Portugal in March 1809. (Wellington was in overall command as Marshal-General of Portugal.) Foreign commanders of the Portuguese army was a well-tried practice, in the 18th century under such good commanders as Lippe, but later foreign commanders had been of little use; in 1796 command was given to the Prince of Waldeck, and after his death to the Prussian Count de Goltz, formerly Frederick the Great's secretary. Britain provided the Portuguese army with its Quartermaster-general in the émigré de la Rosière, formerly of the French army, and Marshal Comte de Viomenil, another French royalist.

Beresford was a splendid administrator. From company level upwards, British officers were introduced, which had the greatest effect in remedying the worst failings of the officer corps, the most useless Portuguese members of which were retired. The organisation was such that any Portuguese field officer had British above and below him, and vice-versa; thus a Portuguese major would have a British senior captain and battalion-commander, and a Portuguese brigade-commander would have two British colonels immediately below him. The old method of conscription was retained (as late as 1811 a British witness described how recruits were herded to their regiments, roped together and under cavalry escort), but conditions improved markedly: better pay, reasonable food, better equipment (much of it from Britain) and fairer discipline brought higher morale, and revealed the innate qualities of the Portuguese soldier. In battle they behaved with courage, and apart from working in manual labour, when a perceived national indolence reduced their effectiveness, they became as valuable members of the army as their British colleagues. The Anglo-Portuguese staff officer William Warre is an excellent guide to the rapid progress made by the army under Beresford's reforms; in 1808 he referred to them as cowards 'who

*Atirador, 5th (Campomayor) Caçadores, 1810. Unlike the remainder of the Portuguese army which wore blue, the Caçadores ('hunters' in Portuguese) wore brown with coloured facings and yellow lace, and the false-fronted 'Barretina' shako unique to Portuguese troops. In 1811, when the number of regiments was increased from 6 to 12, a new uniform was introduced, still dark brown but with black hussar-style braid and a British-style 'stovepipe' shako.*

won't fight 1/16th of a Frenchman with arms, but plunder and murder the wounded', but by 1809 was describing them as 'very obedient, willing and patient, but also naturally dirty and careless of their persons.' By the end of that year Warre reported that under British supervision 'had they justice done unto them in the common comforts . . . clothing and food, they would make as good soldiers as any in the world. None are certainly more intelligent or willing, or bear hardships and privation more humbly.' By 1812 they had won a fine reputation, and even Picton, the sternest of judges, regarded their exertions as equal to those of the British and thus 'deserving an equal portion of laurel'. Wellington recognised that the improvement owed more to the decent treatment in pay and conditions afforded to the Portuguese than to any instruction given them; in other words, Beresford and his assistants found the best way of utilising inherent qualities.

The infantry comprised 24 regiments with territorial designations, each of two battalions (the 21st Regt had only one), each of five companies, one company of the 1st Bn being grenadiers and one in the 2nd light infantry (the latter apparently detached about 1811). Battalion-strength was officially 770, but in practice was often very much less; in 1809, for example, average regimental strength was 1,128 instead of 1,540, with 7 regiments having less than 1,000 men, the 8th (Evora) Regt with only 369 and the single-battalion 21st (Valenza) Regt with only 193 men. There were six light infantry or rifle battalions, styled *Caçadores*, formed by Beresford in November 1808, who were trained in British light infantry tactics and became the equivalent of the British 95th and 5/60th; three more battalions were formed and three others converted from the Anglo-Portuguese Loyal Lusitanian Legion, bringing the total to 12 battalions each of 770 men in five companies, of which one company of each was styled sharpshooters or *Atiradores*. Most of the infantry regiments were linked permanently in 11 brigades (two regiments per brigade: the 20th and 22nd were never brigaded), with the *Caçadores* distributed like the British light troops.

The Portuguese cavalry was the least effective part of the army, due largely to an insurmountable shortage of horses which meant that at least three of the twelve numbered regiments (2nd, 3rd and 12th) were used only as dismounted garrison troops. Regimental establishment was 594 men in 4 squadrons, but field strength rarely approached 300, and no more than 1,300 were ever fit for field service at any time. They fought well on occasion but were unreliable and liable to flee if not bolstered by the presence of British troops; though Wellington's comment 'worse than useless' is perhaps a little harsh.

The artillery was formed in four regiments and greatly improved by Beresford's replacing their 3 and 6pdrs with 9pdrs, and by Alexander Dickson's superintendence. The engineers were of limited use due to the presence of too many senior officers who were unwilling to conduct field-works, and the pontoon-train was crewed by landing-parties from British warships (from 1813 Wellington allowed the employment of Portuguese naval personnel). D'Urban's comment on the commissariat, 'infamous beyond all description', is comprehensive!

The territorial militia was recruited by selective conscription for life, organised as one regiment from each of 48 regions, each regiment of two battalions of 6 companies each, totalling 1,500 men, a figure rarely achieved. Units served for 2, 3 or 6 months at a time, so that no more than a fraction was ever embodied simultaneously; they were ordered not to engage the French if possible, and proved unreliable when they did (as at Guarda), but were valuable for garrison duty, releasing regular units for service with the field army.

# The Hanoverians

The Hanoverian army occupied a unique place in the forces of the many independent German states, by virtue of its close connection with Britain as a result of the Kings of England (from George I onwards) being also Electors of Hanover. Hanoverian troops had served alongside the British even before the Hanoverian succession to the British throne (they formed part of the Allied forces commanded by Marlborough), and the close contacts had brought a number of similarities to the British Army, even though the Hanoverian establishment remained a totally separate entity. In 1775 five infantry battalions went abroad, two to Minorca and three to Gibraltar, where they served alongside the British garrison in the great siege (the 3rd Regt even bore a representation of the 'Rock' upon its colours); in 1787, the 14th and 15th Regts were transferred to the service of the British East India Company and went to serve in India in the British interest.

In matters of dress, the Hanoverian army closely resembled the British, wearing red coats with coloured facings and, on campaign in the 1794 period, 'round hats' as worn by many British units. In 1800 the single-breasted jacket replaced the previous long-tailed coat, and a 'stovepipe' shako was adopted, both in imitation of British style, as was the existence of a royal Foot Guard in addition to the line regiments. The cavalry was organised in a *Leib-Garde* (imitating the British Household Cavalry and wearing red), and both heavy and light regiments of the line in blue uniforms; further evidence of the similarity with the British Army is the fact that the 9th Light Dragoons was titled 'Queen's', and the 10th Light Dragoons 'Prince of Wales'', exactly like the correspondingly-numbered British regiment.

The Hanoverian army was a good, professional body which served alongside the British in the early campaigns of the Revolutionary Wars, Baron von Ompteda (who served in the Foot Guard in the 1794-95 campaign) remarking that 'It will not be denied that eating and drinking are prime articles of faith to the Hanoverian soldier'! (He later became perhaps, the most famous leader of the King's German Legion and died in circumstances of great heroism at Water-

loo.) In June 1803 the French occupied Hanover, the 15,000-strong Hanoverian army being unable to resist. The Convention of Lauenberg (5 July 1803) which disbanded the Hanoverian army permitted its members to go anywhere they wished, with the proviso that they should not again bear arms against France until they had been formally 'exchanged' as prisoners-of-war. (The British government refused to sanction this proviso, so the exchanges never occurred.) Consequently, to utilise the manpower and determination of the Hanoverians, George III authorised the

formation of a corps of foreign troops under Col Frederick von der Decken, to be called (initially) 'The King's Germans', and later, when the corps expanded into a miniature army, 'The King's German Legion'.

From its beginnings in 1803 the German Legion grew rapidly as more units were created to accommodate the influx of recruits who came largely from Hanover, although other German nationals also joined the corps as a way of continuing the fight against Napoleon. By the beginning of 1805 there were four line and two light battalions, a dragoon and light dragoon regiment and five artillery batteries, and when in November of that year Britain made a landing in Germany as a diversion to the French efforts against Austria, the Legion went with them and for some weeks occupied Hanover, Bremen and Verden. When the expedition had to be evacuated after the Austrian defeat at Austerlitz, vast numbers of new Hanoverian recruits returned with them to Britain, which allowed the Legion to be expanded to ten

*Trooper, 1st Hussars, King's German Legion, in Peninsular service uniform, though latterly overalls would have been more common than the white breeches. The horse-furniture and uniform was of British hussar style, in dark blue with scarlet facings and yellow lace, though for the fur busby to have a peak was an unusual variation apparently restricted to the KGL.*

| The Hanoverian Army at Waterloo: | |
|---|---|
| **1st Hanoverian Bde:** | Field-Bns Bremen, Verden, York; Light Bns Lüneburg, Grubenhagen; *Feld-Jäger* Corps |
| **3rd Hanoverian Bde:** | *Landwehr* Bns Bremervörde, Osnabrück, Quackenbrück, Salzgitter |
| **4th Hanoverian Bde:** | *Landwehr* Bns Lüneburg, Verden, Osterode, Münden |
| **5th Hanoverian Bde:** | *Landwehr* Bns Hameln, Gifhorn, Peine, Hildesheim |
| **6th Hanoverian Bde:** | Field-Bns Lauenberg, Calenburg; *Landwehr* Bns Nienburg, Hoya, Bentheim |
| **1st Hanoverian Cavalry Bde:** | Prince Regent's, Bremen and Verden, Duke of Cumberland's Hussars |

*Officer and private of the 1st Light Battalion, King's German Legion; these splendid units wore British 'rifle' uniform in dark green with black facings, though the line battalions wore red jackets with dark blue facings,*
(*print after R Knötel*)

line battalions and five cavalry regiments. The Legion thus became, virtually, the Hanoverian army in exile, though few Hanoverians could be enlisted after the French annexation of Hanover and its absorption into the newly-created kingdom of Westphalia in 1807. Thereafter, recruits to the KGL included foreigners of any description, no longer even exclusively Germans but Poles, Greeks, Italians and others. Nevertheless, despite this dilution of the rank-and-file by men of dubious background, the excellent Hanoverian officers continued to extract the best possible behaviour and discipline from the men under their command, so that the Legion – which was an integral part of the British Army, not merely an Allied contingent under British orders – carved out a reputation in battle which was exceeded by none. Not all the officers were German, as a minority of British officers were taken in; an analysis of the officers holding commissions in 1814, exclusive of staff ranks (e.g. the Duke of Cambridge was nominally Colonel of the 1st Line Bn) appears to show 668 with German (or conceivably Dutch or Scandinavian) names, 91 British, 29 French and 5 Italian.

The Legion spent some time in the Baltic in 1807, during the Hanoverian expedition, and in the following year more than half went to the Peninsula, where over the next six years they established a reputation as among the very best troops in the army. The light cavalry in particular were especially valuable in that unlike most of the British regiments they were trained in 'outpost' duties, the 1st Hussars serving with the Light Division and probably being the best cavalry in the army. (The five Legion cavalry regiments were re-titled: in 1813 the two heavy dragoon regiments were made into light dragoons, and the three light dragoon regiments into hussars, though they had worn hussar uniform from the beginning.) In exploits like the charge of the heavy dragoons at Garcia Hernandez, which provides one of the few instances of cavalry actually breaking infantry in square, the Legion won imperishable laurels. Its highest strength appears to have been reached in June 1812 when it comprised 14,175 men; from first to last around 28,000 men appear to have served in its ranks. As well as with Wellington's Peninsular army, the Legion served in the Mediterranean and Sicily in 1808-11, at Walcheren in 1809, Italy in 1814 and north Germany in 1813-14. After the peace of 1814 the non-Hanoverians were discharged, with the intention that the remainder would form the nucleus of a reformed Hanoverian regular army, but the Waterloo campaign intervened. The discharge of the 'foreigners' resulted in the KGL units in the Waterloo campaign being considerably weaker than their British equivalents (the six line bat-

talions averaged but 420 men each), but this did not prevent them from playing a most heroic role in the battle. Most distinguished was the defence of La Haye Sainte by Major Baring and the 2nd KGL Light Bn, supported by the 1st Light and the light company of the 5th Line Bn. Baring held the French at bay until his ammunition ran out, then with bayonets, until he and but 42 men escaped. Throughout the period, organisation and uniform of the KGL units was like that of their British counterparts.

In addition to the German Legion, the collapse of French influence in Germany as a result of the 1813 campaign allowed a new Hanoverian army to be formed, which contributed a considerable number of units to the Anglo-Allied army in the 1815 campaign. Present in the Waterloo campaign were three regiments of hussars, two foot artillery batteries, 7 'field-battalions' (i.e. regular infantry) and fifteen *Landwehr* (militia) battalions, numbering some 13,000 infantry and 1,600 cavalry, with one field-battalion and 12 *Landwehr*, totalling 9,000, in reserve. Their calibre was adequate (total losses in the campaign were 1,818) but the cavalry in particular were of dubious worth; the Duke of Cumberland's Hussars, in fact, quit the field during the battle and rode to Brussels with tales of Wellington's defeat. As a punishment the unit was broken up and attached to various corps as escorts for the commissaries; the five men attached to Mercer's troop of the RHA he found 'amazingly sulky and snappish with every one'!

# The Netherlanders

Although the army of the Netherlands comprised a considerable portion of Wellington's forces in the 1815 campaign, for the majority of the Napoleonic Wars these areas were under French control and thus contributed personnel to Napoleon's forces. The Austrian Netherlands was overrun in the early stages of the Revolutionary Wars and annexed as part of metropolitan France in 1797. The United Provinces also fell to the French, but existed as an independent French satellite state, initially as the Batavian Republic and, from 1806, as the Kingdom of Holland, to which Napoleon's brother Louis Bonaparte was appointed as king. Louis was something of an unwilling ally to Napoleon and abdicated in 1810, whereupon Holland and its army was integrated into the French Empire. Holland remained part of the Empire until late 1813, when the collapse of French fortunes in northern Europe led to its rebellion and liberation. William Frederick, Prince of Orange (1772-1843), who had lost his principality of Nassau in 1806 when he refused to join Napoleon's satellite organisation of the Confederation of the Rhine, became 'Sovereign Prince of the Netherlands' at that time, the house of Orange being Holland's hereditary ruling family. In 1814, with the separation of the old Austrian Netherlands from France, Belgium was joined to Holland as a new state, the Kingdom of the Netherlands, William Frederick becoming the country's first King, as William I. It was the troops of this newly-created state which took the field with the Allied armies in 1815.

The new army had little time to settle into its new organisation by the outbreak of the 1815 campaign, and the recent campaigning experience of many of the members was sharply contrasting with that undertaken in 1815, for many had, less than two years before, been fighting *with* Napoleon, not against him. There were many Netherlands officers of considerable experience, gained in campaigns with the French army, but although the officer-corps remained loyal to its new sovereign, many of the rank-and-file were doubtless unenthusiastic and perhaps even confused about the change of allegiance. The situation is reflected in the army's command-structure. General Janssens, head of the Ministry of War, had fought against the British both at the Cape and in Java and thus could not be expected to have entertained much sympathy with the British command under which the Netherlands troops served. General David Chassé, arguably the most competent of the Netherlands commanders in the 1815, had begun his service with the Dutch army, but gained most distinction with the French army, fighting with them at Talavera against the British. In 1810 he became a general, and in 1811 a Baron of the Empire. Continuing in the Peninsula until 1813, he then returned to Dutch service and became a Lieutenant-General in 1815, serving with distinction under Wellington at Quatre Bras and Waterloo. At the head of the army was the king, the son of the *Stadtholder* who had taken refuge in England in 1795 and died there in 1806, and William I's eldest son, Prince William of Orange (1792-1849) had known only British service. He had served in the Peninsular War as an aide on Wellington's staff, and had been appointed a major-general in the British Army in 1813 at the age of 21. Now, aged 23, he was in overall field command of the Netherlands troops in the campaign, and in nominal command of the Allied 1st Corps of Wellington's army. The appointment was political, for though the young man was well-meaning he was totally inexperienced in command of troops, and was responsible for a series of ghastly errors in the campaign which sacrificed a number of units to no purpose. Similarly pro-British was the Netherlands Quartermaster-General, Constant de Rebecque, who had also served with the Prince of Orange in the Peninsular War.

Initially, relations between Wellington and the Netherlandish state were not ideal, despite Wellington's association with the Prince of Orange in the Peninsula, the king tending to interfere with planning; but Wellington made his point

*Prince William of Orange (1792-1849), eldest son of King William I, whom he succeeded as King William II in 1840. The young prince was enthusiastic but inexperienced, and when wounded at Waterloo was prevented from causing any further damage by his well-intentioned but ill-advised tactics.*

*Fusilier drummer, Belgian line, 1815. The Netherlands infantry wore blue jackets of British style (except for the shoulder-'wings'), with white facings for all (orange for militia), only the pattern of shako differentiating Dutch and Belgian units, the former having bell-topped caps with front and rear peaks and the Belgian shakos exactly like the British 1812 pattern, save for the 'W' cypher on the plate. The* Jäger *regiments wore similar uniforms but in green with yellow facings, and shakos similarly distinguished, with green plumes (red for flank companies, as for line grenadiers).*

with such firmness that on 4 May 1815 the king (perhaps with some reluctance) appointed Wellington as Field-Marshal of the Netherlands, giving him supreme command over all the Netherlandish forces, removing a considerable obstacle in the planning of the campaign.

The army was divided between Dutch and Belgian units, or, as these names were not in common use at the time, 'North Netherlands' and 'South Netherlands' respectively. Of the Dutch troops, some were probably confused about their status, having so recently marched under Napoleon's banner, and indeed Dutch resistance to France had been lukewarm in the various Allied expeditions to that country, in 1793, 1799 and 1814; though in quality, they were reasonably good. The Belgians had received a promise of independence in 1814 and many applauded the release from Napoleon's yoke; but on finding that their 'independence' was to be an annexation by Holland, their ardour cooled and the attitude of many was one of indifference. With such disadvantages it is surprising, perhaps, that the Netherlands forces behaved as well as they did in the 1815 campaign, even though they were generally the most inferior of all the component parts of Wellington's army.

The Netherlands army made distinction between Dutch and Belgian regiments (being formed to a degree upon 'territorial' lines), but there was only a single establishment, the regiments of both nationalities being integrated. There were 36 numbered infantry regiments, mostly of single battalions, of which the 1st, 2nd, 4th and 7th were Belgian, the 5th, 10th and 11th Dutch East Indian, the 19th-26th and 33rd Dutch colonials, the 16th-18th and 27th Dutch *Jägers* (light infantry or riflemen), the 29th-33rd Swiss mercenaries, the 34th a garrison battalion and the 35th and 36th Belgian *Jägers*. The 28th Regt was from Nassau, and in addition there was a 2nd Nassau Regt, not numbered in the line. 45 militia battalions (numbers of which fought in the campaign) comprised nos 1-20 Dutch and the remainder Belgian. The eight cavalry regiments were numbered consecutively, despite there being different types of cavalry: the 1st and 3rd Carabiniers, 4th Light Dragoons and 6th and 7th Hussars were Dutch (the latter East Indian), and the 2nd Carabiniers, 5th Light Dragoons

and 8th Hussars Belgian. Both militia and regular batteries made up the artillery. Organisation was still basically on French lines; infantry battalions, for example, had six fusilier companies and two of *Flanqueurs* (one a 'heavy' company, like grenadiers, and one a light company), though the Swiss had eight fusilier and two flank companies. Cavalry were organised in four squadrons of two companies each. There was in addition a small unit of *Guides te Paard* (mounted guides) formed as an escort for the commander-in-chief in February 1815.

Probably the best of the Netherlands troops in the 1815 campaign were the two Nassau units, though ironically they had fought for Napoleon as part of the Confederation of the Rhine and at Waterloo still retained their old green uniforms, as worn in the Peninsula. Each battalion comprised four fusilier, one grenadier and one light company, though in the 2nd Regt apparently one of the fusilier companies was designated as riflemen. Both regiments had seen extensive service with the French in the Peninsula, the 1st with Marshal Suchet and the 2nd at Medellin and Vittoria. In December 1813, in concert with the Frankfurt battalion and doubtless as a result of the deteriorating situation in northern Europe, the 2nd Nassau Regt defected to the British. They fought in the Waterloo campaign with great courage and determination, and were regarded among the best elements of the army.

The Netherlands troops engaged in the 1815 campaign numbered some 18,700, with 32 guns, of whom some 466 were killed, 2,054 wounded and 1,627 'missing', the latter including many who absented themselves during the fighting. Several British witnesses remarked on the inordinate number of Netherlanders who accompanied each wounded man from the battle-line, sometimes six or ten 'helpers' to each casualty! Nevertheless, some units behaved very well (though not as effectively as some authors suggest), the stand of Prince Bernhard of Saxe-Weimar and his outnumbered Netherlanders and Nassauers at the early part of Quatre Bras probably saving the Allies from a defeat. Perhaps Fortescue's assessment is the fairest: that under the circumstances in which they had been formed, they could simply never have been expected to be enthusiastic about the war.

# The Austrians, Russians and Swedes

Throughout the Napoleonic Wars, Britain was the only state unwavering in its opposition to Napoleon; but with the exception of the Peninsular War, which exerted a continual drain on French resources, the major campaigns in continental Europe were fought without the significant participation of British forces. The greatest burden of maintaining the war against France fell upon a number of mainland European states, which (by virtue of their opposition to the French if not for other reasons) found common cause with Britain, which throughout the period acted as 'paymaster', providing not only diplomatic support but vast quantities of material help in the form of cash subsidies or loans and even *matériel* to aid the war against Napoleon. In all these campaigns, therefore, Britain played a significant role even though her own forces were not engaged (or engaged only by the presence of token forces, as at Leipzig); but the actual campaigning was undertaken by the armies of the Allied states. The successes of Napoleon's military policy, however, meant that none of these states could remain permanently in opposition; all were allied to France at one time or another, or at least experienced periods of neutrality.

Austria, or more correctly until after Austerlitz, the Holy Roman Empire, was probably the most persistent of the continental opponents of France, experi-

encing repeated defeats yet always returning to the fight until Napoleon's final overthrow. The Hapsburg Emperor Francis II presided over an immense territory, originally stretching from the Austrian Netherlands to Italy and from the Balkans to Poland. From this area was drawn the multi-national *Kaiserlich-königlich Armee*, all the provinces of the Empire contributing regiments and resulting in some confusion in the central administration as some areas of the Empire, notably the 'Hungarian' region, controlled by that kingdom's *Diet* (parliament), the Netherlands, Italian duchies and the Tyrol, enjoyed a degree of administrative autonomy. Successive defeats at the hands of the French reduced the amount of territory held by the Empire, losing recruiting-grounds, and from 1804 Francis II took the title 'Emperor of Austria', and thus became Francis I.

The Austrians first came into contact with the British forces in the Netherlands in 1793, where the excellence of the Austrian troops impressed British observers, and a number of Austrian innovations were consequently introduced into the British Army, ranging from an imitation of their heavy cavalry sabre to the design of the single-breasted infantry jacket and (probably) the first shako. The Austrian forces throughout the period exemplified the earnest, well-disciplined and brave conduct typical of a number of Germanic armies in the 18th century, and it is probably not an unfair reflection that despite somewhat erratic leadership it was the character of the Austrian army which enabled the fight to be carried on for so long. In addition to the many nationalities comprising the Empire – of which the Hungarians, Transylvanians and Croatians formed the 'Hungarian' establishment, different in organisation and uniform from the remainder, styled 'German' regiments, even though these included Poles, Ital-

ians and Netherlanders – a large number of recruits were obtained by voluntary enlistment from the smaller central German states; one estimate suggests that up to half the 'German' regiments were recruited in this way.

Austria sustained the war against France both in northern Europe and Italy until defeated crushingly at Marengo in 1800. In 1805 she again took the field, and was defeated at Ulm and Austerlitz, and again in 1809 at Wagram, after inflicting upon Napoleon his first major setback at Aspern/Essling. Napoleon's marriage to Marie-Louise of Austria reinforced a brief French alliance, during which the Austrians supplied a 'reserve corps' for the attack on Russia; but in 1813 they were among the principal allies who defeated Napoleon in the 'war of liberation' and brought about his first abdication. In 1815 they renewed their attack on Napoleon's return, but only minor actions occurred before his final defeat.

The Empire of Russia was similarly a vast territory, encompassing both Europeans and Asiatics in its army; its massive population resulted in a limitless supply of manpower. Czar Paul I who succeeded his mother, Catherine the Great, in 1796, turned his hatred of the French Revolution into a cause for war, and in 1798 sent three armies into the field, in Italy, Switzerland and the Netherlands, all of which were ultimately unsuccessful despite the genius of the great old general Suvarov. Always unstable, the Czar was recognised as a madman and murdered by a court conspiracy in 1801, to be succeeded by his son, Alexander I. Alexander renewed the war against France in 1805, but after defeats at Austerlitz, Eylau and Friedland (1807) signed the Treaty of Tilsit which formed a Franco-Russian alliance, but the association with Napoleon was always uncomfortable. Alexander's attempts to distance himself from Napoleon were probably a major cause for Napoleon's attack on Russia in 1812, the campaign which destroyed the *Grande Armée*. Russian forces played a major role in the campaigns of 1813-14.

British forces only came into major contact with the Russians in the Netherlands in 1799, so had little opportunity of assimilating any Russian ideas or

*Private, officers and sergeant, Austro-Hungarian fusiliers, in the 1806 uniform which was not completely in use even by 1809. The Austrian army wore their traditional white coat, with white breeches for 'German' regiments and the distinctive light blue for 'Hungarians'. (Print after R v Ottenfeld)*

*Private, Austrian* Jägers, *c. 1800, wearing the* Jäger *version of the 1798-1806 crested helmet (with green crest: for other infantry it was black over yellow). The uniform was grey with green facings; the more familiar head-dress was the later 'Corsican hat'. (Print after R v Ottenfeld)*

*Russian grenadier, 1812, wearing the singular scuttle-shaped shako (kiwer) adopted in that year, with the enormous, thin plume indicative of grenadiers. Russian regiments had worn multi-coloured facings until late 1807, when red facings were adopted by all regiments on the dark green jacket, and regimental distinctives were restricted to the colour of the shoulder-straps, which bore the divisional number to which the regiment was attached. Worn here are the summer 'gaiter-trousers'.*

practices, not that these would have been beneficial. Recruited by conscription and brutally treated like the serfs they were, the Russian soldiery maintained a stoic attitude to beatings from their own officers and NCOs and to the enemy's fire alike. Administration and commissariat were wretched, medical services almost non-existent and leadership frequently injudicious; yet the ordinary soldier remained totally constant in his devotion to duty, his religion, his motherland and his Czar. The army was organised on conventional European lines, but included one valuable resource which was not enjoyed by other nations, in the presence of vast numbers of Asiatic tribesmen, generically termed Cossacks, who provided the army with a most effective light cavalry force, somewhat undisciplined but especially valuable in harassing the enemy. British forces encountered them in Holland in 1814, and reported them almost as dangerous to their friends as to their enemies.

Nevertheless, British observers were always impressed by the Russian troops; John Spencer Stanhope described them as 'a fine hardy race, almost insensible to pain; they were indeed, men of iron . . . They really seemed to be made of different stuff from other men; their frames and sinews were, apparently, as hard as their minds.' The reforms of Alexander I transformed the Russian army from a backward, mid-18th century-style army to one exhibiting in 1805 (in Bunbury's

words) 'very much the outward character of good German soldiers', but never improved the quality of officer, who remained probably among the worst in Europe, without real hope of advancement and with no incentives to do much except drink and idle. Russia's successful commanders were mostly of foreign origin, or who like the old veteran Kutuzov had learned practical soldiering against the Turks.

Sweden had been the leading north European power, but had declined in importance since the days of the great martial monarch Charles XII. With King Gustavus IV a minor, the Swedish regency at first enjoyed good relations with the French republican governments, and in 1800 Sweden joined the 'Armed Neutrality of the North' with Denmark and Russia, to resist British naval actions in the economic war against France. In 1804, however, having developed a hatred for Napoleon, Gustavus took Sweden into the Third Coalition but a quarrel with Prussia prevented any Swedish military action before Austerlitz wrecked the coalition. After Tilsit, Russia invaded Finland and took it from Sweden, part of a Napoleonic strategy to separate Sweden from its British alliance. A British expedition under Sir John Moore was on hand to assist the Swedes, but a quarrel between the king and Moore led to its remaining uncommitted. The loss of Finland caused Gustavus' deposition in favour of King Charles XIII, who adopted as heir the French marshal Bernadotte. Defeats by Russia compelled Sweden to declare war on Britain (November 1810) in the French interest, but it was made clear that the 'war' was only a show until such time as French influence could be thrown off. In July 1812 Britain concluded peace with Russia and Sweden, both countries sanctioning Sweden's attempt to wrest Norway from France's ally Denmark, and Bernadotte, as Crown Prince, led a Swedish army in the 1813 campaign which contributed significantly to the Allied victory at Leipzig.

# The Prussians

Perhaps the most famous of Britain's allies during the Napoleonic Wars, at least from a British viewpoint, is Prussia; though this fame results from only one major military collaboration, in the final campaign of the era, when Wellington's Anglo-Allied army joined with Blücher's Prussians in the Waterloo campaign.

In prestige at least, the Prussian army was perhaps the dominant force in Europe at the beginning of the Revolutionary Wars, basking in the military successes achieved by King Frederick II ('the Great') (1713-86). Not only was Frederick himself undisputedly one of the 'great captains' (whose strategic genius influenced Napoleon), but his career and later reconstruction following the successful but exhausting Seven Years War raised the Prussian army to a position of great repute. Ironically, it was the Frederickian tradition which to some extent prevented the modernisation of the army, so that by the outbreak of the Revolutionary Wars it was still operating along the lines of the mid-18th century, some of the innovations adopted by other states not having touched the Prussians.

Prussia was instrumental in organising the first opposition to the French Revolution, when as early as 1791 King Frederick William II of Prussia and the Holy Roman Emperor Leopold II declared themselves ready to act in concert with other European states to restore the power of the French King Louis XVI. An Austro-Prussian alliance was declared in February 1792 and by July an Allied army was gathering at Coblenz, including 42,000 Prussians, 30,000 Austrians and smaller contingents of Hessians and French émigrés. Command was vested in Karl Wilhelm Ferdinand, Duke of Brunswick (1735-1806) who had served under both Frederick the Great and his own uncle, Ferdinand of Brunswick. The Allied forces invaded France but on 20 September were stopped in their tracks at Valmy by the French generals Dumouriez and Kellermann. Brunswick, unenthusiastic about the operations in which the slow-moving Prussians were out-manoeuvred by the French, was discouraged by the French cannonade against his infantry and retired to Germany. Valmy saved the French republican cause, and despite Allied

*Musketeer, 1st Bn 10th (1st Silesian) Regt, 1815, a unit which collaborated closely with the British Army at Waterloo, on the extreme right of the Prussian advance. The shako covered with oilskin was the most distinctive feature of the uniform of this period.*

successes in the first half of 1793, France was able to maintain the war until success began to swing their way in the autumn of that year. Brunswick retained his command for some time but was unable to co-operate fully with the Austrians, and was defeated at Wissembourg; he then retired from active service for some 13 years. By the beginning of 1795 Prussia was approaching financial exhaustion, and concluded a separate peace with France by the Treaty of Basel.

The following decade and more added little to Prussia's prestige as under her new king Frederick William III (1770-1840), who succeeded his father in 1797, she remained apart from the wars against France. Prussia's reputation might be seen to have suffered from the apparent indifference displayed to the German territories on the left bank of the Rhine, which fell to the French, which contrasted somewhat with Prussia's eagerness to increase her territories to the east, the second and third partitions of Poland (1783 and 1795) almost doubling her size whilst adding little of significance to her standing or real power. During this period of neutrality the internal management of the state did not really benefit, as might have been expected in a period of peace; the army lost the opportunity of campaign experience and the influx of Polish recruits, some disaffected, was not conducive to the maintenance of the previous high standards. Frederick William tried to mollify the more repressive features of his father's regime, but was not prepared to take the field against France even after the occupation of Hanover in 1803.

In 1805 Prussia joined the Third Coalition but withdrew after Austerlitz; but the formation of the Confederation of the Rhine, which was believed might grow into the dominant force in Germany, persuaded Frederick William to form the Fourth Coalition in 1806. In this he was encouraged by his queen, the beautiful Louise of Mecklenburg-Strelitz, whose vehement anti-French sentiments caused her to be styled 'the only man in Prussia'. However, the brief 1806 campaign was a total disaster; recalling old Brunswick and the even more aged Field-Marshal Richard Mollendorf (1724-1806), another of Frederick the Great's generals,

Frederick William III was routed at Jena/Auerstädt, where both Brunswick and Mollendorf were mortally wounded. For another six years Prussia was humiliated, losing half her territory by the Treaty of Tilsit and being reduced virtually to a French satellite.

The catastrophe of 1806, however, proved Prussia's salvation; for it caused the growth of a regenerated patriotism, encouraged by the *Tugenbund* or 'League of Virtue'. The internal administration was reformed radically by the great minister Baron Heinrich v Stein (1757-1831), who was forced by French pressure to flee to Austria in 1809, and his successor Prince Karl v Hardenburg (1750-1822); whilst the army was reformed and reconstructed by the Hanoverian General Gerhard v Scharnhorst (1755-1813) and the Saxon General Augustus Wilhelm v Gneisenau (1760-1831). The former in particular was regarded as the symbol of the increasing tide of German nationalism awakened by the 1806 defeat, which in 1813 resulted in a patriotic fervour which supported the resumption of the war against France. In the event, this was to a degree forced upon Frederick William by the Convention of Tauroggen (December 1812) in which the Prussian general Johann Yorck (1759-1830), commanding the Prussian contingent which had been compelled to act in support of Napoleon's invasion of Russia, agreed with the Russians that the Prussians

*Prussian infantry storm into the blazing village of Plancenoit on the afternoon of the battle of Waterloo; French Chasseurs à Pied of the Imperial Guard give way before the pressure exerted by the Prussians. (Print after C Röchling.)*

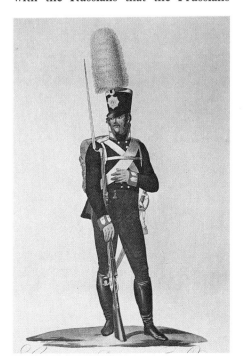

*Grenadier, Prussian Foot Guards, c. 1810, in full dress. The shako is worn here without its service-dress cover, with the enormous 'Busch' plume which distinguished grenadiers, and showing the 'Guard star' badge on the front. (Print after Wolff & Jügel.)*

should become neutrals in the conflict. Frederick William repudiated the Convention, but shortly after abandoned the French alliance and joined the Sixth Coalition. The Prussian army was enlarged by the formation of many new units, including the mobilisation of the *Landwehr* (militia), and buoyed up by the resurgence of patriotic feeling made a significant contribution to the so-called 'war of liberation' in 1813-14, which first expelled French troops from Germany and then invaded France, bringing about Napoleon's abdication in 1814. Frederick William himself was present in the campaigns, including the battles of Bautzen, Dresden, and the decisive encounter at Leipzig.

Prussia gained very considerable territory at the conclusion of peace, and with it a number of 'foreign' regiments whose personnel had fought previously alongside the French; others included the ex-Russo-German Legion, a Russian corps of German ex-prisoners transferred to Prussian service, Saxons, Westphalians and Hanseaticers. The worst shortages of equipment had been remedied by the time of Waterloo (in 1813-14 some *Landwehr* had been barefoot and armed only with pikes), but it was still necessary to field large numbers of *Landwehr* units. Perhaps the most significant part of the Prussian army in the 1815 campaign was its command: Gebhard von Blücher (1742-1819) epitomised the stern fighting qualities of old Prussia (though he was born a Mecklenberger and first served in the Swedish army), had been the last to surrender in 1806 and was a loyal and indomitable ally to Wellington, his nickname Marshal *Vorwärts* ('forward') reflecting his character. To his stubborn and fiery temper was added the calculating brain of Gneisenau, his chief of staff, who though he distrusted the British and was inclined not to support them, nevertheless followed Blücher's instructions and, despite the battering taken by the Prussians at Ligny, moved to reinforce the Anglo-Allied army at Waterloo, which move ultimately decided the campaign.

A significant characteristic in the behaviour of the Prussian army in the campaigns of 1813-14 and the 'Hundred Days' was a totally uncompromising attitude towards the French; having suffered humiliation, occupation and looting by the French armies, the Prussians fully intended to exact their revenge on the people of France and in 1815 it took all Wellington's diplomatic skills to prevent the worst excesses intended by them.

# The Emigrant Corps

The practice of a state employing foreign nationals in its military forces was long-standing, from the great mercenary armies of the 16th and 17th centuries through the 18th century, when many European armies included 'foreign' regiments, such as the Irish in France or the Swiss in Spain. Britain had made great use of such foreign units in the 18th century, though most were 'hired' allies rather than independently-recruited mercenaries; best-known is the employment of Germans (principally Hessians) in the American War of Independence. Though the employment of 'foreign corps' continued throughout the Napoleonic Wars, the 1792–1802 period was somewhat singular in the existence of *émigré* or emigrant corps, whose origin was basically as politically-motivated refugees who fled from France and wished to continue their fight in support of the royalist cause.

Britain was not alone in forming regiments of French *émigrés* and other foreigners; indeed, a large force (styled the '*Armée de Condé*') existed on the continent in the early campaigns, receiving support from Allied nations but almost an independent entity. Those who enrolled in British service, however, varied from the very good to the very bad, as the field from which the troops were recruited was widened to include unreliable mercenaries who enlisted to obtain the bounty and for a chance of plunder, who would desert and re-enlist at the first opportunity. Those entrusted with the task of forming the emigrant corps ranged from French royalists who fought from genuine and sincere conviction, like the Duc de Choiseul and the Prince de Rohan, to minor German nobles or officers desirous of making a profitable deal. Only occasionally did British officers initiate the formation of such units, for example Major Ramsey who formed the York Rangers.

Despite their mixed composition and chequered records of service, almost all the myriad units which served at this period were *bona fide* elements of the British Army, the majority of officers being given the King's commission (sometimes signed by the Duke of York as Commander-in-Chief). No firm demarcation can be discerned even with the so-called 'white cockade corps', those units of Frenchmen who wore the white cockade of the French royal army instead of the black cockade of the British; even their officers received commissions from the king. Other units – apparently for no clear reason – were not even regarded as emigrant corps but purely as British; included in these were Hardy's Royal York Fusiliers, Irwin's York Hussars and Ramsey's York Rangers. It is equally difficult to differentiate between corps on grounds of composition, for even the best units, for example the Loyal Emigrants, the Damas Legion and the Béon Legion, found it difficult to recruit from the genuine political refugees who originally formed their personnel, and diluted their ranks with foreigners of all des-criptions, including the desperate prac-tice of enrolling prisoners-of-war, many of whom only waited for an opportunity to desert back to the republicans. There were some magnificent emigrant corps, sincere and determined in their desire to restore the French monarchy, but the inclusion of such ex-prisoners and un-principled mercenaries tended to pollute the name of the whole. After the dis-astrous expedition to Quiberon in 1795, which annihilated some emigrant corps and was greatly hindered by the presence of many unreliable men, a debate in the House of Commons in 1796 (which voted a further £435,000 to support the surviving foreign corps) brought sharply-conflicting opinions of the worth of the emigrants. Dundas admitted that some untrustworthy units had been disbanded, to which Sheridan added that he saw no reason to keep *any*: 'he saw himself the foreign troops that were encamped near Southampton, dancing the *carmagnol* and singing *ça ira*' (both vehement republican expressions!); 'If these were to experience our liberality, let it be in a different manner from that of marshalling and keeping them as an army, which could answer no purpose.' It should be admitted that whatever the failings of such units (which cost the Treasury vast sums for their mainten-

*Private, York Rangers, 1795, formed by Major GW Ramsey, formerly of the 30th Foot; one of the best of the emigrant corps with a distinguished record in the Netherlands. The unit wore a blue uniform with yellow facings and white buttons, blue breeches, and a peaked black leather light infantry cap decorated with a green plume and a fox's brush running over the top from left to right.*

ance), in the early campaigns many fought heroically and, including experienced soldiers in their ranks, provided many specialist light troops which the British Army could not otherwise obtain, given the decline in light infantry skills which afflicted the regular army. Even the best combat units, though, were prone to indiscipline and pillaging; Abercromby's remark in 1797 that many resembled the *condottieri* of the 16th century has some truth in it. -

The earliest corps were the best, such as Ramsey's York Rangers which was in action as early as autumn 1793. Conceivably the first unit was an abortive one contracted to the Polish Prince Lubomirski, but the senior (and perhaps best) was the Loyal Emigrant of the Comte de la Châtre, raised in England in early 1793 and considered the only one in 1795 safe to be allowed on mainland Britain rather than in the Channel Isles. These and other units were engaged in the Netherlands in 1793–94, and fought with great repute; included among them were the first and only British lancer unit of the entire period, the Comte de Bouillé's *Uhlans Britanniques* (many of the men from the French royal Swiss regiments), the first of several corps formed by Baron Charles Hompesch which bore his name, Choiseul's and Rohan's units. These corps suffered heavily, especially as emigrant corps were shown no mercy by the French republicans, who so resented their exist-

*Officer, probably of the Royal Emigrants. Many of the emigrant corps wore British-style uniform, though with distinctive features; this is scarlet with blue facings and gold lace, and the green plume of a light company. (Silhouette probably by John Buncombe.)*

ence that prisoners and wounded were frequently shot out of hand, as happened to 400 of the Loyal Emigrant who were captured after a valiant defence at Nieuport in July 1794; only 50 survived the massacre.

Some troops were raised during the occupation of Toulon, including the 'Royal Louis', best of the 'white cockade' units; some from Netherlanders, such as Nacquard's Dutch artillery (originally Franco-Dutch in Dutch service, then taken onto the British establishment) and, after the Netherlands was evacuated, from Germany, such as more of Hompesch's units (one of which helped to form the 5/60th Royal Americans) and Löwenstein's. The landing at Quiberon in 1795, in support of a royalist rising, was executed almost exclusively by emigrant corps; but mis-management resulted in an overwhelming defeat despite the sterling performance of many of the 'old' emigrant units. Something over 5,000 landed, of whom perhaps 1,000 were evacuated by the Royal Navy; many ex-prisoners probably deserted, but about 750 captured emigrants were murdered by the republicans. It marked the end of the *émigrés* as a major force.

Thereafter, although some emigrant corps were employed in Portugal, and a 'Dutch emigrant Brigade' raised during the expedition to north Holland in 1799, their main area of employment was in the disease-ridden West Indies, where many units were extinguished by fever. Some corps were actually raised there, from French Royalist settlers, but only Charmilly's and Montalemberts's were 'regular' troops, the others being auxiliary units with names as odd as the Cul de Sac Militia, with some of the San Domingo units formed of Negroes and Mulattoes. Another corps obtained at San Domingo was the remnant of the French 2/87th *Ligne*, the ex-Irish Regt Dillon, whose Irish commander, Major O'Farrell, brought it over to the British in September 1793. It was incorporated into the 'Irish Brigade' of 1794 and by 1796 consisted of 11 officers and 4 other ranks, described as 'annihilated in His Majesty's service', the fate of most of the poor *émigré* corps consigned to the fever-ravaged Caribbean.

Hompesch's Mounted Rifles served in Ireland during the '"98" (with a reputation for cruelty) and in Egypt, but by the Peace of Amiens only a single emigrant regiment was still in Britain, the York Hussars, one of the first and most distinguished. It was disbanded in June 1802, the sad remnant of a large number of devoted French royalists.

## The expedition to Quiberon, June/July 1795, commanded by the Comte de Puisaye and the Comte d'Hervilly. (Statistics are approximate)

**Initial landing**

| Regt | approx strength | survivors |
|------|-----------------|-----------|
| Loyal Emigrants (De la Châtre's) | 600+ | about 121 |
| du Dresnay's | 700 | 45 |
| Hector's ('Marine Royale': largely ex-French naval personnel) | 550 | 56 |
| d'Hervilly's | 1,300 | 307 |
| Rotalier's Artillery | almost 600 | 439 |

**Reinforcement**

| Regt | approx strength | survivors |
|------|-----------------|-----------|
| Infantry of Béon Legion | 250 | 35 |
| Infantry of Damas Legion | 300 | 14 |
| Rohan's Light Infantry | 300 | 84 |
| Salm's Light Infantry | 150 | 18 |
| Périgord's | 150 | 16 |

# The Foreign Corps

As late as 1813 one in eight members of the British regular army was a 'foreigner' (the figure of 27 per cent quoted for this year includes the Portuguese army, and is thus somewhat deceptive). Many British regiments included a few foreigners, though in 1812 scarcely above 400 were serving in the line regiments, of whom many were musicians (European professional bandsmen or Negro percussionists). A small number of officers were non-British: the son of the Duke of Orleans, for example, was killed at Badajoz as Capt Saint-Pol of the 7th Fuzileers, and the Neapolitan Prince Castelcicala was a lieutenant in the 6th Dragoons at Waterloo; and a good number were of American birth though British by nationality, most famous perhaps being Sir William DeLancey, Wellington's Quartermaster-General mortally wounded at Waterloo.

Otherwise, the foreign troops were concentrated into their own regiments, which were styled 'foreign corps' and which included the King's German Legion, already covered. There were in addition a vast number of other units, ranging in quality from the excellent Swiss regiments to the mutinous rabble of Albanians, Greeks, Bulgars and Russians in Froberg's Regt, which was disbanded for mutiny in 1807, and the appalling collection of ex-French prisoners formed into the 'Independent Foreigners' which committed every possible excess at Hampton, Virginia, during the Chesapeake Bay expedition in 1813.

The Mediterranean was the scene of the formation of a number of regiments, most distinguished of which was Stuart's Minorca Regt, composed of Germans and Swiss who had formed the Spanish garrison of Minorca, mostly being Austrian prisoners-of-war 'given' to the Spanish by France. Despite this repeated change of allegiance, the regiment was of first-class quality, served with great distinction in Egypt and was titled 'The Queen's Germans', and in 1805 was taken into the line as the 97th Foot. It served equally well in the Peninsula.

The Swiss regiments also saw much service in the Mediterranean. A number of Swiss corps were formed from the remnants of those who tried to oppose the French occupation, recruited largely by the British minister in Berne; the regiments Roverea, Salis, Courten and Bachmann were amalgamated in 1801 under the colonel of Rovera's, Frederick de Watteville, whose name the new regiment took. It served in the Mediterranean, including with distinction at Maida, and in Spain, and served in Canada in the war of 1812. Another exemplary Swiss corps was de Roll's, formed in 1794-5 under Baron de Roll, an ex-Swiss Guardsman of the French royal army, as were many of his original recruits. It was not as successful as de Watteville's in retaining its Swiss character, as some Germans, French and Italians were admitted, but served well in Egypt, the Mediterranean and as part of a 'provisional battalion' with Dillon's Regt in eastern Spain. The latter was originally an emigrant corps, principally French plus Germans and Italians; it served well in Egypt but suffered from desertion after its reformation in 1803 when 22 nationalities were represented, mainly Italians and Spanish but including even Turks and Albanians. A better Swiss corps was de Meuron's Regt, originally raised for Dutch service but transferring to the British upon the capture of Ceylon in 1795. It served well in India, and the cadre was sent to reform in Europe in 1807, recruiting over 500 Swiss and Germans from French service, captured at Baylen; its service was largely Mediterranean until 1813, when it went to Canada. Its predominantly Swiss/German composition rendered its desertion-rate commendably low.

A number of units were raised in Corsica, including Maclean's Chasseurs (which served at Toulon), the Corsican Light Dragoons and the Corsican Union Regt. (officered in part by British); but the most significant were the two corps of Corsican Rangers, a light infantry unit existing 1799-1802, and distinguished in Egypt, and a re-raised rifle regiment formed by Hudson Lowe (later Napoleon's gaoler on St Helena) which existed from 1803 to 1816, serving extensively in the Mediterranean and at Maida, one of the best of the 'foreign corps'. Like most of the 'foreign' regiments, the Rangers included a number of British officers; in 1814, for example, they had 13 officers

*Private, Royal Corsican Rangers, 1806. The 'foreign corps' mostly wore uniforms like those of the British regiments, excluding such exotic styles as the dress of the Greek Light Infantry or Calabrian Free Corps. The Corsican Rangers were typical, as a rifle corps wearing a uniform virtually identical to that of the British Army's German rifle battalion, the 5/60th, in dark green with red facings and blue breeches; officers had silver lace.*

*Hussar (left) and infantry of the Brunswick Oels Corps. The Duke of Brunswick chose black uniforms and death's-head shako-badge to represent the mission of revenge against the French for which the 'Black Legion' was formed; hence the nickname 'Death or Glory men' bestowed upon them by the British. In 1815 Lady DeLancey described them as resembling 'an immense moving hearse'. (Print after CH Smith)*

with British names, 35 Italian, 7 German and 4 French. At the same time the Sicilian Regt. (raised 1806, served in Egypt in 1807, disbanded 1816) had 34 British officers, 10 French, 3 German and only 13 Italian (including the Catholic chaplain). The Calabrian Free Corps, a useful light regiment, was another formed in Italy, in 1809 from Calabrian insurgents who had sought refuge in Sicily; they served in the Mediterranean and fought well in eastern Spain.

A corps originally of French *émigrés* (most from the *Armée de Condé*) was the Chasseurs Britanniques, formed 1801; it served in Egypt and the Mediterranean, but was considerably distinguished in the Peninsula, especially at Fuentes de Oñoro. Due to an influx of mixed nationalities (Italians, Poles, Croats and Swiss), many ex-prisoners, its desertion-rate was abysmal, and for all its good combat record Wellington ordered that it was never to be trusted on outpost duty.

Similar problems affected the Brunswick Oels Corps. Raised in 1809 by the Duke of Brunswick-Oels (son of the Duke killed in 1806), the 'Black Legion' was originally in Austrian service, but following Wagram the Duke boldly cut his way through Westphalia and was evacuated from Germany by the Royal Navy, a most gallant and audacious feat. Taken into British pay, the Legion was separated into the Brunswick Hussars (which served in eastern Spain) and the Brunswick Oels Jägers, which from 1810 served with Wellington in the Peninsula. Useful in action, their dilution by ex-prisoners-of-war (including Italians, Danish, Croats, Dutch and Poles) caused terrible problems of desertion; Leach of the 95th stated that the British had only a lease on them, whilst Robert Craufurd, complaining of those in his Light Division, announced that any who wanted to desert would be granted an official pass, 'for we are better without such'! In 1815 the reformed 'Black Legion' – in effect

the Brunswick army – served at Quatre Bras and Waterloo, the Duke being killed in the former action. The Brunswick troops in this campaign formed a complete army of cavalry, infantry, light infantry and artillery, and included a nucleus of Peninsular veterans, but were mostly newly-recruited young soldiers inexperienced in combat; under the circumstances they performed creditably.

Greece provided two colourfully-dressed units formed in the Ionian islands, principally from Suliote tribesmen. The 1st or Duke of York's Greek Light Infantry was raised in 1809, though not brought onto the official 'establishment' until 1811; a 2nd Bn was formed in 1812, and although the corps was intended only for the defence of the Ionian islands, it served in Montenegro in June 1812 and at Genoa in April 1814. In 1814 the corps had only 6 British officers (to 2 German, 3 French, 1 Portuguese and 46 Greek or Italian), and wore a uniform styled after Suliote national dress, including a *fustanella* (skirt), and their commander, Major Richard Church (late Corsican Rangers) is believed to have worn a 'Roman'-style helmet with this uniform, the most bizarre British military costume of the period.

Portuguese troops were normally those of their own army, though the Loyal Lusitanian Legion (light infantry plus a light cavalry squadron and artillery battery) was formed partially in Britain from Portuguese emigrants, and served with considerable distinction in the early Peninsular War under its somewhat mercurial (or shifty?) leader, Sir Robert Wilson. It declined in effectiveness after Wilson's return home in 1809, following disagreements with Beresford, and in 1811 the Legion was transferred to the Portuguese establishment as *Caçadores*.

Several corps bore the title 'York' (after the Duke of York), most notably the York Light Infantry Volunteers, raised as the Barbados Volunteer Emigrants in 1803 from the defeated Dutch garrison of Berbice, and supplemented by deserters from the Peninsular War. It served throughout in the West Indies, with some distinction. The Royal York Rangers was formed in 1808 from the Royal African Corps, a penal battalion raised in 1800; the Rangers served exclusively in the West Indies. The Royal West India Rangers was similarly a 'condemned corps', formed of British deserters, criminals and the most untrustworthy ex-prisoners-of-war.

# Chapter Six: STRATEGY AND TACTICS

An important consideration regarding the tactics and strategy of the period is that regarding the organisation of the army, its formation and command-structure. Central to this organisation was the size of Anglo-Allied armies when compared with those of the continental European powers.

From the start of the Revolutionary Wars, most British military operations had been conducted with relatively small forces, and as the wars progressed the differences in size between them and the vast armies ultimately controlled by Napoleon remained marked. For example, at the end of May 1813, at the commencement of the Vittoria campaign, Wellington commanded a grand total of 52,484 British and 28,792 Portuguese soldiers, to which were ultimately added 46,292 Spanish serving under Wellington's direction. This, virtually the entire Peninsular field army, was less than twice the number of men who composed Napoleon's I Corps in the invasion of Russia (approximately 69,000 strong). These comparatively small numbers enabled Wellington to overlook almost everything himself, and to operate with staff minute in comparison with those of the French army. That Wellington was able to control the army as precisely as he did with such a small staff is a tribute both to his organisational skills and to his clear thinking which foresaw almost all eventualities. As he remarked, the whole business of war (as indeed of life) is the ability to judge what was on the other side of the hill, a philosophy as true in its most general application as in its literal.

In the early operations undertaken by the British Army, the largest tactical unit was the brigade, an organisation of two or more infantry battalions, which acted in concert under the command of a 'brigadier'. The latter was not a rank but an appointment; a brigadier might be a general officer, or the senior of the battalion-commanders within the brigade, when the brigadier's own battalion would be led by his second-in-command. The brigade staff was tiny, consisting virtually of only the brigadier's ADCs and his brigade-major, the latter usually an offi-

cer detached from his battalion. All matters of liaison with higher command and administrative functions would be handled by these officers, in concert with the commissaries of the component battalions. When more than one brigade acted in concert, and not under the personal direction of the commanding general, the senior brigadier took over the whole. In the Netherlands expeditions of 1793-94 and 1799, and in Egypt, no higher organisation than the brigade existed, despite large forces being employed. The Duke of York divided his army into 'columns' of two or more brigades, but only on an *ad hoc* basis, whilst Abercromby reverted to the earlier 18th-century practice of referring to 'lines', initially implying those brigades arrayed in the front of the line-of-battle, the second-line, the reserve, and so on. The concept of organising the army into 'Divisions', permanent formations incorporating a number of infantry brigades and their attendant artillery and services, apparently first appeared in the Copenhagen expedition of 1807, when the permanently-organised Divisions were each commanded by a regularly-appointed lieutenant-general.

The army which landed in the Peninsula was basically operated on a brigade level until Moore took control, when he formed the troops under his immediate command into four divisions of two infantry brigades, plus a cavalry brigade. Upon Wellesley's resumption of command in 1809, the brigade system endured until 18 June when a General Order instituted the divisional system which was to be maintained throughout the war, and included the organisation of a cavalry division, sufficient mounted units having been obtained for three brigades to be formed. The four original divisions were increased in number as more troops were received, so that by 1814 there were seven numbered divisions plus the Light Division. Each was commanded by a lieutenant-general, or by the senior brigadier if a general were not available.

Within a Division, certain characteristics were maintained even though it might number two, three or four brig-

ades. Important to Wellington's system was the practice of integrating his units, so that new or weak battalions would not be massed together. Initially, an experiment was made by which the Portuguese were integrated at brigade level, though this did not last beyond 1809; thereafter, excluding the *Caçadores* who served with the Light Division, the Portuguese were brigaded together and the brigades attached at divisional level. A similar practice was applied in 1815, when the less-reliable elements of the army were integrated with the best, so that the former were raised up by the presence of the latter, rather than the best being debased by the worst. Also significant was the attachment to each division, usually to each brigade, of a company of riflemen, principally from the 5/60th, to supplement the skirmishers of the brigade's own battalion light companies. Artillery was at first not sufficiently plentiful for permanent divisional allocations to be made, though companies became associated with particular divisions. Divisional organisations were fluid, according to circumstances and availability of troops, and of necessity strengths were not equal; the last-organised 7th Division, for example, was at first very weak and by virtue of its predominantly foreign composition known as 'The Mongrels'!

Although a 'Corps' system was never applied (the combining of several divisions under independent command, though latterly there were similarities), each of Wellington's Divisions resembled Napoleon's *Corps d'Armée* in that it was a self-supporting entity, with its own staff, commissariat, artillery and reconnaissance facility, in fact an army in miniature if only 6,000 strong. D'Urban compared it with a Roman Legion, capable of performing all operational functions unaided, testimony to the 'Simplicity and Genius' of the army's commander.

*Individual acts of heroism occurred throughout the period: at Arinez, near Vittoria, Lt John G Fitzmaurice of the 1/95th with only two men intercepted a French battery and captured a gun and team. (Print after Harry Payne, executed about 80 years after the event.)*

# Wellington's Strategy

It would be easy to assert, as some did, in the 19th century, that Wellington was the greatest tactical and strategic genius who ever lived. His record is unsurpassed: never defeated, and the conqueror of Napoleon, another candidate for the accolade of the greatest general ever. Yet Wellington was not infallible and, rather than applying some rigid tactical or strategic theory formulated early in his career, his methods appear to be a process of constant evolution, developing with experience and in accordance with the circumstances pertaining to any particular event.

Wellington enjoyed one advantage possessed by many of history's great commanders: what might be termed 'unity of command', in that in all his Peninsular battles, and to some extent in India, the course of the war was decided by him alone. Whilst he had political masters and was mindful of the necessity of diplomacy when dealing with Allied states, he had no military superiors (after Cintra) and enjoyed the command of Allied forces not by some shaky political accommodation but by virtue of regular commissions from the states in question, so that his authority was unquestioned. But though his will was predominant in the field, the guarantee of political support needed success or, at least, no defeat, which increased his responsibilities.

Perhaps the most unjust opinion which could, and has been made of Wellington as a commander is that he was a purely defensive general who stood his ground until his opponents had exhausted themselves, and then counter-attacked. Such an assessment might be justified if operations like Talavera, Torres Vedras and Waterloo are considered superficially, but a more balanced view would be that Wellington applied attack and defence as it was necessary, and indeed was equally capable in offence. His Indian experience founded his offensive spirit, for it was generally acknowledged that the only way of defeating the immense native armies was to rush and overthrow them before they realised what was happening, and at Assaye and Argaum the Marathas were defeated in exactly this fashion by a rapid blow almost as soon as they had been encountered and after a brief personal

reconnaissance had been made. At Köge in Denmark, Wellington used the same tactics with the same effect.

The 'defensive' posture, however, which was applied throughout much of the Peninsular War, was forced upon him by the responsibility of his position. The Peninsular army was the *only* field army Britain possessed, and its defeat would have left the country dangerously over-stretched. Nowhere better did Wellington voice this responsibility than to Stanhope whilst defying the French from behind the lines of Torres Vedras: 'I could lick those fellows any day, but it would cost me ten thousand men and, as this is the last army England has, we must take care of it.' Hence the sometimes over-cautious attitude which, perhaps, prevented the exploitation of victory. Ever concerned with shepherding his resources, the 'defensive phase'

of the Peninsular War was only overcome by taking a risk; yet to achieve the decisive victory which was required, risks were necessary, and the unexpected dash at Salamanca, which wrecked the astonished French army, appears to be Wellington's old penchant for offence overcoming the defensive rut into which he had been slipping. The retirement from Burgos at the end of the 1812 campaign was the consequence of an injudicious advance following Salamanca.

The 1813 campaign was offensive from the start; no longer was the intention of conserving the army and not hazarding a battle, but instead to strike at the French and drive them from Spain. Nor is it correct to assume that this was achieved because Wellington's opponents were inept; some were, and Napoleon's badgering of his subordinates and their lack of co-ordinated action hindered their operations, but they were not, in general, poor commanders. That they were Wellington's

inferiors is more a tribute to his skills than to their shortcomings. Even in apparently 'defensive' battles, Wellington's aptitude for offence is apparent; his very decision to stand at Waterloo was an offensive gesture, when prudence might have suggested a withdrawal, and even in 'defensive' actions the constant changing of units within the battle-line is testimony to his offensive inclination in the field of 'minor tactics'; this is exemplified by the changes which habitually repelled French advances.

If Wellington had no set of perfectly-prescribed strategic or tactical theories, but to some extent learned and adapted constantly, certain features were characteristic. Flexibility was one keynote, as he expressed in his analogy of harness. French plans, he said, resembled a set of leather harness, which looked magnificent until it broke, and was then useless; his system was like a harness of rope, which looked inferior but when it broke he could tie a knot and go on.

Attitude of mind was another significant factor. Before going to the Peninsula, he discussed with Croker how he should conduct the campaign and how he would face the French. He acknowledged that although he hadn't seen them since 1793–94, when they were good troops, he realised that so many years of victory under Napoleon would have made them

*Wellington and his staff in the gathering dusk at Waterloo. Wellington wears his habitual campaign uniform: a low cocked hat covered with oilskin and a dark blue civilian frock-coat, contrasting with the bright uniforms of the remainder.*
*(Print published by R Bowyer, 1816.)*

better. Yet he was not overawed: 'though they may overwhelm me, I don't think that they will outmanoeuvre me . . . I am not afraid of them, and secondly, because (if all I hear about their system is true) I think it a false one against steady troops. I suspect all the continental armies are half-beaten before the battle begins. I at least will not be frightened beforehand.' This was true equally of his army, for the quality of his troops was another major factor in his successes. He described his army in November 1813 as 'probably the most complete machine for its numbers now existing in Europe'; part of this was the innate quality of the individual soldier, but part equally was the organisation he imposed and the high morale which resulted from his deeds. Complete machine though it was, it was also very much 'Wellington's Machine'.

Against 'their system' Wellington employed a number of devices which were characteristically his, most notably the screening of his position from enemy view which time and again undid his

opponents, yet was virtually ignored by all other European commanders. This screening was achieved by two basic methods: firstly by throwing forward a line of skirmishers, to occupy and hold back the French *tirailleurs* (sharpshooters), the British skirmishers being called in only at the last moment before the French attack was mounted; and secondly by concealing the main British position by arraying the army on a reverse slope, often lying down, so that not only were they protected from French fire but the French had no idea who was where. Again and again, French attacks foundered on the unexpected appearance of the British from behind the crest of a ridge, yet the system was not copied; even at Ligny, when Wellington advised the Prussians not to expose themselves or be 'damnably mauled', they persisted in assembling their forces in full view of the French and suffered accordingly. So characteristic was the 'reverse slope' tactic that Wellington even used it to successfully deceive the French into believing that a lightly-held position concealed a large force.

At Quatre Bras, Reille halted before a single unsupported Netherlands division in the belief that the British must be hidden behind it; thus irretrievably losing an opportunity of sweeping aside the opposition.

# On the March

An army's speed of march depended upon circumstances, including the nature of the terrain and the health of the troops. Precise calculations in contemporary manuals are guides only to the speed which could be executed on the parade-ground, and bore little relevance to that attained in the field. Adye, for example, quotes the regulation 'quick-step' ordained by Dundas at 108 paces per minute, each of 30 inches, making 90 yards per minute; 'wheeling step' (for manoeuvre) of 120 per minute, making 100 yards per minute, and 'ordinary step' of 75 per minute. For cavalry, he calculated that at a walk 400 yards would be covered in 4½ minutes, at the trot in 123 seconds and at the gallop 'in about 1 minute', but notes that 'the usual rate of marching' was 17 miles in 6 hours, 'but this may be extended to 21, or even 28 miles in that time.'

It was generally held that the French were superior in marching ability; as Judge-Advocate Larpent noted, 'In marching, our men have no chance at all with the French. The latter beat them hollow.' Yet this is an over-generalisation perhaps affected by the fact that the Peninsular army was at times sickly, with some regiments still suffering from the recurrent Walcheren fever. Excluding the retreats, when commissariat arrangements collapsed, the British Army often moved with much greater success and less wastage than the French. Individual comparisons can be deceptive, but when Junot marched his army from the French border to Lisbon, 640 miles in 43 days, the first 300 at 12 miles a day on main roads and the remainder at 18 miles a day over minor roads, it wrecked his army and caused his cavalry and artillery to be left behind. Wellington moved his army from the Portuguese frontier to Vittoria over the same bad roads at 15 miles a day without damaging the efficiency, due to superior organisation, a more propitious season (summer instead of October/November) and increased experience.

Under unusual circumstances, astonishing feats could be achieved, though nothing surpasses the march of the Light Brigade to Talavera, driven though they were by the sternest of commanders and knowing how desperately they were

required. The traditional calculation of '62 miles in 26 hours' is in error, probably arising from the different measurements of the four types of 'league' used in Spain, varying from 2.63 English miles to 4.21. In actual fact this distance covered would appear to be 42 miles in 26 hours, plus four or five miles beyond Talavera, an astonishing feat nonetheless. Similarly, Sir Charles Vaughan's ride from the Tudela to Corunna, via Madrid and Salamanca, he incorrectly calculated as 790 miles in 9 days; actually it was 595 miles. The speed at which an ADC could convey messages was reckoned at 4 miles in 18 minutes, 12 miles an hour, or with a relay of mounts 60 miles a day. Wellington himself was an amazingly hard rider; he once travelled from Ciudad Rodrigo to Badajoz, 174 miles in 76 hours, a rate not exceptional by his standards.

The ordinary marching routine of the army was perfected in the Peninsula until it ran like clockwork; there was no more 'playing the young soldier' by throwing away knapsack and blanket as Surtees described when with the 56th in the Netherlands! Unlike French armies, which straggled out of formation, scavenging as they went, British units were kept closely together to prevent plundering and maintain cohesion, stragglers who fell out from sickness and exhaustion being swept up by the rear-guard and

those who strayed deliberately being arrested by the provost-marshal. In times of stress draconian measures were adopted to keep the regiments together, such as Craufurd's flogging of those who fell out even on the retreat to Corunna.

The routine in the Peninsula was common to all daily marches. Orders would be passed from the commander, via the Quartermaster General to the divisional commanders, who transmitted them to their brigade-commanders via the AQMGs, and to battalion-commanders by the brigade-majors. The drums and trumpets roused the units generally an hour and a half before daylight, so that a meal could be eaten and camp struck, and the brigades assembled, ready to march off at daybreak. The units would assemble in sections of threes, headed by an advance-guard and a guide with the day's route, and would begin to march in parade-ground order, until after a short time 'March at ease' would be ordered. A five-minute halt was ordered after half an hour's march, and then at hourly intervals, to allow equipment to be adjusted, snacks to be eaten, and for those who had fallen out (with their officer's permission, for calls of nature or whatever) to catch up. After the halt

*Manhandling a piece of heavy artillery. Guns were normally only moved manually – by 'bricole', named from the ropes used – near the enemy. These appear to be light infantrymen assisting the gunners. (Print after WH Pyne, 1802.)*

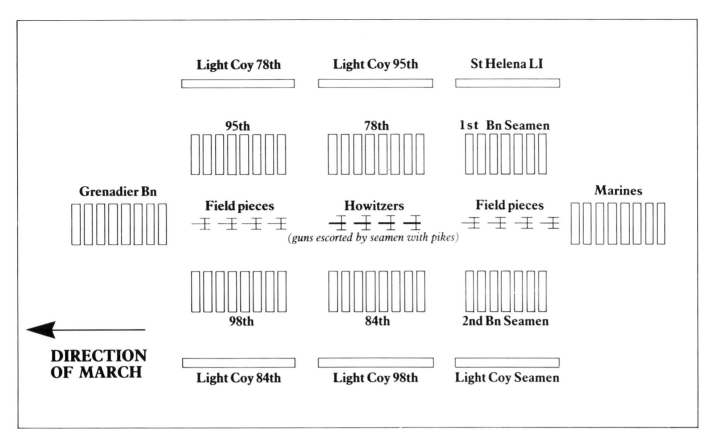

Light Coy 78th   Light Coy 95th   St Helena LI

95th   78th   1st Bn Seamen

Grenadier Bn   Field pieces   Howitzers   Field pieces   Marines

*(guns escorted by seamen with pikes)*

98th   84th   2nd Bn Seamen

← DIRECTION OF MARCH

Light Coy 84th   Light Coy 98th   Light Coy Seamen

*An advance in hostile territory. From an unpublished MS, this illustrates the disposition of the army which marched on Capetown in 1795, led by a composite Grenadier Bn, supported by companies of seamen and marines, with the vulnerable guns and equipment in the centre of the column and flanks protected by deployed light companies.*

the column would recommence marching in step, until 'at ease' was decreed. Music was used to keep up spirits and maintain cohesion.

When not in the presence of the enemy, each battalion sent an officer 24 hours ahead to establish billets or camping-ground for the next night's halt, and another with a fatigue-party in advance of the unit to mark out this area. Arriving at the selected site in the afternoon, the column halted and sent out its picquets, posted its sentries and arranged for its patrols and its point of assembly in case of alarm. Only then was the baggage unpacked, bivouacs built from whatever foliage was available, tents pitched and fires lit. Rations were then collected by each company and the men settled down for the evening to cook their food. (A major improvement introduced by

Wellington was the replacement of the ponderous iron kettle with a light, tin version which could be carried by the men and boiled quicker than the heavy ones, which had to be carried with the battalion baggage.)

Accompanying each battalion was its baggage and rations borne by mules, and its camp-followers. The commissariat problems were enormous; by mid-1813 the army required 100,000lbs of biscuit, 300 head of cattle (travelling on the hoof) and 200,000lbs of forage-corn per day; as each mule could only carry 200lbs of supplies plus its own feed, vast herds were needed, even if the depots were situated only three or four days' march away. In addition to the 150 mules attached to each brigade or cavalry regiment for commissariat stores, each unit had others for its camp-equipment, ammunition, medical supplies and for officers' baggage, these allocated on a sliding scale from ten for a lieutenant-colonel, major seven, captain five, subaltern one, and so on. Though horses' forage could often be acquired locally, the allowance was 14lbs of hay or straw, 10lbs of English hay, 12lbs of oats or 10lbs of barley or Indian corn per horse per day (this was not universal: in

November 1809, for example, the 3rd DG and 4th Dragoons were allowed 12lbs of barley).

In the vicinity of the enemy, or in hostile terrain, columns could move in defensive formation (as illustrated in the diagram of the advance at the Cape), with the vulnerable baggage and artillery forming the centre of the column, protected by infantry and with strong van- and rear-guards, often with light troops deployed on the flanks, with scouting ahead where such was available.

Also accompanying the army were the battalion's womenfolk, permitted on active service at four or six per company, chosen by lot from among the wives of the soldiers. They assisted with the battalion's cooking, washing and foraging, and when widowed usually re-married within a day or two. 'The greatest nuisance' was how one officer described them; they impeded the army's march but, as Bell of the 34th remarked, they 'stuck to the army like bricks' and in difficult times even helped carry the equipment of exhausted soldiers or allowed the sick to ride on their donkeys. They were one of the most remarkable components of a remarkable army.

# The Line

The popular perception of a British victory over the French involves the French advancing in massed column against a 'thin red line', which devastates the French with its musketry and pursues the beaten fugitives with the bayonet. In practice, what really happened is rather more complicated.

'Old Pivot' Dundas decreed in his *Rules & Regulations* that the three-deep infantry line was the ideal formation, for with a two-deep line 'no general could manage a considerable army . . . a line formed in this manner would never be brought to make or stand an attack with bayonets . . . in no service is the fire and consistency of the third rank given up; it serves to fill up the vacancies made in the others in action, without it the battalion would soon be a single rank.' In this formation, each man 'must just feel with his elbow the touch of his neighbour . . . nor in any situation of movement in front, must he ever relinquish such touch, which becomes in action the principal direction for the preservation of his order.' Troops were almost always arrayed in 'close order', the ranks one pace apart; 'open order', two paces apart, was reserved for parade, and 'when the body is halted and to fire, they are still closer locked up' than even close order. This was the manner in which the British Army was trained, fighting in line (which was formed from an approach-march in column), but the three-deep line, for all Dundas' arguments, was soon abandoned. As early as 1801 the two-deep line was given official approval, and in practice was probably commonly used even before that.

Dundas' reasoning was valid for pro-longed fire-fights against enemy lines, but for obvious reasons the two-rank line was more effective against the French columnar attack: by forming two-deep, more muskets could be brought to bear upon the flanks of an attacking column. (Fire *could* be delivered in three ranks, though probably not so effectively.) Vastly greater musketry could be brought to bear from a line than a column: for example, a French division 5,000 strong advancing on a two-company front could fire simultaneously 340 muskets, using only those at the head of the column. Against them, 500 men in a two-deep line could discharge between 6 and 10 shots per yard per minute, a lethal fusilade when directed at a comparatively small target like the head of a column. A significant disadvantage of the two-deep line was the 'shrinkage' which occurred in combat, as gaps were filled by the line closing in towards the centre; but its flexibility was demonstrated at Alexandria when the 28th's rear rank faced-about to repel an attack from the rear. The flanks of the British line might edge forward so that the line became crescent-shaped, musketry being poured into the sides as well as the head of the column, as occurred with the 43rd and 52nd at Busaco. Such columnar attacks could not hope to succeed, for morale was as shattered as the leading ranks by such relentless musketry.

Yet the theory which suggests that firepower alone was decisive in such encounters perhaps over-simplifies. It is possible that some French commanders intended columnar attack to steamroller its way through the opposing line, as the early republican armies had sometimes done, but more likely the column was used merely as a way of hurrying up troops at maximum speed, who would then deploy into line before the fire-fight commenced. That they rarely seem to have attempted this against the British is probably due to a large extent to the fact that owing to the 'reverse slope' disposition of the British, the French didn't know where their opponents were and thus were unable to decide when to deploy; by the time the British appeared over the crest of the hill, it was too late, and the French were routed. Despite numerous defeats the lesson never seems to have been learned; in Wellington's words, they came on in the old style and were beaten off in the old style. The attacks were usually made with heroism, but still came to nought; as Wellington commented to Beresford, 'these attacks in column against our lines are very contemptible.'

It was not by musketry alone that such attacks were defeated, however, for the counter-punch was a vital ingredient, in the bayonet-charge which swept the French away. Despite the bayonet being regarded as the 'traditional' weapon of the British infantry (and the French, and Russian for that matter!) the evidence for its use in combat is very slight, as will be quoted in due course. Rather, it was the psychological shock of the bayonet which counted, and it was generally only used when the enemy was already disordered. As the French columns advanced, their officers shouting patriotic exclamations and drums beating, they would be harassed and raked by British artillery-fire and often skirmishers, and then would appear the silent, almost immobile red wall of infantry before them, the silence contrasting markedly with the fervour within the attacking

## Legend

| | | | |
|---|---|---|---|
| G | Grenadier Coy | Major | M |
| L | Light Coy | Colour bearer | C |
| ● | Officer | Drummer | D |
| ■ | Sergeant | Bandsman | B |
| A | Adjutant | Pioneer | P |
| LC | Lieutenant-Colonel | Colonel | Co |
| ▲ | Staff | Companies | ■ |

*An infantry battalion arrayed in-line in close order. This disposition is shown in contemporary manuals (the companies in two ranks), though as H Dickinson noted in his* Instructions for Forming a Regiment of Infantry *(1798), 'Some trifling Deviations from the "Rules and Regulations, for Infantry Formation and Exercise", as published under the Authority of the Adjutant General, are permitted in most Regiments.' On service the battalion would be commanded by the lieutenant-colonel, whose staff would normally be with the Colour-party in the centre.*

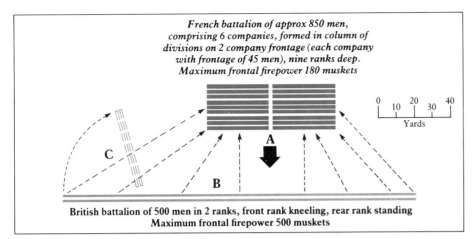

French battalion of approx 850 men, comprising 6 companies, formed in column of divisions on 2 company frontage (each company with frontage of 45 men), nine ranks deep. Maximum frontal firepower 180 muskets

0 10 20 30 40
Yards

British battalion of 500 men in 2 ranks, front rank kneeling, rear rank standing
Maximum frontal firepower 500 muskets

*A diagram showing the basic advantages of the line over a French attack executed by a 'column of divisions', i.e. upon a two-company front. Before the attacking column (A) could deploy, the British line (B) would open fire upon both the head and flanks of the column; and as the column shuddered to a halt under such fire, one wing of the line (C) could swing out to enfilade even more effectively. A wing could be swung in the opposite direction ('refused') to protect the line from flank attack. (Skirmishers between the two formations are not shown, though a large number might be deployed.)*

column. After the crashing volleys of musketry, or after only one, which decimated the head of the column, the British line would cheer (itself a demoralising sound) and cascade down the slope towards the French, who would break and flee before bayonets were ever crossed. Thus, successive attacks might be beaten off with comparatively few British casualties, as the only French normally encountered man-to-man were the wounded, dead or those in flight. Their defeat was as much psychological as stemming from powder and ball.

The success of the line depended upon other factors than merely the shelter and concealment of the 'reverse slope', for that alone was only part of Wellington's system. Equally significant was protection by other units, firstly by the screen of light infantry and riflemen, thrown forward to cover the British position and to oppose the French skirmishers who normally preceded attacks; so numerous could these skirmishers appear that occasionally skirmish-screens were mistaken for the main line-of-battle. (Frenchmen who believed that they had pierced the main British line at Barrosa, for example, had only repelled the skirmish-screen, and when Reynier wrote of being halted only by Picton's 'second line' at Busaco, he mistook the skirmish-screen for the first line.) Equally important was the provision of supporting units to stop up the line should the bayonet-charge come to grief; fortunately, discipline was such that only on the rarest occasions did counter-attacking troops not rally when ordered and return to their original positions to meet the next attack. Finally, protection on the flanks was of paramount importance, either by troops or terrain. Wellington was a master in the use of geographical features, apart from the siting of his positions along a crest where a reverse slope was available; at Talavera one flank rested on thick olive plantations, the other on a hill; at Fuentes de Oñoro the flanks were anchored by a village and steep river-banks. Where such were not available, artillery or cavalry could be used to protect the ends of the line, or the infantry line extended so far that it overlapped the area in which the main French effort would be made, though this latter tactic risked spreading the infantry too thinly over the ground. A line could protect itself by 'refusing' or throwing back one of its flanks. When this cardinal rule of covering the flanks was not applied (which could even be provided by an infantry battalion in column, ready to form square if threatened), disaster could result, as happened to Colborne's brigade at Albuera. That this appalling example occurred when Wellington was not present in person is evidence that his influence was paramount.

The use of terrain extended also into the protection of the army from the enemy's artillery-fire, for the concealment of folds in the terrain almost always protected Wellington's men from the opening French bombardment. Only in the most exceptional circumstances were they exposed to this fire: a Netherlands brigade was decimated at Waterloo by standing on the crest of the ridge, and at Talavera the ground was such that the line had to be exposed in part.

*The line in action: Sir Charles Belson and the grenadiers of his 28th Foot at Quatre Bras, illustrating the formation of the two-deep line, the front rank kneeling 'to receive cavalry'. The 28th are shown correctly in their unique regimental shako, but as in many contemporary hand-coloured prints, the French uniforms are not accurate: no French lancers wore shakos. (Print after Capt G Jones).*

# The Square

The 'British square' has become associated with Wellington and his army, probably from its use at Waterloo; yet it was never exclusively British, square formation being used by almost every army as the universal defence against attack by cavalry.

It was generally held that against cavalry, infantry was powerless unless formed in a square, as musketry alone could not stop a determined charge if a unit's flanks were exposed, when the cavalry could ride-down and shatter a unit. This is not absolutely accurate; infantry in line or column did on occasion repel cavalry attacks, but this depended on their flanks being secure, as occurred when the 5th Foot defeated French cavalry at El Bodon, and the 52nd at Sabugal, for example. Otherwise, infantry had little chance against a determined enemy. With the square, it was the cavalry which had little chance, for the infantry formation presented a bristling hedge of bayonets on all sides, impenetrable to all but cavalry armed with lances, who could thus spear the infantry without getting within reach of the bayonets. Even so, volley-firing from the faces of the square could knock down any lancer who came within this range.

Squares could be formed from column or from line upon any company, i.e. with a 10 company battalion in line three companies would stand fast, the remainder falling back at right-angles and the flanks turning at right-angles again to close the rear of the square (in which case the 'square' might in fact be oblong, with three companies on each of two sides and two on the other sides; Dundas recognised this by writing throughout of 'the

square or oblong'). Sides were normally four-deep, necessitating some contraction of company frontage from a two-deep line, but sides could be two-deep (used when guarding baggage, for example); as for volley-firing in line, the front rank knelt on one knee, in this case with the musket angled upwards to present a hedgehog of bayonets at horse's-breast height. The square was almost invariably hollow, with officers, musicians, colours, etc in the centre (where the wounded would be dragged), and to be practicable needed several hundred men; at Salamanca the 53rd had to retire as they were too few to form square, though in emergencies two depleted battalions might join together to form a single square, though single-battalion squares were the norm. Forming square required precision and considerable discipline under fire, for in the presence of the enemy any disorder could result in disaster. The 42nd at Quatre Bras almost came to grief when French cavalry entered the square before it was completed; they coolly closed the rear face and killed the French trapped inside.

Though a square was proof against cavalry attacks, if the cavalry were accompanied by infantry or horse artillery, as co-ordinated advances should have been, the square could be destroyed by gunnery; as Dundas noted, 'such situation would be critical indeed, and from which nothing but the most determined resistance could extricate them'. Nevertheless, the alternative was what happened to Colborne's brigade at Albuera, which was hurrying forward to stabilise the Allied right flank. The advance was made without any support to secure the flank, and in line; an immense hail-storm helped shield from

view the French 2nd Hussars and Polish 1st Lancers of the Vistula Legion which fell upon them. In a matter of moments the brigade was destroyed; the battalion furthest from the point of impact (1/31st) managed to form square and repel the tail-end of the charge, but of the others, the 1/3rd lost 643 men from 755; the 2/48th 343 from 452, and the 2/66th 272 from 441. (Colborne had intended to form a column to protect the flank, but was over-ruled by his divisional commander.) No incident more clearly demonstrated the necessity of the square in such circumstances. Ideally, in combat squares were arranged in chequer-board fashion, so that their musketry would not strike each other, but this was naturally not always possible to achieve given the circumstances under which squares were normally formed.

On rare occasions squares *were* broken by cavalry, though these were very few, only when the infantry was panicking, unable to fire because of torrential rain or when a cavalry horse fell dead into one face of the square, crushing a hole in the formation. Garcia Hernandez was the most famous incident in which this occurred involving British troops, when the King's German Legion Dragoons broke the French.

A further variety of square was used only in time of total chaos; when a unit was completely scattered, an officer or NCO would cry 'Form rallying square', when the nearest man would run to him, the first two joining his right and left, the next three in front and more behind, so that when about 80 had gathered a tightly-packed mass would result, unable to act offensively but at least safe from being over-ridden. (This was not dissimilar from the tightly-packed 'mass' formation used by the Austrian infantry, but in the

*The formation of a square from line, with a battalion of ten companies, the grenadier company occupying the right flank and the light company the left. The companies would retire in echelon to form the sides of the square, the rear face being closed by the grenadier company. When the light company was deployed as skirmishers, they would normally have sufficient warning of the advance of cavalry to run in before the square was formed, sometimes in two half-companies, one on each flank of the line. Squares could be formed from line or column upon any company.*

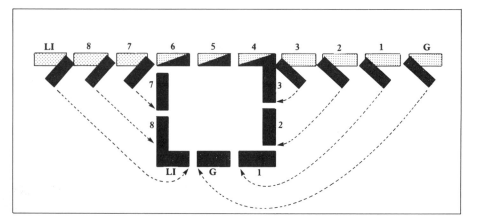

latter case it was a regulated manoeuvre, not an emergency measure as was a British 'rallying square'.)

The square's defensive capability depended to a large extent upon the bayonet, and it is interesting to assess the frequency with which it was used. Leaving aside such desperate mêlées as Colborne's brigade at Albuera, the storming of defended buildings such as La Haye Sainte and the isolated close-quarter skirmishes which occasionally occurred, there are hardly any recorded instances of formed bodies of troops engaging each other with the bayonet. As noted previously, it was the *threat* of the bayonet which proved decisive, a psychological weapon used when the enemy was already shattered or on the point of retreat; one side or other almost always ran before contact was made. Despite numerous exhortations that the bayonet was the infantryman's true weapon, the entire Peninsular War apparently provides evidence of only one

genuine bayonet-fight, and that occurred completely by accident, on 25 July 1813 in the Pyrenees. A contemporary account by a participant of this unique event does not seem to exist, as the British officer in command only published his account in 1839; but the facts would not seem to be in dispute.

Near Roncesvalles the 20th (East Devonshire) Regt of the 4th Division was advancing to repel a French thrust when they encountered French skirmishes. Brigade-commander Maj-Gen Ross called for a company to drive them away, to which Capt George Tovey responded by leading forward his No 6 Coy. (It is interesting to note that this was not, apparently, the regimental light company, evidence that the ordinary companies could skirmish as well.) Tovey brushed aside the skirmishers, advancing with bayonets fixed, in close order and double-quick time. On reaching the edge of a plateau Tovey was astonished to see the head of the French

6th *Léger* (Light Infantry) at ten yards distance, they having just ascended the other side of the plateau. A French officer called on Tovey to surrender, whereupon he shouted to his 70 or 80 men, 'bayonet away, bayonet away,' and they rushed at the head of the French column. The sudden charge threw the French into such confusion that they recoiled down the hill, allowing Tovey's company to regain their regiment with the loss of 11 dead and 14 wounded. A Brunswick officer who witnessed the action declared that it was more like bayonet-drill than a charge, both sides 'fencing' at each other with bayonets; but Tovey's account, supported by Kincaid of the 95th who declared it 'one of the most brilliant feats of the war' (though not an eye-witness), better explains the reason for the French re-coiling, by the impetus of the charge. Tovey remarked on a 'reckless and intrepid' member of his company named Budworth who returned with only the socket of his bayonet on his musket, reeking with blood, declaring that 'he had killed away until his bayonet broke'.

Actual bayonet-fights would appear to have been so rare that those who witnessed them remembered the occasion, such as the incident in which a light company man of the 20th killed three Frenchmen with his bayonet at Maida, or John Rae of the 71st, an old Methodist of 'gloomy disposition', who killed two with his bayonet at Sobral (and shot a third) in 1810.

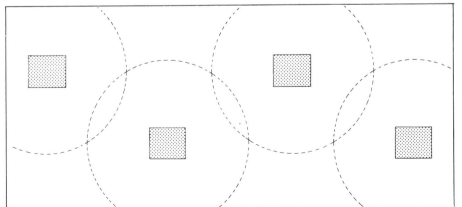

# Light Infantry Tactics

Light infantry skills had never completely withered despite the limited coverage accorded them by Dundas, and it is interesting to note the standard practice of forming light battalions by combining the flank companies of several units. Nevertheless, in the Netherlands the army had found it impossible to come to grips with the clouds of French skirmishers, who retired whenever the British line advanced and continued to harass them with long-range fire, the British light companies and foreign auxiliaries being unable to combat them effectively; even in Egypt, otherwise unengaged British brigades were severely hit by long-range skirmish fire at Alexandria, hardly firing a shot in answer.

The conversion of several regiments into light infantry and their training in this role, inspired by Moore at Shorncliffe, partly remedied the situation, but it is significant that Wellington appreciated the problem from the very first. To prevent the French skirmish-screens approaching his lines, he needed to provide at least an equivalent number of his own skirmishers. As the light infantry regiments were normally concentrated into their own formation, regimental light companies were used for this purpose, supplemented by the rifle companies attached to each brigade, principally the 5/60th but including also Portuguese and miscellaneous German units, and later companies of the 95th

Rifles. The creation and increase of *Caçadore* units, used exclusively as skirmishers, permitted an average Anglo-Portuguese Division of say 5,500 men to deploy as many as 1,200 to 1,500 skirmishers, generally outnumbering and usually outshooting their French counterparts, and completely masking the main body of the army.

The essence of light infantry tactics is perhaps best described by the 1803 *Manual for Volunteer Corps of Infantry*:

'Vigilance, activity, and intelligence, are particularly requisite . . . Rapidity of movement . . . establishes their own security, at the same time that it renders them the terror of the enemy . . . The intelligence chiefly required in a light infantry man is, that he should know how to take advantage of every circumstance of ground which can enable him to harass (sic) and annoy the enemy, without exposing himself . . . In some situations they must conceal themselves by stooping, in others they must kneel, or lie flat upon the ground . . . to gain upon an enemy along hedges, through corn fields, amongst gardens and ditches, almost without being perceived . . . If the regulars advance rapidly upon them, the light troops must recede; and when the enemy is exhausted . . . they must again line the hedges and ditches round him . . . light troops should all be expert marksmen. To fire seldom and always with effect should be their chief study . . . Noise and smoke is not sufficient to stop the advance of soldiers accustomed to war: they are to be checked only by seeing their comrades fall . . .'

This last point was reinforced by Col George Hanger: '. . . though the enemy fired at be not wounded, yet the ball passes so close to him as to intimidate, and prove to him how skilful an opponent he is engaged with . . . provided they are

*Two basic methods of movement were used in skirmishing, either in two lines with the rear rank advancing through the gaps in the front rank, or as here when 'covering' each other: after the front rank man had fired, the rear man moved around him, protecting him whilst he re-loaded. When loaded, the first man said 'ready'; whereupon the second man fired, and they changed places as before.*

*Lt-Gen Sir John Moore (1761-1809), whose training-camp at Shorncliffe was responsible for the re-discovery of British light infantry skills. Though not solely responsible, Moore's influence was crucial.*

*Marksmanship in action: at Astorga the amiable rogue Tom Plunkett of the 95th lay on his back to shoot and kill the French general Colbert (upon his being offered a bag of money to try!).*

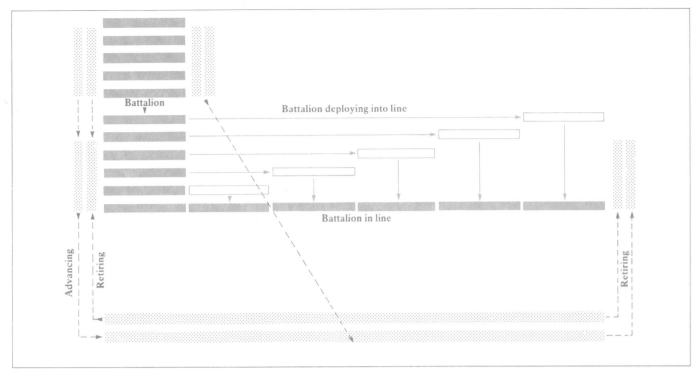

Battalion

Battalion deploying into line

Battalion in line

Advancing

Retiring

Retiring

*A regimental light company masking the movement of a battalion of infantry. The light company advances in two 'wings', one on each flank of the battalion in 'column of companies'. As the battalion deploys into line the light infantry run ahead, forming a two-deep skirmish-chain. When retiring, one wing of the light company would run to each flank, or might pass through intervals between the companies in line.*

not fortunate enough to kill, they are sure to intimidate . . .' Accuracy of the rifle and the excellence of training was such that individual targets could be marked and hit; Landmann of the Royal Engineers recorded a conversation with a German rifleman of the 60th at Vimeiro, asking why he didn't shoot a Frenchman 60 to 80 yards away. The German replied: 'Ton't tisturp me; I want de officer; pecause ter pe more plunder', it being usual for skirmishers to loot the bodies of men they had killed!

Moore trained his men to operate in pairs, so that one man of the two would always be ready to fire. In theory, 'skirmish order' involved men operating quite close together; 'open order' was regarded as having two feet between files, and 'extended order' two paces. All movements were carried out in 'quick time', both motion (controlled by the whistles of the officers and NCOs, and the company buglers) and firing, 'as quick as he can, consistent with loading properly' as Cooper's light infantry manual (1806) remarked. In practice, though, terrain and other circumstances would completely throw out this orderly drill, so that skirmishing often developed into a series of personal encounters such as that described by a sergeant of the 1/ Coldstream Guards light company at Talavera: 'the Skirmishers on both sides singled out their

objects, & thus for 10 or 15 minutes were amusing ourselves shooting at one another as deliberately as if we had been Pigeon Shooting . . . the object I had singled out, & myself exchanged three rounds each, the second of his, hit me slightly on the right shoulder, & after my third he disappeared therefore I conclude he went home!'

Unlike the irregular light troops of some armies, those of Britain were equally capable of fighting in line, hence the organisation of the famed Light Brigades (later Division) in the Peninsula. Originally Craufurd's Brigade of the 3rd Division (1/43rd, 1/52nd, 1/95th) it became the Light Division in February 1810 with the addition of the 1st and 3rd *Caçadores*, Brunswick Oels *Jägers* and a company of 2/95th, plus later the 2/ 52nd, more of the 2/ and 3/95th and ultimately the 17th Portuguese Regt. It became not only legendary for its excellence in every respect, but was probably the finest élite formation existing in Europe. Its original commander, 'Black Bob' Craufurd, was the sternest of disciplinarians (he even had men flogged for falling-out to fill their canteens) but made the division what it was; admired by many despite his sullen demeanour, he was almost universally mourned when killed at Ciudad Rodrigo. The magnificence of his division was a fitting memorial.

# Artillery Tactics

British artillery tactics were governed by the comparative shortage of guns which was experienced virtually throughout the period, and especially in the opening stages of the Peninsular War. The concept of a 'massed battery' used in an offensive role was appreciated – the common belief being that such a concentration of guns had greater effect than the sum of its parts – but 'massed battery fire' was rarely attempted; only at Vittoria was anything like it achieved, and then largely as a result of the restrictions of the terrain rather than any grand tactical purpose. Indeed, Adye's artillery manual stated that artillery was by preference 'separated into many small batteries', but so positioned that all guns could be concentrated 'to produce a decided effect against any particular points' by being positioned so as to sweep the enemy by cross-fire. Though valid in principle, circumstances of terrain rendered this only possible on the most favourable occasions. Instead, Wellington distributed his guns along the front of his line, so as to cover all possible threats, keeping only a very small reserve: at Waterloo, this comprised two Horse troops and a Foot company, which were committed almost from the start. (Shortages of guns meant that not until 1812 was Wellington able to form a small reserve, in addition to the allocation of two field batteries per Division except the Light, which retained its old horse artillery troop, Major Bull's.) This

emphasizes a fundamental difference between Wellington's tactics and those of Napoleon, even though they were initially the result of shortages: whereas Napoleon used artillery in an offensive role, to batter a hole in the enemy line which would then be exploited by infantry and cavalry, Wellington used his guns as essentially a support for his other 'arms'.

Although artillery could expend vast quantities of ammunition in a major action, there seem to be no cases of guns running out, due to the husbanding of resources and the gunners' care to ensure that the maximum number of shots counted, which might mean holding fire until a target appeared through a break in the smoke, or engaging only at medium to short range. At Waterloo no more than 10,000 rounds were fired by 78 guns, averaging 129 each, the highest expenditure being Sandham's company, 183 9pdr and 5½in howitzer rounds. Rates of fire probably averaged two roundshot or three canister per minute (less for the larger guns: a 12pdr might average one shot per minute), though this would decrease as gun-crews took casualties or became tired. *In extremis*, however, when the enemy was dangerously near, almost continuous fire was possible over a short period: in 1777 a competition achieved 12 to 14 unaimed shots per minute. The need to re-position the gun after every shot (due to recoil) slowed the process, Adye calculating the

recoil of fieldpieces between 3½ to 12 feet per shot depending upon the gun and projectile, though as these statistics were measured on a floor of elm planking, on soft ground recoil would be much less. Mercer recalled at Waterloo how his guns recoiled into a 'confused heap' so that at the end their trails were jammed together, the gunners being too exhausted to manhandle them through the mud back into position.

Certain basic rules were observed in the siting and handling of artillery in the field. One of the major points concerned the target: whether or not artillery should attempt to engage the enemy artillery. 'Counter-battery fire' was condemned by Adye's manual in all cases except that in which friendly infantry was suffering more than the enemy's, in which case his artillery might be targeted. Alternatively, a writer in the *British Military Library* (1801) stated that as trained artillerymen were so valuable, it would damage the enemy more in the long term to kill his gunners than his infantry. This has validity, but in practice counter-battery fire seems to have been rare; in fact before Waterloo Wellington specifically ordered artillery to fire only at attacking troops, to conserve ammunition,

*A cross-section through an 'ideal' artillery-position; though it would be a most fortunate battery-commander who found one incorporating all of the most advantageous features illustrated. The arcing trajectory and shell-burst over the advancing enemy indicates the ideal path of 'spherical case-shot' or shrapnel.*

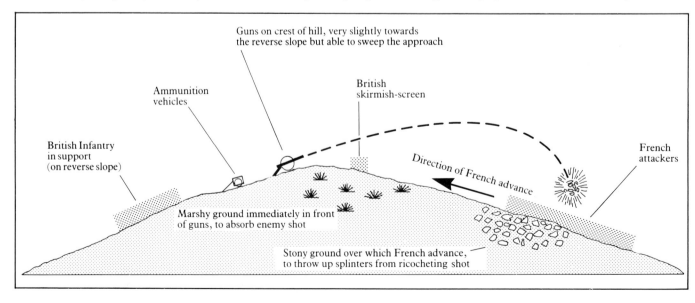

Guns on crest of hill, very slightly towards the reverse slope but able to sweep the approach

Ammunition vehicles

British skirmish-screen

British Infantry in support (on reverse slope)

French attackers

Direction of French advance

Marshy ground immediately in front of guns, to absorb enemy shot

Stony ground over which French advance, to throw up splinters from ricocheting shot

*Recoil was such that as gun-crews tired they might no longer be able to re-position them; Mercer recalled his troop at Waterloo ending in the confused heap above.*

*A feature of all major actions (as at Talavera, right) was the dense smoke caused by the discharge of artillery and muskets, the 'fog of war' which obscured much from view.*

though in the battle Bolton's company certainly engaged French guns which were enfilading the British infantry.

An ideal battery position was in advance of the main line, if possible with some degree of cover in the form of hedges or timber, or 'masked' by cavalry or other troops, who would move out of the line of fire immediately before the battery opened up, so as to reveal the position to the enemy at the last moment. The open space in front should have no 'dead' ground (i.e. hidden from view), with a gentle slope in front of the battery (more than 1 in 5 made the gun difficult to depress); ideally the guns should have been on the crest of a ridge, 'so far back that the muzzles are only to be seen over them' according to Adye, with the limbers and ammunition on the reverse slope and thus hidden from the enemy. Waggons were normally positioned some 50 yards behind the limbers, with a second reserve another fifty yards back, ammunition-waggons moving forward individually to replenish all guns, to expose as few as possible to enemy fire (a single spark could otherwise wipe out a battery's entire ammunition). The ground in front of the enemy would ideally be hard, to help 'ricochet' fire, yet soft around the battery to absorb enemy fire, without stones which might be thrown up by the landing of an enemy shot. A battery would be arrayed in line, with ten to twenty yards between guns, in a staggered line to minimise the danger of enemy 'enfilade' fire sweeping across the entire battery. Firing was often initially by salvo, but thereafter

often at the discretion of each section-commander, according to target and visibility. It was common for guns to act in pairs, firing alternately. If positions were not expected to be moved, temporary earthworks or breastworks might be thrown up, high enough to cover the depth of the carriage, though these were not widely used in the field. The close support of friendly troops was absolutely imperative.

Adye's manual made much of the value of 'enfilade' fire, i.e. taking the enemy in the flank or catching them in cross-fire: 'The shot from artillery should always take an enemy in the direction of its greatest dimension; it should therefore take a line obliquely or in flank; but a column in front', without the battery position being itself exposed to the enemy's enfilade fire. Cross-fire should be directed, he wrote, against the enemy's most critical points, 'the débouchés of the enemy, the heads of their columns, and the weakest points in front. In an attack of the enemy's positions, the cross fire of the guns must become direct, before it can impede the advance of the troops; and must annoy the enemy's positions nearest to the point attacked, when it is no longer safe to continue the fire upon that point itself.'

When in danger of being over-run, evacuation of the position was the best expedient, though this was often hazardous; Mercer's guns were almost captured at Genappe when Uxbridge led them down a narrow lane almost into the French vanguard, whilst at Fuentes de Oñoro Ramsey's horse artillery troop

only escaped by cutting its way in a charge through the French cavalry, a noted epic.

As a last extremity a gun could be 'spiked', the vent being blocked by an expanding nail to render it useless. Before Waterloo Wellington ordered his gunners not to withdraw their guns or 'spike' but before being over-run to remove a wheel and shelter inside the nearest infantry square, running out to replace the wheel and re-commence fire as soon as the enemy retired. This worked well, but Mercer's troop at least disobeyed the order and continued to fire throughout, fearing that if they left their guns the Brunswickers near them would panic and flee.

Appalling ramparts of dead were built up in front of this position, testi-mony to the terrible effect of canister at short range. One gun (Roger's company) was accidentally spiked at Waterloo by an alarmed NCO and was withdrawn to the rear to have the spike drilled out; conceivably its withdrawal, and perhaps the shuttle-service of ammunition-waggons to and from the firing-line, caused Wellington to think some of his artillery ran away at Waterloo, a suggestion patently un-true but one which caused great offence within the corps, one of the Duke's rare aberrations. Close-quarter fighting around the guns was terribly dangerous for both attackers and gunners; as Adye noted, 'Never abandon your guns till the last extremity. The last discharges are the most destruc-tive; they may perhaps be your salvation, and crown you with glory.'

# Cavalry Tactics

It has been said that Welllington was primarily an infantry general, and neglected his cavalry; if so, it was less a reflection upon him than upon other factors, the terrain, the availability of cavalry and their quality. Much of the Iberian Peninsula is not ideal country for cavalry, and the number of regiments Wellington possessed rendered impossible large-scale operations of continental style. The continuing weakness of the Portuguese cavalry, and the general uselessness of the Spanish, meant that only the few British regiments could be relied upon. Only six regiments served at Talavera, and not until 1812 (when he had 15 regiments) was Wellington able to field a cavalry force equal to that of the French, as more regiments were sent out. Consequently, no massed cavalry actions were possible, and although the army's cavalry formed one Division (two Divisions from June 1811-April 1813), the brigades were actually moved about individually under Wellington's personal direction, as he had no cavalry commander he could trust fully; even the worthy Cotton was not allowed independent action.

Consequently, there were few outstanding cavalry actions in the Peninsular War, at least under Wellington's command; there were few actions like Sahagun and Benevente, which owed much to the skill of Paget. Apart from Le Marchant's charge at Salamanca, no other decisive actions can be found; the smaller triumphs, such as Bock at Garcia Hernandez or Lumley at Usagre were of little overall importance. The most valuable work of the cavalry was in the 'outpost' duty, shielding the army and watching the movements of the enemy,

though as this was completely untaught at home it took actual campaign experience for units to become skilled. Best of all were the 1st Hussars of the German Legion, who from March to May 1811 held a 40-mile line against four times their number of French, without losing a man, admitting a French patrol or transmitting a wrong piece of information.

Part of Wellington's mistrust of his cavalry and (more especially) its leaders was a result of failings when it came to action; as Tomkinson of the 16th Light Dragoons wrote with some disgust, each regiment 'estimating its merit by mere celerity of movement', and thus, probably until they had been in combat, lacking the discipline vital for a successful action. Never in doubt was the resolution or quality of the men and horses; the failing was in training, discipline and leadership which held that a madcap gallop straight at the enemy was all that was required. Wellington confirmed this in a letter to Lord John Russell in 1826, in which he said that he considered the British cavalry 'so inferior to the French for want of order, that although I considered some of our squadrons a match for two French, yet I did not care to see four British opposed to four French, and still more as the number increased, and order (of course) became more necessary. They could gallop, but could not preserve their order.'

Cavalry manoeuvres were as complex as those of the infantry, involving a large number of movements to turn line into column, half-column, etc., with titles for these as confusing as 'the open Column changes its Front and leading Flank by the Countermarch of Divisions, each on its own Ground'; for the 'simple' deploy-

ment of column into line, 22 verbal commands were needed (including seven cries of 'Halt'; or eight more commands and three more of 'Halt' for every 'division' in excess of three). In combat these could easily get out of hand, and in the Peninsula there were numerous occasions when victory was turned to defeat by charges careering on unchecked, without a thought of re-forming so as to defend themselves from a counter-charge. Wellington's remarks to Russell may have been unduly harsh, however, for in most cases regiments at fault were seeing action for the first time. Although the 1801 cavalry manual devoted but four pages from 374 to the technique of the charge, its advice was sound: 'When the shock of the squadron has broken the order of the opposite enemy, part may be ordered to pursue and keep up the advantage; but its great object is instantly to rally and renew its efforts in a body.' This was neglected on a number of significant occasions. The 23rd Light Dragoons at Talavera were disordered by falling into a ravine, and then charged on piecemeal instead of re-forming, and were cut to pieces. At Campo Mayor the 13th Light Dragoons scored a major victory and captured the French siege-train, but galloped on, were cut up and lost the captured guns. At Maguilla the

*Deployment into line: a regiment of four squadrons (8 troops) is arrayed in column of 'half-squadrons' (i.e. troops), who deploy into line upon the leading troop, which remains stationary. The succeeding troops face right or left in column of threes, ride parallel with their intended position in the line, face to the front and move alongside the stationary troop, 'markers' having ridden to indicate their correct position. Manoeuvres were complex and subject always to numerous commands.*

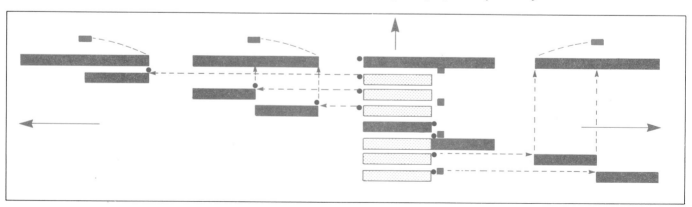

*Horse artillery was designed to provide fire-support for cavalry, but never intended to become involved in mêlées like that at Fuentes de Oñoro, when Norman Ramsey's RHA troop had' to charge through French cavalry to escape.*

3rd Dragoon Guards and 1st Dragoons were left without a reserve and likewise fell to a counter-charge. Significant about the last two actions is that the commanders were both totally incompetent, respectively RB Long and 'Jack' Slade, the latter being commonly regarded as not only 'a damned stupid fellow' (as Paget called him) but a coward. That the regimental officers had little idea of what should have been done is shown by an account of the disaster at Campo Mayor by a participant who thought it wonderful: '. . . the 13th behaved most nobly. I

*A cavalry regiment of four squadrons drawn up in line. Officers commanding squadrons were positioned about a horse's length in advance of the squadron standard; 'supernumerary' officers, sergeants and quartermasters were positioned two horses' distance from the rear rank, 'and their business is to attend to the movements of the squadron, and particularly to the rear rank' according to the regulations. Squadron-standards were not normally taken on campaign.*

saw so many instances of individual bravery, as raised my opinion of mankind . . . the superiority of our English horses, and more particularly, the superiority of swordsmanship our fellows showed, decided every contest in our favour; it was absolutely like a game of prison bars, which you must have seen at school . . The whole way across the plain was a succession of individual contests, here and there, as the cavalry all dispersed . . . it was certainly most beautiful . . .'

After Maguilla Wellington wrote, enraged, to Hill: 'I have never been more annoyed . . . It is occasioned entirely by the trick our officers of cavalry have acquired of galloping at every thing, and their galloping back as fast as they gallop on the enemy. They never consider their situation, never think of manoeuvring before an enemy – so little that one would think they cannot manoeuvre, excepting on Wimbledon Common; and when they use their arm as it ought to be used, viz. offensively, they never keep nor provide for a reserve. All cavalry

should charge in two lines, of which one should be in reserve; if obliged to charge in one line, part of the line, at least one-third, should be ordered beforehand to pull up, and form in second line, as soon as the charge should be given . . .'

At Waterloo, similar disasters occurred; the 'Union' brigade charged on, through its initial target, cut-up French gun-teams and was sadly mauled by French counter-charges. Only after Waterloo did Wellington issue 'Instructions to Officers Commanding Brigades of Cavalry in the Army of Occupation', which set down the *correct* tactics:

(1) A reserve *must* be kept of between half and two-thirds of the whole, to exploit a success or cover a withdrawal.
(2) Deployment should be in three lines, the rear-most line possibly in column but capable of easy deployment.
(3) Against cavalry, the lines should be 400-500yds apart, to allow a defeated first line to retire without disordering the reserve.
(4) Against infantry the second line should be 200yds behind the first, so as to charge the infantry whilst they were re-loading after the charge of the first line.
(5) When a charge is made at a gallop, supports must *walk* and not be carried away with the rest, for cohesion in the supports is vital if they are to be effective.

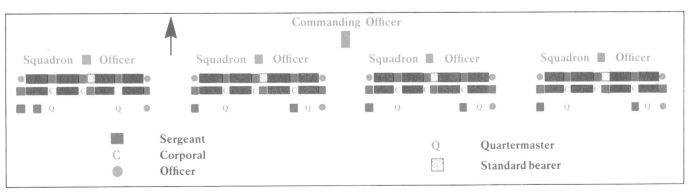

# Defence in Depth: The Lines of Torres Vedras

Few defensive-lines in history have ever been impregnable, from the Great Wall of China to the *Non Plus Ultra* lines erected to confound Marlborough; but few can ever have been as effective as the Lines of Torres Vedras, the greatest achievement in military engineering of the entire Napoleonic era.

The maintenance of the British Army in the Iberian peninsula was dependent upon an uninterrupted flow of supplies and reinforcements from Britain, which in turn depended upon a secure coastal base. Lisbon was the only port which could fulfil this role, so its retention was vital for the maintenance of the war. The security of Lisbon was the primary objective of Wellington's plan for the defence of Portugal, for as early as August/September 1809 he had reported to the British Cabinet that as 'the whole country is frontier', it would only be possible to make the capital and its environs secure. Due to the nature of the terrain to the north of Lisbon, he envisaged two lines of fortification running from the Atlantic coast to a point on the Tagus estuary more than 20 miles north of Lisbon.

On 20 October 1809 Wellington wrote a memorandum to Lt-Col Richard Fletcher, commanding Royal Engineers in the Peninsula, concerning the defence of Lisbon; although the fortifications ultimately built differed slightly from his original intention, it was this document which originated the lines of Torres Vedras, the name of which was taken from one of the largest camps within the system. As Wellington admitted to Fletcher, his plan was not simply to protect the capital, but cover 'the embarkation of the British troops in case of reverse'. It is a remarkable document, covering all avenues of attack, and setting the engineer 21 tasks, ranging from surveying and reporting on the possibilities of defence to the construction of redoubts, establishment of communication-posts and preparation to destroy roads and bridges in case of French advance.

The lines were never planned as a continuous fortification but as a series of mutually-supportive redoubts and gun-emplacements, taking advantage of the mountainous terrain identified by Wellington. He believed that he had but six months to complete the defences, but Massena's delay in advancing led to the lines becoming stronger than envisaged initially, from a means of delaying the advance to an impregnable barrier stretching right across the Lisbon peninsula, the southern (interior) lines 22 miles from sea to sea, and the northern lines 29 miles. Taking advantage of the natural features of the terrain and the often-steep declivities, 152 numbered 'works' or forts were constructed, varying in size and design according to the ground. Some positions were tiny; work no. 37 had provision for only 50 men and three 9pdrs, whilst the largest, no. 14, could hold 1,590 men and was equipped with 14 × 12pdrs, 6 × 9pdrs, 4 × 6pdrs and one 5½in howitzer. The largest complex was the camp at Torres Vedras itself, works nos. 20-22, holding 1,720 men, 10 × 12pdrs, 2 × 9pdrs, 11 × 6pdrs and

## Lines of the Torres Vedras

*(map)*

Atlantic Ocean

to Coimbra

Torres Vedras

River Zizandre

River S Lourenco

Pero Negro

Mafra

Montachique · Bucellas

to Lisbon

to Lisbon

French picquets

to Santarem

Alemquer

Sobral

French encampment

Arruda

Vila Franca

Alhandra

Alverca

French picquets

River Tagus

to Lisbon

N

**Scale:** 0 1 2 3 4 5 Miles

■ Defensive works
▲ Signal stations
☆ Wellington's HQ
⊔⊓⊔ Artificial embankments
Ground over 650 feet

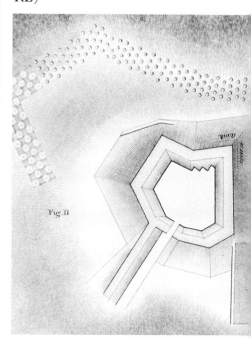

*Plan view of a typical redoubt in the Lines of Torres Vedras, a fortified emplacement with covered approach and entrance at the rear, with* trous de loup *(wolf-pits) to disorder any attacker. (Print after a plan by Lt John Smyth, RE)*

Fig. II

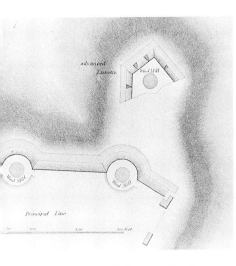

*Plan of a Torres Vedras fortification, showing how existing features of terrain were incorporated in the defences; in this case, three stoutly-built windmills were used as bastions, one being turned into an advanced lunette.*
*(Print after Lt George Hotham, RE)*

*Massena found the Lines of Torres Vedras barring his path a year after the initial plan, on 14 October 1810; 'An impenetrable blend of geography and fortification' as* The Times *described, they wrecked the French army as much as any battle.*

$3 \times 5\frac{1}{2}$in howitzers. In 1812, when the works were fully perfected, they were armed with 534 guns, though the total which could have been accommodated was 628 guns and 39,475 men.

All works were provided with ditches normally 16 feet wide and 12 feet deep, parapets 8 to 14 feet thick, with palisades, gun-emplacements, *chevaux de frises* and abattis (entanglements) and *trous de loup* (wolf-pits); all buildings and timber which might provide cover for an attacker were ruthlessly cleared. At the north-west of the first line a six-mile bog was created by damming the river Zizandre. Where the heights were steep but not accessible, the slope was blasted away; vast abattis were created of interlaced olive-trees, one so large as to block completely the ravine at the head of the Calandrix valley. Each redoubt was closed by a barrier-gate with a wooden bridge; 50,000 trees were used for this work alone. Each work was equipped with a depot of entrenching tools (10 shovels, 6 picks and 3 felling-axes for a 400-man work, for example), and in addition to ammunition-supplies each contained enough casks to provide each man with four quarts of water. Each position had its own bomb-proof magazine, sunk into the ground, lined with timber and covered with sandbags. Abattis were also placed in advance of each fort by some thirty yards, to halt an attacker and provide a 'killing-ground' for the defenders. Wherever possible, each work was supported by the cross-fire of others to make the attacker's task virtually suicidal.

Though Fletcher was an engineer of genius, his professional help was small; no more than 17 engineer officers ever worked at any one time (11 British, 4 Portuguese and 2 Hanoverian), with only 18 trained artificers and 150 men detached from line regiments. They were divided into groups of two or three, to superintend the labour-force of gangs of 1,000 to 1,500 Portuguese militia or peasants, some of whom were 'conscripted' to work more than 40 miles from their homes, yet not one example of unwillingness or unrest was recorded in the year that the construction progressed. The peasants were paid 6 to 10 *vintems* per diem (1/1 to 1/8d in English currency); generally 5,000 to 7,000 were working at any one time. Major John Jones, Fletcher's chief assistant, in his account of the works paid full credit to the Portuguese peasants who performed the manual labour, their excellence being 'more ascribed to regular habits of persevering labour . . . than to the efficiency of the control exercised over them'. Similarly, the peasants 'with their rude means of transport' – ox-carts and human muscle – 'succeeding in transporting 12-pounders into situations where wheels had never before rolled.' The total expense of the entire lines was something less than £100,000, an incredibly small sum for such a massive undertaking.

Jones admitted that the works were 'merely securities for artillery', and the whole plan was to garrison them with Portuguese militia and 'ill-organised peasantry', who though incapable of operating in the field 'being possessed of innate courage, were equal to defend a redoubt'; thus the entire fortification could be defended without depriving the field army of a single brigade; the outer lines could be held by 18,000 men and the inner by 14,000; naturally both did not need garrisoning simultaneously. The field army was to be held behind the lines to attack any French force which did break through; a semaphore system allowed a message to go from end to end of the 29-mile stretch in 7 minutes, and from headquarters to either end of the lines in 4 minutes. As Jones stated, it required a general possessing 'the utmost promptitude, decision and skill', which Wellington had in abundance.

# Coastal Defences – Forts & Martellos

The coastal defences of Great Britain were based on a series of fortresses and shore-batteries covering the areas most vulnerable or of greatest strategic importance. These were essentially static defences; mobile defence-forces were not permanently allocated to any particular area, but depended upon the battalions of militia and regulars in residence at the time, supplemented by the volunteers of the locality. They were not under unified control; those regarded as permanent were governed by the Board of Ordnance, but any classified as temporary 'field-works' were the responsibility of the War Office. The Board interfered in War Office business, and even compelled cities and ports to pay for the construction and maintenance of their own defences. The country was divided into 'military districts' numbered 1 Northern, 2 Yorkshire, 3 Eastern, 4 Southern, 5 South Western, 6 Western, 7 Severn, 8 North Western, 9 Scotland, 10 Ireland, 11 Jersey and 12 Guernsey/Alderney, each commanded by a General Officer with a small permanent staff. The permanent fortifications ranged from newly-built forts like that at Dunbar to ancient defence-works such as Dover Castle, Bamborough Castle, Deal and Walmer Castles, which were strengthened and allocated a large number of heavy guns. The amount of artillery diposed of in this way was immense. In 1805, for example, excluding Ireland and a number of defence-posts for which statistics are apparently unavailable, the total ordnance deployed included 93 42pdrs, 133 36pdrs, 227 32pdrs, 858 24pdrs, 70 20pdrs (in the Channel Isles), 654 18pdrs, 213 12pdrs, 183 9pdrs, 87 6pdrs, 22 4pdrs and 4 3pdrs; plus the following carronades: 26 68pdrs, 40 32pdrs, 84 24pdrs, 84 18pdrs, 101 12pdrs; and 4 each 9 and 6pdrs in Alderney. There were 215 separate positions (counting Alderney and Sark as one each), though some locations had more than one battery (Chatham 13, Dover 7, etc); the size ranged from Narrow Port, Guernsey, with one 9pdr and Swansea with 2 9pdrs, to Portsmouth with 483 guns in ten different emplacements.

Personnel was provided by detachments of regular artillery, stationed in company-sized units or less supplemented by Militia (such as the Royal Pembroke which garrisoned the Landguard Fort near Harwich) and local volunteer companies. The Sea Fencibles (maritime volunteers harshly described by St Vincent as of no other use 'than to calm the fears of old ladies') were also trained to man the batteries, though their main purpose was to crew coasters and floating batteries. There were in addition static garrison and invalid companies of Royal Artillery, one of the latter being formed in 1794 to garrison Bermuda, where it was somehow forgotten and brought home in 1807 when only seven members were still alive, having received virtually no drafts, stores or clothing in all that time.

A unique fortification designed at this time was the Martello tower. Among the defences of Corsica was an ancient circular watch-tower at Mortella Point, which in 1793-94 was twice captured by British forces, having in the interim been handed over to Corsican patrols, who lost it to the French. On the second occasion a four-gun battery at 150yds battered the tower for two days before its 38 men with three guns surrendered, its stalwart defence deeply impressing the British observers. Surveys were made and two similar towers were built at the Cape and one in Nova Scotia, when it was decided to supplement the British coastal defences with a chain of similar towers, known by the corrupted name 'Martello'. The system was not completed until the worst danger of invasion had receded, and thus received much criticism from 'radical' observers like Cobbett who regarded them as a waste of resources, probably costing £2,000 to £3,000 each: 'Here has been the squandering! Here has been the pauper-making!'

A number of different designs were used, both circular and elliptical in plan; the original proposal suggested a height of 33 feet and an interior diameter of 26 feet, the structure constructed with immensely-thick walls with two or three floors and a doorway set half-way up the wall, accessible only by ladder. On the upper storey, a flat, lead-covered roof, were positions for artillery, planned to consist of one heavy gun (24 or 18pdr) and two lighter (or carronades), fixed on traversible mounts to give a 360° arc of fire over the 6-foot parapet. The middle storey was used to house the garrison – usually an officer and 24 men – and the lowest storey for supplies and ammunition. In addition to the ordinary towers or 'bomb-proofs' there were larger 're-doubts' to house 350 men and 11 guns, and a tower larger than the standard

Martello Towers •
Royal Military Canal ⋯⋯
STUDFALL ■
CASTLE

0 1 2 3 4 5 ... 10
Miles

*One of the most important stretches of the southern Martello chain, from Folkestone to Hastings, showing the course of the Royal Military Canal, a 30 mile moat from Shorncliffe to the river Rother at Rye, later extended to Cliff End, to isolate the Romney Marsh area. Its planned gun-positions were never mounted with artillery.*

102

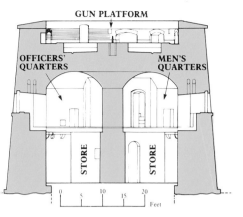

**GUN PLATFORM**

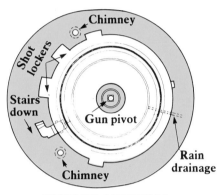

**GUN PLATFORM**

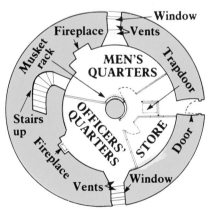

**FIRST FLOOR**

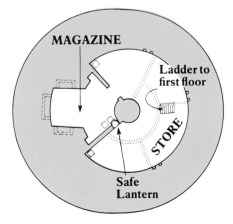

**BASEMENT**

*Elevation and plan of a typical elliptical south-coast Martello, with the thickest part of the wall to the seaward side. Widening towards the base, the walls were at least 6ft thick and made of bricks and 'hot lime mortar' covered with stucco. Flues and stairway began at first floor level; communication with the magazine and stores in the basement was by ladder. Armament was intended to consist of one heavy gun; eastern towers had quatrefoil gun-positions on the roof.*

variety to have four guns. Complete with internal staircase and chimneys, and with an entrenched ditch around, the towers would have provided most sturdy defences, as proved by the demolition of Martello no. 68 at Eastbourne in 1860, which required 50 rounds each from rifled Armstrong guns of 100, 80 and 40pdr variety, immensely more effective artillery than anything used in the Napoleonic era.

The first chain of Martellos, construction of which began in spring 1805, was that along the south coast, Sussex and Kent; when it was completed in 1808 there were eleven 'circular forts' (two guns each) and 73 Martellos (one gun). A second chain was built on the east coast of Essex, 29 Martellos (plus one more to the Sussex chain, at Seaford), the whole finished in 1812, giving a total of 11 forts and 103 Martellos. The east coast towers were larger, with more accommodation, two staircases, four windows instead of two and space for more ordnance, the roof-spaces being quatrefoil-shaped. The eastern ones had more guns, including carronades and 5½in howitzers. The south coast towers were numbered 1-74; those on the east were identified by letters, A to Z and AA to CC. More were built in Ireland, the Channel Islands, a few in Canada and two in the Orkneys (finished in 1818!). Many remain today, some occupied but most silent relics of the Napoleonic invasion-threat.

Few of the coastal defences were tested seriously; the nearest thing to an assault occurred on the Marcouf islands, only four miles from the French coast, which were occupied and fortified in 1795. Garrisoned by 346 men with 20 guns, 5 carronades and a howitzer, an attempt to recapture them in 1798 was beaten off with ease for the loss of one dead and 3 wounded defenders, and the wrecking of the French invasion-boats. The islands were held until the peace of 1802.

*A heavy gun positioned on the upper storey of a Martello tower (which was in fact the lead-covered roof), mounted on a traversing carriage with iron 'truck' wheels upon a central 'pivot', allowing the gun a 360° field of fire over the parapet.*

Apart from internal garrison-towns, there were few 'fieldworks' erected apart from those on the coast, the major project being the Royal Military Canal, intended to facilitate defence. (Cobbett that perpetual critic of the Ministry, was predictably unimpressed, noting in *Rural Rides*, 'Here is a canal . . . to *keep out the French*; for those armies that had so often crossed the Rhine and the Danube, were to be kept back by a canal, made by Pitt, thirty feet wide at the most.') Another exception was the 'Chelmsford lines', a circuit of earthworks the chord of which extended some two miles, from a hexagonal fort at one extremity to the 'Star Redoubt' at Widford at the other. The later 18th century also saw the erection of barracks (in place of the previous practice of billetting troops on landlords and others); there was some opposition to the concept, and the buildings themselves were often dark, insanitary and over-crowded. Barrack-dormitories were shared not only by the men but families as well, with no more privacy than temporary screening by blankets, so that tented camps and hutted bivouacs (as normally used in summer by troops guarding the coast) were more hygenic and generally more popular.

# Chapter Seven: THE ARMIES' CAMPAIGNS

The British Army which embarked on the early campaigns of the Revolutionary Wars was initially small in numbers and mixed in quality. In the earlier 18th century its reputation had reverberated throughout Europe, when commanded by the Duke of Marlborough and in the many brilliant successes of Seven Years War. Since then, its prestige had suffered by the reverses of the American War of Independence, even though such reverses were largely the result of central direction rather than any weaknesses in the regiments themselves. In the decade since the end of the American War, no continental campaigns had been undertaken so that the only active-service experience of the army was among those regiments which served abroad, and only in India was there actually any campaigning. The general standard of the army, if only in experience, had therefore declined to a degree, which was coupled with the usual governmental parsimony which afflicted all British forces, even in the midst of a major war. (It is scarcely credible that an army desperately short of efficient transport, and engaged in a major campaign, should be ordered to send home two of its Waggon Train troops (of which only 12 existed) for disbandment; Wellington refused to comply!).

The state of the army at the beginning of the Revolutionary Wars can be over-exaggerated, as in Henry Bunbury's opinion that in 1793 'Our army was lax in its discipline, entirely without system, and very weak in numbers. Each colonel of a regiment managed it according to his own notions, or neglected it altogether. There was no uniformity of drill or movement; professional pride was rare; professional knowledge still more so. Never was a kingdom less prepared for a stern and arduous conflict and this fact may be fairly taken as a proof that Mr Pitt had entertained no design at engaging in a war with France.' Nevertheless, the rapid expansion of the army when war was declared led to vast numbers of inexperienced men being sent on active service; as the Adjutant-General commented to the Duke of York on a brigade sent to the Netherlands in 1793,

'composed of nothing but undisciplined and raw recruits . . . how they are to be disposed of until they can be taught their business I am at a loss to imagine.' Recruits raised hastily in wartime always included a number of unsuitable men (please 'determine whether my miserable Devils should be discharged or not' as one recruiting-officer had written!), but in addition the quality of officer was not high in some cases. It is always dangerous to quote isolated examples as representative of the whole, but the worst aspects of the system are shown by the story of the light company commander of the 30th Foot, i.e. supposedly the most vigilant officer of the battalion, who kicked a dog on the parade-ground because he was so short-sighted he believed it was a knapsack. (He apologised to the dog when it snapped at him!) Administration and central command was imperfect, and to an extent remained so until the Peninsular War. The rate of expansion of the army may be judged from statistics of the total rank-and-file (corporals and below), including foreign troops: 1793, 38,945; 1794, 85,097; 1795, 124,262; 1800, 140,798; 1801, 149,865. (Totals including sergeants and above may be calculated by adding approximately one-eighth.)

Alone of the European powers, Britain had always to maintain a large proportion of its forces outside Europe, thus limiting the amount of resources which could be employed on a continental campaign. The West Indies in particular exerted a huge drain upon men and resources, and in addition to the various colonial expeditions the British presence in India reduced the numbers of men available for deployment in Europe. A waste of resources occurred throughout the period, but though it is easy to be critical with hindsight (which shows the Walcheren expedition to have been a useless and costly disaster), some of these schemes seemed hopeful at the time; though others, such as the descent on Ostend, were foolish at any time. The amount of resources which were occupied in the colonies is apparent from the official 'establishments' of the army; in these statistics, artillery is counted as

part of the army (though officially it belonged to the Board of Ordnance), and the troops on the Irish establishment (i.e. paid for by the Irish Exchequer) include only those actually *in* Ireland; those 'Irish' units serving in Britain are counted on the 'home' establishment. In 1793 the army was deployed thus: home, 21,074; colonies 18,194; India 10,700; Ireland 12,000. In 1794: home 70,944; colonies, 41,490; India 10,700; Ireland 12,000; foreign troops 33,754. In 1796: home 56,883; colonies 82,182; India 10,718; Ireland 19,012; foreign troops 20,288. In 1798: home 57,275; colonies 34,320; India 22,174; Ireland 39,620; foreign troops 4,807. In 1801 (when the Irish establishment merged with 'home'): home 85,119; colonies 72,829; India 26,219. As troops for continental expeditions were normally taken from the 'home' establishment, the defences of Britain required the mobilisation of the militia and fencibles which sometimes even outnumbered the regular army, but which could not be deployed abroad; the numbers rose from 17,602 in 1793 to 42,803 plus 17,500 Irish in 1794, 66,096 plus 22,698 Irish in 1797 and 137,202 plus 26,634 in 1798. In the latter year this combined total of 163,836, plus 37,539 Irish yeomanry, so outnumbered the regular troops (including foreigners) as to represent 56 per cent of the total military forces.

One factor which should not be overlooked is the use of the Royal Navy, without which the army could not have operated; apart from the obvious fact that any troops leaving Britain on campaign had perforce to be conveyed by sea, the navy was vitally necessary in maintaining supply-routes and communications; hence naval expenditure was often greater than that required to maintain the army.

*The siege of San Sebastian, September 1813; the British battery on Monte Olia fires across the estuary upon the main defences on Monte Urgull. The guns are mounted in typical plank-floored emplacements; more guns are being hauled up with the aid of sailors.*
*(Print by Clark & Dubourg)*

# The Low Countries 1793-1795

Hardly had hostilities with republican France begun than a small British expedition was sent to support the Dutch, who were under attack; British preparations for war had been so poor that only the 1st battalions of the three Foot Guards regiments could be dispatched. Cheered and entertained by the populace on their march, part embarked dead drunk, conveyed to the ships on carts, and their support was little better as reserves and supplies were not available. Even when landed, their initial orders were not to move more than 24 hours' march from the coast, in case instant evacuation should be necessary, so short of regiments was the army. It was obvious that these troops were intended only to hearten the Dutch, and even after the dispatch of three weak line battalions and the Duke of York to take command in March/April 1793, it was not expected that they be used in an offensive role.

It soon became obvious that in the interests of maintaining the anti-French First Coalition, Britain would have to assist the Austrians in the Netherlands in actively fighting the French, so 11 cavalry regiments (so weak that together they numbered only about 2,500) were dispatched to the Netherlands, the Duke of York being appointed commander of an army some 17,000 strong, the bulk being Hanoverians from George III's German electorate. Frederick Augustus, Duke of York (and until 1803 lay-bishop of Osnabruck) (1763-1827) was the king's second son, who had learned his military duties in Germany; from 1795 Commander-in-Chief of the British Army (from which post he resigned in 1809 amid a scandal involving his mistress), he proved an able administrator but was not a gifted general and was unable to rise above the inherent weaknesses of the military system prevailing in the early campaigns. Despite all the imperfections of the army in this unfortunate campaign, the spirit of the troops was good; Bunbury recounts his pleading with Col Maitland of the 1st Guards to get his battalion to retrace their steps to oppose a French advance. Maitland said that his battalion had suffered heavily, was almost out of ammunition, and had marched and fought so hard that it was almost un-

conscious on its feet. At that moment a grenadier roused himself from his exhausted torpor and declared, 'Give us some cartridges, and we will see what can be done'. Maitland called, 'Shoulder Arms!' and the weary troops began to retrace their steps towards the enemy. From the very outset of the great war with France, the calibre of the much-maligned ordinary redcoat overcame all deficiencies of command and central direction.

The Duke's Anglo-Hanoverian army co-operated with the Austrian forces of Prince Friedrich Josias of Saxe-Coburg, who by common consent were much superior to the British in administration and experience. The first Allied objective was the capture of Valenciennes,

which was accomplished, after which the British government insisted that the Duke besiege Dunkirk but first a sharp action was fought at Famars, in which an Austro-Anglo-Hanoverian force made a two-pronged attack against an entrenched French position. It provided the small British contingent with its first combat experience, especially the brigade of Sir Ralph Abercromby (14th, 53rd and a battalion of these plus the 37th's flank companies), operating in the 'Austrian' column of General Ferraris. It was a limited success but gave the British Army the first of its many folklorish incidents produced by the wars of the era, when Lt-Col Charles Doyle of the 14th ordered his drummers to beat the French revolutionary and cut-throat march *Ça Ira* to 'break the scoundrels to their own damned tune'. (This tune, remarkably similar to the British 'patriotic' melody

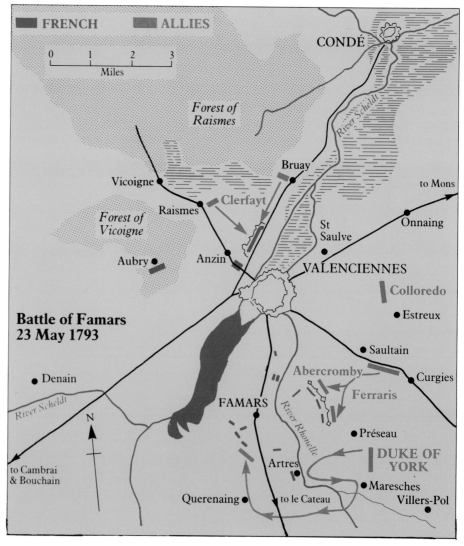

*The Downfall of Paris*, remained ever after the regimental march of the 14th Foot and the West Yorkshire Regiment which it became in 1881.) Following the capture of Valenciennes, the British government ordered the Duke to besiege Dunkirk. On the march on 18 August the Duke received a request from the Prince of Orange to help his Dutch forces recover the town of Lincelles, near Menin, which the French had just occupied. The Duke ordered General Lake's Guards brigade to assist, but arriving to find no Dutch there, Lake attacked immediately with the bayonet and put the French to flight. Fortunately no French counter-attack was mounted as the Duke had left Lake without support, jeopardising the best elements of the army to no purpose.

The siege of Dunkirk had to be abandoned (with the loss of the siege-train) following the defeat by the French General Houchard of the Hanoverian-Hessian part of the Duke's army, commanded by the Hanoverian General Walmoden, at Hondschoote on 8 September, despite a most sterling defence by the outnumbered Germans. Some fighting occurred in the remainder of the year, with the Allies on the defensive, but the Netherlands campaign ended without decisive result. In part this was offset by the capture of the main French naval base at Toulon by an Anglo-Spanish-French royalist force, and the

*A light infantryman, 1791. The traditional items of light infantry dress included a small leather cap and a short-tailed jacket. (Engraving by F D Soiron after H Bunbury)*

*The Duke of York. He resigned as Commander-in-Chief in 1809 following a scandal regarding the disposal of commissions, involving his mistress. (Engraving by Skelton after Beechey)*

occupation of Corsica, though it is interesting to observe that these operations and those against the French West Indies diverted resources which could have gone to the army in the Netherlands, which was constantly ill-provided to the extent that the patriotic 'United Society' had to send vast quantities of clothing to them to prevent the army freezing to death in the winter; it demonstrated the government's inability to concentrate its resources upon one theatre, and by so doing leave all its operations short.

The army at the beginning of the 1794 campaign was in much the same state as it had fought in late 1793, deprived of most of the promised reinforcements; in April it numbered four Guards battalions (one extra formed from the flank companies of the other three), Abercromby's same three line regiments (14th, 37th and 53rd) and 28 cavalry squadrons drawn from 14 regiments, formed in four brigades. Conditions were inauspicious for success, but the campaign was brightened by a number of conspicuous British victories. At Villers-en-Cauchies on 24 April the 15th Light Dragoons and an Austrian hussar regiment charged a body of French cavalry, who wheeled aside to reveal a 'masked battery' and a large body of infantry; the 15th charged on unchecked and routed the whole. (The 15th in so doing saved the Emperor Francis II and his entourage from capture, and eight of their officers were rewarded by the striking and presentation of an Imperial gold medal.) General Mansel with a brigade of British 'heavies' had been criticized for his ineptitude on this occasion, but made amends at Beaumont on 26 April when he charged with Austrian cuirassiers and put to flight a force of perhaps 20,000, capturing 22 guns, though at the cost of Mansel's life. On 10 May at Willems the cavalry again distinguished itself, breaking some French infantry squares (which

had been disordered by artillery bombardment), inflicting between 1,000 and 2,000 casualties and capturing 13 guns.

These successes were few, as the campaign swung against the Allies, resulting both from an improvement in the French forces and the ineptitude of the Austrian supreme command; the Allies were defeated at Tourcoing (18 May) and fought a drawn battle at Tournai (23 May), Allied defeat perhaps being saved by the stalwart conduct of the 14th, 37th and 53rd. In June Lord Moira arrived at Ostend with 7,000 reinforcements (including the 33rd Foot under Lt-Col Arthur Wesley), but they were too few to affect the outcome of the campaign, as French successes multiplied and the Allies began to bicker amongst themselves. The British forces had to withstand another appalling winter in 1794/95, gradually withdrawing through Holland and into Germany, from where the army was evacuated (from Bremen) in April 1795, having suffered some 6,000 casualties in the withdrawal from the Leck, mostly to sickness and exhaustion. The almost total lack of provision for the army in this most bitter of winters, with commissariat, medical and administration totally ineffective, set at nothing the efforts of those officers who did their utmost, among them Wesley of the 33rd whose regiment was one of the best. The nursery-rhyme 'The Grand Old Duke of York' disguises a chaotic end to Britain's first continental campaign of the era; but at least, as Wellington later admitted, it taught him 'how not to do it', though at appalling cost.

# India

The operations undertaken in India diverted a proportion of the nation's resources, though the actual number of troops employed there was not excessive due to the administration of the British territories in the subcontinent being controlled by the Honourable East India Company. Originally a trading company, its original mercantile aims were overtaken as it became almost a sovereign state, with the power to declare war on any of the indigenous Indian states. The Company maintained its own army, a small number of European units and a larger body of native regiments, commanded by British officers and equipped and trained in British style, including even the distinctive red coat. 'John Company' was thus capable of waging war on its own, but from the middle of the century it was usual for a small number of British regiments to be stationed in India, under the command of the Governor-General, to form a reliable nucleus. British warfare in India was conducted on European systems of tactics; but as the British were almost invariably heavily outnumbered, the common expedient was to attack the Indians rapidly whenever the opportunity arose, to give them no time to employ their weight of numbers. This offensive spirit was adopted initially by Wellesley (who arrived in India in 1706

with the 33rd), but was curbed in his European campaigns, where circumstances were very different.

Although the operations in India were against native rulers hostile to Britain, a measure of French influence existed, encouraging hostilities to divert British resources from Europe. The Third Mysore War had ended in 1792 with the defeat of Tippoo Sahib, ruler of Mysore; and in 1795-96 Ceylon was taken from the Dutch, the native king recognising British sovereignty. In 1799 war again erupted with Tippoo, who had been canvassing French support, and the new Governor-General, Richard Wellesley, Lord Mornington (Arthur Wellesley's elder brother) sent two armies into Mysore to crush the ruthless Tippoo. (By this time, Arthur had followed Mornington in altering the family name from 'Wesley' to its earlier form.) The forces included armies from the Madras and Bombay 'presidencies' (the divisions of the East India Company territory), stiffened by British regiments, and the allied contingent of the Nizam of Hyderabad. Command was vested in General George Harris, with young Wellesley of the 33rd in subordinate command, doubtless profiting from his brother's appointment.

On 4 May Tippoo's capital of Seringapatam was stormed, and Tippoo slain.

In May 1800 Wellesley was given his first, small independent command, Company forces plus the 19th and 25th Light Dragoons and 73rd and 77th Foot, to hunt down an obnoxious bandit, Doondia Wao. Not until 10 September was he engaged, Wellesely leading a cavalry charge which scattered the enemy and killed Doondia, an achievement which marked the beginning of Wellesely's rise to prominence and gave him invaluable experience of organising rapid movements and administering his own commissariat. This experience stood him in excellent stead for, now as Sir Arthur, he was given command of the army sent against Holkar of Indore, who had deposed the British-backed hereditary ruler of the Mahrathas, the Peshwa Baji Rao II. The Second Maratha War (1803-05) established Wellesley as a general of repute, his offensive into the Deccan being part of the strategy devised by his brother, now Marquis Wellesley, for a simultaneous operation was launched farther north, in Hindustan, commanded by General Gerard Lake. The Maratha armies were well-equipped and French-trained, Lake's opposing army actually being commanded by a French mercenary, Pierre Perron.

In the Deccan, Wellesley captured Poona on 20 March 1803 and restored the Peshwa; the main Maratha army, of one of the leaders of the Maratha Confederacy, Doulut Rao Scindia, withdrew before Wellesley's small force. Sir Arthur commanded some 11,000 of his own army (only the 19th Light Dragoons and 74th and 78th were Europeans), plus the 9,000-strong Hyderabad contingent (with one European regiment, the Scotch Brigade, later 94th) and a host of allied Mysore and Maratha horse. On 8/11 August Wellesley besieged and stormed Scindia's fort at Ahmednuggur; as a Maratha chief wrote, the English are strange people and their general a wonderful man; 'they came here in the morning, walked over the wall, killed all the garrison, and returned to breakfast.' Continuing his advance, Wellesley some-

*The death of Tippoo Sahib (or Tipu Sultan) (1749-99) at the storming of Seringapatam, 4 May 1799; the British infantry shown wear the 'round hat', often worn with a fur crest, worn as protection against tropical climates. (Engraving by Walker after Singleton)*

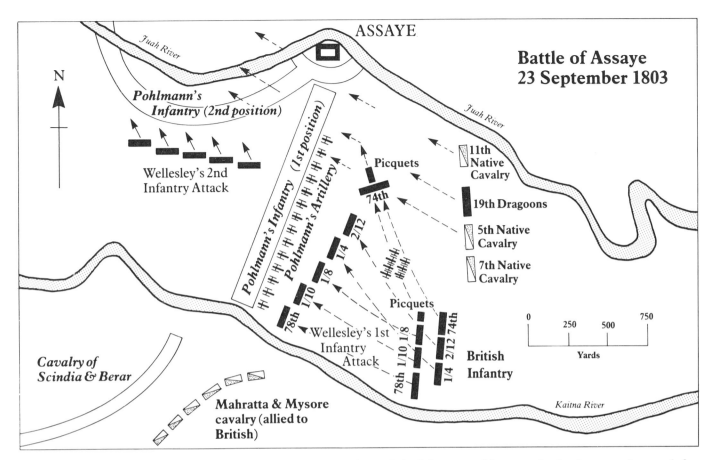

ASSAYE

**Battle of Assaye
23 September 1803**

*Juah River*

*Juah River*

N

*Pohlmann's
Infantry (2nd position)*

Wellesley's 2nd
Infantry Attack

*Pohlmann's Infantry (1st position)*

*Pohlmann's Artillery*

Picquets

74th

2/12

1/4

1/8

1/10

78th

Wellesley's 1st
Infantry
Attack

Picquets

78th  1/10  1/8

1/4  2/12  74th

11th
Native
Cavalry

19th Dragoons

5th Native
Cavalry

7th Native
Cavalry

**British
Infantry**

0    250    500    750

**Yards**

*Kaitna River*

*Cavalry of
Scindia & Berar*

**Mahratta & Mysore
cavalry (allied to
British)**

*General Sir David Baird (1757-1829);
surviving four years in Mysore captivity,
Baird led the storm of Seringapatam in
1799, and lost an arm at Corunna, his last
active command. He is shown here in staff
uniform. (Engraving by T. Hodgetts after
Sir Henry Raeburn)*

what unexpectedly found Scindia's army at Assaye on 23 September, comprising 20-30,000 cavalry, 12,000 European-led infantry and over 100 guns, together numbering 40-50,000 men. Against them, Wellesley had but 7,000 men, including only 1,500 Europeans (19th L.D., 74th and 78th); yet determined to attack rather than be attacked himself. It was a most desperate battle which could have gone either way; Wellesely personally led from the front, losing two horses beneath him, but in the final result the courage of his army, both European and Indian, won the day, though at terrible cost. Some 1,584 men were casualties, 301 in the 74th (which had begun the day with but 500 rank-and-file), whose courage Wellesley never forgot, especially their stand against masses of Maratha cavalry. The one-armed Capt A. B. Campbell of the 74th exemplifies the fortitude shown by the whole army: charging with the 19th, his remaining wrist was broken but he held his reins in his teeth and swung his sword with the injured arm.

Continuing the offensive, Wellesley's army came up with Scindia's forces at Argaum on 29 November 1803. Despite

his troops having been on the march for nine hours, Wellesley again attacked; this time his casualties were only 361, but the Marathas, though 30-40,000 against Wellesley's 10-11,000, were totally routed. The campaign ended with Wellesley's storm of the fortress of Gawilghur on 15 December; his reputation was established. Coupled with Wellesley's successes, Lake's campaign in Hindustan brought Scindia to heel. On 4 September the city of Aligarh was stormed and captured; on 16 September the Marathas were defeated at Delhi; and after a remarkable forced march by Lake's infantry, they were finally beaten at Laswaree on 1 November. Almost a year later, Holkar again took the field but, caught after a two-week, 350-mile pursuit, was defeated by Lake at Furruckabad on 17 November 1804, losing 3,000 dead to only two British, the damage mostly done by the 8th Light Dragoons. After being pursued into the Punjab, Holkar surrendered in December 1805. No other major campaigns occurred in India until the Nepal War of 1814-16, though some disquiet was caused by a sepoy mutiny at Vellore in 1806, which was suppressed rapidly.

109

# The Cape – 1795, and North Holland – 1799

The European situation in mid-1795 was not auspicious; the French had stopped the Allied attack on their territory, the Netherlands had been lost with the British expedition evacuated, and an attempt to support the fading royalist counter-revolution had resulted in a landing of British *émigré* troops at Quiberon, conveyed by the British fleet; it was overwhelmed by the republicans, an example of the recklessness of the government in committing unprepared troops on missions of little hope.

Though Holland was lost, there was a chance of securing the Dutch colonies, especially the Cape of Good Hope, which would sever the French route to India and would help negate the potential danger of Mauritius as a nest of privateers to attack the British India merchant-trade. The first part of the Cape expedition, the 2/78th Highlanders, was despatched in March 1795 under command of Major-General Craig, with a strong reinforcement (2/84th, 95th and 98th) under Major-General Alured Clarke following. Had they found the Cape already occupied by French reinforcements, they were to progress to the Dutch colonies in the east Indies.

The expedition arrived off the Cape on 12 June, whereupon Craig and the naval commander, Commodore Elphinstone, requested the Cape Town authorities to obey a letter they brought from the Prince of Orange and accept British 'protection'; the reply was hostile so Craig sent a message to hurry along Clarke's reinforcement and also bring every spare man from the British base of St Helena. Craig disembarked and occupied Simonstown on 14 July, and began to march upon Cape Town itself with his tiny force, the 78th and detachments of sailors and marines from the fleet, opposed by 800 Dutch regulars and over 2,000 militia. He had no artillery until the arrival of a detachment from St Helena, and was about to be attacked on 3 September when the signal of the fleet's arrival caused the Dutch to hesitate; Clarke's reinforcement had arrived just in time.

When the whole British force had disembarked, eight battalions were formed, the four infantry battalions, a grenadier battalion formed by detaching their grenadiers, two battalions of seamen and one of marines; they marched with the artillery in the centre of an oblong formation, protected by a unit of seamen armed with pikes, with six light companies in skirmish order on the flanks: four from the infantry, one of the St Helena detachment and one of seamen. This serves to demonstrate how, by judicious re-organisation, a force of ostensibly four battalions could be turned into an effective miniature army, and it is testimony to the adaptability of the naval personnel that their light company (commanded by Lieut Campbell of HMS *Echo*) was every bit as effective as the trained light-infantrymen. On 20 August the British forces were given a General Order describing the resistance they might expect from the Cape militia: 'taking advantage of the Irregularity of the Country, to annoy us with a distant & Irregular Fire . . . gaining our flank [and] even getting in our Rear . . . As from this mode of Warfare so much must depend upon our Fire, the Officers will see the necessity of rendering it effectual by attending to the Coolness of the Men, & above all that they do not throw away their ammunition by firing uselessly . . . One Company thus united will be a Match for all the Burgher Cavalry of the Settlement . . .' What is especially interesting is that the tactics described and the counters suggested are uncannily similar to those which would be encountered in the Boer War a century later.

In the event, though the colonists surrounded the column on its march and

*The Cape of Good Hope: this contemporary print shows British ships of war approaching the harbour; the small craft in the foreground flies the Dutch ensign. The forts and defence-works are visible along the shoreline.*

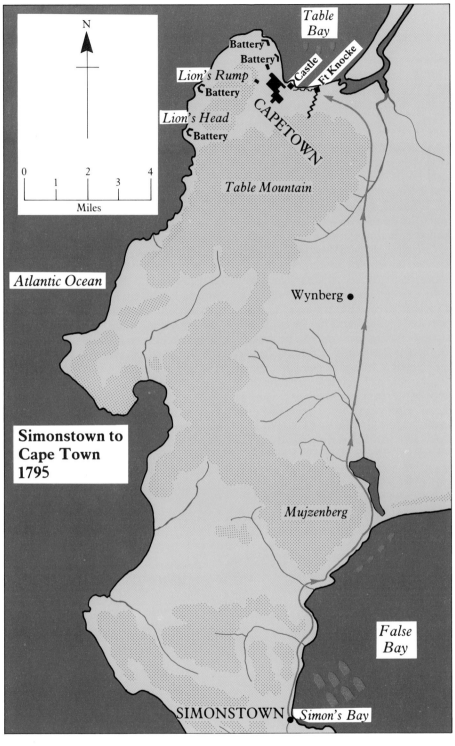

**Simonstown to Cape Town 1795**

kept up a harrassing fire, only one British soldier was killed and 17 wounded in the six-mile march; at Wynberg the colonists attempted to stand, but when the British force deployed they retired and sued for peace. The British force at the Cape was increased, and in 1796 captured a Dutch fleet sent to attempt its re-capture. The Cape was returned to Dutch control in 1803, but permanently re-occupied two years later.

In 1798 a small British and *émigré* force was sent to Portugal under General Charles Stuart, to serve under Portuguese control in response to an appeal for help; but the next major undertaking was an expedition under the Duke of York to north Holland in 1799, in concert with a Russian expeditionary force, hoping to raise popular support to restore the Prince of Orange and expel the French.

The British Army of 1799 was now better prepared with Dundas' system of training now universal; but though some administrative problems had been solved, the supply system remained poor, transportation almost non-existent, and the government persisted in sending troops abroad unprepared for active service, so that great numbers fell sick from cold or privation. In July 1799, in an attempt to increase the number of trained men available, the government passed an Act which permitted volunteers to be admitted from the Militia into certain regiments under privileged terms, in that they would not be required to serve outside Europe nor be drafted to other regiments.

The landing in Holland was made on 27 August, with some 12,000 infantry, 200 cavalry and 600 artillery, the capable Abercromby successfully making a lodgement. Three days later the entire Dutch fleet surrendered, a major success, but the military operations were less satisfactory; co-operation with the Russians was poor, supplies and transport wretched, and the predicted Orange rising never occurred. On 19 September the Duke of York's combined Allied army engaged General Brune's Franco-Batavians at Bergen; the raw British troops fought well but the Russians, many more concerned with drink and plunder, were routed. On 2 October the situation was reversed when the French were beaten, again at Bergen. Many of the British had (on incredibly mistaken orders) left their packs behind and were without water for 24 hours, until a rainstorm relieved them, typical of the mismanagement of support. The Allies were again checked at Castricum on 6 October, which convinced the Duke that further campaigning was pointless. On 18 October, by the Convention of Alkmaar, the Allied forces evacuated Holland, the Duke of York's last active campaign. The imperfections of the supply-system had caused chaos, but improvements could be attempted, and a great advantage had been found by the employment of the Militiamen, who despite their inexperience had performed admirably; a great acquisition to the army, as Abercromby declared.

# The West Indies

The West Indies figured large in the plans of the British government, especially in the period before 1802. The British colonies which had been long-established – principally Jamaica and Barbados, as Trinidad was Spanish, captured in 1797 and ceded to Britain by the Peace of Amiens – was a vital source of sugar, spices, coffee, cocoa and cotton, and the maintenance of the colonies could be guaranteed by the powerful political influence of the 'West India lobby' which represented the mercantile interest. The other territories included the Leeward Islands (principally St Kitts, Nevis, Antigua and Dominica, British), the Windward Islands (Grenada and St Vincent, British, and the French St Lucia), the French Guadeloupe and Martinique, Dutch Curacao and Franco-Spanish Hispaniola or San Domingo (now Haiti). The capture of the islands controlled by Britain's enemies was regarded as vital in depriving those states of the goods and revenue and in increasing British revenue from the Caribbean. The importance of the West Indies at times diverted the government from what might have been regarded as more important military operations; for example, Henry Dundas, the somewhat injudicious Secretary of State for War, wrote to Abercromby in 1793 concerning the lack of support received by the Duke of York's army in the Netherlands, to the effect that the country would never forgive an administration for sacrificing the French West Indies simply 'for the sake of feeding an army under a Prince of the blood'!

Compared to European campaigns, the actions fought in the West Indies were on a small scale, all attacks on enemy islands involving amphibious landings; but West Indian operations proved more costly than a dozen pitched battles, as the fevers prevalent in the area swallowed up vast numbers of men, as many as 80,000 dying or being invalided between 1794 and 1796, of which as many as 40,000 died. Accounts of regiments being decimated within weeks or returning home as skeleton cadres are legion, but only when such statistics are compared with the total garrisons can the enormity of the problem be appreciated. In the Windward and Leeward Islands in 1796, 41.3 per cent of the troops employed *died* (6,585 from 15,928); in the month of October alone, 11.4 per cent (1,273 men) died. The annual ratio of mortality varied from a low of 7.7 per cent in 1813 to over 20 per cent in 1796-97 and 1804, averaging 13.4 per cent between 1796 and 1828. In 1835 Henry Marshall, Deputy Inspector-General of Army Hospitals, calculated that during this period the mortality in the Windwards and Leewards was nine times that of the army in Ireland, and in Jamaica ten times.

Consequently, the West Indies became a most unpopular posting for British regiments; officers wishing to avoid service there found themselves unable to dispose of their commissions at a proper rate, and the rank-and-file always feared joining one regiment only to be drafted to another serving in a fever-hole. To supplement the regular regiments, much use was made of 'foreign corps' ranging from *émigrés* sent from Europe to locally-raised European units previously in enemy service, with some use of bad characters in what were virtually penal regiments. In addition, it was found useful to form regiments of 'natives' under British control, as they were found to endure the climate better than Europeans (from 1810-28 the annual mortality-rate in Jamaica averaged 15.5 per cent for European troops and 5.5 per cent for Negroes). These were originally small independent corps such as Malcolm's Royal Rangers (raised in Martinique in 1794 under Lt Malcolm of the 41st, an early exponent of rifle and light infantry tactics), the Carolina Black Corps and the St Vincent Rangers, though they were re-organised into twelve numbered West India Regiments, reduced to nine by 1804. Their rank-and-file were composed in part of the inhabitants of the West Indies (Negro, Creole or Mulatto), but 'New Blacks' (i.e. newly-arrived African slaves) were enlisted in many; in the 5th West India Regt, for example, only 10.8 per cent of recruits were West Indian Negroes, the remainder being African, with a tiny proportion of Europeans and East Indian lascars. The West Indian regiments were generally good troops, though the 8th Regt mutinied at Dominica in 1802; the 5th was present in the New Orleans campaign.

San Domingo (Haiti), part French, part Spanish, in 1793 was in a state of total anarchy, much of the white population having fled or perished in native revolts, with sections of the French/native population supporting the republican government. A British expedition was landed in 1793 into this horrendous, fever-ridden island, and clung on until

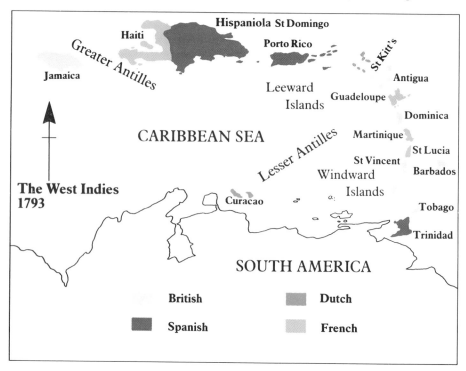

The West Indies 1793

CARIBBEAN SEA

SOUTH AMERICA

Greater Antilles
Lesser Antilles

Jamaica
Haiti
Hispaniola  St Domingo
Porto Rico
St Kitt's
Antigua
Leeward Islands
Guadeloupe
Dominica
Martinique
St Lucia
St Vincent
Windward Islands
Barbados
Curacao
Tobago
Trinidad

British   Dutch
Spanish   French

October 1798. From its geographical position it had some significance, but nothing to justify the expense in money and lives which the British government poured in during the five years' occupation. Eventually, after the ravages of yellow fever and almost uninterrupted violence throughout the island, an accommodation was made with the skilled Negro general Toussaint l'Ouverture (1743-1803) and British forces withdrew; Toussaint eventually united Haiti by occupying the Spanish part, but was overthrown by a French attempt to recover the island and died a prisoner in France. (Like the British, the French forces withered away and left Haiti to a renewed bout of civil war). The abortive and pointless British occupation had cost the Treasury over four millions sterling, and the army countless thousands of lives. It was one of the most futile operations ever mounted.

Elsewhere, the West Indian operations enjoyed more success, as the French colonies of Martinique, St Lucia and Guadeloupe were captured in 1794. In all these operations, which relied totally upon collaboration with the Royal Navy,

*The landing at and capture of Fort Royal, Martinique, February/March 1794, by General Sir Charles Grey. In this print by Clayton the first wave of troops is rowed ashore by seamen; the men in fur caps apparently represent one of Grey's composite grenadier battalions.*

much use was made of additional battalions formed by amalgamating the flank companies of numerous regiments; General Grey's force in 1794, for example, which captured these islands included nine ordinary battalions, three 'grenadier battalions' (elements from 25 regiments) and three similarly-composed 'light battalions'. This considerable effort was to little purpose as the energetic if brutal French mulatto governor, Victor Hugues, recovered Guadeloupe, Grey's expedition being wrecked by disease which cost perhaps 5,000 of the 7,000 troops originally involved. Native revolts occurred in Grenada, St Lucia, and the 'Maroon revolt' in Jamaica, partially inspired by the French; the British were driven from St Lucia and for a time the situation was perilous, the British clinging on grimly against both

the enemy, local insurrections and disease, with army commanders pleading for more troops which the government always promised but rarely sent.

Some of the territory so desperately won was returned to France at the Peace of Amiens, and had to be re-taken again; St Lucia and Tobago in June 1803, for example, and Dutch colonies were also occupied, like Demarera in September 1803 and Surinam in April/May 1804. From this period, British fortunes were in the ascendant, despite sharp fighting which arose from French attempts to re-establish their power (Dominica, for example, was defended gallantly in 1805). It was fortunate, however, that more French resources could not be expended in the West Indies. Though the possession of the islands had succeeded in destroying much of the French West Indian trade, the government had miscalculated at least in the earlier period, never expecting to have to fight not only a few fever-ridden Frenchmen but also much of the Negro population; so that whilst destroying the French West Indian trade, they almost destroyed the British Army as well.

# Egypt, 1801

From 1798 the French 'Army of the Orient' had been campaigning in Egypt and Palestine, operations instigated by the rising star of the French army, Napoleon Bonaparte, with the intention of establishing a French 'empire' and threatening British possession in India by an overland route. Bonaparte was opposed by the forces of the Ottoman Empire which received the assistance of British forces in the Mediterranean. The Royal Navy wrecked Bonaparte's scheme, by Nelson's destruction of the French fleet at Aboukir Bay, and by the Ottoman defence of Acre, commanded by the audacious British naval captain Sydney Smith. Although Bonaparte abandoned his army in late 1799 and returned to France (to make himself dictator and, shortly, Emperor), the French forces remained in Egypt, commanded by General Jean-Baptiste Kléber (1753-1800), and after his assassination by a fanatic on 14 June 1800, by General Jacques-François de Menou (1750-1810).

After a number of abortive plans for attacking the French in the Mediterranean (including an attempt on Cadiz in October 1800, which even went so far as getting the troops into their invasion-barges), the government resolved to accede to Ottoman requests to send an army to expel the French from Egypt. Its urgency was due to the changeable nature of the insane Czar, who since the unsuccessful 1799 campaign in the Netherlands had swung against Britain, and if he succeeded in mobilising a northern coalition against Britain part of the British fleet might have to be withdrawn from the Mediterranean, giving Bonaparte the chance of either reinforcing the French in Egypt or evacuating them. Command of the expedition to Egypt was given to Sir Ralph Abercromby (1734-1801), Britain's most capable soldier of the time. The Duke of York rightly considered him a pattern for the army: an able soldier, he was a humane man of liberal inclination (having refused to fight in America during the fratricidal War of Independence) and would do his duty to the death. His experience in the two expeditions to the Netherlands, in the West Indies and in the Mediterranean must have caused him to doubt the direc-

tion of the government, and especially Henry Dundas; but despite receiving vague instructions for the Egyptian expedition, no man was better equipped to command it.

Abercromby's force numbering some 15,500 fit men (at least 1,500 were sick) left Malta in December 1800, anchoring in Marmorice Bay, 40 miles north of Rhodes, on the 29th/30th, there to meet an expected Ottoman force with which it was to co-operate. (Further reinforcements had been promised from India.) The Turks, however, were totally unprepared, and it was clear that Abercromby was on his own; moreover he was expected to land in Egypt with only the water which could be delivered by the navy, for none was reported available until Alexandria should be captured. Dismayed but undaunted, Abercromby remarked that 'there are risks in a British warfare unknown in any other service' – i.e. the unpreparedness and ignorance of the government – and proceeded to train his troops in the techniques of disembarkation by longboat and cutter, so as to avoid the chaotic scenes which had occurred in Holland in 1799. Even though he calculated that the French might be able to mass as few as 10,000

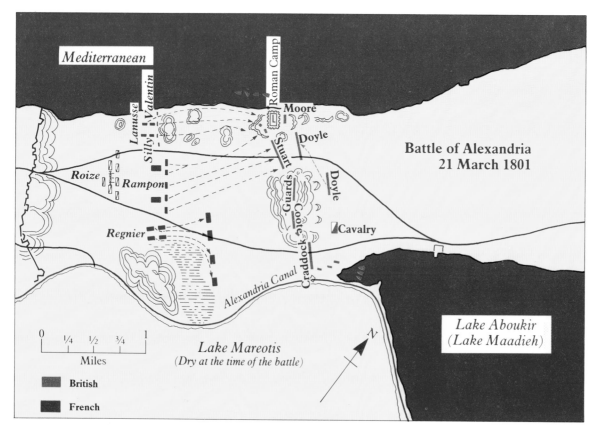

troops to oppose the landing, he knew that his boats were sufficient to land only 6,000 men. (Total French strength was probably around 17,000 fully fit plus 6-7,000 invalids or garrison troops.)

The fleet arrived off Aboukir Bay on 2 March 1801, Abercromby making a personal reconnaissance in a cutter with his capable assistant, Major-General John Moore, who had served with him in the West Indies. On 8 March the weather had moderated enough for a landing to be attempted. As the boats drew in they were caught in a furious cross-fire causing 700 casualties and sinking some boats, but so well-rehearsed had been the landing that within twenty minutes of touching ground, Moore had routed the strong French force and captured their artillery. Abercromby landed his supplies and began a slow advance; his few horses were given to his tiny force of cavalry and his guns (apparently 16 of the 82 with which the expedition was equipped) were dragged agonisingly through the shifting sands by teams of sailors. An encounter battle developed as the advance ran into the French on 13 March; though the French were repelled with the loss of 500 men, their superiority in artillery and cavalry cost Abercromby 1,230 soldiers and 84 sailors killed and wounded. Abercromby was further disadvantaged by a complete lack of intelligence about French strength

*The battle of Alexandria, 21 March 1801; probably the most accurate portrayal of the battle, from an original by Lieut Willermin of the Royal Staff Corps. In the centre foreground Sir Ralph Abercromby struggles with French cavalry and is rescued by men of the 42nd.*

and terrain, and by the fact that both he and his deputy, Major-General Hutchinson, were extremely short-sighted.

Abercromby erected defences to cover an evacuation should it become necessary, and prepared to attack the French positions. On the early morning of 21 March, however, it was the French who attacked and a fierce battle developed, Moore handling the British defence with great skill. Especially savage was a French cavalry charge which pierced the British position, disordering the 42nd Highlanders who lost their formation but stood their ground as individuals, whilst the 28th's rear rank faced-about to fire at the French in their rear; they and a French unit bombarded each other with stones when both ran out of ammunition. As the French rode through the Highlanders they were shattered by volleys from the 40th and Stuart's Minorca Regt, and the last French attack was spent. Abercromby was temporarily captured in this mêlée, but immediately liberated by a man of the 42nd; and towards the close of the battle he was shot

in the thigh. By 9 am the battle was over. Moore reported that his men were without ammunition for an hour, but had the French attacked again, so good was their spirit that they would have replied with the bayonet.

The worthy old Abercromby was carried to the fleet to have his wound attended, covered in a soldier's blanket; his last order before turning command over to Hutchinson was that he must be given the name of the man who owned it, as 'a soldier's blanket is of great consequence' and must be returned. It was typical of the man, who sadly died of gangrene on 28 March.

Blockading the French in Alexandria with some 5,000 British and large numbers of ill-disciplined Turkish irregulars of dubious worth, Hutchinson began an audacious advance on Cairo, which almost provoked a revolt among his officers. The French were now homesick and demoralised, Cairo surrendering on 27 June and Menou at Alexandria on 2 September, his men to be shipped home in British transports. Two days earlier, after a terrible desert march, Major-General David Baird's Indian expedition arrived, too late to be of any use. The Egyptian campaign had ended with British success, due largely to the quality of the troops and their commander. The army was improving: the chaos of the Netherlands was past.

# South America 1806-1807

As soon as the Peace of Amiens was concluded in 1802, as usual the government began to reduce the military and naval forces. When war was resumed exactly a year later the Militia was re-embodied and camps of instruction were established in Sussex, Kent and Essex, the most important being Shorncliffe where Moore began to train his light infantry. An Anglo-Russian attempt to recover Hanover landed on the Elbe in late 1805 but achieved nothing and withdrew; and to protect Sicily from invasion (the realm of Britain's ally, the ex-king of Naples), an expedition under Sir James Craig was sent to southern Italy. The Allied supreme commander, the Russian General Lacy, was a septuagenarian who (according to Bunbury, Craig's Quarter-master-General) spoke with a strong Irish brogue (being the son of an Irish emigrant) and 'showed no trace of ever having been a man of talent or information'; at councils of war Lacy put on his nightcap and went to sleep, leaving his subordinates to decide policy. Naples was indefensible, as the Neapolitan troops were worthless, so the expedition returned to Sicily. A major success occurred in July 1806, however, when Craig's successor Sir John Stuart landed in Calabria and routed a French army under General Reynier at Maida, the first major action against the French on land since Bonaparte's assumption of the title of Emperor Napoleon.

There now occurred an adventure which can only be regarded as an aberration. In late 1805 an expedition was mounted to re-take the Cape, recently restored to the Dutch at Amiens. The troops numbered some 6,360, commanded by Sir David Baird, an officer of skill and experience, escorted by the fleet of Sir Home Popham, a naval officer recognised as an expert at amphibious warfare, well-connected with the government and popular in the navy, if over-keen on prize-money. In January 1806 Baird's force disembarked at the Cape, to be opposed only by some 1,200 Dutch and Waldeck regulars, a unit of French seamen and a rough burgher militia. A sharp skirmish (in which the regulars ran but the seamen and militia fought) decided the issue, and Cape Colony was delivered to Britain on 18 January.

Popham now conceived an incredible plan, probably originating from his contact with the Venezuelan agitator Miranda, who had tried since 1783 to persuade Britain to invade South America and liberate its colonies from Spanish rule, but who the British government recognised as an untrustworthy adventurer. Popham saw great personal advantage in leading a crusade to free the South American colonists, and simultaneously deprive Spain of their annual 20 million sterling income, much of which went straight to Napoleon; perhaps Popham's conversations with leading members of the government, including William Pitt, led him to believe them in favour of this scheme. He therefore persuaded Baird to lend him from the Cape garrison the 71st Highlanders under Col Beresford, the future marshal of Portugal, to accompany his fleet; Popham took the whole of his fleet and inveigled the governor of St Helena to add 400 more men to the expedition, and sailed first for Montevideo, and then Buenos Ayres. Beresford disembarked with his tiny force on 25 June 1806, defeated the half-hearted Spanish resistance and received the surrender of the city, a considerable achievement for the loss of one man killed and a dozen wounded. The million dollars prize money sent home was probably what Popham had really set out to acquire, but Beresford's position was perilous, for the immense Spanish possessions could not be subdued and showed no inclination to accept the British as liberators, even though they seized the chance to throw off Spanish rule. Beresford immediately requested reinforcements from Baird, who allocated some 2,200 men from the Cape.

When dispatches reached home, the government was presented with a *fait accompli*; though the expedition was without sanction, they had little option but support Beresford. (Popham, incredibly, circulated the leading London merchants with a report that he had opened for them a huge new market, attempting, perhaps, to rally support for the expedition.) Beresford found a mounting tide of hostility, led by Santiago de Liniers, a French officer in Spanish service, who had at first co-operated with the British; but the colonists, recognising that the expedition was too weak to fend off any Spanish counter-attack, felt themselves placed in unnecessary hazard and much as they wished to be rid of the Spanish yoke,

*'The Glorious Conquest of Buenos Ayres by the British Forces': engraving by G. Thompson, published 1806, showing the 71st Highlanders landing with naval support; Beresford stands to the right of the furled Colour.*

gathered to attack Beresford. After a brave fight his tiny command was compelled to surrender, before any reinforcements, either from the Cape or from Britain, could reach him.

Now taken up by South American affairs, Secretary of War William Windham organised an expedition under Robert Craufurd, 4,500 strong, to capture the province of Chile and establish a chain of posts across the Andes to link Chile with Buenos Ayres, a plan so utterly absurd as to defy belief. Almost as useless was the instruction given to Sir Arthur Wellesley to prepare a plan for the invasion of Mexico, by Europeans and black troops from the west and from the east by sepoys from India. Fortunately neither expedition came to pass. Meanwhile, a reinforcement for Beresford diverted from Portugal under Sir

Samuel Auchmuty had reached South America, where it picked up Baird's Cape reinforcement which for the past three months had been entrenched at Maldonado, under continual harassment from the colonists. With this weak and sickly force, about 6,300 plus 1,400 seamen, Auchmuty decided to capture Montevideo, which he accomplished on 3 February after a sharp fight.

The government sent a new commander to South America, the ex-Inspector-General of Recruiting, Lt-Gen John Whitelocke (1757-1833), a man of much self-importance but devoid of ability and manners and who was regarded with contempt by the ordinary soldiers from his habit of ingratiating himself with them by the use of obscene language. Despite a further small reinforcement and Craufurd's command,

## Organisation of Whitelocke's army:

**Brig-Gen Sir S. Auchmuty's Bde:** 5th, 38th, 87th Foot.

**Brig-Gen Craufurd's Bde:** 95th Rifles (8 coys), 9 coys light infantry.

**Brig-Gen Lumley's Bde:** 17th Light Dragoons, 36th & 88th Foot.

**Col Mahon's Bde:** 2 sqdns 6th Dragoon Guards, 9th Light Dragoons (both dismounted), 40th and 45th Foot.

Whitelocke's army was not capable of achieving much due to the inability of its commander; yet devoid of transport, with hardly any cavalry, Whitelocke determined to attack Buenos Ayres, leaving his best troops to garrison Montevideo.

From the beginning the expedition was a disaster. Liniers incited the population to resist, and on 5 July 1807 the main attack went in, through the confused streets of the city, the British hungry and unprepared (dismounted cavalry, complete with high boots, were used as infantry; others had muskets so defective that they were instructed to remove their flints). Whitelocke's plan of attack was confused and the force split into many small bodies uncertain of providing mutual support; and though the troops fought with great gallantry, capturing 30 guns and over 1,000 prisoners, some detachments were cut off and forced to surrender. After sustaining almost 3,000 casualties Whitelocke sued for a truce, peace being concluded on 7 July with the British agreeing to evacuate the province. This brought to an end Britain's involvement in South America, ill-conceived and ill-managed from the beginning. Popham was court-martialled and reprimanded; Whitelocke was cashiered and declared 'totally unfit and unworthy to serve His Majesty in any military capacity whatever'. No such censure was heaped upon Windham and the ministers who having chosen the wrong man set him an impossible task.

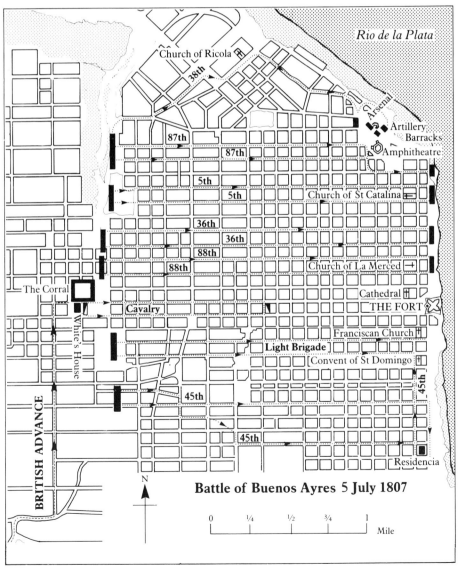

**Battle of Buenos Ayres 5 July 1807**

# Vimeiro – 21 August 1808

1807 marks an important watershed in British military operations during the Napoleonic campaigns, for it saw the beginning of the Peninsular War, Britain's most sustained military effort of the era. Before the Iberian peninsula became the seat of war, however, expeditions were mounted in 1807 to Eygpt and Denmark. The former was a useless adventure ended when a treaty was negotiated with the Ottoman Empire; that against Denmark was to prevent French seizure of the powerful Danish fleet. An expedition of 27,000 men under Lord Cathcart was sent to Copenhagen to pre-empt Napoleon; among the subordinate commanders was Sir Arthur Wellesley, home from his triumphs in India. The Danes made a brave resistance, but their troops were routed – Wellesley being conspicuously successful – Copenhagen bombarded, and the fleet captured.

Portugal refused to participate in Napoleon's 'Continental System', a prohibition of British goods throughout Europe intended to cripple Britain's economy; in retaliation Napoleon deter-

*A famous hero, Piper George Clarke of the 71st played his pipes despite severe injuries at Vimeiro. Aquatint by Clark & Dubourg after Manskirch, incorrectly showing kilts: the 71st wore* truibhs *or grey overalls at Vimeiro.*

mined to invade Portugal via his ally, Spain. Accordingly, General Jean Andoche Junot (1771-1813) was sent with 30,000 men to occupy Lisbon (1 December 1807), the Portuguese royal family fleeing to Brazil after appointing a Council of Regency, which appealed to Britain for help. In March 1808 a further 100,000 French troops marched into Spain; the king, Charles IV, and his ineffectual heir, Ferdinand, were forced to renounce the throne and interned in France. A popular rising in favour of Ferdinand was repressed brutally, and pro-French factions 'elected' as king Napoleon's elder brother, Joseph Bonaparte (1768-1844). Spanish resistance increased, with regional 'juntas' forming armies to oppose the French, but given the wretched state of the regular army, their task was impossible

without support.

Britain responded to their appeals for assistance by sending an expedition. Command was given initially to Sir Arthur Wellesley, recently promoted Lieutenant-General, with about 10,000 men; but as upon reflection this force was deemed insufficient, Sir John Moore (who had recently been sent with 10,000 men to support Sweden, an expedition which failed after disagreements with the mad Swedish king) was directed to reinforce the Peninsular expedition. Moore (1761-1809), the great trainer of light infantry, was a capable general but was politically unacceptable to the government; so, Lt-Gen Sir Hew Dalrymple (1750-1830), governor of Gibraltar, was appointed to command, with Sir Harry Burrard (1755-1813) as deputy; they were both inept.

Wellesley disembarked at Mondego Bay in Portugal in early August 1808. After a week his troops and supplies were ashore and, reinforced by 5,000 men under General Brent Spencer from Cadiz, where they had already been supporting the Spanish, set out for

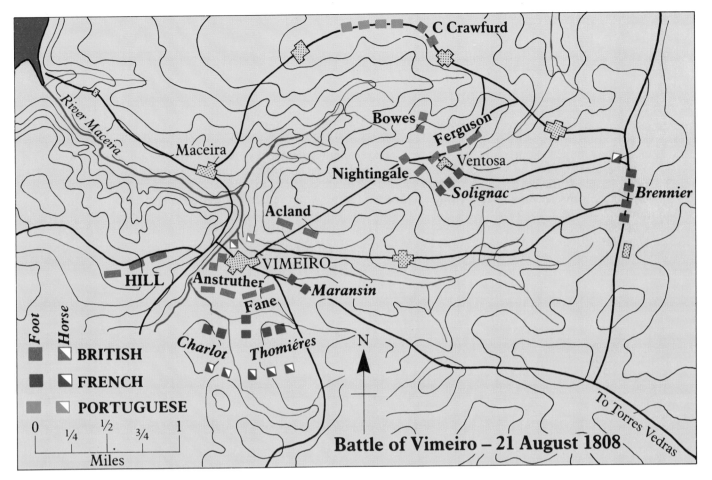

**Battle of Vimeiro – 21 August 1808**

Lisbon; Wellesley's total force was about 14,000. On 17 August he encountered the French general Henri Delaborde (1764-1833) with about 4,400 men at Roliça (known to British annals, due to a typographical error, as 'Roleia'). Delaborde withdrew and Wellesley followed; in the course of the advance, Col Lake of the 1/29th led his battalion into a gully which was assailed from the rear by the French; Lake was killed, his battalion disordered and in danger of being annihilated. To save them, Wellesley ordered a general attack which drove Delaborde off the heights; it was his first victory against the French. Having suffered 487 casualties, he resumed his advance.

Burrard's arrival supplanted Wellesley in chief command, and Burrard mistakenly ordered Wellesley to abandon his plans for advance until Moore arrived. By deciding to spend the night of 20 August aboard ship, Burrard deprived himself of commanding the army next day; and if he instead of Wellesley had won the battle of Vimeiro, history might have taken a different

course. On such small decisions can destiny depend.

Junot was determined to crush the British landing before they could receive reinforcement, and led forward some 13,000 men and 24 guns from Lisbon. He hoped to outflank the British position, but his advance was observed and Wellesley deployed his army along the crest of the Vimeiro ridge in the early hours of 21 August. Junot launched two assaults on Vimeiro hill which made some headway, almost penetrating to Vimeiro village, but the steady musketry of the British infantry drove them away. The only British cavalry present, some 240 20th Light Dragoons, countercharged the retiring French but their initial success turned to disaster as they charged too far. Meanwhile, the French right wing attempted to outflank Wellesley's left, but co-ordination with the attack on Vimeiro village was poor and they too were driven off. Having lost 2,000 men and 14 guns, Junot's mauled army withdrew, Burrard prohibiting any British pursuit despite the fact that Wellesley had suffered only 720 casualties

and that much of the army had been entirely unengaged. A pursuit would have captured Lisbon; but Burrard (who had remained out of action, waiving his right to command) was over-cautious and over-ruled his deputy.

Despite the fact that Vimeiro was a signal victory, and that Junot's position was virtually untenable, Burrard and 'Dowager' Dalrymple (who arrived the following day) agreed to a convention with the French, signed at Cintra on 22 August, by which Junot's army, baggage and plunder was to be evacuated home in British ships, keeping even their arms. This ludicrous treaty ('The Convention that Nobody owns, that saved old Junot's Baggage and Bones' according to the cartoonist Woodward) was greeted with outrage in Britain, and all three British generals were called home to face a court of enquiry, from which only Wellesley was exonerated. It was an inauspicious beginning to the Peninsular War, though Wellesley's position was enhanced both by his victories and by his being most unwilling to the Convention of Cintra.

# Corunna – 16 January 1809

After the recall of Wellesley and his superiors, command of the British expeditionary force fell upon the experienced Sir John Moore, who though his greatest fame is as a trainer and organiser, possessed considerable abilities as a general and aroused the greatest devotion among his subordinates. Yet the situation in the Peninsula at the moment of his assumption of supreme command was daunting. Moore's army was not united – 10,000 were to come from Britain with Sir David Baird – and though the quality was excellent, they were woefully equipped with transport. The government had deliberately not sent the proper stores and equipment, believing that to do so would only cause delays, but trusted to the Spanish for supplies. Moore was meant to join the main Spanish army on their positions along the Ebro, but it was left to him to decide how this was to be achieved; he opted for a march into the interior, his own force from Portugal being joined by Baird's from England, which only after some difficulty was permitted by the Spanish to land at Corunna. But co-operation with the Spanish Moore found to be impossible; the various provincial forces were in dispute, the central Junta was described by Moore in his correspondence with J.M. Frere, British 'Envoy Extraordinary' to the Spanish government, as possessing only imbecility beyond belief, and despite needing Moore's support the Spanish left him without adequate supplies or intelligence. Although he realised that the actual situation in Spain was far different from that which the British government imagined, he determined to play his part and press on, despite the lateness of the season.

Moore's headquarters left Lisbon on 26 October. As his army stumbled along the atrocious roads towards central Spain, and bereft of intelligence or assistance from the Spanish, on 5 November Napoleon himself arrived to take personal charge of operations, determined to end the Spanish war at a stroke. For a few days Moore halted at Salamanca, awaiting the concentration of his army, the artillery and cavalry under Sir John Hope and the Corunna force under Baird. On 28 November news that the Spanish had been routed five days earlier was sufficient to decide Moore to abandon the enterprise, as the Spanish had shown themselves either incapable or unwilling to collaborate; thus, he determined to retreat on Portugal. This decision was correct, but Moore was assailed by appeals from the Spanish and from the British minister not to desert them, and especially one from Madrid, which was intending to hold out against the advancing French.

On 6 December Moore decided to advance against the French communications and take pressure off Madrid; but the commander of that city never bothered to inform him that it had surrendered without striking a blow the day after the despatch of its appeal. Unaware that he had been so cruelly betrayed, Moore pressed on and found that the only French troops in the immediate vicinity were part of the corps of Marshal Nicholas Soult (1769-1851), one of Napoleon's more capable subordinates. He determined to attack and on 21 December his cavalry, commanded by the very able Lord Henry William Paget (1768-1854, later Earl of Uxbridge and Marquis of Anglesey), routed one of

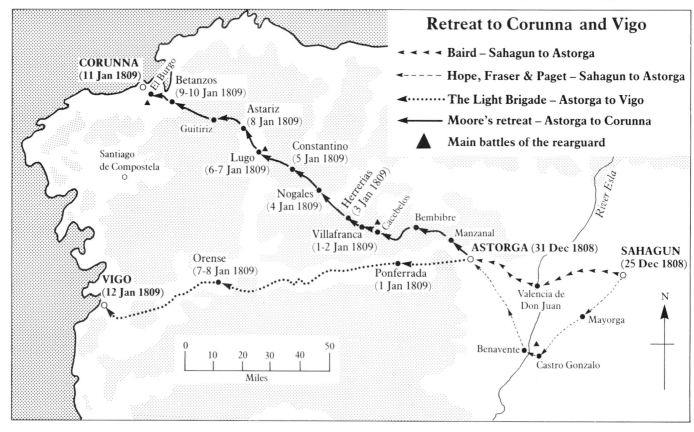

**Retreat to Corunna and Vigo**

◄ ◄ ◄ **Baird – Sahagun to Astorga**

◄- - - - **Hope, Fraser & Paget – Sahagun to Astorga**

◄· · · · · **The Light Brigade – Astorga to Vigo**

◄───── **Moore's retreat – Astorga to Corunna**

▲ **Main battles of the rearguard**

CORUNNA (11 Jan 1809)
El Burgo
Betanzos (9-10 Jan 1809)
Astariz (8 Jan 1809)
Guitiriz
Santiago de Compostela
Constantino (5 Jan 1809)
Lugo (6-7 Jan 1809)
Nogales (4 Jan 1809)
Herrerías (3 Jan 1809)
Cacebelos
Villafranca (1-2 Jan 1809)
Bembibre
Manzanal
ASTORGA (31 Dec 1808)
SAHAGUN (25 Dec 1808)
River Esla
Orense (7-8 Jan 1809)
Ponferrada (1 Jan 1809)
VIGO (12 Jan 1809)
Valencia de Don Juan
Mayorga
Benavente
Castro Gonzalo
N

0    10    20    30    40    50
Miles

*A close-range musketry duel in close formation, without skirmishes as the French attack is thrown back from the British defence-line at Corunna. (Engraving by Clarke after W Heath.)*

Soult's cavalry brigades at Sahagun. Two days later came shattering news: 150,000 French were moving against Moore, and only an immediate retreat could save the army; and a retreat not to Portugal, but to Corunna.

The French were somewhat slow in advancing, and on 29 December Paget and the cavalry rearguard fought a successful action at Benevente during which the commander of Napoleon's Imperial Guard cavalry, Charles Lefebvre-Desnouëttes (1773-1822) was captured by trooper Levi Grisdall of the 10th Hussars. But from this time discipline in Moore's army began to deteriorate as the men became progressively more disillusioned at retiring without a fight; winter was falling, the mountainous roads were atrocious and the army was starving; looting became rife and the rearguard was forced to abandon 1,000 men lying helplessly drunk in Bembibre, most of whom were slaughtered by the French vanguard. Frozen corpses and abandoned equipment littered the line of retreat; camp-followers and soldiers' wives and children died of cold and starvation as the army dragged itself towards Corunna and Vigo. Only the rearguard held together, Paget's cavalry and the Reserve (commanded by his brother, Edward Paget), which turned at bay repeatedly, holding off the French

*Sir John Moore receives his mortal wound at Corunna whilst encouraging his men, a roundshot dreadfully injuring his left shoulder. (Aquatint by T Sutherland after W Heath.)*

vanguard. The best element, the Light Brigade of the 1/43rd, 2/52nd and 2/95th, commanded by the stern disciplinarian Robert 'Black Bob' Craufurd (1764-1812), was sent to Vigo, depriving the army of an invaluable resource, for though they suffered untold privation on their march, they were unmolested. The better battalions held together, especially the Guards and the Highlanders, but others became straggling masses, though NCOs like the redoubtable Sergt. William Newman of the 43rd, who organised an *ad hoc* company and defied the pursuing French cavalry, demonstrated the spirit of the ordinary troops. Moore was horrified by the evaporation of discipline and morale; all he could say in their defence was that when the French appeared the stragglers shuffled together and seemed pleased at the prospect of fighting. Believing the war all but won, Napoleon left the army for France on 1 January 1809.

19,000 weary, ragged and starving men stumbled into Corunna on 11 January, though as usual the Guards marched in rank, in tatters but with parade-ground precision. Troop-transports arrived on 15 January and Moore embarked his sick and what remained of his artillery. Next day, as Moore prepared to evacuate the

remainder, Soult attacked with 20,000 men. The exhausted British infantry formed their ranks with as much composure as if they were exercising in Hyde Park, as one witness remarked. Moore took personal control of part of the British defensive-line covering the harbour and was with the 42nd when a man nearby screamed as a roundshot took off his leg. 'My good fellow, don't make such a noise; we must bear these things better', was Moore's comment. As the Highlanders ran out of ammunition, Moore called on them as 'my gallant countrymen' to remember they still had their bayonets; as they rallied a roundshot struck Moore's left shoulder and almost severed his arm. He was carried back to Corunna where he was told that all along the line the French had been repulsed and that the army could embark in safety. He remarked that it was a great satisfaction, and that 'I hope my country will do me justice.' He was buried on the ramparts next morning, shortly before the ragged and verminous remnants of the army were evacuated by the Royal Navy.

Despite the victory at Corunna, Moore was criticised for what was regarded as a disaster; the total losses during the campaign were about 7,000, but as Moore had reported shortly before his death, he had attracted the entire French army against him, which prevented Napoleon from administering the *coup de grâce* against the Spanish and Lisbon. Despite his mistakes, he had bought time for the war to be continued.

# Portugal and Talavera 1809

Despite Moore's retreat, the government determined to sustain the war in the Peninsula, but as before did not channel all their available resources into the one effort, diverting 40,000 men under the Earl of Chatham to capture the island of Walcheren in the Scheldt estuary, to threaten the French possession of Antwerp. Chatham's army was so decimated by the virulent 'Walcheren fever', a malarial infection, that it was evacuated with no tangible results.

Lisbon remained the main base of operations, and Sir Arthur Wellesley was appointed to command the troops in Portugal, partly on the grounds that as he was so young he could, if necessary, be superceded by a senior general without embarrassing the government. His task was to defend Portugal but not enter Spain without permission from London. Although much of Spain was in arms against the French, the Spanish armies were generally of wretched quality, and though popular risings (such as that which defended Saragossa with incredible fortitude) and the beginning of guerrilla warfare proved to be decisive in bleeding dry the French armies, such

resistance could not oppose the main field armies. In response to a request from the Portuguese Regency, William Carr Beresford (1764-1854) had been appointed Marshal of the Portuguese army to reconstruct it, and though he was a capable administrator it would be some considerable time before the Portuguese would become effective troops. Despite his appointment as Marshal-General of Portugal, giving him complete control over the Allied military forces in that country, Wellesley would have to rely initially upon his British troops. On landing in Portugal on 22 April 1809, Wellesley had about 23,000 men, but was short of artillery and woefully deficient in transport; and the commissariat was largely dependent upon hired Portuguese civilian muleteers and ox-carts. On 18 June Wellesley instituted a new divisional organisation by which the hitherto-independent brigades were integrated into a new command-structure, each division becoming a self-supporting entity, with cavalry attached by brigade rather than remaining together within a single division; the benefit of this was a major factor in the

Peninsular army's attainment of such a standard of excellence.

Two French forces threatened Portugal: Marshal Soult with about 24,000 men at Oporto, and Marshal Claude Victor (1764-1841) with 30,000 near the frontier-fortress of Badajoz. Leaving forces to hold Lisbon and watch Victor, Wellesley advanced towards Oporto, where Soult felt himself protected from attack by the breadth of the River Douro. On 11 May Wellesley slipped his leading elements over the river on four wine-barges, the first troops removing their red jackets so as not to be recognised. By the time Soult had realised what was happening it was too late, and after some resistance the French army began a full-scale retreat. When the pursuit was called off after some ten days Soult had lost around 4,500 men and all his guns and baggage.

After this signal success, which had cost Wellesley only about 150 casualties but which was hardly noticed at home, he was able to consider advancing into

*Exemplifying the recklessness of the British cavalry throughout the period, at Talavera the 23rd Light Dragoons were disordered by a hidden ravine, yet charged on without re-forming, losing 207 from 459 men.*

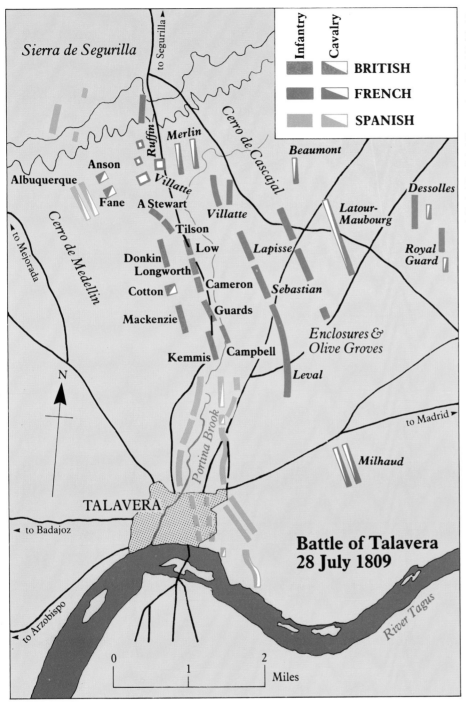

Sierra de Seguilla

to Seguilla

Cerro de Cascajal

Ruffin
Merlin
Beaumont
Anson
Albuquerque
Villatte
Fane
A Stewart
Villatte
Tilson
Low
Donkin
Longworth
Cotton
Cameron
Mackenzie
Guards
Kemmis
Campbell

Dessolles

Latour-
Maubourg

Lapisse

Royal
Guard

Sebastian

Enclosures &
Olive Groves

Leval

Cerro de Medellin

to Mejorada

N

Portina Brook

TALAVERA

to Badajoz

to Arzobispo

to Madrid

Milhaud

**Battle of Talavera
28 July 1809**

River Tagus

0      1      2
Miles

---

Spain to co-operate with the Spaniards. Wellesley obtained sanction from London to enter Spain, and began to collaborate with General Gregorio de la Cuesta (1740-1812), the Captain-General of Old Castille, a man so inept and with planning so chaotic that some British observers suspected him of treachery. Wellesley found it impossible to rely upon Cuesta or his army, but despite continuing transport problems and a lack of both money and credit, he wrote 'The

ball is now at my feet, and I hope I shall have the strength to give it a good kick.'

Wellesley and Cuesta united on 20 July 1809 and agreed to make a joint attack on Victor, who now had about 22,000 men; Wellesley had 21,000 and Cuesta 33,000. When contact was established Cuesta refused to fight on the grounds that it was Sunday, and a golden opportunity was lost; next day Victor retired and Cuesta pursued, Wellesley refusing to move any further until the

Spaniards provided the promised supplies for his half-starved troops. Cuesta returned hotfoot, pursued by 46,000 French under King Joseph Bonaparte and Marshal Jean-Baptiste Jourdan (1762-1833) who had been allowed to reinforce Victor due to the negligence of the Spanish forces. Cuesta drew up his army alongside the British, on the defence-line Wellesley had selected at Talavera. On the night of 27 July the first French attack almost succeeded in driving the British off the summit of the key high ground, the Cerro de Medellin; but though surprised, General Rowland Hill (1772-1842), commanding the 2nd Division (probably the most reliable of all British subordinate commanders in the Peninsula) repelled the French advance.

Early next morning Victor made a renewed attempt, and was again repelled when Wellesley's infantry, hidden on the reverse slope of the ridge, appeared and charged as the French were struggling up the apparently-deserted hill. After a lull in the fighting, Joseph sanctioned Victor's plan for another attempt, and leaving a small force to watch the Spaniards – who did nothing throughout the day – at about 2 pm the French launched a massive assault against Wellesley. It was a desperate fight, especially when the impetuosity of the British Guards brigade caused them to pursue a defeated French column too far, and were only rescued by the 48th which Wellesley had directed in support, foreseeing the problem; his facility to be always at the critical point was amazing. A counter-attack by the 23rd Light Dragoons ended in disaster but though Victor urged a renewed assault, Joseph abandoned the field and retired in the night, having lost a sixth of his men and 17 guns. Wellesley's army was exhausted and mauled, having lost 5,363 men, though was reinforced on the following morning by 'Black Bob' Craufurd and his Light Brigade after an astonishing forced march. With Soult threatening his communications with Portugal and the Spaniards refusing even to furnish food, Wellesley began to withdraw, leaving his wounded in Cuesta's care. Cuesta immediately abandoned them to the advancing French. Desperate though it had been, Talavera raised British morale, was hailed as a triumph in Britain and in reward Wellesley was ennobled as Vicount Wellington of Talavera.

# Busaco – 27 September 1810

The operations with Cuesta in the Talavera campaign were a turning-point in Wellington's conduct of the war. Until then he had expected to act offensively, as an ally of the Spanish; now he realised that to continue in such a manner would be disaster. The small British force must attempt to hold as much of Portugal as possible, whilst gathering their strength, and the Spanish concentrate on holding Andalusia in southern Spain. Such logic was lost on the Spanish Junta, which continued to propose absurd schemes to recover Madrid. General Carlos Areizaga, who had replaced Cuesta, was utterly defeated at Ocaña on 19 November 1809, and on the 28th their remaining army under the Duke of Del Parque was beaten at Alba de Tormes. Wellington was effectively on his own.

The preservation of Lisbon was vital, the Tagus estuary being the route of supplies and reinforcements from Britain; the Royal Navy's control of the sea prevented Napoleon from ever threatening the supply-route. To protect Lisbon, on 20 October 1809 Wellington

initiated the building of the Lines of Torres Vedras, turning the Lisbon peninsula into a gigantic fortress. King Joseph believed the war virtually over; 325,000 French were in Spain, the Spanish field armies were scattered, the British had retired on Portugal and only Andalusia held out, the Junta having installed itself in Cadiz, capital of free Spain. Joseph delayed the attack on Cadiz, allowing the Duke of Albuquerque to gather a small Spanish force and put the city into a state of defence. The useless Junta stood down in favour of a three-man council of Regency in the name of the interned Ferdinand VII, and Wellington sent a small British contingent to stiffen the defence. Though Cadiz was never seriously threatened, until mid-1812 60,000 French were squandered in trying to blockade it.

In May 1810 Marshal André Massena (1758-1817) took command of the French 'Army of Portugal', one of France's ablest generals who had recently lost the sight of an eye when Napoleon shot him when hunting

(typically, Napoleon's loyal chief-of-staff, Alexandre Berthier, was blamed!). Looting was almost *de rigeur* for French commanders, but Massena was more avaricious than most; many were also embarrassed by his mistress, Henrietta Leberton, who accompanied him dressed as an officer on his staff. Wellington realised that his only chance lay in fighting on his own terms, and the longer he could delay Massena's advance the more complete would be the defences of Lisbon; so he made no attempt to relieve the Spanish garrison of Ciudad Rodrigo, which Massena invested in late June 1810. Rodrigo was one of two vital border-fortresses guarding the entry to Portugal; Badajoz covered the route to the south. Rodrigo surrendered on 9 July; the next objective was the Portuguese fort of Almeida, to get at which the French Marshal Michel Ney (1769-1815) had to brush away Craufurd's Light Division, posted along the Coa. Ney, commander of the strongest Corps (6th) of Massena's army, and nicknamed 'bravest of the brave', was as rash as 'Black Bob' and bungled the opportunity given him by Craufurd's delay in retiring, and the French were roughly handled at the

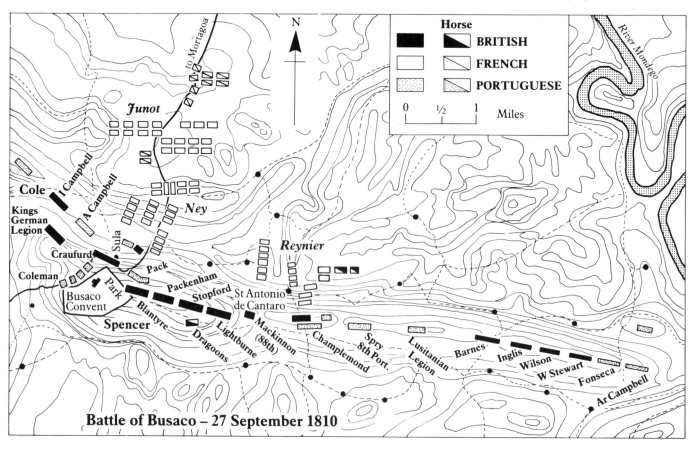

**Battle of Busaco – 27 September 1810**

*The French advance recoils before the appearance of the British over the crest at Busaco with their volleys of musketry followed by a controlled bayonet-charge. (Aquatint by T. Foldry after R. Westall).*

bridge of the Coa by Craufurd's magnificent 'Light Bobs'. Almeida, however, fell when a shell exploded its magazine, and Massena was free to advance. Wellington awaited him on a wonderful defensive position, the long and steel hill of Busaco, a short way from Coimbra.

On 27 September the French attacked the ridge, a decision amazingly foolish as it could have been outflanked (the Portuguese brigade instructed to block the road never received Wellington's orders), but as the Anglo-Portuguese army was deployed hidden on the reverse slope, as usual, Ney decided that it was held only by a rearguard; Massena himself hardly bothered to check and ordered a frontal assault. On the reverse slope of the long ridge were deployed 26,843 British and 25,429 Portuguese with 60 guns; Massena had about 63,000 men and 114 guns, and ordered Ney to attack the British left, whilst the 2nd Corps of General Jean Reynier (1771-1841) attacked the right. Reynier attacked in the early morning of 27 September, hitting the British line where it

*General Sir Rowland Hill (1772-1842) was Wellington's most trustworthy deputy in the Peninsular War, universally liked and nicknamed 'Daddy' for his concern for his men. (Portrait by J. W. Pieneman, 1821).*

was held by the 3rd Division of Sir Thomas Picton (1758-1815), a bluff professional who had served as governor of Trinidad, resigning over allegations of using torture in interrogation, and had been invalided home from Walcheren. Picton was an uncompromising man known as an eccentric (he wore his night-cap at Busaco and his civilian tophat in other battles) but an ideal subordinate for a hard fight; his men, led by the formidable 1/88th (Connaught Rangers) threw back Reynier's attack, and as the morning mist lifted and revealed no threat on the extreme right, Leith's 5th Division wheeled and attacked the French in the flank.

Unaware of Reynier's defeat, and thinking he had reached the crest, Ney ordered his own corps to attack. Pushing back the British skirmishes; it seemed to the French that the ridge ahead of them was almost unoccupied, and they were within ten yards of the summit when Craufurd called on his 1/52nd to avenge Moore; the British line appeared over the crest and hurled back the French in total confusion, the columns not having chance to deploy but tumbling back down the hill in chaos.

Having suffered 4,500 casualties, Massena abandoned his attack; as the French withdrew on 29 September Wellington continued his retreat, the

British and Portuguese having suffered (by an amazing coincidence) only 626 casualties each. Having stood at Busaco only to check the French advance and to give the Portuguese 'a taste for an amusement to which they were not before accustomed' (i.e. victory), Wellington withdrew within the lines of Torres Vedras, having evacuated the area in front of it and stripped it of resources. Massena, having no idea of the presence of the defences, was appalled; he realised that he could not break through but was loath to retreat, and sat outside the lines, his army slowly starving, isolated from support and with small detachments vulnerable to massacre by the vengeful Portuguese guerrillas and the *ordenança*, the feudal *levée-en-masse*. 65,050 Frenchmen had entered Portugal; by early March 1811 they were reduced to probably only 40,000 by which time Wellington's 34,000 British (in October) had increased to 43,000, comfortable and well-fed after a winter's rest behind the lines. On March Massena gave up the struggle and began to withdraw, having hung on far longer than Wellington thought possible. The Lines of Torres Vedras wrecked the French plans more than any battle, and increased the growing disillusionment with the war which afflicted the French army. Portugal was saved.

# Albuera – 16 May 1811

As Massena retired in the spring of 1811, Wellington pursued, but the situation was not yet such that he could make an all-out offensive. The final action of Massena's retreat was fought at Sabugal on 3 April, when Sir William Erskine (generally regarded as insane) needlessly exposed Beckwith's brigade of the Light Division to the attack of three French divisions; Beckwith held on and the appearance of the 3rd Division routed the French. On 9 March the southern gateway to Portugal, Badajoz, surrendered to Soult's army operating on the southern Portuguese frontier, compelling Wellington to divide his army. Hill was on leave, so Wellington detailed Beresford with 20,000 men to observe Soult and if possible recapture Badajoz, whilst he commanded in the north. Massena, determined to relieve the blockade of his Almeida garrison, advanced with some 48,000 men; Wellington met him with 37,504 men at a well-chosen position, along a ridge at Fuentes de Oñoro. On 3 May Massena made an unsuccessful attack, and on the 5th tried again. Wellington hung on in hard fight, and Massena marched away on 10 May, the French garrison of Almeida being evacuated without opposition. Wellington was dissatisfied with the battle, remarking that Napoleon's presence would have defeated them; but the French had now been expelled from Portugal.

As Soult marched to the relief of Badajoz, Beresford took up a position across his path at Albuera, on a low run of hills rising to 'the heights' at the southern end. Beresford's army numbered 10,449 British, 10,201 Portuguese and 14,634 Spaniards, the latter mostly from the army of General Joachim Blake (1759-1827), one of the better Spanish generals; the Portuguese were untried and the Spanish of dubious quality. Beresford was not the most able of generals, but was beset by a series of misfortunes, and his later critics perhaps tended not to do him justice; he held his centre with his most reliable troops, the British 2nd Division, the Portuguese were on the left, the Spaniards on 'the heights' at the right (the least likely place for an attack), with the weak 4th Division in reserve. Two German Legion battalions were thrown forward into Albuera village.

*Marshal Beresford at Albuera: a man of great physical power, he seized and threw down a Polish lancer who attacked him. In this engraving by T Sutherland after W Heath, Beresford wears the blue of the Portuguese army; the lancer incorrectly is shown in red.*

Soult arrived on the evening of 15 May 1811 with over 24,000 men, and believing that Beresford was alone, determined to swing around 'the heights' and interpose himself between Beresford and Blake's presumed approach. His tactics, thus based on an incorrect premise, almost succeeded; on the 16th he made a diversionary attack on Albuera village whilst the bulk of the French army assailed 'the heights'. Beresford requested that Blake send half his army to protect the flank, but Blake sent only four battalions under General Zayas supported by the Allied cavalry, of whom only the 700 British were reliable. As the attack developed, Beresford began a frantic reorganisation, sending the 2nd Division towards the flank; meanwhile, most unexpectedly, Zayas' troops (Spanish Guards and the Regt. 'Irlanda')

126

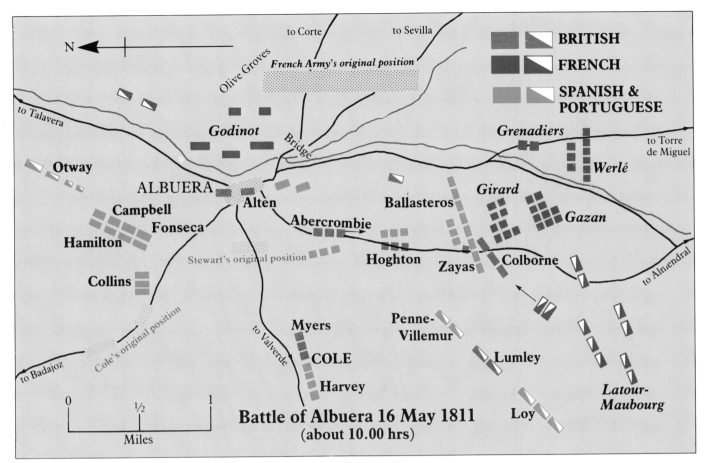

to Corte    to Sevilla

N

French Army's original position

to Talavera

BRITISH

FRENCH

SPANISH & PORTUGUESE

Olive Groves

Godinot

Bridge

Grenadiers

to Torre de Miguel

Werlé

Otway

ALBUERA    Alten

Campbell

Fonseca

Hamilton

Collins

Abercrombie

Stewart's original position

Ballasteros

Hoghton    Zayas

Girard

Gazan

Colborne

to Almendral

Cole's original position

to Badajoz

to Valverde

Myers

COLE

Harvey

Penne-Villemur

Lumley

Loy

Latour-Maubourg

0    ½    1

Miles

**Battle of Albuera 16 May 1811**
(about 10.00 hrs)

*Gilt plate with silver devices from an officer's shoulder-belt, 48th (Northamptonshire) Regt. Both battalions of the 48th fought at Albuera and suffered appalling casualties: the 1st Bn (Hoghton's Bde) lost 280 out of 497, the 2nd (Colborne's Bde) 343 out of 452.*

heroically held off the French attack. Colborne's brigade (1/3rd, 2/31st, 2/48th, 2/66th) of the 2nd Division moved up in support, drove off the French attack and went after them with the bayonet; Colborne, an officer of great skill, prepared to form one battalion into square to protect his flank but was over-ruled by his impetuous divisional commander, William Stewart. Out of a hailstorm, the French 2nd Hussars and Polish 2nd Vistula Lancers fell upon the exposed infantry and massacred them; the 31st, furthest from the charge, managed to form square and save themselves. The others were annihilated, the 3rd losing 643 men out of 755. An attempted counter-charge by two British squadrons was also cut to pieces. Even Beresford became involved in the melee, unhorsing a lancer who attacked him.

The second of Stewart's brigades came up and defied 8,000 French for more than half an hour. Its commander, General Hoghton, who had deliberately changed into a red coat to make himself more conspicuous, was killed, and all three battalion-commanders went down, Ingis of the 1/57th exhorting his men to

'die hard'. Beresford was loath to commit his reserve to end this butchery, so it was left to the Deputy Quartermaster-General of the Portuguese army, Henry Hardinge, to plead with the commander of the 4th Division, Lowry Cole, to save them. Though acting without orders, Cole rushed his men forward into a tempest of artillery fire, the Fusilier Brigade (1/ and 2/7th, 1/23rd, Allied light battalions) and some sterling Portuguese. With the only orders being 'Close up, close in, fire away' the fusiliers rolled forward, driving the French before them; 1,045 from 2,015 fell within half an hour, but they were, as Napier observed, 'astonishing infantry'. Having lost about 8,000 men, Soult withdrew, but the cost was appalling; Beresford's army was shattered. It was perhaps the most heroic day in British military annals, a day won by the courage of the ordinary soldier, most of whom now lay dead, in places piled three feet deep. The 2/7th had 85 men under arms at the close, out of 568; Hoghton's and Colborne's brigades when amalgamated just scraped up two weak battalions. As Wellington observed, 'another such battle would ruin us'.

127

# Ciudad Rodrigo – 1812

Albuera was the last major action of 1811, the year when the Peninsular War began to slip away from Napoleon. By the middle of July 1811 the French had 354,461 men in Spain, plus 8,298 more in reserve at Bayonne, but though they outnumbered their 'regular' opponents greatly, their six armies were unable to co-ordinate their operations, partly due to the intransigence of the commanders who would not even take orders from King Joseph (knowing that such orders must come from Joseph's chief-of-staff and thus be inferior!), and partly due to the nature of the terrain and the distance between the main theatres of war. The 'Army of the South' (Soult), 'Centre' (Joseph) and 'Portugal' (commanded by Marshal Auguste Marmont (1774-1852), who had replaced Massena) might expect to act in concert; but Marshal Louis Suchet's 'Army of Aragon', General Dorsenne's 'Army of the North' and Marshal Jacques Macdonald's 'Army of Catalonia' were occupied in holding down those provinces, and fighting both the small Spanish 'regular' armies, which were never completely overwhelmed, and the guerrilla war. It was this last which really exascerbated what Napoleon termed his 'Spanish ulcer'; fought with horrifying brutality on both sides, it disrupted communications, wrecked the already parlous supply-lines and made Spain a feared posting for the disillusioned French army, whose attitude was summarised by the graffiti: 'This war means death for the men, ruin for the officers, a fortune for the generals.' One estimate put the French loss to guerrillas at one hundred men *per day* throughout the war.

Ironically, the war between British and French was fought with a degree of civility; away from the pitched battles, unnecessary loss of life was usually deplored, so opposing sentries conversed and even drank together. The engineer Landmann described one meeting in which a French sentry, after swigging the British sentry's rum, with characteristic Gallic bonhomie kissed the Englishman; it almost caused bloodshed when the horrified British sentry exclaimed 'what sort of pranks would you be after?!'. George Napier of 52nd demonstrates the officers' attitude: 'there is never any personal animosity between soldiers opposed to each other . . . it strikes you as very odd that men should shake hands with each other, drink and eat together, laugh and joke, and then in a few minutes use every exertion of mind and body to destroy one another . . . I should hate to fight out of personal malice or revenge, but have no objection to fight for *fun and glory*.' Even at the Coa, Napier signalled a French officer to go back, 'not liking to fire at a single man'; when the Frenchman pressed on and was killed, there was universal lamentation in the British ranks, many saying 'God bless his soul'. . .

There was no chance of the Anglo-Portuguese forces capturing either Ciudad Rodrigo or Badajoz with their antiquated siege-train, and fighting was desultory, Wellington's manoeuvres leaving him open to defeat in detail, the

*Sir John Colborne of the 52nd, later Baron Seaton (1778-1863), unequalled as a regimental commander.*

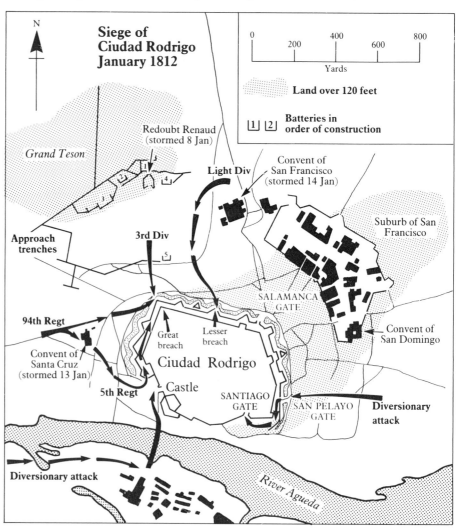

128

French nearly winning a sharp action at El Bodon on 25 September, and Hill surprising General Jean-Baptiste Girard at Arroyo dos Molinos on 28 October, Girard jumping upon his hat in fury at being caught unprepared. In the south, earlier in the year, the redoubtable old Thomas Graham of Balgowan (1748-1843), a violent francophobe who was aged 46 before he embarked on a military career, won a significant battle at Barrosa on 5 March 1811. His 15,000 men (5,200 of them British, the remainder Spanish) marched from Tarifa to disrupt the French blockade of Cadiz. They were met by 7,000 of Victor's army; the Spaniards either abandoned the British or remained as spectators, leaving the small British contingent to defeat them unaided, losing 1,238 men but winning great fame in the process, Sergt. Patrick Masterson of the 2/87th capturing the 'Eagle' of the French 8th Line, a much-heralded achievement.

In contrast to the French, Wellington enjoyed a 'unity of command' unavailable to his enemies, being in sole control of the Allied field army. By this time his forces were approaching the peak of

*The storm of Ciudad Rodrigo; this engraving by T Sutherland after W Heath accurately depicts the confusion, horror and carnage of the most terrible type of combat of this period, 'the imminent deadly breach'.*

efficiency – 'probably the most complete machine for its numbers now existing in Europe' as he was to write in November 1813 – though still deficient in siege-train, engineers and commissariat. By the turn of the years 1811-12 he was ready to assume the offensive, the border fortresses of Ciudad Rodrigo and Badajoz needing to be captured before moving into Spain. Marmont's army had been depleted to support Marshal Suchet's efforts in eastern Spain – he captured Valencia on 9 January – and the sieges could be undertaken without serious threat of disruption.

Siege-warfare progressed in an accepted manner, the besiegers first severing the garrison's communications, then building breaching-batteries to open gaps in the defences and digging 'parallels', trenches which were pushed ever nearer to the walls. With virtually no trained sappers, manual labour was done by the infantry, supervised by the few engineer officers, whose mortality-rate was appalling. By the conventions of the period, when a breach was deemed 'practicable' – i.e. capable of being stormed – the garrison could surrender without impugning their honour. The alternative was to suffer an assault, costly to the attackers and with the garrison not entitled to quarter. Due to the potentially suicidal nature of an assault, it was usual not to detail any particular unit to lead the attack, but to assemble a

'forlorn hope' of volunteers taken from the division allocated the task. (The term 'forlorn hope' was of great antiquity, perhaps deriving originally from the Dutch expression for 'lost party'.) Officers who survived could expect promotion, but even among the rank and file there was always a great surplus of volunteers, the men jealous of the honour of leading the attack.

On 8 January 1812, in atrocious weather, the siege of Rodrigo began with the 'breaking of ground' around it. Marmont cdalculated that he would need about a month to assemble enough men to relieve it; but it fell faster than could have been predicted. The outlying works were stormed in succession and the breaching-batteries opened on 14 January. 34 24pdrs and 4 18pdrs fired 8,950 and 565 rounds respectively and the operations proceeded without a hitch, despite the severity of the weather; the cold was such that it was said that sentries in the trenches froze to death overnight. The work progressed at twice the pace Wellington had hoped despite the exertions of the garrison, and by the evening of 19 January two breaches were opened. One was to be assaulted by the 3rd Division, the other by the Light; two diversionary attacks were to distract the garrison on the opposite side of the defences. The 3rd Division suffered heavily from the explosion of a mine (which killed the division's senior brigadier, General Mackinnon), but the Light Division, against heavy fire, pushed over the rubble of the breach and stormed inside, George Napier of the 52nd having instructed his men to unload their muskets, 'because if we do not do the business with the bayonet, without firing, we shall not be able to do it all'. The garrison, assailed from both breaches, laid down their arms and the governor, General Barrié, retired to Rodrigo's medieval castle and capitulated at the first summons. Following the capture, the criminally-inclined of each battalion (the 'incorrigibles' as Colborne termed them) went on an expedition of pillage and drunkenness. The losses suffered in the assault were 59 officers and 503 other ranks, the most grievous being that of Robert Craufurd, shot through the spine as he directed the Light Division. Though hated by many, the loss of this stern and stalwart general was severe.

# Badajoz – 1812

Following the fall of Rodrigo, Marmont suggested that he move south to help shield Badajoz, the next obvious target; he was told that it was Soult's responsibility and that he should mind his own business. Wellington (created an Earl after Rodrigo) knew that Marmont had insufficient supplies to attempt an operation against Rodrigo, so moved to besiege the great southern fortress. Attacks on Badajoz had failed in 1811: now, despite a continued shortage of engineers (which he had attempted unavailingly to remedy), Wellington determined to make nothing stand in his way. It was to cause probably the blackest day in the annals of the British Army.

Badajoz was strongly-fortified and well-garrisoned (so that Soult believed it safe), and the additional defences installed by the French – mines – were revealed to Wellington by a French sergeant-major of engineers who changed sides after having been insulted by his captain; but Governor Armand Phillipon (1761-1836) was a skilful commander and his troops good. The fortress was invested on 16 March 1812, and an outlying work, Fort Picurina, was stormed on 25 March for the loss of more than half the attackers. Its capture allowed the main breaching-batteries to concentrate upon the weakest part of the defences, the south-east section between the San Roque and Trinidad bastions. In all, Wellington's siege-guns comprised 16 24pdrs, 20 18pdrs and 16 24pdr howitzers; they used 80,000 sandbags, 1,200 gabions (wicker baskets filled with earth, making portable defences) and 700 fascines (bundles of wood), with as many as 1,800 men working every night, the parties being drawn from the various Divisions in rotation. Total ammunition expenditure was 35,346 rounds, including 18,832 from the most effective 24pdrs, 1,826 shells and 2,659 rounds of grape or canister in anti-personnel fire.

On 4 April Wellington received news that Soult was approaching, which would mean reducing the besieging force to augment that 'covering' the siege; Marmont was executing a brief raid into Portugal, which Wellington disregarded completely. On the morning of the 5th two breaches looked practicable, but the assault was delayed as the garrison was attempting to build new defences behind the breaches; the bombardment continued and opened a third breach. The assault was timed for the evening of 6 April, the 4th and Light Divisions to assault the Trinidad and Santa Maria breaches, whilst several diversionary attacks were to be made, one on the opposite bank of the Guadiana river against Badajoz's fortified bridge-head, and the 5th Division against the San Vincente bastion on the opposite side of the defences from the breaches. The 4th Division's trench-guards were to rush the San Roque *lunette*, and at the last moment an extra diversionary attack was permitted, at Picton's entreaty that his 3rd Division be allowed to storm the old castle by escalade, whilst the garrison was occupied defending the breaches. On the evening of the assault, the garrison's effectives numbered 157 officers and 3,921 men, and the able Phillipon had turned the breaches into a nightmare, filling the ditches with entanglements, caltrops (spikes to pierce the feet), beams studded with nails and *chevaux de frises*, beams with sword-blades driven through. The time of the assault was delayed from 7 pm to 10, allowing the French to fill the ditches with combustibles to illuminate the attackers.

The attack was probably the most terrible combat of the age; the horrors of it left survivors unable to find words to describe it. In the confined spaces before the breaches, part of which the French had innundated so that the leading attackers jumped into the ditches and drowned, a tempest of shot and fire was poured onto them. One allusion is found in several reminiscences: that the breaches as nearly resembled the mouth of hell as any sight within man's compass, 'as if the very earth had been rent asunder and

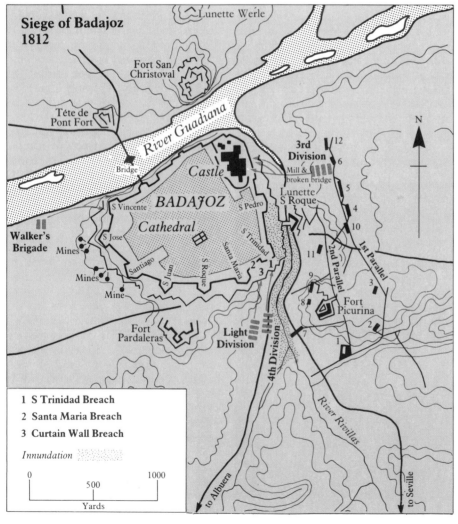

**Siege of Badajoz 1812**

Lunette Werle

Fort San Christoval

Téte de Pont Fort

River Guadiana

Bridge

Castle

BADAJOZ

Cathedral

S Vincente

S Pedro

S Jose

Walker's Brigade

Mines

S Juan

Santiago

S Roque

Santa Maria

S Trinidad

Mines

Mine

3rd Division

Mill & broken bridge

Lunette S Roque

12

6

5

4

10

11

2nd Parallel

1st Parallel

9

8

Fort Picurina

3

2

7

1

Fort Pardaleras

Light Division

4th Division

River Rieillas

N

to Albuera

to Seville

1  S Trinidad Breach

2  Santa Maria Breach

3  Curtain Wall Breach

*Innundation*

0          500          1000

Yards

130

*Vereker M Hamilton's painting 'The Forlorn Hope at Badajoz' exemplifies a style of battle-painting prevalent in the Victorian era: artistically of the very highest standard, but deficient in accuracy of uniforms and regiments depicted.*

its central fires were bursting upwards uncontrolled' as Kincaid of the 95th wrote; 'as if the mouth of the infernal regions had opened to vomit forth destruction' wrote Costello of the same regiment. Napier thought it was 'so dreadful in all its circumstances that posterity can scarcely be expected to credit the tale', whilst Harry Smith, who positively enjoyed a battle, later noted that 'There is no battle, day or night, I would not willingly react, except this. The murder of our gallant officers and soldiers is not to be believed.' From ten until midnight more than 40 separate attacks were made, until the dead and wounded lay heaped in the ditches, and Wellington finally recalled the dazed survivors. Almost one in three did not return.

With the garrison thus occupied, both escalades unexpectedly succeeded, Leith's 5th Division at San Vincente and Picton's 3rd at the castle, though not without heavy fighting during which Picton was shot in the groin. Either attack would have caused the fall of the city, but the French continued to mount a strong resistance until the 3rd Division, having secured the castle by scrambling up on ladders, with Picton hobbling at their head, burst out into the town. Phillipon retreated to the citadel, but soon surrendered, though he and his two daughters escaped murder only by the efforts of British officers who slashed at their own enraged men. After the carnage of the assault, what folllowed was even worse.

There was an ancient tradition that according to the 'rules of war' any army compelled to assault a fortress should have the right to plunder it. Plunder was an accepted facet of military life: the dead were robbed on the battlefield, and in most armies no check was made upon theft from the civil population (in the British forces, under normal circumstances, every effort was made to prevent such crime). After the fall of Badajoz, however, anarchy prevailed. It is difficult to explain what happened by rational means; that the troops regarded it as their right after such an assault might excuse theft, but it was accompanied by uncontrolled license, brutality, rapine and murder upon the civilian inhabitants (who correctly or not were regarded as all pro-French). It would be charitable to regard the culprits as temporarily unhinged by the horrors of the assault, or maddened by the alcohol they stole; others blamed the hard core of bad characters in every regiment, or the camp-followers who stole in after the fighting. For two days the troops within the city ran uncontrolled in an orgy of violence. Kincaid was as numbed by what he saw as by the assault: 'The shouts and oaths of drunken soldiers in quest of more liquor, the reports of fire-arms and crashing in of doors, together with the appalling shrieks of hapless women, might have induced anyone to believe himself in the regions of the damned.' Officers and the more responsible men who tried to protect the civilians were threatened, attacked or murdered; while the wounded lay heaped and unattended in the breeches, the pillage continued. Harry Smith thought that 'Civilized man, when let loose and the bonds of morality relaxed, is a far greater beast than the savage, more fiend-like in every act'; he rescued a young Spanish noblewoman who became his wife (giving her name to the town of Ladysmith, scene of a later celebrated siege), but few such romantic tales came from Badajoz. As one horrified witness remarked, his blood froze at the sights he witnessed in the streets of Badajoz.

Late in the afternoon of 7 April, Wellington sent Power's Portuguese brigade into the city to scour it of any remaining looters (many had already returned to their camps, exhausted and loaded with booty); the provost-marshal erected a gallows in the cathedral square, the threat of which stopped the pillage; or perhaps, as Napier suggested, the perpetrators were simply sated. The road to Spain lay open, but at what a cost.

# Salamanca – 22 July 1812

Possession of the frontier fortresses not only secured Portugal but allowed Wellington to advance into Spain. Despite the assassination of the British prime minister, Spencer Perceval, by the maniac Bellingham in the House of Commons lobby, the Tories stayed in power under Lord Liverpool, preventing the possibility of a Whig ministry abandoning the war. The army in the Peninsula was growing stronger and was both experienced and better-equipped, though the main deficiency, a corps of trained sappers which had been instigated immediately after the disasters of Badajoz, could not yet take the field. Conversely, the French situation was deteriorating; command was at last centralized officially under Joseph, with Jourdan as chief of staff, but the various army commanders paid little heed (Soult refused point-blank to assist Marmont if he were attacked), and not only could few reinforcements be expected, but Napoleon was withdrawing some of the best elements for his attack on Russia. There was now no hope of re-entering Portugal, as Marmont's siege-train had been captured at Rodrigo and Soult's was occupied in the fruitless siege of Cadiz. Wishing to help Cadiz, Wellington decided to strike at Marmont; if he were driven away, Soult would have to evacuate southern Spain or be isolated. Diversions were made by effective amphibious

landings in the north, collaborating with the huge guerrilla bands, and in the east an Anglo-Sicilian landing was planned by Lord William Bentinck (1774-1839) – 'not right-headed' – and led by Sir John Murray (1768-1827), a most inept general, which won a minor victory at Castalla and almost captured Tarragona, but was generally a failure in every respect except that it occupied Suchet's attention.

Wellington began his advance from Rodrigo on 13 June 1812, knowing that as Marmont had concentrated his 50,000-strong army, shortage of supplies would force him to move; taunted for being battle-shy, Marmont at last lurched forward and almost caught Wellington off-balance, but then he retired on Salamanca. Wellington learned via an intercepted document that King Joseph was marching with a reinforcement for Marmont; thus he knew that when the armies combined he would be at a disadvantage and must strike at Marmont immediately. With the opposing forces marching towards Salamanca in sight of each other, the opportunity for action was always there, but Marmont believed Wellington to be a purely defensive general and felt secure.

On 22 July, about 2½ miles from Salamanca, Marmont interpreted a dust-cloud as Wellington's retreat and thought he might hazard a stab. In fact, only

Wellington's baggage was retreating; his entire army was concealed on the reverse slopes of high ground, anchored by two hills known as the Greater and Lesser Arapils, waiting for the one chance to defeat Marmont before his reinforcement arrived. Marmont had 49,646 men and 78 guns; Wellington 51,939 and 60 guns. Marmont occupied the Great Arapil, intending to 'pin' the supposed rearguard, whilst the remainder of his army began to execute an outflanking march to cut communications with Portugal. This necessitated almost the whole French army marching strung-out across Wellington's front. Wellington was eating a chicken-leg as he peered through his telescope at this procession. He exclaimed either 'That will do, by God!' or, to his Spanish liaison officer and friend Miguel de Alava (1771-1843, probably the only man present at both Trafalgar and Waterloo, albeit on different sides), 'Marmont is lost!' First, Wellington ordered the 3rd Division (temporarily led by his brother-in-law, Edward Pakenham, 1778-1815, later killed commanding at New Orleans, Picton being absent) to block the front of the French column of march and smash the first of Marmont's eight divisions. The next two divisions, assailed by Leith's 5th Division and Le Marchant's cavalry, fell in the same manner – though Le Marchant was killed – and Marmont wounded by a shell. Bertrand Clausel (1772-1842) assumed command and organised a counter-attack which severely mauled Lowry Cole's 4th Division, but Beresford (who was wounded) led Spry's Portuguese brigade to throw back the French. As the remainder of the Allied army came up, the French were swept away; the Great Arapil was taken, and only one French division, that of Maximilien Foy (1775-1825) was able to cover the retreat, allowing the escape of only 20,000 men still in any order. Their total losses were about 14,000, half of whom were captured; Allied losses amounted to 3,129 British, 1,627 Portuguese and 6 Spaniards. Wellington was rewarded with another step in the peerage (to

*Edward Paget (1775-1849) was one of Wellington's best subordinates, but unfortunate: he lost an arm at Oporto (1809) and was captured on the retreat from Burgos (illustrated). Engraving by Dubourg after Atkinson.*

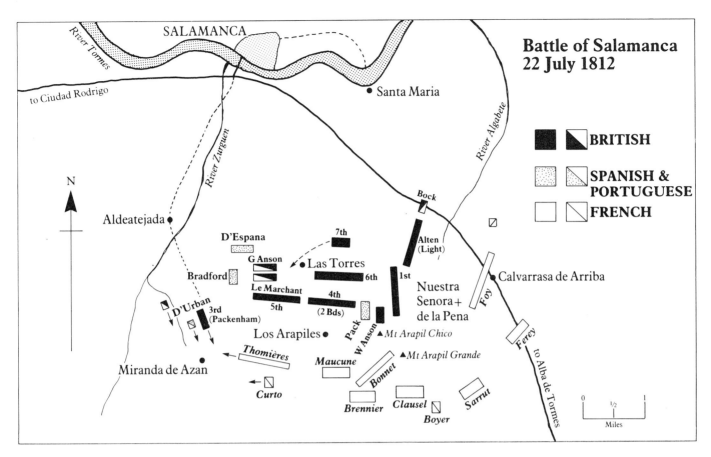

**Battle of Salamanca
22 July 1812**

BRITISH

SPANISH &
PORTUGUESE

FRENCH

SALAMANCA

to Ciudad Rodrigo

*River Tormes*

*River Zurguen*

*River Algabete*

Santa Maria

Aldeatejada

D'Espana

7th

Bock

Alten
(Light)

G Anson

Las Torres

6th

1st

Calvarrasa de Arriba

Bradford

Le Marchant

4th

Nuestra
Senora +
de la Pena

Foy

D'Urban

3rd
(Packenham)

5th

(2 Bds)

Pack

W Anson

▲ Mt Arapil Chico

Ferey

to Alba de Tormes

Los Arapiles

Miranda de Azan

Thomières

Maucune

Bonnet

▲ Mt Arapil Grande

Curto

Brennier

Clausel

Boyer

Sarrut

0    1/2    1
Miles

*Typical of the stalwart but unheralded
regimental officers who formed the
backbone of the Peninsular army was
Hugh Harrison, an Irish officer who
served with the 1st Bn. 32nd (Cornwall)
Regiment at Salamanca (where one-third
of thier officers fell), and who was severely
wounded with them at Waterloo.*

Marquis), but more importantly had
proved that the war in the Peninsula
could be won, which in turn tended further to dishearten the French.

The 'Army of Portugal', still under
Clausel, was wrecked, and the pursuit
included one further action on 23 July,
when the German Legion Dragoons succeeded in doing the near-impossible and
breaking squares of infantry at Garcia
Hernandez. King Joseph abandoned
Madrid, into which Wellington made a
triumphal entry on 12 August simply to
put new heat into the Spanish. Joseph
ordered Soult to his assistance; Soult
replied that he didn't think the king
really meant the order, so would stay in
Andalusia! Wellington determined to
capture Burgos, by which he hoped to
contain Soult and Joseph; but he was ill-
equipped for the task, his siege-train
comprising three guns only, still woefully short of sappers and with a tired
army, and unwilling to risk another
assault as costly as that of Badajoz. In
late August Soult finally condescended
to move and by early October had joined
Joseph, Jourdan and Suchet near Valencia. The meeting was stormy – Soult had
accused Joseph of treachery, Joseph had

begged Napoleon to have Soult arrested
– but their combined armies marched on
Madrid, aiming to cut off Wellington
from Portugal. On hearing the news, and
now threatened also by the 'Army of
Portugal', Wellington began his retreat
from Burgos. He assembled his forces,
some 65,000 strong, on the old battlefield at Salamanca; on 15 November
Soult, given command of the armies of
the South, Centre and Portugal, had
80,000 men but declined to engage.
Wellington's retreat recommenced,
bringing with it memories of Corunna,
as divisional generals made appalling
errors; William Stewart decided he
knew better than Wellington and almost
got his 1st Division lost, and the incompetent Quartermaster-General Gordon –
temporarily replacing the able George
Murray – left the army without supplies.

Soult abandoned the pursuit when
Wellington reached Ciudad Rodrigo
after a retreat of great privation. It was a
sad end to a successful year; but the
French were demoralized, Joseph was in
only temporary re-occupation of a hostile
capital, and Wellington had thrown off
the reputation of being exclusively a
defensive general.

# Vittoria – 21 June 1813

In 1813 the situation became critical for the French, as more men were withdrawn to the war in Germany; Soult was also recalled. Wellington now prepared to expel the French from the Peninsula, as he admitted to Earl Bathurst (Secretary for War) on 11 May: '. . . I shall not be stronger throughout the campaign, or more efficient . . . I cannot have a better opportunity for trying the fate of a battle . . .' A fortnight later his field army numbered 52,484 British and 28,792 Portuguese. In addition, he had some 46,000 Spaniards under his command, exclusive of the large bands of irregulars.

The advance began in late May, turning the French defensive-line exactly as Wellington had planned, and he continued to advance, constantly out-manoeuvering the French. Joseph, who abandoned Madrid finally on 17 May, fell back upon the line of the River Ebro; Jourdan proposed to cut Wellington's communications with Portugal, but Joseph, obsessed with following Napoleon's advice to keep open communications with France, continued to retire. In the event, the communication with

Portugal was no longer important, for Wellington now directed that his supplies should come via the northern Spanish port of Santander. Even at this critical period, he found time to beg the Spanish government to grant an amnesty to those Spaniards 'who have been induced by terror, by distress, or by despair' to support Joseph; he calculated that this would undermine what little support Joseph still had among the Spanish people.

The French were out-manoeuvred so comprehensively that few delaying-actions were fought, the Allied advance being so swift and audacious that they were forced to abandon the line of the Ebro. Wellington's offensive, one of his greatest strategic triumphs, had driven the French back from Salamanca for the loss of 29 Allied soldiers killed, and at such a speed that much of the French reserve could not join Joseph before the decisive battle of the campaign. Joseph's army halted at Vittoria, to the north of the Ebro, on 19 June, to give a chance for additional detachments to join. All three French armies (South, Centre and Portugal) were present, together numbering

about 63,000, and in addition they were encumbered by an immense train of camp-followers and convoys bearing the plunder extracted from Spain over several years. The force was immobile on 20 June as Jourdan was stricken with fever, but on the following day he began to adjust the dangerously separated disposition of the army, when he was informed that Allied troops were approaching.

Wellington divided his army into four parts. On his extreme left, Sir Thomas Graham with the 1st and 5th Divisions was to swing around and cut the road from Vittoria to France, severing the French retreat. The left-centre, under the Earl of Dalhousie (Picton's 3rd and Dalhousie's 7th Divisions) was to link Graham to the main striking-force, the 4th and Light Divisions under Wellington's personal control; and on the extreme right, Hill with the 2nd, Silveira's Portuguese and Morillo's Spanish Divisions, was to occupy the attention of much of the French forces. Wellington knew that

*Vittoria: as the French retreat, pressed by British infantry, Allied troops begin to plunder the French baggage (mid-ground, left centre); Wellington and his staff observe from the extreme left.*

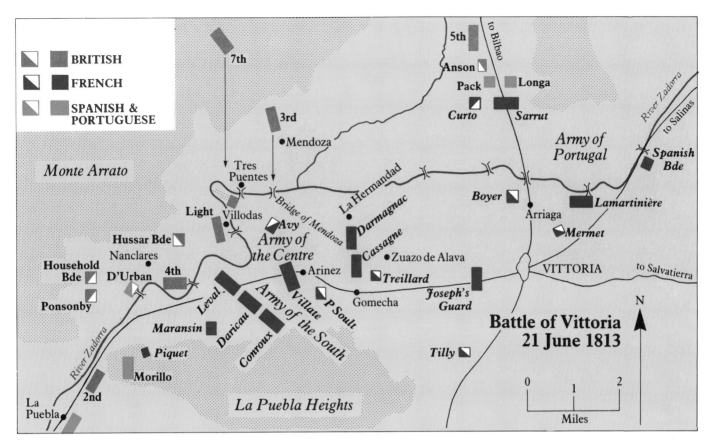

**BRITISH**

**FRENCH**

**SPANISH &
PORTUGUESE**

7th

5th

Anson

Pack

Longa

Curto

Sarrut

*Army of
Portugal*

River Zadorra

to Bilbao

to Salinas

3rd

Mendoza

*Monte Arrato*

Tres
Puentes

Light

Villodas

*Avy*

*Army of
the Centre*

Bridge of Mendoza

La Hermandad

*Darmagnac*

*Cassagne*

Boyer

Arriaga

*Mermet*

*Lamartinière*

Spanish
Bde

Hussar Bde

Nanclares

Household
Bde

D'Urban

4th

Arinez

Gomecha

Zuazo de Alava

*Treillard*

*Joseph's
Guard*

VITTORIA

to Salvatierra

Ponsonby

Leval

*Army of
the South*

Villatte

P Soult

N

*Maransin*

*Daricau*

*Conroux*

*Piquet*

**Battle of Vittoria
21 June 1813**

*Tilly*

Morillo

2nd

La
Puebla

River Zadorra

*La Puebla Heights*

0          1          2

Miles

the operation was complex and might miscarry, but was convinced he could win a victory; he had about 70,000 men.

Jourdan believed that the movements on his right were feints, and organised his resistance accordingly, detaching a division to the south, from where there was no danger. On his left was the Army of the South; the Army of the Centre was in the centre, and the Army of Portugal on the right. On the French left, Hill began the battle by making progress and occupying the heights which commanded the dispositions of the Army of the South. In the centre the action was delayed as Wellington waited for Graham to get into position; when, upon finding a bridge over the river Zadorra which Jourdan had left unguarded, the Light Division and Picton's 3rd (which its fiery commander brought up unordered, Dalhousie's 7th being delayed) crossed the river. The French left wing was now assailed by both Hill on the extreme left, and Picton and the Light, and though they attempted to form a second defensive-line were forced back in the direction of Vittoria. On the French right, Graham successfully blocked the road to Bayonne, and with this avenue of retreat closed Joseph and Jourdan were compelled to order a

withdrawal eastwards, towards Pamplona. The small Army of Portugal, which had resisted Graham so stoutly, retired in good order; in the remainder all cohesion was lost and the withdrawal became a rout. Total Allied losses were 5,158, and those of the French only about 8,400, but such statistics conceal the

*To remedy the shortage of small change available in the Peninsular army, from 1812 the issue of copper token-coins was authorised, bearing Wellington's portrait. This 1813 halfpenny describes him as Field-Marshal, and thus post-dates Vittoria. Britannia appears on the reverse.*

scale of the defeat. Joseph's army was shattered, and he was able to save only one gun and one howitzer, the former of which was captured two days later. The entire baggage and treasury, choking the French line of flight, fell into Allied hands, which was largely the reason that the pursuit was so ineffective. Wellington was outraged at the conduct of 'our vagabond soldiers' who 'have got among them about a million sterling in money . . . instead of . . . getting rest and food to prepare them for the pursuit' they spent the night 'in looking for plunder'. The consequence was, that they were incapable of marching in pursuit of the enemy, and were totally knocked up . . . The 18th Hussars are a disgrace to the name of soldier, in action as well as elsewhere . . .'

To be fair to the 'vagabond soldiers', officers were employed equally in seeking 'souvenirs'; the 14th Light Dragoons took Joseph's silver chamber-pot for use as a punch-bowl in the mess, and among the booty was Jourdan's bâton as Marshal of France. Wellington sent it to the Prince Regent as a trophy; by return, he received his own appointment as Field-Marshal of Great Britain. The Peninsular War was effectively decided.

# The Pyrenees and Southern France

Outraged at the defeat of his armies in Spain, Napoleon laid all blame on the hapless Joseph, who was ordered to retire, and Soult was given overall command of what remained of the French forces in Spain, to bar the access into southern France. In the east, Napoleon was soon to be overwhelmingly defeated and France invaded from that direction by Austrian, Russian, Prussian and Swedish forces, but Soult performed prodigies. To the 50,000 men and one howitzer Joseph had salvaged, he added the garrisons of northern Spain and assembled the 'Army of Spain' of 79,000 and 140 guns, the old and new meaningless titles such as 'Army of Portugal' having been discarded. Two fortresses barred the route through the Pyrenees into France, San Sebastian and Pamplona; Wellington blockaded the latter and commenced operations in late June 1813 against San Sebastian, an excellent harbour which could be used for the delivery of supplies. His major problem was the mountainous terrain which made the rapid transfer of troops extremely difficult, and as he admitted to Hill on 14 July, 'how ticklish our affairs are on the right'; in other words, Soult could achieve a local superiority against any part of Wellington's line along the Pyrenees.

Wellington believed that Soult would try to relieve San Sebastian first, given the commencement of the siege so on receiving news that Soult was attacking the passes of Maya and Roncesvalles on his right, he regarded it as a feint; it was not. Soult massed his entire strength, achieving 'local superiority', in an attempt to reach Pamplona, realising that it must be done quickly before his supplies ran out, attacking at Sorauren on 28 July. They were beaten off thanks to Wellington's presence, in most bitter combat, described by Wellington in one of his most memorable phrases: 'I never saw such fighting as we have had here . . . the battle of the 28th was fair *bludgeon* work . . .'; only with difficulty did Soult extricate his army, minus 13,000 lost. San Sebastian fell on 31 August after a violent assault, which cost 1,696 British and 577 Portuguese casualties and the unfortunate city was then sacked. Soult's efforts to relieve it on the day of the attack were repelled by the Spanish (surprisingly unaided) at San Marcial, and the retreating French were valiantly held up at the bridge of Vera over the Bidassoa by the Horatius-like but vain heroism of a 95th Rifles picquet.

Above: *The last, unnecessary battle of the Peninsular War, Toulouse cost Wellington 4,558 casualties to only 3,236 French, ending Soult's valiant but unavailing defence of the French frontier. (Engraving by T Sutherland after W Heath)*
Below: *Having fought their way across the Pyrenees, the British Army gazes on France in early 1814, a fitting reward for the suffering and endeavours of the Peninsular War. (Print after A Dupray)*

Soult gave up Spain for lost though Suchet was still established in the east, echoing Napoleon's statement of December 1813, that he did not want Spain 'either to keep or give away'! It is greatly to Soult's credit that he handled his limited resources in a somewhat hopeless situation as well as he did, however. Wellington fought his way across the Bidassoa, Pamplona falling on 30 October. On 9 November, decoying Soult into believing that he was about to fall upon his right, Wellington's forces stormed past the French defences along the river Nivelle. By his own admission, it was one of his best operations; now the army could escape the severe Pyrenean winter by being established on the French side of the mountains. Wellington sent home all the Spaniards except Morillo's Division (under British pay and control) to prevent the plundering of France; as he wrote to the Spanish General Manuel Freyre on 14 November (in French, as his correspondence with the Spanish usually was), 'I have not come to France to pillage; I have not had thousands of officers and soldiers killed and wounded for the remainder to plunder the French . . . my duty, and the duty of us all, is to stop plunder, especially as we mean to supply our troops from the resources of the country.' In fact, the Allied army behaved so well in southern France that the French inhabitants accorded them more co-operation than they gave their own army.

On 10 December Soult attacked Wellington at the Nive; after four days the French were repelled. This was some

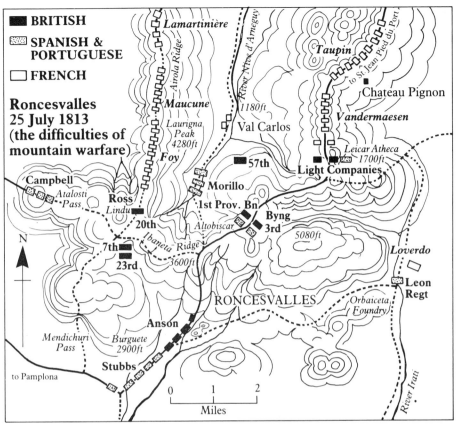

of the most severe combat of the war; on 13 December at St Pierre, with the French 'playing Old Harry' as George Bell of the 34th said, Hill declared 'Dead or alive, my lads, we must hold our ground.' More than one witness described the road *literally* running with blood.

When the winter weather moderated in early 1814 Wellington began his advance towards Bayonne, again outwitting Soult by fabricating a pontoon-bridge over the tidal estuary of the Adour using hired boats. Soult concentrated his army at Orthez, but was forced back upon Toulouse on 27 February, and his demoralized troops began to desert in droves. In the action at Orthez Wellington received his only injury in battle (apart from bruising by a spent ball at Salamanca) when a grapeshot knocked his sword-hilt against his leg. He occupied Bordeaux on 12 March, whilst Soult took his army into the defences of Toulouse. Napoleon bowed to the inevitable and abdicated on 6 April 1814; but it was almost a week before the news reached the southern front, and the last great battle of the war was fought unnecessarily on 10 April. Wellington assaulted the defences of Toulouse, which the French defended resolutely;

Soult abandoned his position, hoping as a last resort to join Suchet's army to the east, but on 12 April the news of Napoleon's abdication arrived. Wellington received it with a rare show of emotion, saying 'Hurrah!', spinning on his heels and snapping his fingers. Soult concluded an armistice on 17 April, ending the Peninsular War.

The 'Spanish ulcer' was a major factor in Napoleon's defeat, and for him it was a constant drain upon men, *matériel* and morale in a war which was almost impossible to win, given the French command-structure and the constant hostility of the population. But these alone could never have defeated the French; credit must go to arguably the greatest British soldier, perhaps the greatest of the age, and to his magnificent army, to whom he announced the cessation of hostilities by a General Order on 21 April, returning 'his best thanks for their uniform discipline and gallantry in the field, and for their conciliating conduct towards the inhabitants of the country'; and added that he trusted they would leave 'with a lasting reputation, not less creditable to their gallantry in the field than to their regularity and good conduct in quarters and camp.' That reputation has never faded.

# America and Canada 1812-1815

The 'War of 1812' between Britain and the United States of America was a tragic and unnecessary conflict, which diverted many of Britain's resources from the more important campaigns against Napoleon. There had been friction for some years between Britain and the United States, arising from the British insistence of searching 'neutral' shipping for contraband, in support of the 'Orders in Council' and blockade intended to combat Napoleon's 'Continental System', and from the impressment of American merchant seamen by the Royal Navy. On 19 June 1812 President Madison declared war on Britain, supposedly to defend the 'freedom of the seas', but hoped to use the opportunity to conquer Canada, knowing that it was weakly-defended and appreciating the logistical difficulties involved in reinforcing the British army in Canada, when Britain was fully engaged in the Peninsula.

The defences of Canada were weak indeed; at the outbreak of war the garrison consisted of four regular battalions (8th, 41st, 49th and 100th Foot), the 10th Veteran Bn, and a locally-raised 'regular' unit, the Newfoundland Regt, which together with a few artillery companies totalled only 4,450 men, to defend a 1,600-mile frontier. There was in addition the locally-raised Canadian militia, who, though largely ill-trained and not fully equipped were in general to acquit themselves with much greater credit than their American equivalents: a large proportion of the American army was newly-formed and inexperienced, and with the one notable exception of Andrew Jackson had few leaders of consequence. In the opening stages of the war, along the US/Canadian border, one commander of great skill and energy

appeared: Major-General Isaac Brock (1769–1812), who had arrived in Canada in 1802 as commander of the 49th and whose last combat experience had been aboard Nelson's fleet at Copenhagen. To this charismatic leader goes the credit for repelling the American invasion of Canada in late 1812, as the Governor-General at Quebec, the French-American Sir George Prevost, was militarily inexperienced.

Though the Americans planned to attack, they were initially forced onto the defensive by the British capture of Fort Dearborn (now Chicago), its garrison being massacred by 'British' Indians after their surrender; and on the following day, 16 August, the inept American General William Hull surrendered Detroit without resistance, upon the appearance of Brock with a tiny force. Despite chaotic lack of co-operation within the American command, Major-General Stephen van Rensselaer crossed the Niagara with a sizeable force, to establish a bridgehead for a full-scale invasion of Canada. Brock was equal to the task and defeated the Americans at Queenston on 13 October, succeeding with meagre resources but at the cost of his life.

From early 1813 the war widened from the Canadian border to campaigns in the west, north and south. British reinforcements were conveyed across the Atlantic as soon as they could be spared – units which would have been employed more valuably in the Peninsula – and as the war in Europe drew to a close, many more ex-Peninsular regiments were sent to America, a necessary dissipation of strength but one which did not bring the successes which might have been expected, due in part to mediocre command and to the growing confi-

dence of the American leaders and their forces. In the north, the Americans planned a two-pronged assault on Upper Canada, which ended in defeat after the Americans burned York, capital of Upper Canada (now Toronto) on 24 April – which achieved nothing but hardened the Canadian will to resist – and captured Fort George at the mouth of the Niagara. The Americans were routed at Stony Creek (6 June) but British success was nullified by Prevost's defeat at Sackett's Harbor, the US arsenal on Lake Ontario on 28/29 May 1813. An American operation against Montreal was defeated at the Chateaugay River (25 October) and Chrysler's Farm (11 November), but a renewed offensive defeated a small British force at the Chippewa River (5 July 1814). A drawn battle was fought at Lundy's Lane (25 July), which was a strategic success for the British, and following the arrival in Canada of British reinforcements all further plans of invading Canada were discounted. Similarly, Prevost's invasion of the USA via Lake Champlain was blocked at Plattsburg (11 September 1814), and the comprehensive defeat of the British naval squadron on the lake deprived Prevost of his amphibious capability.

In the west, the Americans under General William Henry Harrison prepared to recapture Detroit, despite a sharp defeat at the Raisin River (22 January 1813). Later in the year Harrison and Commodore Oliver Perry, whose squadron defeated the British ships on Lake Erie on 10 September, recovered Detroit

*The burning of Washington by British forces under Maj-Gen Robert Ross, 24/25 August 1814. Naval and staff officers (left) direct infantry through the streets as sailors (in 'round hats', right) break into a building prior to its burning.*

*The battle of New Orleans, 8 January 1815. In the foreground of this print of the unavailing British attacks, Thornton's Bde (85th Light Infantry, 5th West India Regt, marines and seamen) are seen storming an American advanced battery.*

(29 September) and defeated a small British force at the Battle of the Thames (5 October), though no further profit was made as Harrison's militia was ordered to disband and his regulars to go to the Niagara area; Harrison resigned in disgust.

In the Chesapeake Bay area, the increase of British troops freed from the Peninsular War allowed Major-General Robert Ross to occupy Washington, routing the American defenders at Bladensburg (24 August 1814) and burning the White House and the Capitol in Washington on the following day. Another amphibious attack, on Baltimore, met stiffer resistance (12–14 September), during which fighting Ross received a mortal wound, and the British expedition withdrew on 14 October.

In the south, a small British expeditionary force arrived off New Orleans in late November 1814. They were opposed by a hastily-assembled American force under the command of the Americans' most capable commander, General Andrew Jackson. Commanded by Wellington's brother-in-law, Edward Pakenham (a brave officer and capable subordinate if not distinguished in overall command), the British forces landed on 13 December 1813 and penetrated to within seven miles of New Orleans. Jackson prepared an entrenched posi-

tion along the abandoned Rodriguez Canal, south of New Orelans, which Pakenham attacked in force on 8 January 1815. Though many of Jackson's defenders were militia or volunteers, his position was strong, and Pakenham's frontal assault was without tactical skill. The British regiments advanced with extreme heroism against the entrenchments, but the assault was hopeless; 2,100 casualties were suffered and Pakenham killed for the loss of 7 Americans killed and six wounded. A week later the British withdrew; though with awful irony peace had already been signed, at Ghent on 24 December 1814, making New Orleans a tragic, unnecessary battle.

Throughout the war, the Royal Navy had imposed a blockade on the United States which almost bankrupted that country. The tiny US Navy scored some remarkable victories over the hitherto invincible British, a result of the comparative greater power of the American warships and, perhaps, of the complacency among the Royal Navy, which was used to beating the French virtually every time they met. The most famous action, though, was the defeat and capture of USS *Chesapeake* by Capt Philip Vere Broke of HMS *Shannon* off Boston on 1 June 1813, which re-established the reputation of the Royal Navy.

# Quatre Bras – 16 June 1815

The statesmen of Europe were engaged at the Congress of Vienna when news was received that Napoleon had escaped from Elba, where he had been exiled. Probably he intended no more than to inflict sufficient damage on the Allied nations to persuade them to accept a negotiated peace; but the allies determined to dethrone him permanently. They declared him an outlaw and formed the Seventh Coalition against him, determined to field between 500 and 800,000 men, financed by Britain; but their plan to attack France would take time to prepare and only the forces already in the Netherlands could effectively oppose Napoleon's new 'Army of the North' of some 124,000 men. Stationed in Belgium was an Anglo-Netherlands force of about 95,000, and a Prussian army of 124,000, commanded respectively by Wellington – now a Duke, the highest rank in the British peerage – and old 'Marshal Vorwärts' himself, Gebhard v Blücher (1742-1819), one of Napoleon's most determined and uncompromising opponents.

The army which Wellington returned to command from the Congress of Vienna (where he had been a British representative) was far from being the Peninsular army; he attempted to obtain some of his old Portuguese troops, but without success. The nucleus of the army was the British contingent, some of which had been in the Netherlands in the previous year with the expedition led by Sir Thomas Graham, but these battalions were in general weak. The best were old Peninsular corps like the 1/23rd,

51st, 1/52nd, 1/71st, 1/91st and 95th, but many men of these had been discharged after the war, and had been newly-recruited; others, like the 3/14th and 2/59th were very young and very inexperienced. Unlike the Peninsular infantry, much of which had been sent to America, the cavalry had no such calls upon them but they too included inexperienced regiments: for example, the 2nd Dragoons (Scots Greys) had not been on active service since 1795. The King's German Legion, excellent troops as always, were so reduced in numbers by the discharge of non-Hanoverian other ranks that their battalions had to be reduced from ten companies to six.

The remainder of Wellington's army was composed of Netherlanders and Germans. The Netherlandish troops were either young and inexperienced, or had recently fought on Napoleon's side and were unenthusiastic about their new king; their commander, the Prince of Orange, who had served in the Peninsula on Wellington's staff, was eager but inexperienced in command and generally inept. The German contingents were those of the re-created Hanoverian army – some 'regulars' but mostly *Landwehr* (militia) and most inexperienced; the small Nassau contingent, officially part of the Netherlands army, fine veteran battalions which were the best of that nation's troops; and the Duke of Brunswick's small army, including some veterans of his previous 'Black Legion' but with regiments newly-created with mostly young soldiers in their ranks.

Wellington complained constantly about his inability to obtain the officers he wanted for subordinate commands, and as in the Peninsula he was denied some of those he requested; some of his Peninsular generals were unavailable (Pakenham dead at New Orleans, Lowry Cole on his honeymoon, Murray in America), but many of his old companions were present, including De Lancey as Deputy Quartermaster-General, the audacious Colquhoun Grant as head of intelligence, and for the first time the most capable British cavalry general, the Earl of Uxbridge (the Lord Paget of the Corunna campaign) whose family quarrel with Wellington (he had eloped with the Duke's sister-in-law) had prevented his serving earlier.

Central to Wellington's plan of campaign was his organisation of the army, in the mixing of experienced with raw troops and reliable with doubtful. The army was divided into three Corps, the 1st under the Prince of Orange, the 2nd under Hill and the Reserve actually commanded by Picton (his official command was the 5th Division). Within this organisation, British and foreign troops were intermixed, so that only in the 1st Division was the composition entirely British. The brigading was even more subtle; for example, in the 3rd Division, some young British troops were supported by experienced German units; in the 2nd, 5th and 6th Divisions, where the British were all veterans, the Hanoverians were all *Landwehr*. Similarly, in the Netherlands divisions there was a mixture of young and old, Dutch and Belgian; and it is interesting to note that Johnstone's brigade, detached to cover the far right flank at Waterloo and uninvolved in the combat, comprised two non-veteran battalions (2/35th, 1/54th), the young and weak 2/59th, plus one old Peninsular battalion (1/91st), exemplifying perfectly the system of making the best of a mediocre army.

Wellington and Blücher concentrated their armies south of Brussels; they were aware of Napoleon's tactic when faced with two opponents, of interposing him-

*The battle of Quatre Bras. The village of Quatre Bras is in the left mid-ground; the Highlanders in the foreground are members of Kempt's or Pack's brigades, hurried up on the Allied left in support of the original Netherlands and Brunswick defence-line.*

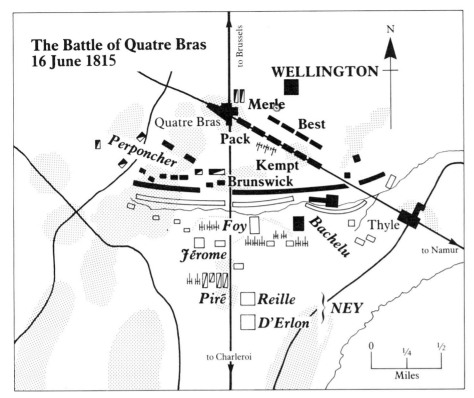

## The Battle of Quatre Bras
## 16 June 1815

*The Black Watch at Quatre Bras. In the midst of the action the battalion commander, Sir Robert Macara, was wounded. As four of his men were carrying him from the field they were surrounded and made prisoners by French cavalry; but seeing from his decorations that Macara was apparently an officer of rank, they callously cut down his attendants and killed him. Only three of the 19 most senior 42nd officers were unscathed in the campaign. (Engraving after Jones.)*

self between the two, 'pinning' one with a minority of his army, destroying the other with the bulk of his forces and then returning to defeat the first. It was vital, therefore, that Wellington's and Blücher's armies be mutually-supportive. A possible difficulty existed in the presence of the efficient Gneisenau, an ideal chief-of-staff to Blücher but a man who distrusted the British; he was less inclined to act in a supportive role but in the event and to his credit followed Blücher's plans.

Napoleon crossed the frontier rapidly on 15 June and took the Allied commanders by surprise; Wellington, attending the Duchess of Richmond's ball in Brussels that evening, remarked that 'Napoleon has humbugged me, by God!', but set the army in motion immediately. He had determined to occupy a defensive position previously reconnoitered, the ridge of Mont St Jean, south of the village of Waterloo on the Brussels-Charleroi road, but his advance positions were further south, at the crossroads of Quatre Bras. The Prussians were concentrated to the east, at Ligny, where Napoleon fell upon them on 16 June.

A subsidiary part of Napoleon's army, commanded by Ney, was sent to Quatre Bras to hold the Anglo-Dutch whilst Napoleon defeated Blücher; but Ney progressed slowly, being valiantly resisted by Prince Bernhard of Saxe-Weimar and about 8,000 Netherlanders. Throughout the action, more elements of Wellington's army came up, though even at the close only 36,000 were present. Initially the position was desperate, with only part of Picton's division and the Brunswick corps assisting Bernhard's steady Nassauers and doubtful Netherlanders. The Duke of Brunswick was killed and his troops forced back; a Netherlands cavalry brigade ran, and Wellington himself was almost captured, jumping his horse over a line of 92nd Highlanders to safety. The fighting was desperate; the 1/42nd and 2/44th were caught by French cavalry before they could form square, the latter turning their rear rank and fighting back-to-back and the Black Watch closing the square and killing the French cavalry inside. The Prince of Orange, resenting the perceived 'interference' of the experienced Picton, ordered four battalions into line, suicidal in the presence of cavalry; the 69th was ridden down, lost a Colour and ceased to exist as an operational unit, and two other battalions (33rd and 2/73rd) scattered. The arrival of more troops (including the ever-reliable British Foot Guards) allowed Wellington to counter-attack and regain almost all the lost ground by the time the battle ended at 9 pm. Ney had lost some 4,000, Wellington 4,800 (including 2,275 British) but in the wider context the French had lost a great opportunity due to Ney's slowness and confusion in the French command.

# Waterloo – 18 June 1815

Wellington withdrew from Quatre Bras to keep in touch with the Prussians on his left, as they retired after being very severely handled by Napoleon at Ligny. Blücher was ridden-over, and was unceremoniously hustled away after the army; until he recovered Gneisenau was left in command. His inclination was to retire on Liége to reorganise, but in the event he stood by Blücher's word and agreed to support his allies, ordering a retreat upon Wavre, within striking distance of what would be Wellington's position, the ridge of Mont St Jean, just south of Waterloo.

The Anglo-Netherlands withdrawal from Quatre Bras was harassed by the leading elements of the French army on 17 June, but the only real difficulty occurred at Genappe, where in the narrow, crowded streets the 7th Hussars were roughly handled by French lancers, but were rescued by a charge of the Life Guards. The position Wellington had selected was a low ridge which intersected the Charleroi/Brussels road at right angles, providing his favourite 'reverse slope'. At the far right a weak British brigade protected the army's flank. The main line was anchored by three fortified strongpoints: on the left flank, the villages of Papelotte, La Haye and Frischermont, garrisoned by Nassauers; in the centre, on the main Brussels/Genappe highway, was the farm of La Haye Sainte, into which

Baring's 2nd KGL Light Bn was thrown, supported by a unit of 95th Rifles in a sandpit a short distance along the road. Forward of the right flank was the strongly-built château of Hougoumont, garrisoned mainly by the light companies of the British Guards, who held the right wing of the line and sent in reinforcements to Hougoumont throughout the day. The remainder of the army was drawn up to the rear of the ridge, along a slightly-sunken road which followed the crest, with thick hedges providing an additional defence. Wellington was determined to stand here and await Blücher's promised arrival on his left flank. It is usual to regard Waterloo as a defensive battle; but within the framework of that defence, Wellington used his resources aggressively, moving units around the field to plug gaps where they occurred, and as usual displayed his remarkable facility of being wherever his personal direction was most required.

Both sides spent a wretched, wet night, with Napoleon drawing up his forces on rising ground opposite the Anglo-Netherlands position. Wellington's forces numbered around 63,000, of which 21,000 were British, 5,000 German Legion, 20,000 Netherlanders, around 11,000 Hanoverians and about 5,500 Brunswickers; with 156 guns. Napoleon's forces numbered about 72,000 with 246 guns, a greater advantage than the figures suggest given the

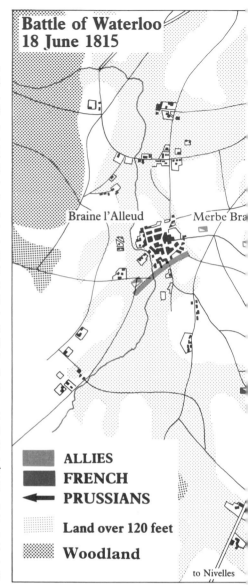

**Battle of Waterloo 18 June 1815**

Braine l'Alleud   Merbe Bra

■ ALLIES
■ FRENCH
← PRUSSIANS

Land over 120 feet
Woodland

to Nivelles

*The defence of Hougoumont was perhaps the most vital part of the battle of Waterloo, anchoring Wellington's right wing and consuming a large part of Napoleon's resources. The light companies of the British Foot Guards comprised the main garrison of Hougoumont, but support was given by reinforcements from the Guards immediately to the rear of Hougoumont. Though driven from the château woods and gardens, the Guards clung on to the blazing buildings throughout the day. In this illustration, reinforcements from the 2/2nd (Coldstream) Guards emerge from the woods to counter-attack the French attempting to force the main gate at Hougoumont, which was that closed by Lt-Col James Macdonell of Glengarry, 'the bravest man at Waterloo'. (Painting by Denis Dighton)*

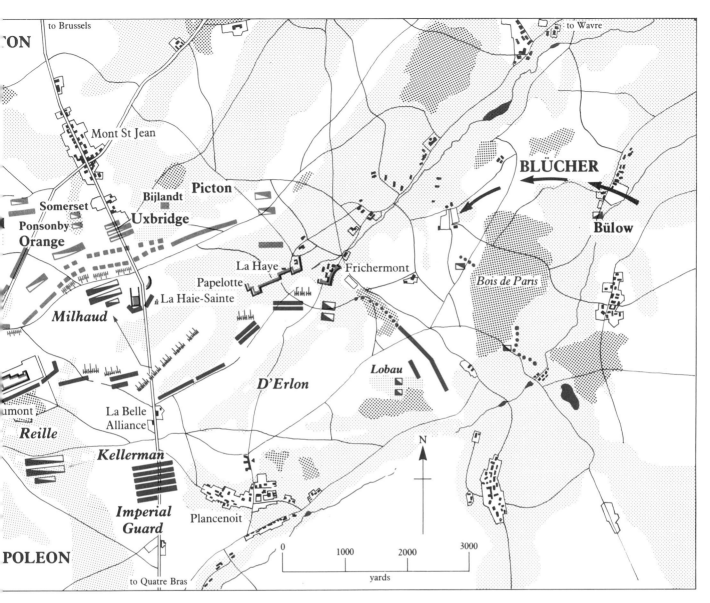

to Brussels

Mont St Jean

**Picton**

Bijlandt

**Uxbridge**

Somerset

Ponsonby

Orange

La Haye

Papelotte

La Haie-Sainte

*Milhaud*

*D'Erlon*

La Belle
Alliance

*Reille*

*Kellerman*

*Imperial
Guard*

Plancenoit

POLEON

to Quatre Bras

to Wavre

**BLÜCHER**

**Bülow**

Frichermont

*Bois de Paris*

*Lobau*

N

| 0 | 1000 | 2000 | 3000 |

yards

quality of some of the Allied troops. Napoleon had no clear view of Wellington's dispositions due to the usual 'reverse slope' tactic, though Soult (miscast as his chief-of-staff when an independent command would have been wiser) warned him that '*l'infanterie Anglaise en duel, c'est le diable*'. Napoleon thought he knew better and unfairly rounded on Soult to the effect that he only thought Wellington was a good general because he had beaten him so often, whereas he, Napoleon, knew that Wellington was a bad general and that the British were bad troops, and the battle would be only an '*affaire d'un déjeuner*'. Whether arrogance or said to bolster his general's morale, it was a great error, as was the delegation of almost all battlefield authority to the impetuous Ney. The result was

not a battle of manoeuvre but (in Wellington's terms) a 'pounding match'.

At about 11.50 am on 18 June the battle began with the assault of Hougoumont by the division of Napoleon's brother, Jérôme Bonaparte, intended as a diversion to draw in Wellington's reserves and leave his army vulnerable to a blow through the centre. But Napoleon had not considered the quality of the Guards defending the château, who clung on tenaciously to the burning buildings throughout the day, drawing in progressively more of Napoleon's troops as Jérôme continued to assault the strongpoint; instead of depleting Wellington's reserves, it had that effect on Napoleon's. Early in the action, a party of the French 1st *Léger* (Light Infantry) outflanked the château and

broke in the northern gate behind the axe-wielding Lt Legros; after a desperate fight Lt-Col James Macdonnell personally heaved the gate shut.

Napoleon assembled a 'massed battery' to bombard the Allied line, but due to Wellington's 'reverse slope' dispositions, its effect was greatly negated though one Allied brigade, Bylandt's exposed Netherlanders, broke and fled under the bombardment. Shortly before Napoleon launched his first main attack on Wellington's centre, he learned of the appearance of Prussian troops far to his right. To hold them off he ordered a defensive flank to be established around the village of Plancenoit, in his right rear, which consumed increasing numbers of troops throughout the day; but due to abysmal roads, mud and a fire which partially blocked the road at Wavre, the Prussians took many hours to arrive, their rearguard valiantly holding off Marshal Emanuel Grouchy whom Napoleon had ordered to prevent their reinforcing Wellington.

Napoleon ordered the first main attack on Wellington's position at about 1.30 pm, d'Erlon's Corps, which advanced in massive, unmanageable columns. Raked by artillery fire, the infantry pushed the Allied skirmishers back and engaged Baring's German Legion in La Haye Sainte; the Prince of Orange, thinking they should be supported, again ordered a battalion into line (the Hanoverian Lüneburgers), and as at Quatre Bras they were destroyed by French cavalry. Struggling up the ridge, the French attack was halted by the disciplined musketry of Picton's Division, though Picton himself was killed by a shot through the head. A conspicuous figure in his customary civilian greatcoat, 'roundhat' and spectacles, the bluff Welshman had been severely wounded at Quatre Bras but had deliberately concealed his injury to command his Division at Waterloo; his was a grievous loss.

As the French attack faltered, Uxbridge launched a counter-charge by the British Household Cavalry and 'Union' brigades (1st, 2nd and 6th Dragoons) which was at first brilliantly successful, breaking all but one of the French Divisions, capturing two 'Eagles' (most famously that of the 45th *Ligne*, by Sgt Charles Ewart of the Scots Greys) and 3,000 prisoners and chasing the remainder back towards the French lines. The whole mass careered on, through the 80-gun 'massed battery' and resisting all orders to rally (such was the pride in the individual regiments that members of the 1st Dragoon Guards refused to obey the command to rally from an officer of the mere Royal Dragoons!). When disordered and their horses 'blown', they were duly cut to pieces by French cavalry; among those killed was Sir William Ponsonby, commander of the Union brigade, whose small horse had stuck in the mud; Lt-Col James Hamilton of the Greys, who had both arms cut off and rode with the reins in his teeth; and John Shaw of the Life Guards, a renowned bare-knuckle prizefighter who attacked the French with fists and helmet after his sabre broke.

At about 3.30 pm Ney mistook a re-

*British infantry in square repel charges by French cuirassiers in the mid-afternoon; note the Congreve rockets visible over the buildings in the centre, which apparently are intended to represent La Haye Sainte. (Engraving by R Reeve after W Heath)*

arrangement of Wellington's line for a withdrawal, and ordered forward the first of numerous French cavalry charges, executed without infantry or artillery support, over glutinous terrain and often executed at a walk, with as many as 10,000 troopers on a 700-yard front, rendering manoeuvre impossible. Never had the French cavalry behaved with more heroism, as they tried to break the squares formed to greet them; each charge was assailed by artillery-fire, the gunners then sheltering within the squares until the cavalry began to retire, then returning and blasting them with canister again; Cavalié Mercer of the Royal Horse Artillery compared them to grass being mown down by a scythe. (His troop remained with their guns throughout, creating a wall of dead in front of their position, as to retire would have caused the raw Brunswick battalions nearby to panic.) British cavalry delivered some counter-charges, but the infantry bore the brunt of the attacks. By 4.30 pm Wellington could hear firing from his far left, indicating the arrival of the Prussians, Blücher commanding in person, but stout defence of Plancenoit by Napoleon's Young and Middle Guard held them off, at least for a time.

Before the Prussians were fully in action, however, the most critical moment of the battle occurred with the fall of La Haye Sainte, as Ney at last co-ordinated cavalry, artillery and infantry in a major attack. Baring's German Legion in the farm ran out of ammunition, and tried to hold the buildings with bayonets. The Prince of Orange, attempting relief, repeated his two earlier errors by ordering the 5th and 8th KGL line battalions to advance in line; and as before, they were caught by French cavalry and the 8th destroyed. At last, Baring with his surviving 42 riflemen evacuated La Haye Sainte, opening the Allied centre to the French onslaught. Moving up artillery, Ney assailed the line with a storm of iron, raking the British battalions still clinging to the ridge. The 2/30th and 2/73rd were so reduced that they had to combine to form a square, as did the 33rd and 2/69th. Colin Halkett, commander of the British 5th Bde, begged Wellington to allow him a few moments' respite to reorganise his four battalions, but Wellington told him that 'every Englishman on the field must die on the spot we now occupy.' The endurance of the

dwindling band of redcoats along the ridge was beyond belief.

At this juncture the battle hung in the balance, as Wellington's centre came under increasing pressure; some raw 'foreign' battalions only held together by the presence of a thin line of British cavalry deliberately formed in their rear to check their flight. This was the moment for a final effort, but when Ney asked Napoleon for more troops, the Emperor replied 'do you think I can

*John Colborne's 52nd Light Infantry prepares to advance at the critical moment of the last French attack, ordered on by Wellington; at the right is an officer and rifleman of the 95th.*
*(Print after George Jones)*

make them?'; for now the pressure from the Prussians in Plancenoit on his right flank was intense. Against the depleted Anglo-Netherlanders virtually the last French reserve was now committed: seven battalions of the Imperial Guard, who had never before suffered defeat. Two immense columns began to ascend the ridge, mistakenly not against that part of the line most shattered; instead, one column approached Maitland's Guards Division, lying hidden amidst the standing corn. The smaller column drove back the 30th and 73rd, but for once the Netherlanders stood firm and the attack withdrew. The stronger column came within 40 yards of the Guards, where as usual Wellington was in command at the critical point. Whether he said 'Up Guards and at them', or more likely 'Stand up, Guards' and 'Now, Maitland, now's your time!', the effect was the same: the British appeared as if from nowhere and poured musketry into the Imperial Guard; witnesses described the writhings of the column as corn blown before the wind. The column wavered as its head was decimated, and at that moment John Colborne wheeled his 1/52nd and enfiladed their flank; it was peculiarly appropriate that this crucial manoeuvre should be executed by Moore's old regiment, those most stalwart members of the Peninsular Light Division.

The Imperial Guard disintegrated and began to flee back down the slope; Wellington ordered a general advance, shouting to Colborne to 'Go on, go on! They won't stand. Don't give them a chance to rally!' The cry '*La Garde recule!*' rose from the French army, and the sight of the defeat of the Guard put the remainder to flight. The Prussians finally burst out of Plancenoit, and as

night drew on Wellington and Blücher met at the appropriately-named inn of La Belle Alliance, in the rear of Napoleon's position, the old Prussian remarking '*Quelle affaire*' (about the only French he knew) and apologising for smelling of gin and onions, with which he had dosed himself to recover from his fall at Ligny.

The Prussians conducted the pursuit, for Wellington's army was both exhausted and shattered. About 15,000 were casualties, the bulk from the British battalions which, like the 27th, were now lying 'dead in a square' on the ridge. Peninsular veterans were stunned, for only in the breaches at Badajoz had such carnage ever been experienced. Wellington's staff was decimated; Uxbridge had lost his leg at Wellington's side (reputedly saying, 'By God, sir, I've lost my leg!'; at which the Duke glanced at him and replied, 'By God, sir, so you have'). The 1/27th had but three officers out of 19 unscathed; the 28th one officer above the rank of lieutenant. Halkett had replied to the Duke by saying 'we stand here until the last man falls'; and they had. As he began to receive the casualty-returns, Wellington broke down and wept; as he said, nothing but a battle lost can be half so melancholy as a battle won.

Many reasons have been advanced for Napoleon's defeat, including his own failings and the presence of the Prussians, and certainly their arrival turned the day; as Sir Hussey Vivian remarked (commander of the 6th Cavalry Bde), 'those are most unjust to the Prussians who refuse them their full share of the credit'. In 1816 Baron v Müffling, Wellington's Prussian liaison officer, gave another reason: 'There is not perhaps in Europe an army equal to the British . . . The British soldier is vigorous, well fed, by nature highly brave and intrepid, trained to the most rigorous discipline, and admirably well armed. The infantry resist the attacks of the cavalry with great confidence, and when taken in the flank or rear, British troops are less disconcerted than any other European army. These circumstances in their favour will explain how this army, since the Duke of Wellington conducted it, has never yet been defeated in the open field.' One other reason was voiced by Wellington himself: 'By God, I don't think it would have done if I had not been there.'

A copper halfpenny minted privately in Kent in 1795 bore the inscription 'God Bless the Wooden Walls of Old England'. The 'wooden walls' – the ships of the Royal Navy – were arguably the most important part of Britain's war effort, and consequently expenditure on the Royal Navy often outstripped that on the army, even at those times when a large military presence was required overseas (though by the later stages of the Peninsular War, the balance had swung towards the army).

The reason for the importance of the navy is explained simply by geography: as an island, Britain's foreign commerce depended wholly upon her merchant fleet, and to protect which her naval forces were vital. British trading-ships ranged over the globe, from the icebound ports of the far north to the tropics where the climate was (in a memorable contemporary phrase) only a sheet of paper from hell; although the East India Company maintained a small 'naval' contingent to protect her own merchantmen, virtually all this responsibility fell upon the Royal Navy, which at times was considerably stretched. Equally significant, and certainly consuming more resources, was the 'war of commerce' waged actively against France in support of the 'Orders in Council' (November/December 1807) which were decreed as a counter to Napoleon's 'Continental System'; by which Orders all neutral vessels proceeding to or from a hostile port should be required to pay a levy imposed by Britain or have their goods confiscated. This was basically an extension of the blockade of French ports which had been in course throughout, to restrict France's maritime capability. The differing results of the blockades and 'war of commerce' engaged in by France and Britain reflect the respective capability of the navies. From the outbreak of war to 1800 a mere 2½ per cent of British trade was stopped by the French efforts, and the Continental System (by which all European ports under French influence were closed to British trade) caused a drop in British exports of less than 9 per cent in 1807, a temporary effect as in 1808 British exports increased by

27 per cent! So ineffective was the French attempt to destroy British commerce that the tonnage of the merchant fleet rose from 1,512,231 in 1804 to 2,072,244 in 1809, and both imports and exports peaked in 1810. Despite the Continental System, smuggling was so rife that British trade with Europe flourished. Conversely, French overseas commerce was virtually annihilated by British naval supremacy; in 1812-13 foreign commerce represented only 5.3 per cent of the Empire's total produce (in francs 378 million out of a total of over 7,034 million), and that would be almost exclusively over land.

The Royal Navy's other role was offensive, against the French and their Allied naval forces. Their initial duty was to prevent the possibility of French invasion of Britain; although a landing was achieved in Ireland and, less seriously, in Wales, neither were able to receive reinforcement due to the presence of the British fleet, and other attempts at invasion never reached the coast. Though Napoleon's overall strategy had caused the abandonment of his plans to invade Britain even before Trafalgar was fought, the virtual annihilation of the fleet engaged assured that the opportunity would never again arise, despite the ambitious plans to create a navy even more powerful than Britain's, which were proceeeding almost up until the fall of the Empire. Of equal importance was the British navy's role in confounding Napoleon's wider strategical plans; the destruction of the French fleet in Aboukir Bay marooned the French 'Army of the Orient' in Egypt and ended Napoleon's dream of creating an overseas empire, and the destruction of the Danish fleet at Copenhagen caused the 'Armed Neutrality of the North' to collapse. The latter is an example of the 'war of commerce' in that the main threat of the Neutrality was in the interruption of vital supplies imported by Britain from the Baltic – grain (to compensate for bad British harvests which forced the price of wheat per 'Winchester quarter' to 138/1d in 1801, its highest for the period; it had been 48/4d in 1790), and timber for the shipyards.

Throughout the period, the Royal Navy attacked and captured hostile bases throughout the world, reducing the French and their allies' colonies to a minimum; and even more important was their support of every land campaign undertaken by Britain during the period. Of necessity, ships were required to transport the military forces to their theatre of operations, be it Egypt, India or the Peninsula, but their role was far more than simply as a transport service, for every land campaign required a constant process of re-supply. In some campaigns, almost everything had to be landed by ship, at least initially (even the army's water after the landing in Egypt), and though it was usually possible for the military forces to purchase provender from the area of campaign, naval support in the supply of reinforcements and munitions was invaluable for the maintenance of the war, and on occasion even had a strategic effect in itself; for example, the establishment of Santander as Wellington's supply-base in the later stages of the Peninsular War was entirely due to the navy's total domination of the sea, and the frequent raids on the east coast of Spain occupied large numbers of French troops required elsewhere. So dominant was the Royal Navy over their continental opponents that the minor defeats in the single-ship actions of the War of 1812 caused an outcry, so used had Britain become to the navy being successful in every engagement. A measure of the domination is provided by the statistics that in the period of the wars, the French navy lost some 90 'capital' ships (50 guns or more); only one British ship of similar nature was captured and not recovered. If some of Britain's military successes were spectacular, then the Navy's overall record was matchless.

*HMS* Victory *at Trafalgar: Admiral Lord Nelson's immortal flagship in the midst of the action. The wreckage of damaged ships with survivors clinging to what floated was a common feature of major naval engagements, as shown in the foreground of JMW Turner's painting.*

# Ships' Crews

One of the most obvious ways in which the Royal Navy was superior to those of other continental states was in the quality of its training and personnel, much of which devolved upon the expertise of the officer corps. At the head was the naval equivalent of the Horse Guards, the Board of Admiralty. The Lords Commissioners of the Admiralty consisted of a number of board members, headed by the 'First Lord' (usually a politician) and the 'First professional Lord', a distinguished senior officer. All orders emanated from this body (though naturally the difficulties of communication gave the commanding officers of overseas stations virtually independent command over their own fleets), and it is remarkable that a total Admiralty office staff as small as under 60 (including the gardener!) could run all naval matters with a high degree of efficiency. This was perhaps less due to the seven Lords Commissioners (of whom often only the First Lord or 'professional Lord' would be present to attend to routine business) than to the Board Secretary, the Admiralty's senior civil servant in whose name most orders were issued; most famous (and capable) of these incumbents was probably Evan Nepean, who signed all but the most important orders and commissions, which required the assent of three Board members.

Unlike the navies of some continental states, officers of the Royal Navy had to be adjudged competent seamen before they could be commissioned. A lieutenant's commission could not be awarded until the appropriate examination had been passed, and it was not possible to take the examination until six years had been spent at sea, two of which had to be in the position of midshipman or master's mate; thus, candidates would usually be taken to sea at a very early age as a 'captain's servant' or 'volunteer' to gain time at sea; frauds were attempted to short-cut the process but after 1794, when volunteers first received pay, the scope was much reduced. All these 'cadets' (this term was not used) were enrolled independently of the Admiralty; selection of a 'volunteer' depended wholly upon the individual captain, so that his young pupils were usually the offspring of friends, relations or influential contacts. From the earliest stage, therefore, the influence of 'patronage' was great, and extended up to the very highest ranks; captains might ally their careers to a particular admiral, who would in turn favour his own followers or 'family' over those of another Admiral, and the interchange of favours was commonplace. The system was potentially open to great abuse, and though undoubtedly some careers suffered unfairly as a result, in general it worked remarkably well.

The position of midshipman was usually the first step on the ladder of promotion, and this lowest of 'officers'' rank was occupied by young men gaining their experience at sea or, having passed the examination for lieutenant, awaiting a vacancy or who lacked the necessary influence to rise in rank. Some midshipmen were less than fourteen years of age,

*A seaman in 'shore rig': the uniform of seamen was unregulated, so that each man purchased his own clothing on shore, or as 'purser's slops' bought at sea. The straw 'round hat' was the universal head-dress, often tarred in northern climates, and the short blue jacket had an opening 'mariner's cuff' to enable it to be rolled up. The loose trousers could similarly be rolled up, and it was customary at sea to have bare feet, allowing for a better grip on the sanded decks and rigging.*
*(Engraving after CH Smith).*

but most were in their twenties; midshipmen of forty years were not uncommon and one was approaching 60 before he was given his lieutenancy (having told the examination board to be damned when they set him an insoluble problem!). The examination for lieutenant could not be taken before the age of 20 (later 19), though there was a degree of latitude in practice, and paid attention not only to theory but practical seamanship, which allowed those of unusual talents of leadership and seamanship to pass even though they might be weak on mathematics or navigation, or 'rum in their nauticals' as the saying went. Having gained a lieutenant's commission, the new officer began to progress up the Navy List ('Sea Officers' List'), his promotion being dependent upon the attraction of his superiors' notice or 'influence'; seniority alone could not guarantee promotion so that a man might languish in the lieutenants' list for 40 years or more. By the rules of promotion, a lieutenant could command only an 'unrated' ship (i.e. usually less than 20 guns); anything larger required the promotion to commander, who commanded 'sixth-raters'. For ships of 32 guns and above (frigates to line-of-battleships) the commander was a 'post captain'; command of such automatically resulted in the officer being 'made post' with the rank of captain. (The intermediate step of commander was not essential; a favoured lieutenant could step up immediately to captain.) In this sense 'captain' was a rank; though by convention the commander of *any* vessel was called 'captain'. Progress up the captains' list was by seniority, eventually rising automatically through the three grades of rear-admiral, three of vice-admiral and two of admiral, if the officer lived long enough, though in many cases these steps were achieved only after many years on the 'half-pay' list.

Because there were insufficient commands for the large number of qualified officers, before the war less than a quarter were actually employed, and even during the war many languished on half-pay, awaiting an appointment which might never come, for a commander could not be given less than a sixth-rate ship nor an unemployed captain revert to a commander's position. Officers on half-pay – virtually enforced if often temporary retirement – might not be inactive; Capt Charles Napier R.N.

## SHIPS' CREW:
### The number of crew varied from ship to ship, even of the same 'rating', but the following were typical statistics:

| 'Rate' | Guns | Seamen | Marines |
|---|---|---|---|
| 1st | 100-110 | 875 | 1 captain, 3 subalterns |
| 2nd | 90-98 | 750 | 1 captain, 3 subalterns |
| 3rd | 80-74 | 650 | 1 captain, 3 subalterns |
| 3rd | 64 | 650 | 1 captain, 2 subalterns |
| 4th | 50 | 420 | 2 lieutenants |
| 5th | 32-44 | 300 | 1 subaltern |
| 6th | 20-28 | 200 | 1 subaltern |
| Sloop | 16-18 | 125 | 1 sergeant |

In addition to the officers listed above, it was usual for the complement of marines to equal the number of guns.

served at Busaco (where he was wounded) 'not having a ship at that time and being too active and enterprising a fellow to remain at home idle waiting for one', having attached himself to the 52nd as an 'amateur'. In 1812 Capt Nesbit Willougby served in the Russian army as a colonel! Thus, naval officers could have chequered careers and despite periods of unemployment might achieve high rank. William Tremlett was typical: he entered the navy aged 11, was discharged in disgrace as a midshipman, was re-admitted and made lieutenant by age 17. After a number of distinguished actions, as a captain he was transferred to land to command the Cromer Sea Fencibles (not popular appointments) where he had the distinction of being crippled by a shot in the foot from his own men. Back in a sea command, he received the rank of General in the Spanish Army for his services off the Peninsula, but after his ship was wrecked off the Ile de Rhé in 1809 never served again, yet survived to reach admiral's rank 43 years later.

Although bound by the 36 Articles of War, enforceable by Court-Martial and death penalty, at sea a captain was in total command of his ship, unless it was acting in concert with others whose commanders were his seniors. This gave a degree of latitude to his conduct not available to military officers, especially if a frigate captain on a 'cruise', i.e. looking for any tempting target. The responsibility was awesome, but the system worked remarkably well and threw up only a few lunatics or tyrants, most in-

famously Capt Pigot of HMS *Hermione* who was murdered by his crew – a forgivable offence in the circumstances – but who then did the unforgivable and handed the ship to the Spaniards. The Admiralty was extremely strict with those guilty of irregularities, and a minority of cases were appalling, such as that of Lieutenant Leaver of HMS *Martial*, court-martialled in 1814 and found not guilty of flogging to death a ship's boy named Ansell but convicted of pouring cold water over the boy and confining him to the 'coal hole' at a time when mortally ill.

The Royal Navy's need for seamen was insatiable. The authorized strength of the navy rose from 45,000 at the outbreak of war to 110,000 seamen and 20,000 marines in 1800, and losses were considerable: in the major actions less than 1,900 were killed but over 85,000 died of disease, accident or shipwreck. To maintain this continual supply of men, the government resorted to three forms of recruitment: volunteers, the 'Quota', and impressment. Volunteers were the most acceptable: seamen who enlisted and were paid a cash bounty. The Quota Act was introduced in 1795, by which each county had to provide a number of recruits calculated upon its population or pay a fine, so that the civic authorities either offered a bounty to fill their quota with volunteers or in some cases remitted the sentences of malefactors providing they agreed to go to sea. The most infamous mode of recruitment, however, was the 'press gang' or,

*A Royal Navy captain of three years' post, c. 1805, in a typical seagoing 'undress' uniform. Until 1857 only naval officers had an authorised blue uniform, introduced in 1748 and progressively re-styled, the original white facings being withdrawn in 1795. Gold lace was worn on full dress uniforms, but in 'undress' the only decoration was the gold epaulettes, of which two were worn by captains of three years' post and one by those of under three years. The hat by this date was generally worn 'fore-and-aft'.*

more correctly, the Impress Service.

The impressment of seamen into the King's service was used as early as the 13th century, and involved the forcible abduction of men irrespective of their circumstances (providing that they were not apprentices, under 18 or over 55 years, though these terms were not observed rigorously). Although merchant seamen were the preferred target (being already trained), press-gangs ranged far inland to conscript unwilling civilians; though equally common was the practice of stopping merchant-ships en route to port and taking off any likely men. The Impress Service was highly unpopular in some quarters; the *Morning Chronicle* claimed in 1798 that manning the navy in this manner was so absurd that even Swift in *Gulliver's Travels*, 'though he drew occasionally upon his imagination to heighten or multiply follies, he could not stretch so far as this'. Until the impressed men reached their ships, they sometimes had to be forcibly restrained from absconding; in June 1798 it was reported that 15 had suffocated whilst locked in the hold of a tender lying off the Tower. Resistance to the press-gang was sometimes fierce; a veteran of the 'Glorious 1st of June', Peter Martin, was hanged near Chester in 1798 for shooting a member of the press-gang from HMS *Acteon* in the Mersey, and as late as 1812 Midshipman Thomas Benny was indicted for discharging a musket whilst under attack from those objecting to the press.

*Nelson mortally wounded at Trafalgar: Denis Dighton's painting depicting the upper deck of HMS* Victory *illustrates the appearance of all sections of the crew, including seamen, marines and petty officers, one of whom (wearing blue and a 'round hat') is sharpshooting in the centre foreground.*

Though the impress was unpopular, there was no realistic alternative for producing recruits; the Sea Fencibles (the maritime 'home guard') had been intended for use as a reservoir of experienced seamen to serve in an emergency, but when requested hardly any came forward. These men were exempted from the press (indeed, in 1812 they actually operated a 'hot press' on the Thames) but later in that year when their 'protection' from impressment was withdrawn, the London watermen apparently ceased work rather than risk the press-gang, so that 'the whole of the business below bridge is at a standstill, and the Baltic fleet outward, is detained'. The number of felons drafted into the navy was probably less than popularly believed, though numerous cases are recorded such as that in January 1814 when 'two little boys . . . neither of them twelve years of age and seemingly much younger' were sent to the Impress Service at Tower Hill as their last chance of 'reformation' (having broken a window and stolen a handkerchief). It is impossible to arrive at any definitive proportion of pressed men to volunteers, as numbers of those impressed from merchant ships at sea might choose to volunteer rather than be conscripted (thus receiving the bounty); but whatever the case, the system did work satisfactorily, and as each ship's crew was

mutiny' discipline was not one of the seamen's complaints. Other punishments varied from 'starting' (blows struck by a rope's-end wielded by a petty officer) to execution for such crimes as mutiny. Officers who exceeded their authority were dismissed after court-martial, even so illustrious a hero as Sir Edward Hamilton (who audaciously recovered the surrendered *Hermione*) being dismissed for tying men to the rigging, and

*Private, Royal Marines, c. 1805. Each ship had a complement of Royal Marines, in effect the Navy's military force, who in action acted as sharpshooters and formed the nucleus of landing-parties. Another purpose for their presence aboard ship was implied by the fact that they slept between the officers' quarters and the seamen: to protect the officers from the danger of mutiny. Their uniform consisted of a red infantry-style jacket with blue facings (white before 1802), a 'round hat' with white-and-over-red plume and military overalls. Lace was white with red and blue stripes; gold for officers.*

discharged at the end of its commission the conscription was only for a limited period. Apart from the dangers of combat, life at sea with the Royal Navy was easier than in many merchant ships, as the very much larger crews meant that the individual's work-load was less than it would have been aboard a merchantman, and whilst life was spartan and provisions rough, at least the quantity of food was usually sufficient.

Foreigners were also enrolled in the Royal Navy; over ten per cent of the crew of HMS *Victory* at Trafalgar, for example, was non-British, including at least 15 nationalities, many Americans among them and even a Russian, an African, Swiss, Scandinavians and West Indians. Americans were officially exempt from impressment, providing they had a 'protection' issued by an American consul, but the issue of these was uncontrolled and many British seamen declared themselves American to escape the press. The ignoring of such fraudulently-obtained 'protections' was one of the causes of the War of 1812.

Discipline was imperative if ships' companies were to be effective in action, and its enforcement was the subject of much criticism by those unaware of conditions at sea. Until 1806 captains were not officially entitled to order more than a dozen lashes (though many ordered more), and brutal though the process was of beating with a cat o'nine tails, it was regarded by even the ordinary seamen as a necessary method of enforcing discipline. Even at the time of the 'great

in another infamous case a captain was cashiered for having marooned a member of his crew on a desert island.

Promotion from the 'lower decks' (where the seamen lived) went from 'landsman' (i.e. an untrained recruit) to ordinary and able seamen (some of whose responsibility determined their title, e.g. 'captain of the foretop') to those possessing special skills, sailmakers, carpenters, etc, who were termed 'idlers' from their being excused the standing of watches. The 'petty officers' were appointed by the captain, but the higher ranks or 'warrant' officers were Admiralty or Navy Board appointments: gunner, boatswain, carpenter, master-at-arms, etc, plus the more exalted posts 'of wardroom rank' (i.e. those who lived with the 'commission' officers): purser, surgeon, chaplain and the master (or 'sailing master'), arguably the most important man on the ship, responsible for navigation and the production of charts. The purser was responsible for all victuals and clothing, and was financially responsible for his accounts.

# Ships-of-the-Line

The principal ships of the Royal Navy were those known as 'ships-of-the-line' or 'line-of-battle-ships', virtually floating gun-platforms, heavily armed and used for offensive operations against the enemy fleet. These ranged from the older 50-gun ships to the huge three-deckers mounting in excess of 100 guns, all of which were allocated a 'rating' according not to the size or actual number of guns carried, but of the number of ports or 'perforations' from which guns could be fired (thus a ship-of-the-line with most of its guns removed to take extra stores – said to be 'en flûte' – retained its original rating). The rating could be deceptive, however, as additional guns were usually carried; carronades, for example, did not form part of the 'rated' armament so that a '50-gunner' would actually carry 62 guns, and so on. The first four rates were all ships-of-the-line, the 98-gunners and above with three decks and others two. Although ships' armaments varied within the 'rates', typical statistics for guns are noted on p.154.

Dispositon of guns varied from ship to ship, but typical arrangements were as follows: for a 100-gunner, lower deck 28 × 32pdrs; middle deck 28 × 24pdrs; upper deck 28 × 12pdrs; quarter-deck 12 × 12 or 6pdrs; forecastle 4 × 12 or 6pdrs. For a two-decker 74-gunner: lower deck 28 × 32pdrs; upper deck 28 × 18pdrs; quarterdeck 14 × 12 or 9pdrs; forecastle 4 × 12 or 9pdrs. Carronades were carried on the quarterdeck and forecastle.

In fleets of any size, the flagships were 1st- or 2nd-raters, and the bulk of the fleet was composed of 74-gunners, which were preferred to the 64s by virtue of their additional armament. Fourth-raters of 50 or 60 guns were used only in emergencies, as they were generally not sufficiently strong to sail in the line-of-battle and lacked the manoeuvrability to engage enemy frigates; although it is interesting to note that the 50-gunner HMS *Leander* played an important role in the battle of Aboukir Bay, slipping into the line of anchored French ships. The bulk of the Royal Navy's ships-of-the-line were built in Britain, the most famous yard being that at Buckler's Hard near Portsmouth. The preferred material was English oak, but as a typical

*Officer, 2nd (Queen's Royal) Regt, 1794, wearing the ordinary scarlet infantry uniform with the regimental blue facings and silver lace. Detachments of troops were sometimes used as marines aboard ship, even cavalrymen on rare occasions. The 2nd Foot illustrated served at the 'Glorious First of June'; Mather Brown's famous painting of Lord Howe at the battle aboard HMS* Queen Charlotte *also illustrates the death of the 2nd's Lt Neville.*

74 might require 2,000 trees, or around fifty acres, Italian and Baltic oak was also acceptable. With a gun-deck 182 feet long and an extreme breadth of 48 feet, and a displacement in excess of 1,600 tons, construction of such a ship was a massive undertaking, and as the war progressed the price rose dramatically, for example from around £12 per ton at the start of the war to over £20 per ton. Vast amounts of materials other than wood were used; apart from about 43 tons of 'cordage' (rigging) and nine tons of sails (including spares), the material used for sealing the woodwork and filling the joints might run to 30 tons of pitch, tar and oakum. The hull below the water-line was normally clad in sheet copper – more than 12 tons for a '74' – to protect the hull from the boring teredo worm which otherwise could literally eat out the bottom of a ship; metal cladding was infinitely better than the painted mixure ('black stuff' or 'white stuff') used as protection before the introduction of coppering. Even the paint required would add a further four tons or more. It is interesting to note that, contrary to popular belief, the colour-scheme of black with yellow 'strakes' along the lines of the gunports was not an officially-adopted or universal colour-scheme, though it became very common in the post-Trafalgar era. From 1780 ships were officially allowed to be painted black or yellow (all-black sides would tend to make the ship appear smaller and tempt the enemy to attack), but colour-schemes depended upon captains' preference. At Aboukir Bay, for example, the British fleet included a variety of colours: six were plain yellow and five yellow with a black strake between upper and lower gunports. HMS *Culloden* was yellow with two black strakes; *Zealous* red with a narrow yellow stripe, and *Minotaur* red with a black strake between upper and lower gunports. HMS *Theseus*, a 74gun two-decker, was yellow with a black strake between upper and lower gunports and in addition had an ingenious addition: the hammock-cloths on each side (which in action acted as rudimentary splinter-shields immediately above the upper-deck guns) were painted yellow with black shapes to resemble gunports, giving the enemy the impression that the ship was a three-decker! Additional decoration such as gold-leaf ornamentation had to be de-

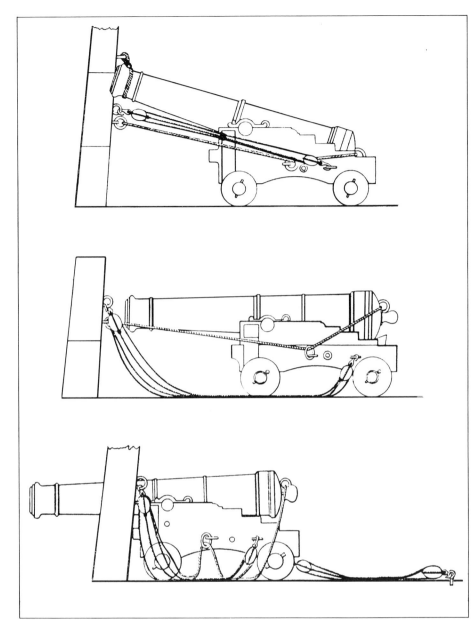

which the victorious ship was attached) received one-eighth, and the victorious captain two eighths. The 'commission' officers, master and surgeon shared an eighth; the warrant officers and master's-mates shared another; the midshipmen, mates, inferior warrant officers and marine sergeants shared another; whilst the remainder of the company shared two-eighths. This was an unequal division (the Admiral's and captain's shares were reduced after 1808) and resulted in some Admirals and officers becoming extreme-ly wealthy (especially those in lucrative stations such as the West Indies), but gave rise to the most famous naval cartoon of the period, in which a seaman prays before battle that the enemy's shot be distribut-ed like the subsequent prize-money, the lion's share among the officers! (The intricacies of the prize-money system were such that in April 1807 an Act of Parliament was passed to allow a share of the prize-money for ships captured at Genoa and Savona by Admiral Lord Keith to be shared with the crew of allied ships which also participated, in this case naval units of the Kingdom of the Two Sicilies. The Act was widened to authorize the sharing of prize-money with all 'Ships or Vessels belonging to any Foreign States, Allies, or Auxiliaries of His Majesty' which collaborated with the Royal Navy, a remarkably fair sys-tem by which any such sum was paid by the Prize Agent to the London minister of the nation in question.)

Britain's fleet, as befitted a power which regarded itself as primarily mari-time rather than land-based, was excep-tionally more powerful than any of its continental rivals; in 1790, for example, the Royal Navy possessed 195 ships-of-the-line against only 81 by France, 72 by Spain, 44 by Holland and 38 by Denmark, but such figures, though published dur-ing the period, are extremely deceptive. In 1794, in fact, 100 ships-of-the-line

frayed out of the captain's own pocket.

Although the majority of line-of-battle-ships were British-built, a con-siderable proportion was always represen-ted by ships captured from the enemy, either in combat or after the occupation of enemy harbours like Toulon or Copenhagen. Great importance was laid upon the acquisition of enemy vessels, by the Admiralty as a quick way of increasing the fleet, and by members of the navy who received 'prize money' for each capture. There were two varieties of financial reward for the capture of an enemy vessel; the first, 'bounty' or 'head' money, was an equal payment to each member of the crew at the rate initially of £10 per gun on the captured

vessel, later to £5 per head of enemy crew (so that, for example, a 64 gun ship might yield £640 to £650 for the victorious crew, divided equally). This sum was small compared to 'prize money' distri-buted when a captured enemy ship was 'bought in' by the Admiralty; when all contents and the ship itself were calcula-ted, many thousands of pounds might eventually be paid to the capturing crew (shared equally with the crews of any British ships within sight; even if an approaching ship fired not a gun, it was regarded as part-captor as its very appear-ance might have persuaded the enemy to surrender). The total value of the prize was divided into eighths; the Admiral commanding the fleet (or station to

153

were actually in commission (nine of them weak 50-gunners); eight were employed as 'guardships', hospital or prison-hulks (including three '50s'). The remaining ships were either repairing, building, or not in commission. Of the 92 ships-of-the-line in actual service, 12 were in the West Indies, 3 in the East Indies and 1 in African waters; 41 were in port and fitting-out, so that the immediately-disposable total which the Admiralty could deploy were 18 in home waters and 19 in the Mediterranean. The resources were thus stretched thinly, and remained so virtually throughout the period. (The cost and frequency of repair often outstripped the financial outlay of building; HMS *Victory*, for example, cost on average almost £10,000 a year to maintain her between 1790 and 1805, half as much again as she had cost to build in 1765.)

In 1794, of the ships-of-the-line, eight were captured foreign ships, five French, two Dutch and one Spanish (HMS *Gibraltar*), only two of which were in commission as battleships (*Gibraltar*, 80, and *Argonaut*, 64). This number of foreign ships increased rapidly during the Revolutionary and Napoleonic Wars, however, and thus is explained the strange naming borne by many British ships, as their orignal titles were only changed if a Royal Navy ship of the same name already existed or if the foreign name had political overtones; thus the Royal Navy had ships-of-the-line titled *Salvador del Mundo* (Spanish, 112 guns), *Rivoli* and *Marengo* (74 guns, French ships named after Napoleon's

victories!), and *Tre Kronen* (the Danish *Trekroner*, 74 guns). Typical of changes of name was that of the French 74 *Peuple Souverain*, a name politically unacceptable; instead it became HMS *Guerrier* (keeping the French style), whilst others like the 74-gun *Hoche* received truly British names, in this case *Donegal*. HMS *Achilles* was a British-built 74, but at Trafalgar fought alongside an ex-French 74 which retained the name *Achille*; there was in addition at that battle a 74 in the French fleet bearing the same name). This naming-system rarely worked in reverse due to the small number of British ships captured by the enemy, though *Swiftsure* was an exception: an ex-British 74 in the French fleet at Trafalgar, it was recaptured at that battle, in which an HMS *Swiftsure* also fought in the British fleet (when recaptured, the old *Swiftsure* was re-styled HMS *Irresistible*). *Berwick* was another example; captured by the French in March 1795, it was re-taken at Trafalgar but sank. Classical or foreign names were beyond the comprehension of most British seamen, so that HMS *Agamemnon* became 'Old Eggs and Bacon', *Bellerophon* 'Billy Ruffian' and *Téméraire* 'Timmy Roar', for example!

Most of the captures taken into the Royal Navy were ships of the smaller variety, but they included a considerable number of 1st-4th rates. By capture, the navy gained from France 1 120-gunner, 8 80-gunners, 26 76-gunners, 1 64-gunner and 1 50-gunner (the last the recaptured HMS *Leander* lost in 1789 and retaken at Corfu by the Russians in

1799); from Spain 2 112-gunners, 3 80-gunners and 5 74-gunners; from the Dutch 1 74-gunner, 1 72-gunner, 1 70-gunner, 3 68-gunners, 8 64-gunners, 3 56-gunners and 2 54-gunners; and from the Danes 2 84-gunners, 12 74-gunners, 1 64-gunner and 1 60-gunner. The largest capture was 15 Danish ships-of-the-line at Copenhagen in 1807, 7 Dutch at Camperdown and 7 at the Texel in 1799, 6 French at Aboukir (of which two fought under British colours at Trafalgar, *Tonnant* and *Spartiate*) and four at Toulon in 1793. As different nations built different styles of ship, some of the foreign designs were found to be even better than those native-built (French frigates, for example, were especially prized), and in addition to commissioning captured ships, especially good designs were copied: HMS *Cambridge*, for example, was a duplicate of the Danish *Christian VII* captured at Copenhagen (and itself commissioned into the Royal Navy without a change of name), whilst the *Northumberland*, which conveyed Napoleon to St Helena, was ironically a copy of the French *Impérieux*. Other British ships with French names were home-built, the most famous perhaps the *Foudroyant* and the *Ville de Paris*.

Set against these acquisitions were considerable British losses, though very few were as a result of enemy action. Among these losses, 25 ships-of-the-line were wrecked (including HMS *Leopard* whilst acting as a troopship), 7 were accidentally burned (including the captured French 80-gunner *Ça Ira*, which retained its name despite its political overtones), 7 were captured by the enemy, 4 foundered (including the 64-gunner HMS *York* which disappeared in the North Sea) and one accidentally blown up (the 64-gun HMS *Ardent* off Corsica in 1794). No 1st-raters were lost during the period, the largest ships lost being 98-gunners, HMS *Boyne* accidentally burned and *Impregnable* and *St George* wrecked. Many of the ships-of-the-line were of considerable age; of those existing in 1794, at least 25 were more than 30 years old, including HMS *Anson* (built 1743); older ships were generally kept 'in ordinary' (i.e. not in commission or used as storeships, hospitals, guardships, etc), though HMS *Valiant* was still serving with the Channel fleet in 1794, having been built in 1759. The ships at Aboukir Bay, for example, dated from

### 'Rating' of ships:

| Rate | Guns | cannon (pdrs) | | | | | | | carronades (pdrs) | | | |
|------|------|----|----|----|----|----|----|----|----|----|----|----|
| | | 42 | 32 | 24 | 18 | 12 | 9 | 6 | 32 | 24 | 18 | 12 |
| 1st | 110 | 28 | – | 28 | – | 30 | – | 18 | 2 | 6 | – | – |
| 2nd | 98 | – | 28 | – | 30 | 40 | – | – | 2 | – | 6 | – |
| 3rd | 80 | – | 26 | – | 26 | – | 24 | 4 | 2 | – | 6 | – |
| | 74 | – | 28 | – | 28 | – | 18 | – | 2 | – | 6 | – |
| | 70 | – | 28 | – | 28 | – | 14 | – | 2 | – | 6 | – |
| | 64 | – | – | 26 | 26 | – | 12 | – | – | 2 | 6 | – |
| 4th | 60 | – | – | 24 | – | 26 | – | 10 | – | – | – | – |
| | 50 | – | – | 22 | – | 22 | – | 6 | – | 6 | – | 6 |

(Though the above table was published in 1802, the 42pdr had generally fallen from use by the 1790s, a heavy piece which needed a larger crew but was no more effective than the 32pdr)

being absorbed by a system of ropes and pulleys which allowed the gun to be run out through the gunport before firing. The British adoption of flexible rammers allowed the guns to be fired even when tight against an enemy ship, the presence of which prevented the gunners from ramming with a stiff ramrod, a great advantage over French ships when grappled together.

Carronades were named from the factory of their initial manufacture (Carron ironworks at Falkirk) and were short, large-bore guns generally used for anti-personnel fire at short range, requiring a smaller powder charge and their shot travelling more slowly, thus inflicting more casualties by the production of splinters. Known as a 'smasher', a carronade could produce most horrendous casualties at close range, approximating to the effect of a giant shotgun. Their carriages were usually not wheeled but on a slide, to facilitate traversing and absorb recoil. The short range of the carronade was probably the reason for its not counting in the 'rating'; its failings were demonstrated when HMS Phoebe used her 18pdrs at long range to batter USS Essex into submission, never drawing close enough for the Essex to employ its armament of 32pdr carronades.

Projectiles used at sea were like those used on land, though other varieties existed: bar-shot, chain-shot, expanding- and knife-blade shot were all used for destroying rigging, expanding or whirling like a flail through the air. Incendiary-shells were used, though almost as effective was hot-shot, round-shot heated red-hot in a brazier or oven before firing, which could smoulder for hours when imbedded in the enemy's woodwork. True grapeshot (as different from 'heavy case') consisted of a number of iron balls lashed in a canvas bag around an iron pillar, and 'langridge' was a number of iron bars in a bag or tin, both useful against either personnel or rigging.

1762 (HMS *Defence*), 1778 (*Alexander*), 1780 (*Leander*), 1781 (*Goliath*), 1783 *Culloden*, 1785 (*Zealous, Audacious, Majestic*), 1786 (*Bellerophon Theseus*), 1787 (*Vanguard, Swiftsure, Orion*), and 1793 (*Minotaur*).

The larger ships of war were virtually floating artillery-platforms, and although naval ordnance was basically similar in construction to that used on land, there were several significant differences. Most obvious was the weight of shot: whereas 12pdrs were the heaviest normally employed in the field, naval guns (not having to manoeuvre) were much heavier, the 32pdr being the principal weapons of 70-gunners and above once the 42pdr of the 1st-raters had been phased out. Usually

one 'nature' of gun was kept on each deck (to facilitate ammunition-supply for one reason), with the larger guns nearer the waterline for stability. The gun-barrels were like those of land ordnance, but ignition was by means of detachable flintlocks, introduced in 1755, obviating the need to keep slow-matches burning by every gun and thus reducing the risk of fire. All powder was made up into flannel cartridges for ease of loading, a gun-crew numbering up to twelve plus a ship's boy to fetch powder from the magazine. For protecting the gunmetal, the usual coating of warm coal-tar mixed with seawater was applied. Gun-carriages were low, wooden structures with small wheels (trucks), recoil

# Frigates

Of all types of ship, it was said (by Nelson among others, that the one of which the fleet could never have enough was the frigate. In naval warfare they fulfilled a role similar to that of the light cavalry on land: reconnaissance, message-carrying and harrying the enemy in minor actions. Styled 'the eyes of the fleet', frigates were fast-moving, extremely manoeuvrable ships used in conjunction with the main battle-fleets to discover the position of the enemy and carry reports between fleets and bases; and though most carried considerable armament, they were invariably ordered to remain at the periphery of a 'fleet action', as they were insufficiently strong to take on a ship-of-the-line. Frigates were equally invaluable in harrying the enemy merchant trade, assisting in blockading enemy ports, launching raids against shore installations and, perhaps above all, operating against the enemy's frigates. From the very outset of the Revolutionary Wars, the majority of 'single-ship' actions, or actions involving only a handful of craft, were primarily fought by the fleet's frigates, with almost universal success; for in such actions the Royal Navy's personnel, superior training, seamanship and gunnery counted for more than even in a 'fleet action', and until the British engaged the vastly more powerful and equally well-crewed American frigates in the war of 1812, frigate combat was a matter of almost unrelieved success. Indeed, it has been suggested that one reason why the Americans were able to win a number of significant encounters was because the Royal Navy had become lax, being so used to defeating the French that they believed all nations were equally vulnerable to the British mastery of their trade. Certainly against the French most of the major successes (after the great fleet actions) were fought by frigates, which being so fast and manoeuvrable

*A naval gun on a wooden 'sea service' carriage with 'truck' wheels, utilising elevation by quoin. This typical iron 12-pdr is of the pattern used throughout the period, irrespective of size, which varied from the 42pdr (10ft long, weighing 67cwt) to the 6ft 6pdr weighing 6½cwt. Range at 2° elevation was 1,200yds, rising to 2,150yds at 7°.*

could usually outsail any enemy ship-of-the-line which they encountered. (Theoretically a ship-of-the-line with all canvas set might achieve a greater speed than a frigate, but in practice this was more than compensated for by the additional manoeuvrability attained by the frigates and their expert crews.)

Frigates were 5th-raters, carrying between 32 and 44 guns (plus carronades); in their case there was even greater divergence between rating and actual number of guns carried, in that a '44' might carry 48 *plus* carronades. The French *Prévoyante*, captured in May 1795 and taken into British service, was ostensibly a 36-gun frigate (carrying 24 but pierced for 40 when captured en flûte); in British service it was rated as a '36' but actually had 56 guns, including carronades!) Crews for 32-44-gunners officially consisted of 300 seamen, 1 Marine lieutenant and 1 Marine per gun; though it should be remarked here that (as with many ships) the crew was often very much under-strength.

In 1799 Britain possessed a total of 226 frigates, but of these only 176 were in commission (deducting those held 'in ordinary', i.e. in reserve and not operational, and those repairing); of these, 9 were 'guardships' and 69 in port and fitting-out, leaving a disposable total of 98. Of these, only 32 were in home waters, 18 in the Mediterranean and the remainder spread around the globe, 30 in the West Indies. During the war captured vessels represented a large proportion of the total frigates in service: of those taken into the Royal Navy, 90 were French (including re-captured British frigates), 17 Dutch, 13 Spanish, 9 Danish, 2 Venetian and 1 US (*Chesapeake*); the most significant mass-captures were the 9 Danish frigates taken at Copenhagen in 1807 and 6

French at Toulon. Against this, British losses were considerable, among them being 59 wrecked, 15 captured (3 by the USA, but not including HMS *Vestale*, 36, recaptured after one day in French hands in 1796, but including one captured after being grounded and one burned after capture), 4 foundered, 3 accidentally burned, 2 destroyed to prevent capture, 1 burned as unserviceable, 1 accidentally blown up, *Hermione* handed to the Spanish after a mutiny and *Mediator* expended as a fireship at Basque Roads.

As with ships-of-the-line, foreign designs of frigate were copied, especially French whose shipwrights produced magnificent vessels (better, in fact, than the standard of most French crews deserved); *Hyperion*, for example, was copied from the French *Magicienne*, but despite being slightly enlarged still suffered from lower decks but 51 inches high, the 'living space' in frigates and smaller craft being even more cramped and uncomfortable than in larger ships.

Smaller than frigates were a large variety of ships, classified as 6th-raters (20 to 28 guns), sloops (18 guns) and others; the established crew was 200 seamen and a Marine lieutenant for a 6th-rate and 125 seamen and a Marine sergeant for a 16- or 18-gunner, with the usual one Marine per gun. The 6th-raters and less represented a large proportion of the navy's vessels; in 1794 there were almost 50 6th-raters and well over 100 others, and by 1799 of the total of 788 vessels, 345 were sloops and less (303 out of 646 actually in commission), the majority of which were deployed in home waters. The large number of such vessels resulted in a variety of bizarre ship-names such as *Black Joke*, *Charming Molly*, *Clinker*, *Haddock* and *Plumper!* 6th-raters were three-masted two-deck-

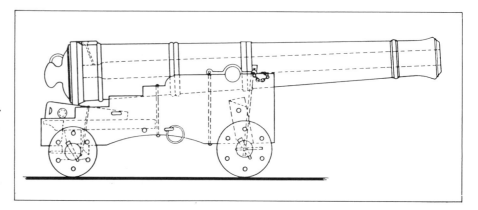

ers, but with armaments usually on the upper deck only. The term 'sloop' covered ships with one to three masts; two-masted vessels were often referred to as ketches or brigs, though the terminology was not fully constant. Brigs were normally two-masted, square-rigged boats with a 'lugsail' attached to the mizzenmast by a 'gaff' yard. Cutters were single-masted, gaff-rigged boats (ie with the sail 'fore-and-aft'), with a square topsail, and the normal jibsails which extended from the foremast to the bowsprit on all vessels. Schooners were two-masted boats with square-rigged sails on the foremast and gaff-rigged on the mizzenmast. Xebecs, Mediterranean craft, had three masts, the fore- and main-mast square-rigged but the mizzen with a triangular lateen sail. 'Bomb ketches' were two-masted sloops, the mainmast often square-rigged and the mizzen with a square topsail and a gaff, and instead of a foremast with one or two large mortars installed, principally for use in bombarding coastal installations or harbours. The term 'gunboat' covered everything from a four-gun cutter to a longboat mounting a single gun on the prow, used mainly in coastal waters. Privateers (ie civilian vessels sailing under a 'letter of marque'

which made them virtually legalised pirates providing they attacked only enemy ships), were usually sloops and smaller, often carrying larger crews than normal to permit captured vessels to be sailed home as prizes.

Many of the larger frigate-actions are well-known, but some of the fiercest were fought by the much smaller vessels, such as HM Packet *Antelope* which sailed from Jamaica in November 1798 carrying mail and passengers for England. Off

*The first successful frigate-action of the war was fought by Edward Pellew, one of the most distinguished Royal Navy officers of the period, whose HMS* Nymphe *(36) captured the French frigate* Cléopâtre *(36) in the English Channel on the early morning of 17 June 1793.*

Cuba she encountered the French privateer *Atalante*, flying the red flag of no quarter. *Antelope*'s commander, Lieut Curtis, had but 21 men plus passengers, including a French Royalist ex-naval officer. The privateer fired a broadside and attempted to board; Curtis was killed in the first exchange and his first mate wounded (the second mate had died of fever), so command devolved upon boatswain Pasco and the French officer, Nodin. The latter took the helm and defended the stern with a boarding-pike and musket whilst Pasco and his tiny band, plus French civilian passengers, held off the 65 men of *Atalante*. The French decided to withdraw after their attempts to board met with failure, but with incredible audacity Pasco lashed the yards together, holding the ships firm. Having lost about 47 men out of their 65, the privateer struck her colours, and Pasco took her a prize back to Jamaica; *Antelope* lost 3 killed and 7 wounded. Few actions were more creditable than *Antelope*'s defence by a mixture of British seamen and French gentlemen especially with the vessel commanded by a warrant officer, and as in so many actions involving the smaller craft, it demonstrated the qualities which led to the Royal Navy's reputation being unmatched throughout the period.

### Armaments of frigates and smaller craft:

| Ship | Guns (pdrs) | | | | Carronades (pdrs) | | | |
|---|---|---|---|---|---|---|---|---|
| | 18 | 12 | 9 | 6 | 32 | 24 | 18 | 12 |
| 44-gun frigate | 20 | 22 | — | 6 | — | — | 8 | — |
| 36-gun frigate | 26 | 2 | 8 | — | 8 | — | — | — |
| 32-gun frigate | — | 26 | — | 6 | — | 6 | 6 | — |
| 28-gun 6th-rate | — | — | 24 | 2 | — | 6 | — | — |
| 24-gun 6th-rate | — | — | 22 | 2 | — | 2 | 6 | — |
| 20-gun 6th-rate | — | — | 20 | — | — | — | — | 8 |
| 18-gun sloop | — | — | — | 18 | — | — | — | 8 |

### Ships in full commission, 1794 and 1814:

| | 1794 | 1814 | Av. tonnage |
|---|---|---|---|
| 44-gun frigates | — | 1 | 1,400 |
| 40-gun frigates | — | 6 | 1,200 |
| 38-gun frigates | 11 | 51 | 950-1,050 |
| 36-gun frigates | 18 | 51 | 930-950 |
| 32-gun frigates | 37 | 12 | 750-900 |
| 28-gun 6th-rate | 22 | — | 600 |
| 20-24 gun 6th-rate | 10 | 25 | 500 |
| 4-18-gun vessels | 76 | 360 | 70—450 |

# Shipyards and Equipment

The navy maintained a number of important bases throughout the United Kingdom, the most important being Deptford, Woolwich, Chatham, Sheerness, Portsmouth and Plymouth: there were also home bases not developed to full dockyard status, such as Deal. In addition, an established naval presence existed in almost 50 ports, in the staff of the Impress Service. Other bases were scattered around the globe, some permanent (like Gibraltar and Jamaica) and others, as in the Mediterranean, being moved according to circumstances.

Provision of the navy's equipment was largely in the hands of private contractors, though official supervision was strict to ensure that ships and equipment were of the desired standard. (Ships were not normally built in the colonies, except at Bombay from 1801.) The most vital commodity was wood, and the depletion of Britain's oak-forests was a cause of considerable concern. By 1791 the annual consumption of timber was around 200,000 tons for the merchant service and over 270,000 tons for the navy; small wonder, then, that accession to the forests of the Baltic area was regarded as vital, hence the efforts to defeat the 'Armed Neutrality of the North'; or that Admiral Cuthbert Collingwood would have his pockets full of acorns when ashore, which he planted in likely places to provide the next-but-several generation of ships! (Equally important commodities from the Baltic were pitch and hemp.)

Ordnance was also provided by private contractors, subject to 'proving' by official inspectors (including test-firing); but a number of defective guns were 'proved' as combat-worthy despite official testing., For example, when one of HMS *Collosus'* 32pdrs burst (probably at Lorient) the remaining guns were tested at Woolwich. The first six burst on the first shot with a full charge, and the remainder were scrapped immediately; apparently the ship's gunner had had to fire with less than the correct charge in action! (Three years later the ship, a 74-gunner built in 1787, was wrecked off the Scillies, taking to the seabed Sir William Hamilton's priceless collection of classical Greek vases.) The difficulty of supplying an adequate number of guns resulted in even major ships having incorrect armament at times; in 1790, for example, HMS *Gibraltar* (an 80-gun ex-Spaniard) instead of 32pdrs carried 26pdrs on both gundecks, and thus had difficulty fitting guns to carriages.

Rations were the responsibility of the Victualling Board and comprised a set allocation of one pound of bread and one gallon of beer per man per day. Other food was issued on set days: on Sundays, 1lb pork and ½ pint pease; Mondays, 1 pint oatmeal, 2oz butter, 4oz cheese; Tuesday, 2lbs beef; Wednesdays, ½ pint pease, 1 pint oatmeal, 2oz butter, 4oz cheese; Thursdays, as Sundays; Fridays, as Wednesdays; Saturdays, no extra ration to supplement the bread and beer. When other commodities were available,

they were issued on the following scale: 4lbs flour = 4lbs beef; 3lbs flour, ½lb raisins (or ¼lb currants) and ¼lb suet = 4lbs beef or 2lbs pork and pease ('but are not to be issued in lieu of the latter, except unavoidable') ½lb sugar = ½lb butter; 1lb rice = 1lb cheese or 2 pints oatmeal; 1 pint oil = 1lb butter or 2lbs cheese); 1 pint wine, or ½ pint brandy, rum or arrack = 1 gallon beer; 1lb fresh beef = 1lb salt beef, but 1½lbs fresh beef = 1lb pork. In addition, each man received ¼ pint vinegar each week. When flour, suet and raisins were available they were to make up no more than half the beef ration, and be issued only on 'beef day'; only when 'unavoidable' were they to be issued on 'pork day'. When any deficiencies were found in the barrels containing the meat (14 pieces weighing 112lbs per barrel), including the bone but with the 'salt shaken off', the master was permitted to issue 'as much beef and pork as will make up the deficiency'. It is interesting to note the difference in rations accorded to soldiers aboard ship: as above, except that six soldiers received the ration of four sailors (the sailors requiring extra nourishment to do their work, the soldiers doing little aboard ship), and that 'No wine or spirits are to be issued to the troops while in port, nor at sea, till after all the beer is expended': obviously soldiers were less trusted with fierce alcohol than sailors!

These quantities were supposed to be served out by 'full weights and measures', but were actually calculated as 14oz pounds. Issue of rations was the responsibility of the ship's purser, who was poorly paid but allowed to make a profit of 12½ per cent on all except tobacco (10 per cent) and 'slops' (clothing) (5 per cent). His additional profit, made illegally but though recognised rarely prevented, was in the further eighth made by issuing 14oz pounds. A purser required a good business sense and considerable capital (he had to lodge hundreds of pounds – dependent upon the size of ship – with the Navy Board as a 'bond' before he received his appointment), and the additional illegal profit was permitted to defray the frauds perpetrated by the victual-suppliers (whose short-measures only became apparent at sea, when the casks were opened) and the deterioration

---

*The vast quantity of material required by each ship is demonstrated by the approximate weights of stores (excluding victuals) for a typical 74-gun ship-of-the-line:*

| | |
|---|---:|
| Spars, standing and running rigging, cables (22in and 13½in): | 48 tons |
| Anchors (2 67cwt bower, 67cwt sheet, 67cwt spare, 16 cwt stream, 8cwt kedge): | 14.6 tons |
| Iron ballast: | 80 tons |
| Shingle ballast: | 387 tons |
| Guns: lower deck 78½ tons, upper deck 56 tons, quarter-deck and forecastle 22½ tons: | 157 tons |
| Gun carriages: | 15¾ tons |
| Grapnels: | 1½ cwt |
| Coal: for cooking | 20 tons |
| Wood: | 6 tons |
| Boats: 1 launch, 1 pinnace, 1 barge, 2 cutters, 1 jolly-boat. | |

of provender, some of which might be many years old before it was eaten, hence the universal tales of 'bread' (ship's biscuit) full of weevils, slimy butter and maggoty cheese. The stories of cheese so hard that it could be carved like wood, and in one case even used to ship a mast, are probably scarcely exaggerated! (The rations of butter and cheese were not so generous as the above implies: butter was weighed in pounds of 12oz and cheese 9oz, the deficiency in the proper weight being compensated by improved quality; one of the main grievances of the 'great mutiny' was that naval rations should be weighed as on shore, i.e. in 16oz pounds.) The issue of wine was generally made in the Mediterranean and West Indies (where rum might substitute also), was known as 'black strap' and was somewhat unpopular; the rum was normally diluted into 'grog' by the addition of three-parts water to one of rum.

Quantities of victuals required for a ship were thus immense: for example, a typical '74' provisioned for four months would carry approximately 8½ tons of beef and the same of pork, 30 tons of bread, 1½ tons of butter, 2 tons of cheese, 6½ tons of oatmeal, 6 tons of pease, 1½ tons of raisins, 500 gallons vinegar, 50 tons of beer, 250 gallons of

*Devonport dockyard, c1793. One of the principal Royal dockyards, Devonport was established by William III in 1689 and until 1824 was known as Plymouth Dock; not until 1832 was it accorded the status of parliamentary borough. It maintained two volunteer regiments, the Loyal Plymouth Dock Infantry and the Plymouth Dock Cavalry.*

brandy, 1,800 gallons of wine, 6 tons of flour, 6cwt of suet, 220 tons of water, 20 tons of coal and 6 tons of wood (for cooking). Officers' rations were separate and provided by the individual, some livestock often being kept aboard to enable them to dine if not in style at least reasonably well.

The dockyards and contractors were infamous for corruption, as an official enquiry of 1803 proved; some of the frauds were quite staggering in scale, such as a cooperage contract which cost more than 27 times the material's value, and swallowed countless thousands of government funds whilst maimed seamen were allotted the most miserable of pensions. Conversely, Rear-Admiral William Bradley was sentenced to death (commuted to banishment) in 1814 for defrauding the postmaster-general of £3.8s.6d.; he had been unemployed for five years due to an 'unsettled state

of mind'.

The Admiralty maintained a system of communication by semaphore linking the main depot of Portsmouth with London, a chain of 24 stations by 1796, erected by Lord George Murray, Admiralty Director of Telegraphs, each station having a wooden framework on which letters were displayed. Admiral Popham's system adopted in 1803 was a two-armed device, which in 1806 transmitted a message from London to Portsmouth in two minutes, and a similar system was installed (with limited success) in Portugal during the Peninsular War. The main disadvantage was that all such systems were static (though Congreve used two windmill-arms to transmit messages at Menin in 1793), as were the beacons established in the maritime counties to warn of invasion. The beacon-system, probably no more elaborate than that used to warn of the Armada's approach in 1588, worked well in practice except that it was liable to 'false alarm', as in 1804 when the beacon-post at Home Castle mistook an agricultural fire in Northumberland as the signal of French invasion, and set off the beacon-chain. If nothing else, it provided evidence of the alacrity and enthusiasm with which the volunteers marched to their assembly-points.

The tactics of the Royal Navy were to a large extent dominated by the maxim of 'attack', which differed markedly from those commonly adopted by the French. French admirals believed that combat should only be initiated if a successful result would achieve something more than merely the destruction of the enemy fleet; conversely, to the British the capture or sinking of the enemy was an end in itself, and thus the British ships habitually engaged the enemy if there existed the remotest possibility of victory. This policy was remarkably successful; the only major defeat occasioned by injudiciously engaging a superior enemy occurred off Grand Port, Mauritius, in 1810, which cost Britain four 36-gun frigates (*Magicienne* and *Sirius* destroyed to prevent capture, and *Néréide* and *Iphigenia* captured; these were recovered some three months later when Mauritius was taken). Some of the 'single-ship' defeats in the War of 1812 were also caused by British overconfidence, underestimating the heavier firepower and competency of the American frigates.

These differences in the attitude towards combat dictated the manner in which fleets engaged. The French generally attempted to disable the enemy's masts and rigging, to prevent them pursuing at the end of the action, whereas British gunnery was directed generally upon the enemy's hull, either to sink the ship, dismount her guns, kill the crew or make her indefensible. The result was usually that British ships often lost spars, masts and had their sails and rigging shot to pieces, but lost very many fewer men than their French opponents, whose gun-decks might be utterly devastated. Casualty-figures for Trafalgar are revealing; despite the superior gunnery of the British ships and the great superiority in handling them, the targetting must have been responsible to a considerable degree for the disparity between the fleets. Worst-hit of the British ships were HMS *Victory* (57 killed, 75 wounded), *Royal Sovereign* (47 killed, 94 wounded) and *Téméraire* (47 killed, 76 wounded); the French *Bucentaure* had 197 killed and 85 wounded, the

Spanish *Santissima Trinidad* 216 and 116, *San Agustin* 184 and 201. Sixteen of the Franco-Spanish ships lost around 200 or more, with total casualties of almost 7,000; total British casualties for 27 ships were around 449 killed and 1,214 wounded. Similarly, French to British casualties at the 'Glorious First of June', amounted to approximately six and a half to one.

The theoretical range of 'Sea Service Iron Guns' tested in 1796 was a maximum 2,150yds (with a charge of 1/3 the weight of shot), but in practice fire was normally most effective when the enemy was within 400yds. It was not uncommon for guns to be 'double-shotted', firing either two roundshot or one ball and one round of grapeshot, in which case the maximum range was reduced to 500 and 600yds, respectively. A 32pdr carronade tested in 1798 had a maximum range of 1,087-yds, though the effective range in which they were usually employed was much nearer to the 32pdrs' maximum range with a 2lb charge at point-blank (ie 0° elevation), which was 330yds. Rate of fire similarly varied with circumstances: three broadsides in 90 seconds was recorded, and at Trafalgar HMS *Victory* fired three in two minutes, but under combat conditions at sea the firing of broadsides depended more upon the position of the target than upon the performance theoretically attainable. The rolling of the ship was an additional factor, and it was possible to cause roundshot to ricochet off the surface of the sea and strike the enemy in an upward direction if the broadside could be timed correctly with the roll. As on land, the discharge of a number of cannon produced dense clouds of smoke which obscured targets, and as both the target and the firer were usually moving, instead of firing a mass broadside a ship's guns might fire in a rolling barrage as the target came into view, or 'as the guns bear'.

Very few ships were sunk by gunfire, though a shot-holed vessel was always prey to bad weather such as the storm which sank many of the captured vessels after Trafalgar; a greater danger was fire and the consequent explosion of magazine, such as that which destroyed

*L'Orient* at Aboukir and the French *Achille* at Trafalgar (the latter caused by the shrouds being set alight by her own musketry). More common was the capture of ships, either by a captain striking his colours if his ship were no longer defensible, or by boarding. The latter involved most vicious hand-to-hand fighting in which all members of the crew swarmed aboard the enemy, when fierce combat would occur until the boarders were evicted or the boarded ship surrendered. It is somewhat ironic that excluding cavalry charges, probably more literal 'hand-to-hand' combat occurred at sea than on land, given the great infrequency with which bayonets were crossed. Throughout an action, a ship would have marksmen stationed on the upper deck and sometimes amid the shrouds, firing down upon the enemy's deck, involving seamen armed with muskets as well as marines; the most famous victim of such tactics was Nelson himself, shot by a French sniper from the *Redoutable*. Because of the danger of musket-flashes setting light to the sails, the stationing of marksmen in the 'fighting tops' was often discouraged in the Royal Navy.

In boarding actions, all members of the crew might be involved irrespective of their own specialist duties; and the British maintained no separate naval artillery personnel. The Corps of Royal Marines was the navy's military force, but the associated Royal Marine Artillery was formed in 1804 only to man the navy's bomb-vessels in place of the Royal Artillery detachments which had done the job previously. (The Royal Marines represented a considerable proportion of the navy's personnel, ultimately 31,400 out of a total of 147,000.)

*Trafalgar, 21 October 1805. This painting illustrates to good effect the confusion which could result in battle, with ships running aboard one another and pounding with broadsides at the closest range. Collisions were common when ships had become partially dismasted and were thus no longer in control; in such circumstances a captain might strike his colours to prevent the further slaughter of his crew.*

# Breaking the Line

For some considerable time, the accepted method of engaging an enemy fleet at sea had been the formation known as 'the line-of-battle', in which the fleets would be arrayed in line astern, drawing progressively nearer to the enemy until within effective gun-range. As ships-of-the-line had little firepower which could be directed either forward or aft, the way of best utilising their offensive capability was to approach the enemy broadside-on, so that all the guns on one side of the ship could fire simultaneously. As codified in 'fighting instructions', the line-of-battle became an almost inflexible rule; as a British manual of 1744 noted, it was regarded as the 'basis and formulation of all discipline . . . has had the test of long experience, and has stood the stroke of time', and captains who deliberately broke the line ran the risk of court-martial. Whilst it might be said that the line-of-battle generally prevented any major defeat, it equally made decisive victory extremely difficult, for in theory the preservation of the enemy's line-of-battle allowed them to utilise their maximum firepower as well.

For a long time it had been recognised that the maximum damage would be inflicted upon the enemy (and the least suffered) if the enemy could be 'raked', ie firing a broadside as the guns bore not upon the enemy's thick sides but into his bow or stern; this manoeuvre, long employed in single-ship actions, was known from the respective positions of the ships as 'crossing the "T"'. It had a dual advantage: first, the enemy could reply only with his bow- or stern-chasers, a very small number of guns, and secondly that a shot striking the enemy's stern would pass right along the length of the ship (there being no substantial bulkheads), causing a vastly greater amount of damage than had the same shot struck the side. So effective was this tactic that it was possible for a ship thus assailed to be turned into a shambles by one broadside delivered at close range, and effectively knocked out of the fight. Although this tactic was employed in small actions, the insistence of the maintenance of the emasculating 'line-of-battle' prevented the use of 'crossing the "T"' in the wider application of a fleet action, as the tactic it would have involved, that of 'breaking the line' of the enemy, might involve a hazardous approach in which the enemy fleet would be able to use their broadsides while the attackers would be approaching bow-on, unless the enemy line were broken by swinging each ship from line-of-battle through the gaps in the enemy line.

It is sometimes stated that Horatio Nelson was responsible for the widespread use by the Royal Navy of the tactic of 'breaking the line', but though he gave it a new dimension, its roots lie further back and much of the credit would appear due to John Clerk, whose *Essay on Naval Tactics* was published in 1804, though his theory was formulated many years before, and was the subject of a long critique in the *Morning Chronicle* in November 1798, in the wake of the victory of Aboukir Bay. Clerk, who 'though he was never at sea, always attended very much to maritime affairs', observed that whenever single ships or small squadrons engaged the enemy, 'they were always an overmatch for the enemy' as a result of 'the most skilful seamanship, intrepidity and perseverence, attended with uninterrupted success.' Yet when large fleets met, the result was always negative: the French 'whose system was to batter and destroy our rigging, and then escape unhurt themselves' made off as soon as the British had been so damaged as to prevent their pursuing: '. . . our fleets . . . have been invariably baffled – nay, worsted, without ever having lost a ship, or almost a man.' Though this was an over exaggeration, the general principle was true: by ranging the fleet 'along the line of the enemy, until the van of our fleet came opposite the rear of his, thus our ships run the gauntlet of the enemy's whole fleet, giving them an opportunity to

*Breaking the line: diagram A shows the tactic at its most basic, with the attackers maintaining a 'line-of-battle' until each ship turns into the gap between the enemy ships, raking their stern and bow before laying alongside for close action. Diagram B illustrates the perfection of the technique, the attacker approaching in columns, cutting the enemy line and overwhelming the centre and rear before the van could reverse its course and assist. Because of the difficulty which the van of a fleet might encounter and the delays which would result in performing this reversal of course, the concentration upon the centre and rear could enable an inferior force to destroy a superior fleet, a maritime version of the military tactic of gaining 'local superiority', which formed the cornerstone of Napoleon's system of warfare.*

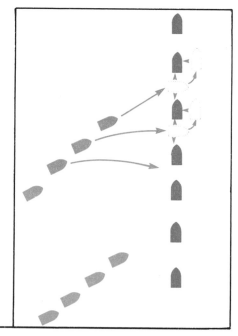

cripple each ship as it passed.'

Clerk's solution was to advocate that instead of preserving the 'line-of-battle', the British should break through the enemy's line, 'and cutting off one division of his fleet from another, so as to prevent the enemy from being able to extricate himself' would be 'a certain means of, either capturing the division you have cut off or of bringing on a general engagement.' Clerk printed a few copies of his treatise in 1782 for circulation among his friends. One of these, it was said, found its way to General Debbieg, known as a forward-thinking tactician, who loaned his copy to Sir John Jervis (later Earl St Vincent). Jervis read it and asked Debbieg where he might buy a copy. "'It is not to be bought," answered the General; "I had this copy from the author, who is a particular friend of mine; he had but a few copies printed, all of which he has given away among his friends." "Since that is the case," said Sir John Jervis, "you shall not have this copy back again; it is too good a thing for you, who are a landsman, I will keep it to myself.'"

The effect of Clerk's essay appears to have been profound; when Lord Rodney was asked his opinion of it, he supposedly answered, 'You shall see what I think of it whenever I am so happy as to meet the

*Breaking the line at Trafalgar: the British fleet approaches in column and cuts the French line-of-battle in two places, bringing about Nelson's 'pell-mell battle' in which the skill of the crews and ship-handling could tell. (Painting by N. Pocock)*

French fleet again; for I am determined to follow it'; and Duncan, who received an original copy, told Clerk that he should re-print it as naval officers were circulating hand-written copies among themselves. The *Morning Chronicle* in October 1798 noted that 'the manoeuvre of *breaking the line*, formerly considered as the most desperate system, appears now to be reduced to a system . . . with certainty and success. The skill of our seamen in working their ships, is said to give our fleets a superiority in their performance of this which the fleets of no other nation have presumed to emulate.' The results of this manoeuvre were demonstrated at the Battle of the Saints (1782) and Camperdown, for example, the victors of both (Rodney and Duncan) acknowledging their debt to Clerk's theory. The tactic was especially effective in severing the rear of the enemy fleet, which could be overwhelmed before the remainder could reverse their course and come to their assistance. Nelson's tactics at

Trafalgar, by employing *two* columns to break the enemy line in two places and laying alongside the rearmost enemy ships (or creating the 'pell-mell battle' he desired) was an extension and culmination of Clerk's system, owing much to Nelson's 'degree of masterly boldness . . . and a dauntless intrepidity'; but, as the *Chronicle* remarked, this was also due to the 'superiority of our seamen, a topic much insisted on by Mr Clerk, and from which he promises certain suc-cess whenever our fleets can be brought into close engagement with the enemy.' Without this excellence of ship-handling, gunnery, training and discipline, and the determination to engage the enemy, these tactics could not have succeeded to the same degree, which is probably why they were only used to effect by the Royal Navy.

A similar standard of excellence was demonstrated when seamen were employed on land, either as gunners (manning the breaching-batteries at San Sebastian, for example) or even as infantry; though they were most useful in executing raids, at times they even served (with considerable competency) in organised units, such as at the Cape in 1795 when the light company formed of seamen was described as being just as effective as the expert light infantry.

# Frigate Tactics

The majority of actions fought by the Royal Navy throughout the Napoleonic era were not large 'fleet actions' but encounters between single ships or small squadrons, in which the superiority of the ships' crews usually told over their opponents. The tactics employed by the British commanders were usually simply to attack at the first opportunity and rely upon their skill in seamanship and the excellence of their crews to decide the business. The majority of these actions were fought by frigates and smaller vessels, and were of great ferocity; when HMS *Phoenix* (36) captured the French *Didon* (40) off Cape Finisterre on 10 August 1805, the British captain Thomas Baker reported that the action lasted three hours, 'never without pistol-shot' (i.e. with pistol-range the whole time), 'during which our ropes were cut to pieces, our maintopsail yard shot away, and most of our masts and spars severely wounded', until *Didon* 'became a perfect wreck' and struck her colours with a loss of 71 men. (*Phoenix* had suffered from *Didon*'s superior manoeuverability and for 45 minutes was locked in a position which prevented her guns from reaching the Frenchman.)

The example was set for British superiority in such actions by the encounter between HMS *Nymphe* and the French *Cléopâtre* (both rated as 36: *Nymphe* actually carried 32 guns and 8 carronades) on 17 June 1793, when Capt Edward Pellew (one of the most renowned British naval officers of the period) opened the action with a cheer of 'Long Live King George'. After a considerable battering *Cléopâtre* became unmanageable and ran aboard *Nymphe*, whereupon Pellew boarded and within ten minutes had beaten into submission the considerably more numerous French crew. *Cléopâtre*'s captain, Mullon, mortally wounded by a roundshot, was found upon his own quarterdeck trying to eat his copy of the French signal-manual; by mistake he was devouring his own commission. Such actions required a considerable degree of skill in weapon-handling, and all seamen were trained in close-quarter combat. Each ship's contingent of marines (armed as infantry with muskets and bayonets) were in the forefront of such combat, but the sailors were equally employed in boarding, when they carried cutlasses, short boarding-pikes (kept in racks around the base of the masts), pistols (equipped with hooks for carrying on the waist-belt) and boarding-axes, colloquially known as 'tomahawks'.

Some of the exploits were audacious to the point of incredulity; Thomas Cochrane, most famous of frigate-captains, made his name in 1801 when his sloop *Speedy* (14 / 4-pdrs) captured the Spanish *Gamo* (32); despite having 54 men to the Spaniard's 319, Cochrane boarded with his entire crew (less two boys and the surgeon)! Cochrane led his crew aboard with blackened faces (resembling pirates and enhancing their fearsome appearance) and screaming like banshees; his first act was to lower the Spanish colours, so that the enemy wondered if their officers had surrendered, and traditionally it was said that as the Spanish wavered in the face of so furious an assault, Cochrane shouted down to surgeon Guthrie at the helm of *Speedy* to send another fifty men aboard. If true, the ruse worked and the Spaniards surrendered despite the unwounded outnumbering Cochrane's crew by almost seven to one (*Speedy* lost 3 dead and 9 wounded; *Gamo* a total of 55 casualties). A similar disparity in strength occurred in October 1799 when Edward Hamilton of HMS *Surprise* (32) recovered Pigot's captured *Hermione* from Puerto Caballo, Venezuela, a port defended by three castles and 200 guns, by rowing in his ship's boats and towing out *Hermione* for a cost of 11 men wounded (against over 400 Spanish casualties), an incredible exploit for which he was knighted (and later, after his capture while returning home to convalesce, it probably hastened Napoleon's agreement to his rapid exchange); yet this audacious commander was later court-martialled and dismissed from the service for brutality to his crew.

More usual were encounters between warships of approximately equal strength, such as that between HMS *Amethyst* (36) and the French *Thetis* (44) on the night of 10 November 1808. Capt Michael Seymour of *Amethyst* noted that after chasing *Thetis* from first sight, the Frenchman tried to board and for over an hour was locked to *Amethyst*, 'the fluke of our best bower anchor having entered her foremost main-deck port'. The savagery of the action is only hinted at in Seymour's account, for *Amethyst* lost her mizzen-mast and was 'much damaged and leaky' with two feet of water in the hold at the end of the fight. 'After great slaughter' while the ships were fast together, *Thetis* was boarded and captured despite her enormous crew (330 sailors and 103 soldiers), of whom 135 were killed and 102 wounded; *Amethyst* lost 19 killed and 51 wounded, and was in so parlous a state that *Thetis* had to be taken in tow by the newly-arrived HMS *Shannon* after the conclusion of the action. *Thetis* was ablaze, 'wholly dismasted' and 'dreadfully shattered', and her captain killed, yet when Seymour boarded, her acting captain, Dédé, attempted to defend the quarter-deck alone. As Seymour wrote of his crew, 'No language can convey an adequate idea of the cool and determined bravery shown by every Officer and man of this ship; and their truly noble behaviour has laid me under the greatest obligation.' (Five months later Seymour captured another French frigate, *Niemen*, 44, in a most desperate fight which left both ships with only the foremast standing.)

Disparity of size was often of little consequence in curbing the offensive spirit; in July 1808 HMS *Seahorse* (38) engaged two Turkish frigates and a galley in another night action, 15 minutes' 'hot fire at half pistol-shot distance' leaving the *Ahs Fezan* (24) 'in a state of the greatest distress and confusion, with her sails mostly down, and just before we had left her she had partially blown up forward.' *Seahorse* then made after the larger ship, *Badere Zaffer* (52) and by early morning had devastated her as well. Capt John Stewart noted that 'knowing the character of the people' (ie Turks) he waited until daylight to board, after he 'poured a broadside into her stern.' The Turks lost 165 killed and 195 wounded from 500; *Seahorse* had five killed, ten wounded, and lost her mainmast. Even the absence of wind could not discourage British captains; when the sloop HMS *Kingfisher* captured the French privateer *Hercule* in June 1808,

*Proficiency in hand-to-hand combat was essential for the crews of Royal Navy ships, especially those of frigates whose opportunity for boarding was frequent. This print of the cutlass-drill, after Rowlandson, was published in 1814.*

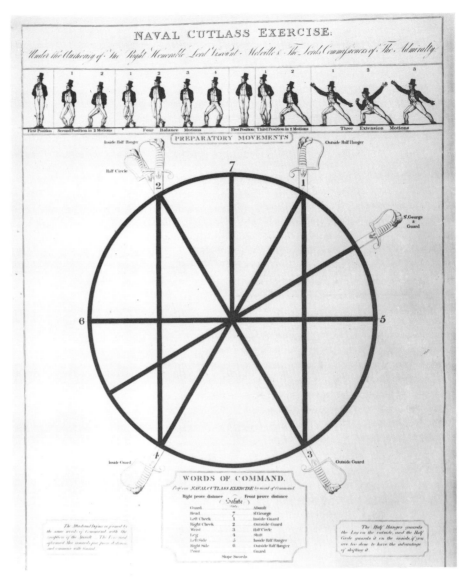

Capt Hepenstall had to chase the Frenchman by using his 'sweeps' (oars), and overhauled him that way.

Not only frigates were involved in such small-scale actions; in March 1812 HMS *Victorious* (74) and *Weazel* (18) encountered the French *Rivoli* (74), *Jena* (18), *Mercure* (18), *Mameluke* (10) and two gunboats in Italian waters. Capt Andrew of *Weazel* blew up the *Mercure* and then had the audacity to engage the *Rivoli* with his sloop, giving three broadsides, before *Victorious* bombarded the Frenchman for two hours. Though 'rendered perfectly unmanageable' and with her mizzen down, *Rivoli* kept two guns on her quarterdeck in action until, with 400 casualties, she surrendered, *Victorious* having lost 42 killed and 99 wounded, 'neither ship having been above half musket-shot distance from each other during the whole of the action, which only ceased at intervals, when the ships were hid from each other by the fog and smoke, and were not able to see the flashes of each other's guns.' Two months later, HMS *Northumberland* (74) and the gun-brig *Growler* (12) intercepted *Rivoli*'s erstwhile companion *Mameluke* (then mounting 18 guns) with the frigates *Arianne* and *Andromache* (both 44) which were operating as commerce-raiders. By skilful seamanship, *Northumberland*'s captain, Hon Henry Hotham, though under fire from strong shore-batteries all the time so that his sails and rigging were shot to pieces, forced all three French ships to run aground, and had the satisfaction of seeing all three blow up before he took his leave, a victory of sailing-skill rather than gunnery; *Northumberland* lost 5 killed and 28 wounded. In April 1806 the frigate HMS *Sirius* engaged a French squadron of 9 vessels, together mounting 97 guns, when only the usual damage to the British ship's sails prevented her from capturing more than the sloop *La Bergère* (18).

Especially later in the war, French ships became unwilling to risk combat with British vessels. (A measure of British superiority may be gathered from the fact that from the outbreak of war to the Peace of Amiens, Britain lost 6 frigates to the enemy, including one captured in a neutral port and *Hermione* to mutiny, against which Britain's enemies lost around 115 to the Royal Navy.) Consequently, the British in many cases resorted to what were termed 'boat actions': the rowing of ships' boats into French anchorages and either destroying or capturing the enemy vessels. A typical incident was that recounted by Capt George Mundy of HMS *Hydra*, who chased three French polaccas (lateen-rigged Mediterranean craft: *Eugène*, 16; *Belle Caroline*, 10; *Carmen de Rosario*, 4) into the harbour of Begu, Catalonia, in August 1807. Anchoring *Hydra* in the harbour (on a 'spring' to enable the ship to swing around even when anchored), Mundy engaged the shore-batteries and sent 50 seamen and marines in boats to make a landing. Despite heavy fire from shore and other craft in the harbour, the landing-party scrambled up a cliff and captured the main shore-battery, when the British split up, part to retain the position and harrass the remaining defensive-positions, whilst *Hydra*'s 2nd Lieut Drury took the rest to capture the town! This having been accomplished, Drury then boarded the three polaccas and, reinforced by other boats from *Hydra*, warped them out of harbour (ie dragged by cables, which were attached to rocks in enemy possession). As Mundy noted of his crew, 'I feel perfectly incapable of writing a panygeric equal to their merits', for this action was completed for the loss of one man killed and six wounded. Astonishing though this appears, numerous boat-actions were equally audacious and successful.

# Chapter Ten: THE NAVY'S CAMPAIGNS

Although most attention is given to the great naval engagements of the period, these events comprised only a fraction of the navy's efforts in the wars against republican France and Napoleon. Much of their work is now largely forgotten, such as the boring months spent blockading French ports, suffering foul weather and the morale-sapping inaction resulting from the French unwillingness to venture out. Convoy-duty was another disliked chore, attempting to escort fleets of independently-minded merchantmen across the Atlantic to protect them from commerce-raiders. Transporting troops and maintaining their supply-routes was equally significant, as was the constant battle against French privateers and merchantmen.

Naval officers commanding small squadrons or even single ships were subject only to their written orders; their responsibilities were often immense yet errors could result in court-martial or removal to languish in the half-pay lists. Diplomacy was involved when dealing with foreign powers, though few emulated that of one commodore who accompanied a request to a foreign potentate with a 'gift' of a 32 lb shot wrapped in a cloth! (The unfortunate recipient, not expecting the present to be heavy, dropped the gift upon his toe; but the intended point was made.) Sidney Smith (1764-1840, received his knighthood in Swedish service, and after escaping from the notorious Temple prison in Paris following an abortive raid on Le Havre, was re-employed in the Royal Navy as commander of HMS *Tigre* (80). Sent to the Mediterranean to serve under Nelson, he was given virtually an independent command, during which he landed in Syria and was largely responsible for the successful defence of Acre against Bonaparte. He concluded the convention of El Arish upon his own authority, was wounded in command of the naval landing-parties at Aboukir, was employed on secret service, captured Capri and helped the Portuguese royal family to escape to Brazil, yet his prickly attitude brought him into conflict with virtually all his superiors. His active service ending in 1814, he was present at Waterloo in the capacity of spectator! Few of his naval contemporaries were quite so colourful, but it is interesting to note that Thomas Cochrane (1775-1860), one of his few rivals for audacity and for annoying higher authority, after a career of heroic brilliance was convicted (unfairly) of complicity in the notorious Stock Exchange fraud which gave his enemies the opportunity of revenge, and for the succeeding 15 years he plied his skill with the greatest success in the infant navies of Chile, Peru, Brazil and Greece.

In addition to the more conventional services at sea, landing-parties of sailors and marines frequently fought on land, often with great effect, though rarely were they organised on purely military lines as at the Cape in 1795, when there were insufficient marines to compensate for the lack of *bona fide* soldiers. Operating in small detachments, such landing-parties of seamen and marines performed many raids and minor actions of great distinction and no little strategic effect.

For example, on New Year's Day 1807 four frigates approached the island of Curacoa, giving the Dutch garrison five minutes to surrender. When this capitulation did not occur, landing-parties first captured a frigate, a sloop and a schooner, then two forts, and took possession of the island for the loss of 3 dead and 14 wounded. In January 1809 HMS *Confiance* and 500 Portuguese troops captured Cayenne (including a canoe-borne assault of two forts!) for the loss of 2 killed and 22 wounded. In August 1810, 140 seamen and marines and 40 soldiers of the Madras European Regiment scaled and captured the fort at Banda Neira in the Spice Islands ('our brave fellows swept the ramparts like a whirlwind'), suffering no casualties but capturing 120 cannon, 700 regular troops and perhaps 800 militia.

In all their operations, the Royal Navy operated virtually unaided, for the naval forces of allied states were often negligible; Austria, had only minimal maritime forces (none after 1806), including an English commander, Ernest 'von' Williams; Naples had nothing more powerful than four 74s, and other powers which maintained significant navies such as Spain, Russia and Turkey rarely co-operated with Britain, most of their contact with the Royal Navy occurring when these states were opposed to Britain. For example, by the quirks of international relations British and Russian fleets co-operated against the Ottoman Empire off the Dardanelles in 1806-07 (culminating in the Russian victory at Lemnos in June 1807, in which no British forces were engaged), though a year later HMS *Centaur* and *Implacable* were responsible for the capture and burning of the Russian *Sewolod* (74) when Anglo-Russian friendship lurched into hostility after Tilsit. Portugal's navy, though considerable in size, played little part in the war, contrasting greatly with the participation of her army.

*Samuel Drummond's painting 'Death of Nelson' (showing the wounded admiral being carried from his quarterdeck) depicts the horror and confusion aboard a ship of the line under heavy fire.*

---

### Typical distribution of Royal Navy ships (excluding hired vessels protecting British coastal shipping); for the month of Trafalgar (October 1805):

| | |
|---|---|
| In port: 140 ships | Iberian Peninsula/Gibraltar: 1 |
| English & Irish Channels: 157 | Mediterranean: 55 |
| Downs & North Sea: 163 | Hospital & prison ships: 20 |
| West Indies: 44 | On secret expeditions: 5 |
| Jamaica: 32 | Guard ships: 14 |
| North America, Newfoundland: 33 | Out of commission: 137 |
| East Indies: 32 | Building: 68 |

# The Glorious First of June – 1 June 1794

In the early years of the Revolutionary Wars, French naval fortunes reached their lowest point, when the emigration of officers and the suspension of others for royalist associations or forebears left their fleets largely leaderless and riddled with incapables, mutiny, wretched efficiency and disorderly crews. The Anglo-Spanish occupation of Toulon, the main base in the Mediterranean, in 1793 cost France most of her Mediterranean fleet, at least 13 serviceable ships-of-the-line.

The first great naval battle of the period occurred in a French attempt to avert the famine brought on by the bad harvest of 1793 and the disorder of the Revolution. A large amount of grain was purchased in the United States and a convoy of 125 vessels was loaded to take it to France, and the Brest squadron, commanded by Admiral Louis Thomas Villaret de Joyeuse (1748-1812) was ordered to escort it in. Britain, having learned of the convoy, sent Admiral Earl Howe to intercept it. 'Black Dick' Howe (1726-99), ex-First Lord of the Admiralty, had first been to sea 54 years before, and though old was vastly experienced. When Villaret de Joyeuse sailed from Brest, Howe was soon in pursuit, having been awaiting the arrival of the convoy. Howe had originally been allotted 34 ships-of-the-line and 15 frigates, but had to detach eight to escort a British convoy America-bound, which left him with 26 ships and the smaller attendant vessels (including the bizarrely-named hospital-ship *Charon*, doubtless a great comfort

to any wounded who realised it was named after the boatman who ferried the dead over the Styx!). Howe had three 1st-raters of 100 guns, including his flagship *Queen Charlotte*, four 98s, two 80s, and 17 74-gunners. The French fleet included Villaret de Joyeuse's massive flagship *Montagne* (120), three 100s, including the *Républicain* and *Révolutionnaire*, both of which had been renamed because of republican fervour (their previous names, *Royal Louis* and *Bretagne*, being politically unacceptable), four 80s and 18 74s; thus both fleets had 26 vessels each.

On 28 May 1794 Howe came up with the French 400 miles west of Ushant, and forming his fleet into two lines-of-battle, with his four fastest 74s in a 'light division' between the fleet and the French, attempted to bring them to action. The French were unwilling to engage and only in the evening, four hours after Howe had signalled 'general chase', did the first fighting occur, when *Révolutionnaire* was battered into submission; but as no British ship attempted to board she slipped away and was towed into Rochefort by the *Audacieux*, which had come up to reinforce the French after the battle was joined. HMS *Audacious* was so cut-up in her rigging that she had to retire from Howe's fleet. Next morning the fleets engaged again, Howe ordering his ships to break through the enemy's line, but due to gunsmoke his order was missed by a portion of his fleet, and despite *Queen Charlotte* herself

piercing the French line-of-battle, the manoeuvre was patchy and complicated by rough sea which made ship-handling difficult, and Villaret Joyeuse came up to rescue the ships cut off by Howe's attack. Thick fog prevented fighting on 30/31 May; by extraordinary chance, Howe's youngest daughter sailed right through the French fleet on a passage from Lisbon to Ireland, without ever realising the French were there!

The morning of 1 June found the fleets still within sight of each other; some French ships had departed and others had come up, so that 26 French ships faced 25 British (effectively 24: HMS *Caesar*, leading the British line, tacked too early and missed the French, taking no part in the battle). Howe's orders were for each British ship to seek-out its French counterpart, and break through the French line under its target's bow, though in the event only a quarter of the fleet managed it when the engagement began about 9.30 am. The British approached in line, *Caesar* in the lead (and, when she mis-manoeuvred, *Bellerophon*, a famous '74' known to her unclassically-minded seamen as 'Billy Ruffian'); *Queen Charlotte* was approximately in the middle of the column, with the aptly-named *Thunderer* (74) bringing up the rear. *Montagne* was similarly in the centre of the French line. *Queen Charlotte* executed the intended tactical manoeuvre perfectly, bearing down on the French almost at right-angles and cutting between *Montagne*'s stern and

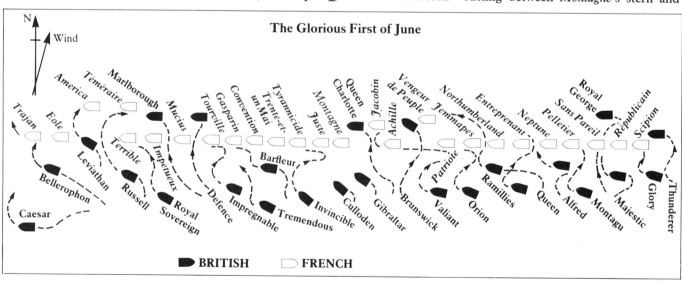

**The Glorious First of June**

N — Wind

Trajan · Eole · America · Téméraire · Marlborough · Mucius · Toureille · Gasparin · Convention · Trente-et-un Mai · Tyrannicide · Juste · Montagne · Queen Charlotte · Jacobin · Achille · Vengeur de Peuple · Northumberland · Jemmapes · Entreprenant · Neptune · Pelletier · Sans Pareil · Royal George · Républicain · Scipion

Caesar · Bellerophon · Leviathan · Terrible · Russell · Impétueux · Royal Sovereign · Defence · Impregnable · Tremendous · Barfleur · Invincible · Culloden · Gibraltar · Brunswick · Valiant · Patriote · Orion · Ramillies · Queen · Alfred · Montagu · Majestic · Glory · Thunderer

◖ **BRITISH**   ◗ **FRENCH**

*Britain's safeguard: a halfpenny token issued by the Deptford ironmonger Thomas D Haycraft (whose initials appear below the date): 'Prosperity to the Wooden Walls of Old England'. The 'wooden wall' shown is the stern of a ship-of-the-line bearing the name 'Royal George'.*

*The battle of Ushant, or 'the Glorious First of June' (1794) was a limited success; yet it was heralded in Britain as a signal triumph less for its consequences than for being the nation's first victory in the war against republican France.*

*Jacobin*'s bow, blasting both with her broadsides as she did so. The French were so surprised by this manoeuvre that when the British cut the line and pulled alongside the French starboard (having approached from port), they found the French starboard gunports closed and their broadsides not ready to fire. *Montagne* fired hardly a shot in return until she put on more sail and pulled ahead. A similar lack of preparation afflicted the French '74' *Vengeur du Peuple*, two ships astern of *Montagne*, which was assailed by HMS *Brunswick*. *Brunswick* held herself close to the Frenchman by her anchor, and for three hours (being able to fire by the use of flexible rammers) smashed the *Vengeur* to matchwood. Eventually the ships broke apart and *Vengeur* sank, her crew defiantly shouting '*Vive la liberté*' as the dismasted hulk went down, though many of her crew were rescued by British boats at great risk to themselves.

At 10.13 am Howe signalled 'general chase' as the French began to pull away, and due to the imperfect execution of Howe's plan Villaret de Joyeuse managed to extricate 19 of his ships, including five which had to be towed away, three of which (*Scipion*, *Jemmappes* and *Mucius*) were totally dismasted. Howe's fleet had also suffered quite severely (so as to prevent effective pursuit), 11 ships having severe damage to their rigging and two (*Defence* and *Marlborough*) being totally

*Richard, Earl Howe (1726-99); First Lord of the Admiralty 1783-88, Admiral of the Fleet 1796. (Engraving by WT Fry after G Dupoint)*

dismasted. Six French ships were captured, the 80-gunners *Juste* (which had been engaged by *Queen Charlotte*) and *Sans-Pareil*, and four 74s. Lord Howe was exhausted (as might be expected for a man of his years) and not at all the stately figure which appears in Mather Brown's famous painting: at the conclusion of the battle he was black with gunpowder and had to be supported by his officers. British losses were considerable, 290 killed and 858 wounded, *Marlborough* with 29 dead and 90 wounded, *Brunswick* with 44 and 14, and *Queen* with 36 and 67 being worst hit; Captain Harvey of *Brunswick* and Hutt of *Queen* were mortally wounded, and Montagu (of HMS *Montagu*!) was killed. Against this, the French suffered over 7,500 casualties (including prisoners).

In one sense the 'Glorious First of June' was a French success in that the grain convoy got through; but tactically it was the first in a series of startling British successes, vindicating the tactic of breaking the line, imperfectly though it was executed; though by engaging the entire enemy fleet, many were allowed to escape whilst the rearmost British ships could only engage towards the end (*Thunderer*, for example, suffered no casualties). Howe was duly lauded for his great success but admitted generously that it was his 'brave lads' who were responsible for his victory.

# Cape St Vincent – 14 February 1797

Few major actions occurred for the two years after the battle of the First of June. Admiral Hotham twice engaged the French Toulon fleet in 1795 and took a couple of French ships-of-the-line, but these were due more to French ineptitude (when *Ça Ira* collided with another French ship) than to Hotham's ability. It did foil the projected French invasion of Corsica, however, and Capt Horatio Nelson (1758-1805) of HMS *Agamemnon* greatly distinguished himself. In June 1795 Lord Bridport captured three French ships-of-the-line in an engagement with Villaret de Joyeuse off Ile de Groix (near Lorient), but Bridport's lack of aggression allowed the remaining 9 to escape. The French disrupted the Newfoundland fishing industry when a squadron evaded the British blockade, but much less success attended an attempted invasion of Ireland, part of which was prevented by bad weather from landing, and the bulk of the remainder was captured by the Royal Navy.

In August 1796 Spain allied herself to France by the Treaty of San Ildefonso. With the powerful Spanish fleet now ranged alongside that of France, British operations in the Mediterranean were no longer tenable; Corsica and Elba were evacuated, and the Mediterranean fleet, now commanded by Sir John Jervis (1735-1823) who had replaced the ineffectual Hotham, moved to Gibraltar and transferred its operations to the Atlantic; Jervis, possibly Britain's greatest admiral of the period after Nelson, was both capable and vastly experienced. An invasion of Britain still appealed to France's military planners, and in pursuance of a somewhat grandiose scheme (in which the French and Dutch fleets would co-operate), a Spanish fleet set sail from Cartagena in early 1797.

Jervis was near Cadiz, off Cape St Vincent, when on 14 February a frigate signalled the approach of an enemy force. Jervis had 15 ships-of-the-line: 2 100-gunners (*Britannia* and his own flagship, HMS *Victory*), two 98s, two 90s, eight 74s (including Commodore Nelson's HMS *Captain*), and the 64-gun *Diadem*. He had no intelligence of the strength of the approaching Spaniards, and as an increasing number appeared, *Victory's* Capt Calder informed the admiral of the strength in view: from eight to 20 to 25; Jervis stopped the count, saying that the die was cast and if there were 50 he would still engage them. In fact there were 27, commended by Admiral José de Cordova who flew his flag in the giant *Santissima Trinidad*, at 136 guns the largest ship afloat. The fleet included six 112-gunners, two 84s, and 18 74s, giving a theoretical superiority of 2,308 guns to Jervis' 1,232; yet Cordova was singularly ill-prepared for a fleet action, his crews poor and the fleet not in battle formation, being widely separated into two groups. Jervis determined to exploit this error in disposition by preventing them from uniting: he arrayed his fleet in a column, plunged into the gap and engaged the larger group of 19 ships.

Cordova was in no mood to risk a battle, so the main body began to make off in the direction from which Jervis had come; thus, to bring them to battle, Jervis had to reverse his own course. Broadsides had already been exchanged, and the combination of gunsmoke and the fact that *Victory* was in the centre of the British column made it difficult for Jervis to judge the right moment for ordering the British fleet to tack. In the event, he delayed the order too long, giving the Spanish main body what would have been a vital advantage; Jervis intended his fleet to retain its line rather than each ship turning at the same moment. Commodore Nelson, third

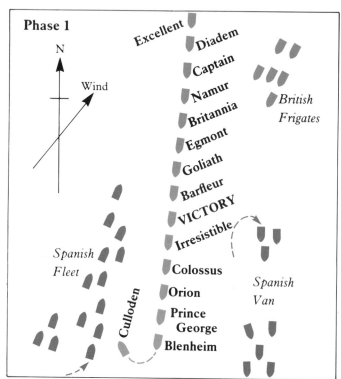

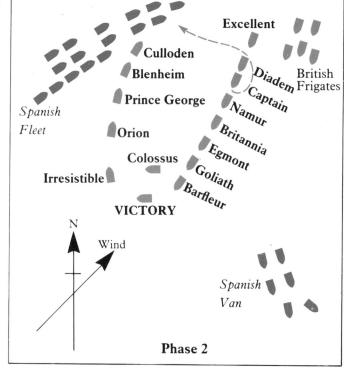

from the end of the British line in HMS *Captain*, appears to have realised the danger and broke away from the line-of-battle on his own initiative and attacked the head of the Spanish fleet. HMS *Excellent*, the rearmost ship, commanded by Nelson's close friend Cuthbert Collingwood, followed his lead, and at about 1.30 pm a furious battle began, *Captain* engaging the *Santissima Trinidad* as HMS *Culloden*, the leading ship of the British line, came up to Nelson's assistance: the audacious manoeuvre of attacking the head of the Spanish fleet had been decisive.

HMS *Excellent*, whose gunnery was matchless, opened fire on the *Salvador del Mundo* (112) and then engaged the *San Ysidro* (74) until the latter struck her colours; then Collingwood sailed on to assist Nelson, whose *Captain*, partially dismasted, was engaging the *San Nicolas* (80). In order to avoid *Excellent*, *San Nicolas* collided with *San Josef* (112) and *Captain* ran aboard the stern of *San Nicolas*. Nelson himself led a boarding-party of sailors, marines and members of the 69th Foot who were aboard *Captain*, and *San Nicolas* was captured. Finding that *San Josef* was inextricably entangled in *San Nicolas'* rigging, Nelson threw his boarding-party into that ship as well – 'Nelson's Patent Bridge for Boarding' as it became known! – and *San Josef* was captured similarly. *Santissima Trinidad* actually struck her colours to HMS *Orion*, *Irresistible* and the persistent *Excellent*, but the remainder of the Spanish fleet came up and the giant flagship was able to limp away. Having captured four ships – *Salvador del Mundo* had also struck – Jervis ordered the abandonment of the mêlée and brought his fleet back into line.

Only five British ships had been very heavily engaged: *Captain*, *Excellent*, *Culloden*, *Blenheim* and *Prince George*, which together suffered 65 of the 73 British sailors killed in the battle (227 were wounded). The flagship lost only one man killed; his blood had showered Jervis, alarming all who saw him but not the admiral, who calmly called for an orange to rinse his mouth! Spanish losses (including prisoners) amounted to some 3,800, 200 casualties having been suffered in the flagship alone. Cordova considered whether to renew the action next day, but on enquiring he found three of his ships (including two of his surviving 112s) totally unfit to fight and his flagship a wreck, so limped into Cadiz. Five of the British ships were damaged, but only *Captain* was partially dismasted, having lost the fore topmast.

St Vincent was a considerable success which raised British morale at a time when the situation appeared unpromising. Though Jervis has been criticised for not continuing the action, at little cost he had frustrated the Spanish plans, and he deserved his earldom of St Vincent for his determination in attacking the vastly superior enemy fleet; but the real victory had been achieved by Nelson's disobeying of orders.

# Camperdown – 11 October 1797

Between the battles of St Vincent and Camperdown occurred the greatest potential threat to the navy during the period: the 'great mutiny'. It is unclear why the genuine grievances of the seamen should have come to a head at this moment – the influx of non-seamen brought in by the Quota Acts received some blame – but it is not surprising that protests were made about the appalling conditions under which the seamen existed. They made no complaint about discipline or flogging, but concentrated their demands (very reasonably) on the fact that they were usually cheated out of a portion of their rations and the fact that they had received no increase in pay since Cromwell's era.

The trouble broke out in the Channel fleet at Spithead in April 1797, though the 'mutineers' (in modern parlance 'strikers' would be a more appropriate term) behaved with remarkable restraint and declared from the outset that they would willingly suffer double the hardship they had experienced rather than

the Crown of England be in any way jeopardised. Nevertheless, there was some bloodshed aboard HMS *London* (three men were killed and Admiral Sir John Colpoys was called a 'damned bloody scoundrel' to his face), but the grievances were recognised as just and were remedied, Lord Howe visiting each of the disturbed ships in turn with news of improvements in pay and granting a royal pardon to those involved. More serious was an outbreak of dissent among the ships off the Nore (in the Thames Estuary) in May/June led by an impressed neurotic of some education and skill at oratory, Richard Parker. Whether or not Parker was an instigator or whether his shipmates simply pushed him forward as an articulate spokesman, he declared himself 'President of the Floating Republic' and hoisted the red flag of mutiny, and dissent spread to the North Sea fleet at Yarmouth, originating on HMS *Director* whose captain, William Bligh, was plagued with mutiny throughout his career, on the *Bounty* and

in New South Wales, which raises a question over his tact! An element of politics crept into Parker's demands, and the fleet attempted to blockade London, but talk of handing the ships to the Dutch caused the seamen to revolt against their leaders. Ship after ship returned to their duties and the mutiny collapsed; 29 ringleaders (including Parker) were hanged.

The Dutch fleet was an important part of the French plan to invade Britain, and the blockading of them in port was the responsibility of the North Sea fleet under Admiral Adam Duncan (1731-1804), a gigantic, fierce and experienced Scottish seaman. When the disturbance at the Nore spread to Yarmouth, only

*Camperdown: towards the close of the action, Admiral Jan Willem de Winter's flagship* Vrijheid, *a dismasted wreck, is about to surrender to Admiral Adam Duncan's flagship* Venerable *(centre, partially obscuring from view the* Vrijheid*). (Engraving after R. Dodd.)*

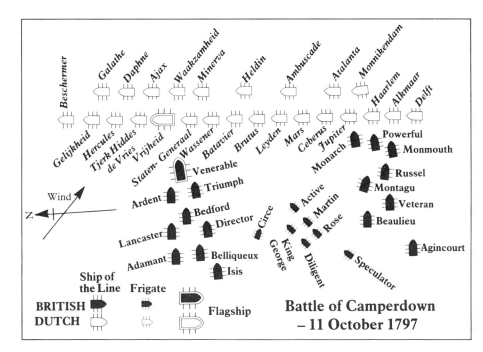

**Battle of Camperdown – 11 October 1797**

Wind

Z

Ship of the Line    Frigate

**BRITISH**
**DUTCH**

Flagship

Dutch ships (top line): Beschermer, Galathe, Daphne, Ajax, Waakzamheid, Minerva, Heldin, Ambuscade, Atalanta, Monnikendam, Haarlem, Alkmaar, Delft

Dutch ships (second line): Gelijkheid, Hercules, Tjerk Hiddes de Vries, Vrijheid, Staten-Generaal, Wassener, Batavier, Brutus, Leyden, Mars, Ceberus, Jupiter, Monarch, Powerful, Monmouth

British ships: Venerable, Triumph, Ardent, Bedford, Director, Circe, Active, Martin, Rose, Russel, Montagu, Veteran, Beaulieu, Lancaster, Adamant, Belliqueux, Isis, King George, Diligent, Speculator, Agincourt

two ships were prepared to sail out with Duncan, his flagship *Venerable* and HMS *Adamant*: so for three days Duncan blockaded the entire Dutch fleet in the Texel with these two, making signals to an imaginary battle-fleet over the horizon. (Duncan was no orator but a practical seaman whose blunt manner had prevented his own ship from mutinying, and he held a ringleader of *Adamant* over the side of the ship with one hand, telling the crew to look what an insignificant wretch was attempting to deprive him of his command!) The Dutch fleet sailed out of the Texel in October 1797, intent on joining the French Brest fleet and landing in Ireland.

Most of the North Sea fleet was re-equipping when the Dutch left the Texel, but they were summoned by a cutter and put to sea immediately, sighting the Dutch off Camperdown (Kamperduin, north of Haarlem) in the early morning of 11 October 1797. Duncan had 16 ships-of-the-line, seven 74s (including his flagship HMS *Venerable*), seven 64s and two 50s, seven of which had been mutinous but now behaved as if nothing untoward had occurred. The Dutch (Batavian) fleet was commanded by Admiral Jan Willem de Winter and included 17 ships-of-the-line plus frigates, with four 74-gunners (including the flagship *Vrijheid*), five 68s, two 64s, four 56s and two 44s. Unlike the French or Spanish, however, their crews were not half-hearted or inept, but as stout as

their British counterparts, with ships evenly-matched, and hence the battle was one of great ferocity.

De Winter formed his fleet into two lines, the ships-of-the-line nearest to the British and his 8 frigates furthest away. Straining to catch the Dutch before they approached so near to the shore to prevent his ships cutting their line, Duncan's fleet became somewhat disordered but resolved itself into two groups; and exactly as at the First of June, Duncan signalled that his ships should 'pass through the Enemy's line and Engage from to Leeward'. By coincidence the attack resembled that adopted at Trafalgar, two columns assailing a line. The signal for 'Close Action' gave the captains to understand that each ship should seek an opponent when the mêlée became general; only HMS *Agincourt* (64) held back and took no part in the action (her captain was court-martialled as a result). The signals from the flagship were confusing, however; Capt Inglis of HMS *Belliqueux* (64), a prickly Scot, threw his signal-book on the deck and damning the signals ordered his helmsman simply to 'gang into the middle o' it'.

The first British column into action, at about 12.30 pm, was that led by Admiral Onslow in HMS *Monarch* (74), which cut the Dutch line three ships from the rear, and the four rearmost ships found themselves assailed by all but one of the ships in Onslow's column (*Agincourt* hanging back). The Dutch

rear was overwhelmed, the four rear ships-of-the-line being captured as well as the large frigate *Monnikendam* (44) which bravely tried to assist the outnumbered rear. At about 12.45 pm Duncan's column, led by the flagship *Venerable*, broke the Dutch line five ships from the head of the column, attacking the *Vrijheid*, despite the Dutch *Staten-General* attempting to block his passage. The remainder of Duncan's column swarmed over the Dutch van, but *Venerable* was left for almost two hours fighting up to four Dutchmen unaided. HMS *Triumph* turned the Dutch *Hercules* (64) into a blazing wreck, but the fight was still desperate even though HMS *Ardent* (64), her captain dead and crew devastated, bravely attacked *Vrijheid* to take pressure off the flagship. Had *Agincourt* come up (being unengaged) from the other column, *Ardent* might not have been shattered.

At about 2.30 pm de Winter observed through a break in the smoke that action at the rear had ended, and as the only unwounded officer on *Vrijheid's* deck personally tried to signal for assistance; the halyard was shot out of his hand by a broadside from Bligh's HMS *Director*, newly-arrived from the rear column. *Vrijheid* was a floating shambles, but when challenged to surrender they replied 'What do you think?'. A British boat rowed over and took possession, de Winter being transferred to *Venerable* where Duncan clasped his hand rather than 'take a brave man's sword'. The capture of the flagship ended the action. Eleven Dutch ships were captured, plus the sloop *Galatea* and including the frigate *Embuscade* (32), of which the *Delft* (56) sank and the *Monnikendam* beached. The Dutch fleet was thus effectively destroyed, with over 1,100 casualties (plus prisoners); but so well had they fought that Duncan lost 203 killed and 622 wounded and his ships were in no state to pursue: though like the British the Dutch had directed their fire against the enemy's hull and thus the British sails and rigging were largely undamaged, so shot-battered were *Ardent's* masts that not a sail could be hoisted and she had to be towed home. Nonetheless, it was a signal victory which earned Duncan a well-deserved viscountcy, and proved that even against such tough opposition the Royal Navy remained invincible.

173

# The Mediterranean, 1798

British presence in the Mediterranean had been considerable from the beginning of the war, to a degree in support of the 'Kingdom of the Two Sicilies', whose monarch, Ferdinand IV, ruled both Sicily and the southern part of Italy, centred on Naples. The British had undertaken a number of significant operations such as the occupation of Corsica and the capture of most of the French Mediterranean fleet upon the Anglo-Spanish occupation of Toulon. The alliance of Spain and France, however, had caused the British to evacuate the area and not until 1798 was a considerable British presence restored when Horatio Nelson – now a Rear-Admiral – was ordered to investigate the large French military and naval concentration around Toulon and other southern ports.

Since St Vincent, Nelson's career had not been particularly distinguished, his expedition to Tenerife in July 1797 (to capture a Spanish treasure-ship) being unsuccessful and costing him an arm. He was, however, a superbly able subordinate to Earl St Vincent (Jervis) who commanded the British fleet stationed off Cadiz. The preparations in the southern ports were those for Bonaparte's Egyptian expedition, part of a somewhat impractical scheme for establishing a French oriental empire and perhaps threatening the British presence in India. It involved a very considerable fleet, transports for around 35,000 men and a naval squadron commanded by Admiral François Paul Brueys d'Aigalliers (1753-98), who had been restored to command after being cashiered on 'aristocratic' grounds in the purges which crippled the French navy in the early Revolutionary Wars.

Bonaparte's fleet set sail in mid-May and totalled some 72 warships (of various sizes) and around 400 transports. Undetected by Nelson (who was hindered by bad weather and lack of concrete intelligence) the French stopped at Genoa, then sailed to Malta which was occupied after a brief resistance from the Knights of St John. The island was garrisoned by the French (in order to use it as a mid-way base to secure communications with Egypt) and some of the warships were detached from the main fleet, so that Brueys' strength was re-duced from 15 ships-of-the-line to 13. Fatally embarrassed by a lack of reconnaissance facility – he had no frigates and only one brig – Nelson tracked across the Mediterranean in a vain attempt to find the French, then headed towards Asia Minor and then back to Sicily, having only by the smallest margin missed encountering the French at sea. On 1 July, therefore, the French arrived off Alexandria and were able to disembark without hinderance from the Royal Navy. It was exactly a month later that Nelson returned to Alexandria, to find only transports in the harbour and no battle-fleet, but shortly after Brueys was discovered at anchor in Aboukir Bay, near the Rosetta mouth of the Nile delta.

Brueys had anchored his ships in what he considered a strong position, in a line only a short distance from shore, protected by shoals and overlooked by a shore battery. His fleet numbered 13 ships-of-the-line, including the 120-gun flagship *L'Orient*, three 80-gunners (*Franklin, Tonnant* and *Guillaume Tell*) and nine 74s. His four frigates (one 44-gunner, two 36s and their 48-gun flagship *Le Diane*) were anchored in a second line closer in towards the shore.

Nelson's fleet was slightly larger in numbers – 14 ships-of-the-line – but had nothing larger than a 74-gunner and included one weak 50-gunner (HMS *Leander*); his only other vessel was the *Mutine* brig (18), commanded by Thomas Masterman Hardy, later Nelson's companion as captain of HMS *Victory*. Nelson's flagship was HMS *Vanguard* (74), and the fleet included five veterans of the First of June and three of St Vincent, *Orion* and *Culloden* having fought in both battles. Brueys believed that the British would not attack immediately (thus some of his crews were ashore) and in any case was confident of the strength of his position.

Nelson and his captains, after the tedious and frustrating chase across the Mediterranean, were in little mood to wait, however, and were determined to attack, intent on taking advantage of the wide distance between the French ships, and moved into action without even waiting to form an official 'line-of-battle'. The British negotiated successfully the shoals in their approach to the French fleet, though HMS *Culloden* ran aground on a sandbank and thus took no part in the action, reducing the battle to thirteen aside. An important factor in Nelson's conduct of tactics was the freedom he gave his captains to use their initiative, knowing that he, as commander, could not observe everything from his place in the flagship. It demanded mutual trust and confidence between admiral and captains, and Nelson was able to inspire both. He referred to his subordinates as a 'Band of Brothers', and rarely can any commander and his deputies have enjoyed such a beneficial relationship.

In the late afternoon of 1 August 1798 the leading elements of Nelson's fleet came into action, led by HMS *Goliath*. Her captain, Thomas Foley, discovered that the space left between the French ships would allow him to manoeuvre through the French line and attack from the landward side, so he cut the line and was followed by a number of ships which began to bombard the port side of the French fleet; not expecting such a manoeuvre, the French had concentrated their preparations to the guns on their starboard sides, and were thus somewhat unprepared. Dusk was drawing on by the time Nelson's *Vanguard* came into action, and lacking the light for more complicated manoeuvering (and with gunsmoke increasing the obscurity), the remainder of the British fleet sailed down the seaward side of the French fleet as originally intended; trapping the French between two fires was largely fortuitous, so that instead of simply overwhelming the van as Nelson had intended, almost the entire French fleet was subjected to a furious cannonade. So skilfully did the British manoeuvre and anchor that much of the French gunnery could not be brought to bear upon them. Nevertheless, the fight was extremely fierce, and HMS *Bellerophon*, after engaging the huge French flagship alone for about an hour, drifted away as a dismasted wreck with almost 200 casualties. Obscured by the gathering dusk, the progress of the battle was not easily discerned.

Nelson was wounded and temporarily blinded in his one good eye (by the flow of blood from an iron splinter which

*The Battle of the Nile, or Aboukir Bay, 1 August 1798. With part of Nelson's fleet having cut the line, the Royal Navy was able to successfully assail both sides of the anchored French fleet (centre, with sails furled).*
*(Painting by Norman Wilkinson)*

struck him above his sightless eye), and though the French van had been overwhelmed, the centre was heavily engaged and the rear virtually untouched. (Though fainting from pain and shock, Nelson remained in command: great physical courage was not the least of his attributes.) At this moment, however, three more British ships came into action: *Leander*, which had been endeavouring to drag *Culloden* clear of the sandbank, and *Alexander* and *Swiftsure*, which had lagged far behind the original attack. These three ships probably turned the day, especially the little *Leander*, for her captain, Thomas Thompson, sailed her into a gap in the French line caused by the French *Peuple Souverain* (74) having drifted from the line-of-battle after her main cable had been cut by a shot. *Leander* was thus able, at no risk to herself, to glide into the French at right-angles and rake both *Franklin* and Brueys' flagship *L'Orient*.

The scene on *L'Orient*'s deck was horrific and appalling; Brueys had lost both legs but continued to direct the battle until a ball from HMS *Swiftsure* cut him in two. The flagship began to burn, so fiercely that the pitch began to melt on *Swiftsure*'s side, but her captain, Benjamin Hallowell, declined to move away as he believed that if *L'Orient* blew up the safest place would be nearby, so that the

explosion would arch over the top of *Swiftsure*; thus he remained in place, drinking ginger beer on his quarterdeck, until *L'Orient* did explode at about ten at night in one of the most awe-inspiring scenes from the age of sail. The explosion remained imprinted on the memory of all who witnessed it, and it effectually brought the battle to a close. (It also provided Felicia Hemans with the material for her most famous poem, 'The Boy Stood on the Burning Deck'.) Commodore Casabianca and his son both perished when *L'Orient* sank, taking with it the looted treasures of the Knights of Malta. The fire was started, it was said, by smouldering wadding from *L'Orient*'s own guns setting light to buckets of paint which the crew had omitted to clear away before action.

Fewer than 900 casualties had been inflicted on the British fleet; the severest loss was that of *Bellerophon*, 49 dead and 148 wounded. (Among the most lamented casualties was Capt GB Westcott of HMS *Majestic* (which with 193 casu-

alties had suffered almost as severely as *Bellerophon*), whose talents raised him from humble birth, from cabin-boy to captain. It was said he only embarked on a naval career after, as a child, demonstrating his skill at splicing a rope when helping to repair a windmill from which his father, a country baker, purchased flour.) Virtually the entire French fleet was destroyed. Three ships-of-the-line tried to escape next day; *Guillaume Tell* with Admiral Villeneuve (later Nelson's opponent at Trafalgar) and *Le Généraux* succeeded, but *Le Timoléon* grounded and was burnt, and two frigates also got away (*Le Diane* and *Justice*); the other two had tried to engage the British and had been sunk, *La Sérieuse* by Sir James Saumarez's HMS *Orion* and Foley's *Goliath* early in the battle, and *L'Artémise* towards the end. Of the remaining ten, nine were captured and one had blown up; as Nelson remarked, 'victory' was not a strong enough name for such an event. The annihilation of the French fleet was not only a stunning blow in itself, but also marooned Bonaparte's expedition in Egypt and at a stroke destroyed his plan of oriental conquest. Well might the *Morning Chronicle* make the pun on the 'Battle of the Nile' (the common name for the battle in Aboukir Bay): 'might not it be justifiable to speak and write his title Lord Nile-son?'

# Copenhagen – 2 April 1801

Aboukir Bay had been a staggering success (the First Lord, Earl Spencer, had fallen flat in the Admiralty at the news), and in October 1798 Sir John Borlase Warren intercepted and destroyed an attempted French landing in Ireland. Success in the Mediterranean was followed by inconclusive operations centred on Naples which occupied Nelson for some two years with little effect, though Sicily was secured from French capture. However, the next major action occurred in the Baltic as the British response to the 'Armed Neutrality of the North', a compact between Russia, Denmark, Sweden and Prussia to contest the British practice of stopping and impounding neutral shipping which might be used to succour France. The league posed a very serious threat to Britain's Baltic trade (including the supply of timber and other materials such as pitch and hemp needed to maintain the fleet, as well as grain), so early in 1801 a fleet was despatched under Admiral Sir Hyde Parker (1739-1807), who had commanded in Jamaica from 1796 to 1800 a somewhat vacillating commander, to deliver an ultimatum to Crown Prince Frederick, regent for the insane Danish king Christian VII. The Danes refused to comply with the request that they withdrew from the Armed Neutrality, and British strategy was thus directed towards the dismantling of the Armed Neutrality piecemeal, to remove either Denmark or Sweden from the alliance before the Russian Baltic fleet broke free from the ice which held them in port.

Parker's fleet comprised 20 ships-of-the-line and some 30 smaller vessels, but his greatest asset was his second-in-command, Horatio Nelson, who since his return from the Mediterranean had been commanding a division of the Channel fleet. Diplomatic negotiations broke down on 23 March 1801, but it was not until a further week had passed that the fleet proceeded down Copenhagen Sound, close-in to the Swedish shore to avoid the attentions of the Danish shore batteries; the Swedes decided not to initiate action and their batteries remained inactive.

The defences of Copenhagen were impressive with 18 moored ships and more at hand: there were eight 'blockships' (moored ships with cut-down masts), of which seven were ships-of-the-line with 52 to 74 guns, and one an ex-merchantman with 26; five floating batteries with between 18 and 24 guns; one unrigged 74 (*Saelland*) and two fully-rigged ships-of-the-line (*Trekroner*, 74 and *Danmark*, 70); two 22-gun praams (flat barges), a 6-gun corvette, two 18-gun brigs, a 20-gun transport, two frigates of 22 and 40 guns, and eleven 4-gun gunboats. The shore batteries, especially those of Trekroner fort, were also most formidable. Because of the shoals off each shore, Parker was reluctant to commit his larger ships lest they run aground, so gave Nelson a squadron of 12 ships-of-the-line plus support vessels with which to make the attack, Nelson transferring his flag from the 98-gun *St George* to the *Elephant*, 74. The squadron comprised seven 74s, three 64s, one 56 (William Bligh's HMS *Glatton*, experimentally armed entirely with carronades, which Nelson did not favour), one 50, six frigates, three brigs, seven bomb-ketches and two fireships. The remainder of the fleet remained out of range.

At first light on 2 April 1801 the twelve British ships-of-the-line having spent the night anchored near to the Danes began to sail upon the moored defences. At the very commencement HMS *Russell* (74), *Bellona* (74) and *Agamemnon* (64) ran aground and were able to play only a minor role in the battle, their only fatalities being caused by the explosion of *Bellona*'s own guns. At about 10.30 am the action commenced as the nine surviving ships-of-the-line engaged their selected opponents, and the frigates engaged the Trekroner battery. The Danes fought with great

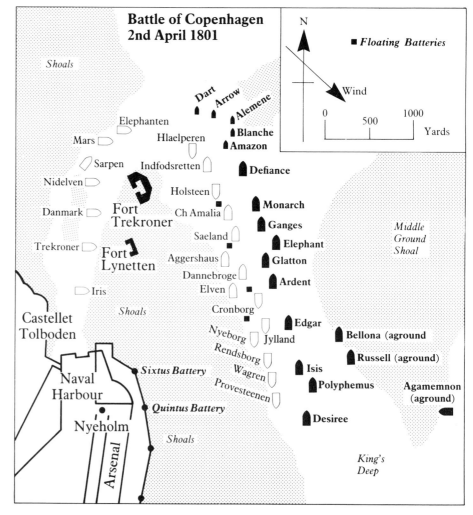

**Above:** *Copenhagen, 2 April 1801: the British fleet sails in upon the Danish line, with HMS* Polyphemus *(left) bringing up the rear;* Bellona *and* Russell *are aground in the right foreground. (Engraving by E.W. Tomkins.)*

**Below:** *Horatio Nelson (1759-1805), Duke of Brontë, created a viscount for his victory at Copenhagen: probably the greatest naval commander in history and Britain's greatest sailor. (Engraving by Robinson afer Hoppner.)*

resolution, more able to ferry the reinforcements from shore to replace their casualties and their stalwart conduct made the task a hard one; against any other opponent but the determined Nelson, they would probably have conducted the defence successfully.

The Danish commander, Johan Fischer, flew his flag in the blockship *Dannebroge* (60), but when that was set afire transferred to *Holsteen* (60); when that ship surrendered Fischer moved to Trekroner fort. The leading British ship-of-the-line was HMS *Defiance*, Nelson's *Elephant* being third in line. About 1 pm, when the British cannonade was at last beginning to tell, Hyde Parker decided that success was not possible, knowing that three ships were aground, and signalled Nelson to break off the action. The frigates nearest to Parker obeyed the signal with some dismay, HMS *Amazon* (38) being racked by gunfire as she withdrew, killing her captain, the highly-rated Edward Riou. Nelson, however, was in no mood to repeat Parker's signal and ordered his own – 'close action' – to remain flying. When his attention was again drawn to his superior's signal, he put his telescope to his blind eye and said that really, he saw no signal. As at St Vincent, his disobeying of orders resulted in victory. By damning Parker's signal – which apparently he did on

several occasions – Nelson's force remained in action and, being on the point of victory at the moment that Parker signalled, continued to blast their targets. By this time about eight of the Danish ships were either wrecked, taken or drifting, and by another hour all that remained in combat were the *Jylland* (54), *Holsteen* (with but few guns still firing) and *Dannebroge*, blazing but with three guns still in action. So heroic had been the Danish defence that the 58-gun blockship *Provensteen* only surrendered when 56 of her guns had been dismounted.

Nelson proposed a truce in a letter he wrote himself whilst under fire, addressed to 'the Brother of Englishmen, the Danes', pleading for a cessation of fire to prevent him having to burn the captured ships. It was accepted, and the battle ended. All the Danish ships engaged were either captured or destroyed; the resolute conduct of the Danes resulted in fearsome casualties, 1,035 Danes, 944 British; worst hit was HMS *Monarch* (74), with 57 dead and 163 wounded.

The destruction of the Danish fleet effectively ended the threat of the Armed Neutrality, but ironically the assassination of the Czar (12 March) would have done the same, without the bloodshed of Copenhagen. Nevertheless, it raised the reputation of Nelson and the Royal Navy to new heights.

# Trafalgar – 21 October 1805

One further encounter of note occurred before the war was temporarily suspended by the Peace of Amiens: Sir James Saumarez twice engaged the Franco-Spanish off Algeciras, British supremacy being confirmed in the second action, though the enemy's most serious loss came from their own ineptitude. HMS *Superb* (74) fired a broadside at the Spanish *Real Carlos* (112) as it passed; *Superb*'s shot flew over the Spaniard and struck another first-rate, *San Hermenegildo*, which presumed that *Real Carlos* was responsible. The two huge Spaniards then engaged each other until both blew up!

With the renewal of the war, Napoleon conceived an ambitious plan for the invasion of Britain, involving the assembly of a huge 'Army of England', centred on Boulogne, and the construction of a vast flotilla of invasion-barges to be used to transport the troops across the Channel. This required the French to gain temporary control of the Channel; as the chances of defeating the Royal Navy were remote, it was decided that the British defenders should be lured away, whereupon the French fleet would return rapidly and cover the invasion before the British fleet could catch up.

On 29 March 1805 the fleet of Vice-Admiral Pierre de Villeneuve (1763-1806) slipped out of Toulon under the cover of bad weather and evaded the British blockade; Nelson, commanding the watching fleet, mistook their destination and sailed further into the Mediterranean, and was thus far behind when the Frenchman's true destination became apparent. Picking up a Spanish fleet under Admiral the Duke of Gravina (1756-1806), Villeneuve sailed for the West Indies and, when he was sure that the British were following, reversed his course and returned to Europe. The new First Lord, Admiral Lord Barham (1726-1813) ensured that the Franco-Spanish would be intercepted on their return, and on 22 July Sir Robert Calder (1745-1818) fought an inconclusive action off Cape Finisterre, allowing Villeneuve to harbour with the loss of two ships. Nelson, angry at having missed an opportunity of a fleet action, went home for a short leave.

Although by now Napoleon had abandoned his plan of invasion, he bullied Ville-neuve by accusations of cowardice into putting to sea again, and the Franco-Spanish 'Combined Fleet' sailed to Cadiz, shadowed by a British squadron under Admiral Sir Cuthbert Collingwood (1750-1810). Nelson re-joined the fleet aboard his flag-ship HMS *Victory*, and Villeneuve, threatened with dismissal, again put to sea. The combination of Napoleon's lack of understanding of the realities of naval warfare and the deficiencies of the French navy had set them up for defeat.

Leaving Cadiz on 19 October, Villeneuve headed for the Mediterranean to raid Malta's supply-routes, but finding an unexpected British presence barring his way off Cape Trafalgar in the early morning of 21 October, he ordered a return to Cadiz. The 'Combined Fleet' numbered 33 ships-of-the-line, 18 French (four 80-gunners and the rest 74s) and 15 Spanish, including the gigantic *Santissima Trinidad* (130), two 112s, one 100, two 80s, one 64 and the remainder 74s. Nelson had 27 ships-of-the-line, including three 100-gunners, four 98s, one 80, three 64s and the rest 74s. The most valuable British asset, however, was Nelson himself, for his leadership qualities had turned his captains into a 'band of brothers' who understood perfectly what he intended to do. In an extension of the tactic of cutting the enemy's line, Nelson planned to assault the French line with three columns at right-angles (in the event only two columns were formed), to overwhelm the enemy's rear and centre

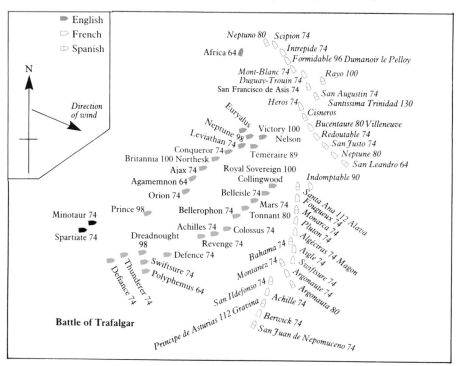

Battle of Trafalgar

178

before the van could retrace its course and return to support. The result would be a 'pell-mell battle', which, said Nelson, would 'surprise and confound the enemy' and allow the British superiority of gunnery and ship-handling to be utilised to the greatest effect.

Shortly after mid-day on 21 October the battle began, Nelson having hoisted his immortal signal 'England expects that every many will do his duty' (an unnecessary exhortation!) and 'Engage the enemy more closely'. His own (windward) column was led by HMS *Victory*, and rather than expose the admiral to unnecessary danger, *Victory's* captain, Thomas Hardy, signalled the next ship in the column (HMS *Téméraire*, Capt Eliab Harvey) to overtake and to attack. Nelson walked to *Victory's* stern as *Téméraire* drew alongside and sharply reminded Harvey of his 'proper station' astern of *Victory*! However, it was the column led by Collingwood which first broke the Franco-Spanish line, in HMS

*Trafalgar, 2.30 pm: Victory's column penetrates the Franco-Spanish fleet. Victory (out of sight, left) is followed by Téméraire (left, entangled with the dismasted Redoutable); Fougueux burns behind. Boats in the foreground rescue men from the shattered Santissima Trinidad (right). (Print after WL Wyllie.)*

*Royal Sovereign* (100) which for a period was engaged by no fewer than five enemy ships. He was seconded by the succeeding ships, HMS *Bellisle*, which though suffering severe damage to masts and rigging took the first trophy, the Spanish *Argonauto* (80). Within an hour, *Victory's* column was in action, the flagship first aiming for the huge *Santissima Trinidad* but transferring its attention to *Bucentaure* (80) when Villeneuve's admiral's flag was seen flying from her. *Victory* cut the line and began to batter *Bucentaure*, but was herself engaged by the French *Redoutable* (74), commanded by perhaps the best captain in the French navy, Jean Lucas, who had trained his crew to a degree largely unknown in French service. About 1.30 pm a marksman in *Redoutable's* fighting-tops sighted the slight figure in the medal-covered coat walking *Victory's* quarterdeck and brought him down with a musket-shot. Nelson had refused to change his bejewelled coat and now fell, shot through the spine. He was carried below to the stygian gloom of *Victory's* cockpit with a handkerchief over his face, so as not to dishearten the crew who idolised him; but though he knew the wound was mortal he continued to issue orders.

This was the French fleet's only success, for the tactic – which its architect had styled 'the Nelson touch' – proved brilliantly successful. Though several of

the British ships were badly damaged, the Franco-Spanish fleet was destroyed. The fighting was extremely severe; at one time, for example, *Redoutable* was almost on board HMS *Téméraire*, with *Victory* on the other side, and the French *Fougueux* having collided with *Téméraire*, which boarded and captured her. By the time the Franco-Spanish van had reversed their course, the centre and rear had been overwhelmed as Nelson had planned, and those ships which were able made off. Nelson died at 4.30 pm, in the knowledge that a great victory had been won, that Villeneuve was captured when *Bucentaure* was taken, and that 15 enemy ships had struck. Two more were taken from the French Admiral Dumanoir's van when it tried briefly to avert the disaster, and one other (*Achille*, 74) blew up at 5.30 pm, having been set afire by the marksmen in her own fighting-tops, which effectually ended the battle. Nelson's last words were typical of him: 'Thank God I have done my duty'.

About 450 British sailors were killed and 1,100 wounded; the Franco-Spanish lost some 14,000 men, but only four of the 17 prizes survived the storm which arose on the night of the battle. Although the plan of invading England had been abandoned before Trafalgar, the overwhelming British victory meant that never again would it be contemplated.

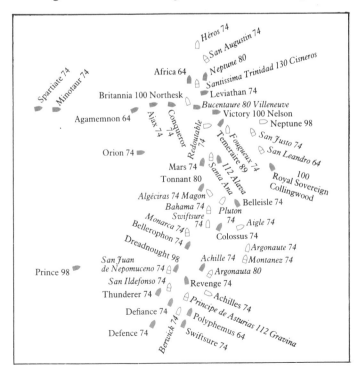

# The Naval Campaigns – 1806-15

Following Trafalgar, British naval supremacy remained unchallenged despite Napoleon's earnest attempts to increase his fleet to the point where it might mount a serious challenge. There were, however, no great sea-battles of the Trafalgar mould, French morale never having really recovered despite the excellent quality of the ships they built, and (as Admiral Sir Edward Pellew remarked of the Toulon fleet in 1811), their calibre increasing as a result of adopting 'too many of our arrangements'! Nevertheless, the Royal Navy's task post-1805 was much more than merely combatting the French commerce-raiders (which were not fully mastered until 1813), blockading and providing support for military operations; a number of significant actions occurred quite apart from those in support of the acquisition of enemy overseas territory.

Soon after Trafalgar four of Dumanoir's surviving ships (*Formidable*, 80, and three 74s) were intercepted and captured by four 74s under Sir Richard Strachan; one of these, *Duguay-Trouin*, survived as HMS *Implacable* until after World War II, when she was scuttled. The remaining Trafalgar survivors were handed to Britain when they were taken by Spanish patriots at Cadiz upon the outbreak of the Peninsular War. Though reluctant to engage in a major action, French squadrons sometimes evaded the blockades to raid British commerce, such as Admiral Leiségues' foray from Brest with five ships. He was caught by Admiral Sir John Duckworth at Santo Domingo on 6 February 1806; three were captured and two destroyed. Throughout this period, Britain lost not one ship-of-the-line to enemy action (but 12 to wreck or accident); in fact the only one taken by the French from the renewal of hostilities was HMS *Calcutta* (54) off Sicily on 26 September 1805 (and that was destroyed at Basque Roads in 1809!).

Less successful were British naval operations against the Turks in support of Russia, an attempt to force the Dardanelles by Duckworth early in 1807 being mauled before it was abandoned. Greater success attended a second expedition against Copenhagen, in September 1807, this time mainly military, which resulted in the capture of virtually the entire Danish fleet including 16 ships-of-the-line and 10 frigates, a useful addition to Britain's naval resources. In the Mediterranean France made a minor gain with the capture of Capri, but their attempt on Sicily was easily beaten.

As the French were unwilling to engage the Royal Navy in a major battle, increasing use was made of coastal raids upon French harbours to compel them to fight. An attempted French expedition to the West Indies in 1809 resulted in the most spectacular of these, when Admiral Willaumez's French squadron, having been intercepted on its break-out from Brest, ran for cover to Basque Roads or Ile d'Aix, a 'safe' anchorage near Rochefort. Together with the Rochefort squadron the French fleet, now blockaded in, numbered 11 ships-of-the-line and 4 frigates. The position was beset with shoals and an enormous cable supported on buoys acted as a boom to prevent entry to the anchorage, and was thus considered impregnable. Impregnable, that is, to all but the Royal Navy; Admiral Lord Gambier (1756-1833), commanding the blockading squadron, was joined by Britain's most audacious frigate-commander, Thomas Cochrane (1775-1860), who organised an attack with fireships and frigates. (His raids on the enemy coast and destruction of shipping had become legendary). On the night of 11 April 1809 Cochrane blew up the boom and sent 20 fireships into the anchorage; the French ships cut their cables and ran, and in the darkness and confusion all but three stuck fast on the shoals. Cochrane engaged with his frigates, and destroyed four ships-of-the-line and a frigate, but Gambier's caution prevented his committing his larger ships and the remainder managed to escape up the Charente estuary. Nevertheless, it emphasized the complete dominance of the Royal Navy over the French. (After a career of unrelieved success, Cochrane was cashiered for alleged implication in the 'Great Stock Exchange Fraud' of 1814; thereafter he employed his immense talents in the service of various South American republics.)

Smaller but equally impressive were the 'frigate actions' in which single ships or small squadrons attacked the French wherever they might be found. One of the most significant of these was the action at Lissa (13 March 1811) in which four British frigates under the command of Capt William Hoste of HMS *Amphion* engaged eleven Franco-Venetian vessels including four frigates. In a fierce action, no enemy vessel larger than a brig escaped, plus the frigate *Flora* which made off after she had struck her colours, an act so dishonourable that Hoste wrote to her commander requesting that he obeyed the laws of war and handed over his ship; the request was refused! Other actions which were typical and which earned some notoriety included the capture of the French frigate *La Piedmontaise* by HMS *St Fiorenzo* (8 March 1808) in which the British commander, Capt George Hardinge, was killed (brother of Henry Hardinge whose actions saved the day at Albuera); and Capt Jahleel Brenton's HMS *Spartan* beating off twelve Neapolitan craft on 3 May 1810, despite *Spartan* being so short-handed that a Royal Engineer passenger and the purser each had to command a division of guns.

British dominance was challenged sharply by the infant United States Navy during the tragic and unnecessary War of 1812. Although the Americans possessed nothing larger than frigates, their crews fought with the same spirit as those of the Royal Navy, and their ships were superb. Although officially frigates, the American ships combined the manoeuvreability of the smaller vessels with a firepower akin to that of a smaller ship-of-the-line; thus in ship-to-ship frigate-actions they were sometimes 50 per cent more powerful than their British opponents. In any case, the huge imbalance in the respective navies was levelled by the British preoccupation with the war against Napoleon; when the War of 1812 began, for example, only one British ship-of-the-line and six frigates were on the eastern American seaboard, and thus American commerce-raiders were able to wreak considerable havoc throughout the period of hostilities.

Even more significant were the frigate actions in which the U.S. Navy's well-managed and more powerful ships inflicted a number of startling defeats upon British ships whose captains had, per-

*The largest frigate action of the period, the battle of Lissa (13 March 1811) was a comprehensive defeat of a Franco-Venetian squadron by William Hoste's frigates Amphion, Active, Cerebus and Volage. Hoste flew the signal 'Remember Nelson'. (Engraving after R. Dodd)*

haps, grown complacent at the frequency with which their opponents (the French) were defeated with ease. It was a rude shock, therefore, when the USS *Constitution* (44, alias 'Old Ironsides') shattered HMS *Guerrière* (38) on 19 August 1812 off Nova Scotia, to be followed by another victory over HMS *Java* (38) off Bahia, Brazil, on 29 December, with Stephen Decatur's USS *United States* (44) capturing HMS *Macedonian* (38) in the interim. As *The Times* shrieked in March 1813, 'Five hundred merchantmen, and three frigates! Can these statements be true; and can the English people hear them unmoved?' The situation was severe, for not only was British commerce being ravaged by numerous small American warships and privateers, it was even said that the French were taking new heart by the proof that the Royal Navy was *not* invincible, and Napoleon ordered his new frigates to be built to resemble the splendid American designs.

The War of 1812 henceforth stretched Britain's naval resources to the limit, as over 100 vessels were diverted from the war with France to blockade the American ports (in the event with great success, as America's trade was wrecked and the country brought to the verge of bank-

ruptcy); and on 1 June 1813 the Royal Navy's reputation was recovered by a stunning victory off Boston. HMS *Shannon* (38), trained to the peak of efficiency (especially in gunnery) by her captain, Philip Vere Broke, challenged Capt James Lawrence of USS *Chesapeake* (36), who eagerly sailed out of Boston confident of inflicting another defeat on the British. Within fifteen minutes *Cheseapeake* was wrecked by *Shannon*'s gunnery, her sailing-master killed and Lawrence wounded mortally, and Broke personally led the boarding-party which captured the shattered American frigate. The victory raised British morale and though the American commerce-raiders remained so troublesome that British ships were only safe in escorted convoy, no more significant reverses were suffered before the sad war was brought to its conclusion.

The remaining operations were direc-

ted towards the acquisition of French overseas territory, such as Martinique (captured in June 1809 by an Anglo-Spanish expedition), Mauritius and Réunion in December 1810; and in support of the various military operations in Europe, such as the abortive landing at Walcheren in 1809 and, more significantly, in the Peninsular War. British mastery of the sea alone enabled Wellington to transfer his home base from Lisbon to Santander, and the supply-routes held open by the navy throughout the war were even more significant. Minor naval actions against small squadrons and individual vessels continued throughout the war, with almost unrelieved success, the four frigates lost in an injudicious action at Grand Port in August 1810 being the only major setback. The final actions of the war occurred on 25 May 1814, when the French xebec *Aigle* (6) was captured by the boats of HMS *Queen Elizabeth* (74) off Corfu; and, during the 'Hundred Days', the frigate *Melpomène* (40) off Ischia. Exemplifying the superiority of the Royal Navy, the latter was captured by HMS *Rivoli* (74), ironically named after one of Napoleon's victories and herself a captured French ship.

# Amphibious Operations

The fact that Britain is an island meant that all military operations had to be conducted in concert with the Royal Navy. It was even found more convenient to move troops around Britain by sea, the trip from (say) Edinburgh to London being faster by coaster than by marching the troops the same distance. Little use was made of inland waterways, however, though a number of 'marches' were made by barge; even this was hazardous such as the trip of the Tarbert Fencibles along the river Suir in 1799, which cost 58 lives when a boat sank.

Transportation of troops by sea was the responsibility of the 'Board of Transport' of five naval captains and a secretary. The merchantmen they chartered for this service were frequently unsatisfactory both in condition and crew, and healthy men were frequently embarked in ships infected with disease, so that sickness spread, often with devastating results (worst were the vessels which transferred Irish recruits to Chatham, voyages notorious for their mortality rate). The supply of merchantmen was at a premium so the Board laboured

under great difficulties; but some of their charters were appalling. Many transports had drunken or incompetent masters and crew, and on at least one occasion an infantry captain had to navigate a ship from the West Indies to England (he arrived safely in Ireland, though believed the mouth of the Mersey was the Downs; though for an unskilled mariner it was a great achievement). Latterly, old 50- and 60-gun ships were used as troop-transports ('*en flûte*', i.e. with part of the armament removed), but the only really healthy and comfortable troop-transports were those of the East India Company, which as usual spared little expense to make their vessels the best of any, very different from the strictures placed by the Board of Transport upon the ships it chartered from other sources.

Apart from major operations (like Portugal and Egypt), amphibious descents upon enemy coasts ranged from the brilliantly successful to unmitigated disasters. Small raids conducted by frigate-crews created many problems for the French; the acquisition of French

*'Landing troops and guns': a print after a painting by Thomas Rowlandson, 1801, showing the landing of heavy artillery pieces, the guns dragged by teams of seamen whilst the Royal Artillerymen rest in the foreground.*

overseas territories depended upon successful operations of the larger scale, whilst those like Quiberon or Walcheren were both ill-conceived and ill-executed, though such failures were generally occasioned by failures in the military operations rather than any breakdown in the amphibious stage of the landing. It is perhaps surprising that the actual process of landing troops generally passed off successfully, given that there were no specially-designed landing-craft of any description, ships' boats or cutters being the general means of transporting troops from sea to land in those cases where a regular port was unavailable. (The landing under fire in Egypt, for example, was a considerable achievement.)

Amphibious operations profited greatly from cordial co-operation between the military and naval commanders, though inter-service rivalry sometimes spread to acrimony, as evidenced by an amazing order recorded in the *United Service Journal* in 1831:

'Lt-Gen Prescott's Orders, St Pierre, 16 June 1794.

'Whereas, Vice-Admiral Sir John Jervis has given orders, I am told, frequently, here on shore, and particularly, by a note dated off Point Petre, June 11th, 1794, which must have arisen from great ignorance, or great presumption and arrogance. If from ignorance, poor man! he is to be pitied; but if from presumption and arrogance, he is to be checked. It is therefore Lt-Gen Prescott's orders, that in future no attention whatever is to be given to such Notes, or Orders, and his signature to such, to be as little regarded, as that of John Oakes, or Peter Styles'.

Whereas the expeditions to Quiberon and Walcheren are perhaps the most famous of the failed amphibious expeditions, one which demonstrates the difficulties is the attack on Ostend in 1798. Home Popham (of South American expedition fame) advanced the idea that a significant blow could be delivered against France if the lock on the recently-completed Bruges-Ostend canal were

*'Landing troops in the face of the enemy': a scene probably from the eastern Peninsular seaboard, the British infantry disembarking from ships' boats. (Print by Dubourg after J A Atkinson)*

destroyed a mile from Ostend, this waterway being a convenient route for the transportation of supplies and troops, preparatory for any intended invasion of England. The plan received backing from the War Office. Ideally, the raid could have been accomplished by an audacious frigate-captain and his crew, but a much larger descent was planned, despite obstructions from the Admiralty at every turn (either from dislike of Popham or from a realisation of the hazards). Thus delayed until 14 May, the expedition sailed from Margate escorted by a naval flotilla under Popham's command, with no less than about 1,400 troops, including the 11th Foot, four light companies of the 1st Guards, four from the 2nd and 3rd Guards, the flank companies of the 23rd and 49th Foot, 100 Royal Artillerymen with six guns and nine men of the 17th Light Dragoons, commanded by Major-General Eyre Coote. (The Guards were presumably hazarded on this venture because of the shortage of trained men available, demonstrating the weakness of the home forces.) The expedition did not arrive off Ostend until the early hours of 19 May, and an approaching gale led Popham to suggest a postponement. As intelligence suggested that the area was but weakly garrisoned, however, Coote landed immediately, the troops being dumped ashore without any regard to the previously-decided order of disembarkation. By five in the morning all had

landed save the 1st Guards (whose transport had strayed en route), and Coote advanced to the lock in face of light opposition and blew it up. By eleven the force was back on the beach without having suffered a casualty; but the gale had risen to such a pitch that Coote's men had to entrench themselves in the sandhills and wait for the storm to abate, though quite unprepared, calling on the citadel of Ostend to surrender to pass the time (they refused).

By dawn on 20 May the beach-head was being assailed by French troops on all sides, and for two hours Coote held his defensive perimeter, until he was severely wounded. His deputy, Major-General Burrard, believing that further loss of life was pointless, surrendered. 163 of the expedition were casualties, and over 1,100 taken prisoner; and though the government hailed the destruction of the lock a great success, in fact it had little effect on the internal navigation between Holland and France. The War Office blamed the Admiralty for causing delays which compelled it to be undertaken in bad weather; but it was suspected that Secretary Huskisson had agreed to the plan simply to put heart into the Cabinet. But to use a contemporary phrase, the game was obviously not worth the candle.

Though many succeeding amphibious operations were successful, ineptitude continued to plague the minor expeditions such as Lord Blayney's landing at Fuengirola in October 1810 in an attempt to capture Malaga; the incompetent general was surprised and captured on the beach with half the 89th. A similar disappointment were the operations on the east coast of Spain in 1813, especially the abortive attempt on Tarragona. The fault here was in the commander, the ineffective Sir John Murray, of whom Wellington wrote that he lacked 'sound sense. There is always some mistaken principle in what he does . . . what I cannot bear is his leaving his guns and stores; and, strange to say, not only does he not think he was wrong in so doing, but he writes of it as being rather meritorious, and says he did it before . . . The best of the story is, that all parties ran away . . . Sir John Murray ran away; and so did Suchet . . .' Throughout the period, the main cause of failure of such operations was not the calibre of the troops, but inept leadership.

# *Appendix*

## Order of Battle: Vittoria

The organisation of the army is demonstrated by the Order of Battle of Wellington's Anglo-Portuguese forces for the Vittoria campaign:

**Cavalry:** Hill's Bde: 1st & 2nd Life Guards, Royal Horse Guards
Fane's Bde: 3rd Dragoon Guards, 1st Dragoons
Ponsonby's Bde: 5th Dragoon Guards, 3rd & 4th Dragoons
Grant's Bde: 10th, 15th & 18th Hussars
Anson's Bde: 12th & 16th Light Dragoons
Long's Bde: 13th Light Dragoons
Alten's Bde: 14th Light Dragoons, 1st KGL Hussars
Bock's Bde: 1st & 2nd KGL Dragoons
D'Urban's Bde: 1st, 11th & 12th Portuguese Cavalry
Campbell's Bde: 6th Portuguese Cavalry

**1st Division:** (Howard)
Stopford's Bde: 1/2nd Guards, 1/3rd Guards, 1 coy 5/60th
Halkett's Bde: 1st, 2nd & 5th Line Bns KGL, 1st & 2nd KGL Light Bns

**2nd Division:** (Hill)
Cadogan's Bde: 1/50th, 1/71st, 1/92nd, 1 coy 5/60th
Byng's Bde: 1/3rd, 1/57th, 1st Provisional Bn (2/31st, 2/66th), 1 coy 5/60th
O'Callaghan's Bde: 1/28th, 2/34th, 1/39th, 1 coy 5/60th
Ashworth's Bde: 6th & 18th Portuguese Line, 6th *Caçadores*

**3rd Division:** (Picton)
Brisbane's Bde: 1/45th, 74th, 1/88th, 3 coys 5/60th
Colville's Bde: 1/5th, 2/83rd, 2/87th, 94th
Power's Bde: 9th & 21st Portuguese Line, 11th *Caçadores*

**4th Division:** (Lowry Cole)
Anson's Bde: 3/27th, 1/40th, 1/48th, 2nd Provisional Bn (2nd & 2/53rd), 1 coy 5/60th
Skerret's Bde: 1/7th, 20th, 1/23rd, 1 coy Brunswick Oels
Stubb's Bde: 11th & 23rd Portuguese Line, 7th *Caçadores*

**5th Division:** (Oswald)
Hay's Bde: 3/1st, 1/9th, 1/38th, 1 coy Brunswick Oels
Robinson's Bde: 1/4th, 2/47th, 2/59th, 1 coy Brunswick Oels
Spry's Bde: 3rd & 15th Portuguese Line, 8th *Caçadores*

**6th Division:** (Pakenham)
Stirling's Bde: 1/42nd, 1/79th, 1/91st, 1 coy 5/60th
Hinde's Bde: 1/11th, 1/32rd, 1/36th, 1/61st
Madden's Bde: 8th & 12th Portuguese Line, 9th *Caçadores*

**7th Division:** (Dalhousie)
Barnes' Bde: 1/6th, 3rd Provisional Bn (2/24th, 2/58th), 9 coys Brunswick Oels
Grant's Bde: 51st, 68th, 1/82nd, Chasseurs Britanniques
Lecor's Bde: 7th & 19th Portuguese Line, 2nd *Caçadores*

**Light Division:** (Alten)
Kempt's Bde: 1/43rd, 1/ & 3/95th
Vandeleur's Bde: 1/52nd, 2/95th
Portuguese: 17th Line, 1st & 3rd *Caçadores*

**Silveira's Division**
Da Costa's Bde: 2nd & 14th Portuguese Line
Campbell's Bde: 4th & 10th Portuguese Line, 10th *Caçadores*

**Pack's Bde**
1st & 16th Portuguese Line, 4th *Caçadores*
Bradford's Bde: 13th & 24th Portuguese Line, 5th *Caçadores*

*The Battle of Vittoria, 21 June 1813. This print by Terry & Pound, though not executed by an eye-witness, is perhaps a more accurate portrayal of the appearance of a Napoleonic battlefield than many more 'artistic' compositions: obscured by smoke (the 'fog of war') and with the position of troop-formations not clearly evident. These factors greatly influenced the reliability of eye-witness accounts which describe anything more than events which occurred in the witness' immediate vicinity; as the Duke of Wellington remarked, a participant was as capable of giving a complete account of a battle as a dancer was able to describe exactly all the events of a ball.*

# Chronology

(The events listed are those which had most bearing upon British involvement in the Revolutionary and Napoleonic Wars.)

## 1769
1 May – *Birth of Arthur Wesley, probably at Merrion St, Dublin.*

## 1787
17 March – *Arthur Wesley commissioned as ensign, 73rd Highlanders.*

## 1793
1 February – *France declares war on Britain.*
14 April – *British capture of Tobago.*
28 June – *Allies capture Valenciennes.*
27 August – *Anglo-Spanish expedition occupies Toulon.*
30 September – *Arthur Wesley commissioned lieutenant-colonel, 33rd Foot.*

## 1794
23 March – *British capture of Martinique.*
2 April – *British capture St Lucia.*
21 April – *British complete capture of Guadeloupe.*
1 June – *Admiral Howe defeats Villaret de Joyeuse at 'Glorious 1st of June'.*
15 September – *Wesley's first action, at Boxtel in the Netherlands.*
10 December – *French recapture Guadeloupe.*

## 1795
14 April – *British Netherlands expedition evacuated from Bremen.*
18 June – *British quit St Lucia.*
27 June – *Anglo-émigré landing at Quiberon; evacuated 21 July.*
16 August – *British complete capture of Cape of Good Hope.*

## 1796
5 February – *British capture Ceylon.*
25 May – *British re-occupy St Lucia.*
2 November – *British evacuation of Corsica following Franco-Spanish alliance; British leave Mediterranean on 1 December.*
16/30 December – *Abortive French expedition to Bantry Bay.*

## 1797
14 February – *Admiral Jervis defeats Cordova at St Vincent.*
17 February – *British capture Trinidad.*
22/24 February – *Abortive French landing at Fishguard, Pembrokeshire.*
16/24 April – *Spithead mutiny.*
12 May/15 June – *Nore mutiny.*
11 October – *Admiral Duncan defeats de Winter at Camperdown.*

## 1798
8 May – *British re-enter Mediterranean.*
19 May – *Abortive British landing at Ostend.*
23 May – *The '98 rebellion in Ireland.*
12 June – *Defeat of Irish rebels at Vinegar Hill.*

1 August – *Nelson annihilates French fleet at Aboukir Bay, marooning Bonaparte's Egyptian expedition.*
22 August – *General Humbert's French expedition lands at Killala Bay, Mayo.*
25 August – *Humbert defeats Lake at Castlebar.*
8 September – *Humbert surrenders to Cornwallis at Ballinamuck.*
15 November – *British capture Minorca.*
3 December – *Introduction of Income Tax to finance British war effort.*

## 1799
10 March – *British forces sent to garrison Sicily.*
17 March – *Bonaparte besieges Acre: defence led by Sydney Smith.*
5 May – *Wellesley appointed governor of Seringapatam after the fall of the city.*
27 August – *Anglo-Russian army lands in north Holland.*
19 September – *Allies defeated at first Battle of Bergen.*
2 October – *French defeated by Anglo-Russians at second Battle of Bergen.*
6 October – *Allies defeated at Castricum.*
18 October – *Convention of Alkmaar by which Anglo-Russian army leaves north Holland.*

## 1800
21 January – *Convention of El Arish between French and Anglo-Ottomans in Egypt; war resumed after its repudiation.*
19 June – *Abortive British raid on Belle Isle.*
26 August – *Abortive British raid on Ferrol.*
5 September – *British capture Malta.*
10 September – *Wellesley defeats the bandit Doondia Wao.*

## 1801
1 January – *Act of Union between Britain and Ireland.*
8 March – *British landing at Aboukir.*
21 March – *Abercromby defeats Menou at Alexandria.*
2 April – *Nelson destroys Danish fleet at Copenhagen, virtually ending the League of Armed Neutrality.*
27 June – *British capture Cairo.*
6 July – *Sir James Saumarez fights inconclusive action against French at Algeciras.*
12 July – *Saumarez defeats Franco-Spanish fleet in second battle of Algeciras.*
2 September – *French in Egypt surrender.*
1 October – *Britain and France sign preliminaries of peace.*

## 1802
27 March – *Peace of Amiens between Britain and France.*
29 April – *Wellesley appointed Major-General.*

## 1803
16 May – *Britain declares war on France.*
3 June – *French capture Hanover.*
22 June – *British capture St Lucia.*
30 June – *British capture Tobago.*
11 August – *Wellesley captures Ahmednuggur.*
20 September – *British capture Demerara.*
23 September – *Wellesley wins victory of Assaye.*
29 November – *Wellesley wins victory at Argaum.*
15 December – *Wellesley captures Gawilghur.*

## 1804
5 May – *British capture Surinam.*
7 May – *William Pitt again becomes Prime Minister, having resigned on 14 February 1801.*

## 1805
30 March – *Admiral Villeneuve sails from Toulon.*
14 May – *Villeneuve reaches Martinique.*
22 July – *Admiral Calder intercepts Villeneuve off Cape Finisterre.*
18 August – *Villeneuve puts in to Cadiz.*
21 October – *Nelson defeats Villeneuve off Cape Trafalgar as the Franco-Spanish fleet attempts to return to Cadiz.*
4 November – *Surviving French ships defeated off Rochefort.*

## 1806
8 January – *British capture Capetown.*
23 January – *Death of William Pitt.*
6 February – *Admiral Duckworth defeats Laissaque's French squadron off San Domingo.*
12 May – *British capture Capri.*
17 June – *British expedition to Buenos Ayres.*
4 July – *Sir John Stuart defeats Reynier at Maida in Calabria.*
8 October – *Sydney Smith raids Boulogne.*
21 November – *Napoleon proclaims blockade of Britain by Berlin Decrees.*

## 1807
7 January – *Orders in Council in reply to Berlin Decrees.*
3 February – *British capture Montevideo.*
3 March – *British abandon attempt on the Dardanelles.*
17 March – *British landing in Egypt.*
28 June – *British landing at Buenos Ayres.*
5 July – *Whitelocke surrenders at Buenos Ayres.*
16 August – *British landing in Denmark.*
29 August – *Wellesley defeats Danish army at Kjöge.*
7 September – *Danish capitulation following bombardment of Copenhagen.*
19 September – *British expedition to Egypt withdrawn.*
30 November – *French occupation of Lisbon.*
17 December – *Milan Decree against Britain confirms the 'Continental System'.*

## 1808

**1 August** – *British expedition disembarks in Portugal.*

**17 August** – *Wellesley defeats Delaborde at Roliça.*

**21 August** – *Wellesley defeats Junot at Vimeiro.*

**30 August** – *Convention of Cintra; British commanders recalled to face court of enquiry.*

**4 December** – *Napoleon enters Madrid as Moore retreats to Corunna.*

## 1809

**16 January** – *Moore defeats Soult at Corunna.*

**17 January** – *Evacuation of Moore's army from Corunna.*

**24 March** – *British capture Martinique.*

**11/12 April** – *Cochrane attacks French fleet in Basque Roads.*

**22 April** – *Wellesley arrives to command British forces in Portugal.*

**12 May** – *Wellesley forces the passage of the Douro at Oporto.*

**6 July** – *Wellesley appointed Marshal-General of Portugal.*

**27/28 July** – *Wellesley wins victory at Talavera.*

**30 July** – *British landing at Walcheren.*

**4 September** – *Wellesley becomes Viscount Wellington of Talavera and Wellington.*

**20 October** – *Wellington instigates building of the Lines of Torres Vedras.*

**9 December** – *British evacuate Walcheren.*

## 1810

**4 February** – *British capture Guadeloupe.*

**17 February** – *British capture Amboyna.*

**23/28 August** – *British naval defeat at Ile de France.*

**27 September** – *Wellington defeats Massena at Busaco.*

**10 October** – *Massena halted by Lines of Torres Vedras.*

**2 December** – *British capture Ile de France.*

## 1811

**4 March** – *Graham's victory at Barrosa.*

**13 March** – *Hoste defeats Franco-Italian naval force off Lissa.*

**3 April** – *French evacuate Portugal.*

**3/5 May** – *Wellington defeats Massena at Fuentes de Oñoro.*

**16 May** – *Beresford defeats Soult at Albuera.*

**18 September** – *British capture Java.*

## 1812

**19 January** – *Wellington captures Ciudad Rodrigo.*

**6 April** – *Wellington captures Badajoz.*

**11 May** – *Prime Minister Spencer Perceval assassinated.*

**19 June** – *USA declares war on Britain.*

**22 July** – *Wellington defeats Marmont at Salamanca.*

**12 August** – *Wellington enters Madrid.*

**16 August** – *British capture Detroit.*

**18 August** – *Wellington elevated in the peerage to Marquess.*

**17 September** – *Wellington besieges Burgos.*

**13 October** – *American invasion of Canada defeated at Queenston.*

**19 November** – *Wellington returns to Portugal.*

## 1813

**4 March** – *Wellington appointed a Knight of the Garter.*

**24 April** – *Americans burn York (now Toronto).*

**23 May** – *Wellington advances into Spain.*

**28/29 May** – *British defeated by Americans at Sackets Harbor.*

**1 June** – *HMS Shannon captures USS Chesapeake.*

**21 June** – *Wellington defeats Joseph Bonaparte at Vittoria.*

**26 July/1 August** – *Wellington defeats Soult at the Pyrenees.*

**31 August** – *Wellington captures San Sebastian.*

**10 September** – *British squadron defeated by Americans on Lake Erie.*

**5 October** – *British defeated by Americans at Battle of the Thames.*

**7 October** – *Wellington forces the passage of the Bidassoa; France invaded.*

**25 October** – *British defeat Americans at Battle of the Chateaugay.*

**10 November** – *Wellington defeats Soult on the Nivelle.*

**11 November** – *British defeat Americans at Chrysler's Farm.*

**10/13 December** – *Wellington defeats Soult on the Nive.*

## 1814

**27 February** – *Wellington defeats Soult at Orthez.*

**12 March** – *Wellington enters Bordeaux.*

**10 April** – *Wellington defeats Soult at Toulouse, four days after Napoleon's abdication.*

**11 May** – *Wellington elevated in the peerage to Duke.*

**5 July** – *British defeated by Americans at Chippewa.*

**25 July** – *British defeat Americans at Lundy's Lane.*

**24 August** – *British defeat Americans at Bladensburg.*

**24/25 August** – *British burn Washington.*

**11 September** – *British advance defeated at Plattsburg and on Lake Champlain.*

**12/14 September** – *Abortive British attack on Baltimore.*

**13 December** – *British expedition arrives at New Orleans.*

**24 December** – *Treaty of Ghent brings peace between Britain and USA.*

## 1815

**8 January** – *British attack on New Orleans defeated.*

**1 March** – *Napoleon returns to France.*

**15 June** – *Napoleon invades the Netherlands.*

**16 June** – *Wellington defeats Ney at Quatre Bras; Napoleon defeats Blücher at Ligny.*

**17 June** – *Wellington withdraws to Mont St Jean.*

**18 June** – *Wellington and Blücher defeat Napoleon at Waterloo.*

**22 June** – *Napoleon abdicates.*

**7 July** – *Wellington and Blücher enter Paris.*

**22 October** – *Wellington appointed Commander-in-Chief of all Allied Armies of Occupation in France.*

*Waterloo, 18 June 1815. Denis Dighton's painting shows French cavalry making one of their many attacks upon Wellington's position, the British infantry having formed square. In the foreground, French cuirassiers approach the British infantry, who wear the oilskin shako-cover commonly used on active service. The front rank are in the position 'prepare to receive cavalry': on one knee, with fixed bayonets presented at horse's-breast height. At the left is a fieldpiece of the Royal Foot Artillery, with members of its crew dead and wounded around it (the remainder would be sheltering by the square); in midground can be seen the French Grenadiers à Cheval of the Imperial Guard, and Hougoumont burns in the background.*

# Glossary

The following includes a number of colloquialisms which may be encountered in contemporary sources but which are not immediately intelligible; the glossary concentrates on those terms used in British service, though the language of fortification made extensive use of foreign terms, principally French.

**Abatis:** barricade of felled trees.

**Aide-de-Camp:** junior staff officer attached to a general.

**Ammuzette:** large-bore firearm or 'wall piece'.

**Armed Association:** local volunteer corps raised for the protection of its own locality.

**Ball (as in 'ball ammunition'):** musket-ball *or* cartridge.

**Banquette:** firing-step behind a parapet.

**Barbette:** a cannon was 'en barbette' when able to fire over a parapet without using an embrasure.

**Bastion:** (1) a four-sided fortification; (2) a design of uniform-lace, following the same shape.

**Batardeau:** dam to retain water in a fortress-ditch.

**Battalion company:** 'centre' company of an infantry battalion.

**Battery:** gun-emplacement; later came to refer to an artillery unit of 6 guns.

**Bengal lights:** carcass composed of saltpetre, sulphur and red orpiment.

**Blacking ball:** blackening-agent for equipment.

**Bomb:** mortar-shell; loosely applied to all explosive projectiles.

**Bombardier:** junior NCO, Royal Artillery.

**Breastplate:** small metal badge worn on a shoulder-belt.

**Breastwork:** protective parapet or barricade.

**Bricole:** (1) rope or strap used for manhandling a cannon; (2) a cannon fired 'en bricole' when the shot struck a sloping revetment.

**Brigade:** (1) tactical formation of two or more battalions; (2) artillery company.

**Brown Bess:** affectionate name for British military musket; 'to hug Brown Bess': to serve as a soldier.

**Brown George:** an 'ammunition' loaf, or military issue of bread.

**Caçadore:** Portuguese light infantry (lit 'hunter').

**Canister:** artillery ammunition comprising lead balls in a tin.

**Cap:** general term for military head-dress.

**Caponnière:** covered communication-trench from an enceinte to a detached work, or a casemated fortification projecting across a ditch for delivering flanking-fire.

**Capsquare:** metal plate securing the trunnions of a cannon to the carriage.

**Captain-lieutenant:** officer commanding the company nominally led by the battalion colonel.

**Carbine:** short cavalry musket.

**Carcass (or carcase):** incendiary or illumination-shell.

**Carronade:** large-calibre, short-range cannon.

**Cascabel:** knob at sealed end of a cannon-barrel.

**Casement:** chamber in a fortress-wall.

**Case-shot:** canister.

**Cavalier:** raised battery, usually inside a bastion.

**Centre company:** 'battalion company'.

**Chemin des Rondes:** sentry-walk around the top of a revetment.

**Cheval-de-frise:** barricade made of stake- or blade-studded beams.

**Chinese light:** illumination-flare composed of nitre, sulphur, antimony and orpiment.

**Chock:** quoin.

**Chosen man:** lance-corporal.

**Citadel:** four- or five-sided strongpoint.

**Clash pans:** cymbals.

**Clinometer:** instrument for measuring the incline upon which a cannon stood.

**Club:** hair-dressing used by grenadiers, a queue doubled-back upon itself.

**Coehorn (or Coehoorn):** small mortar.

**Colour-sergeant:** senior NCO, rank instituted 1813.

**Commissary:** supply-officer.

**Company-sergeant:** Colour-sergeant, Royal Artillery.

**Comrade:** one of a pair of light infantrymen.

**Cornet:** cavalry second-lieutenant.

**Corps:** (1) a tactical unit of two or more divisions; (2) generic term for *any* military unit.

**Counterscarp:** slope or retaining-wall on outer side of ditch.

**Countersign:** password.

**Covered way:** fire-step along a ditch.

**Crapaud:** British nickname for Frenchmen.

**Croppy:** Irish rebel; 'croppyism', support for United Irishmen.

**Death or Glory men:** nickname for Brunswick Oels corps (from their badge).

**Desaguiler:** light fieldpiece named after its designer.

**Dispart:** half the difference between the diameter of a gun-barrel at the base-ring and the swell of the muzzle; generally 1/56 of the length.

**Division:** tactical formation of two or more brigades.

**Dolphin:** lifting-handle on a cannon-barrel.

**Draft:** system of breaking-up a unit to transfer personnel to other corps.

**Dumpling:** short-barrelled pistol.

**Embrasure:** opening in a parapet to allow gunfire through the wall.

**Enceinte:** fortress-wall or perimeter.

**Enfilade:** fire from a flank.

**En flûte:** a ship-of-the-line with most guns removed.

**Ensign:** infantry second-lieutenant.

**Enthusiastics:** nickname for 4th Division, Peninsular War.

**Envelope:** continuous enceinte.

**Evolution:** drill-movement.

**Expense magazine:** small magazine placed near a battery.

**Family:** general's staff.

**Fascine:** bundle of brushwood used in fortification.

**Fausse-braye:** low outer rampart.

**Felloe (or felly):** curved segment of a wheel.

**Fencible:** home-defence unit similar to regular army.

**Fighting Division:** nickname for 3rd Division, Peninsular War.

**Fire Ball:** illumination-flare comprising rosin, sulphur, alum powder, starch, saltpetre, mealed powder and linseed oil.

**Firelock:** musket.

**Fireworker:** artillery technician.

**Fixed ammunition:** artillery projectile with propellant and wooden 'sabot' attached.

**Flank company:** grenadiers and light infantry of a line battalion.

**Fly:** rapidly-moving infantry waggon.

**Forlorn hope:** first storming-party into a breach.

**Fugelman:** soldier during drill from whom the remainder took their time.

**Gabion:** earth-filled wicker basket used in fortification.

**Gallery:** mine-tunnel.

**Galloper:** light, shafted fieldpiece without a limber.

**Garland:** wooden framework holding roundshot.

**Gentleman's Sons:** nickname for 1st Division, Peninsular War.

**Glacis:** slope descending from a fortification.

**Gorget:** decorative crescent-shape plaque worn by officers around the neck.

**Grand Rounds:** main nightly inspection of sentries.

**Grapeshot:** artillery ammunition of a number of medium-sized iron balls.

**Grog:** mixture of rum and water.

**Guerite:** sentry-box, originally one sited on ramparts.

**Gun-metal:** 'brass' of cannon, generally 8 or 10 parts tin to 100 parts copper.

**Half-brigade:** half an artillery company.

**Half-pay:** pay accorded an officer who held a commission but had no employment.

**Handspike:** lever used to manoeuvre a cannon.

**Housings:** horse furniture.

**Howitzer:** short-barrelled cannon designed for high-angle fire.

**Instrument (or Desagulier's Instrument):** device for discovering internal cracks in cannon-barrel.

**Jaggers:** nickname of 5/60th (anglicization of German *Jägers* = riflemen).

**Jingling Johnny:** musical instrument of bells on a pole.

**Johnny Newcombe:** a newly-enlisted soldier or one unused to campaigning.

**Knapsack:** infantry pack.

**Laboratory:** room or tent where powder was made into cartridges.

**Langridge:** coarse grapeshot.

**Light Ball:** illumination-flare.

**Light Bobs:** nickname for light infantry.

**Limber:** two-wheeled carriage connecting cannon with gun-team.

**Linstock:** pike holding slow-match.

**Lobster:** colloquialism for a soldier (from the red coat).

**Local Militia:** part-time 'home guard' formed 1808.

**Lunette:** triangular fortification on or beyond a glacis.

**Magazine:** (1) storage-place for ammunition; (2) extra cartridge-box.

**Marching Division:** nickname for 6th Division, Peninsular War.

**Match:** impregnated burning-cord for igniting cannon.

**Marquis:** large tent, now 'marquee'.

**Militia:** home-defence force raised partly by ballot.

**Mongrels:** nickname for 7th Division, Peninsular War.

**Mosquito trousers:** breeches and gaiters in one

piece.

**Mother Shipton:** tall 'round hat' named after Yorkshire witch.

**Music:** regimental band.

**Musketoon:** light musket.

**Nature:** weight or classification of an artillery piece.

**Necessaries:** personal kit.

**Observing Division:** nickname for 2nd Division, Peninsular War.

**Old Trousers:** British nickname for French drum-call '*Pas de charge*'; thus 'here comes Old Trousers' = 'the French are charging'.

**Ordenanca:** Portuguese militia.

**Outpost:** outlying picquet; scouting-work in general.

**Parallel:** siege-trench running parallel to enemy fortification.

**Park:** artillery reserve.

**Parole:** (1) system of releasing prisoners-of-war from confinement on their promising not to escape; (2) password.

**Pelisse:** (1) furred hussar jacket; (2) officer's braided frock-coat.

**Petard:** explosive device for blowing-in a gate.

**Picker:** wire needle for clearing musket touch-hole.

**Piece:** any cannon (orig 'fieldpiece').

**Pioneer:** regimental artificer or carpenter.

**Pioneers:** nickname for 5th Division, Peninsular War.

**Picquet:** infantry outpost or sentinel.

**Portfire:** holder for match.

**Post:** outpost, sentinel.

**Prepared ammunition:** ball and propellant in a cartridge.

**Present:** to 'present fire' = to aim.

**Prog:** colloquialism for food.

**Prolonge:** rope attaching cannon to team to obviate unlimbering.

**Provisional Cavalry:** similar to Fencible Cavalry.

**Provisional corps:** composite units formed from detachments.

**Queue:** (1) pigtail-hairstyle; (2) tobacco plug shaped like a pigtail.

**Quick-match:** quick-burning match.

**Quoin:** wooden block used for elevating a cannon-barrel.

**Rampart:** earth or masonry wall forming main defence of fortress.

**Ravelin:** triangular detached fortification in front of a fortress-wall.

**Recruiting regiment:** one formed to be split up immediately and the men drafted to other regiments.

**Redan:** V-shaped fortification.

**Redoubt:** detached fortification, or a redan in a bastion.

**Reinforces:** reinforcing-bands on a cannon-barrel.

**Revetment:** retaining-wall of a fortification.

**Round hat:** short 'topper' with wide or upturned brim.

**Running ball:** musket-charge without wadding.

**Sabot:** wooden shoe on 'fixed ammunition'.

**Sap faggot:** fascine eight inches thick, three feet long.

**Sap roller (or 'gabion farci'):** gabion rolled in front of a sapper to shield him from enemy fire.

**Sea Fencibles:** naval home-defence volunteers based in sea-ports.

**Sentinel:** sentry.

**Serpent:** woodwind musical instrument.

**Shell:** (1) explosive artillery projectile; (2) sleeveless jacket.

**Skilly:** thin, watery soup.

**Slow-match:** slow-burning match.

**Spadroon:** straight-bladed, light sword.

**Spatterdash:** long gaiters.

**Spherical case:** shrapnel shell.

**Spontoon:** half-pike.

**Stirabout:** stew or stock-pot.

**Stock:** leather strip worn around the neck.

**Storm-poles:** palisade planted on a scarp, projecting horizontally or slightly downwards.

**Subdivision:** one artillery-piece, crew and waggon.

**Substitute:** militiaman paid to serve in place of one selected by ballot.

**Suffocating pot:** sulphur/nitre composition, when ignited causing distress to the enemy, or used for fumigation.

**Sugar-loaf:** any tall, cylindrical head-dress.

**Supporting Division:** nickname for 4th Division, Peninsular War.

**Sweeps:** (1) nickname for 95th Rifles (from dark uniform); (2) (nautical): oars.

**Tarleton:** fur-crested light dragoon helmet, named after General Banastre Tarleton.

**Terreplein:** wide upper part of a rampart.

**Time-beater:** percussion-musician.

**Tin helmet:** lightweight cavalry helmet for tropical use.

**Toise:** old French unit of measurement, used for measuring fortifications; = 6.395 English feet.

**Tow Rows:** nickname for grenadiers (from the chorus of the march *British Grenadiers*).

**Triangle:** framework of spontoons to which a prisoner was tied before flogging.

**Truck:** small, solid wheels for artillery carriage.

**Trunnions:** projecting-lugs on a cannon-barrel, fitting onto the carriage.

**Turban:** cloth strip around a helmet.

**Valenciennes composition:** incendiary mixture of saltpetre, sulphur, antimony and Swedish pitch.

**Vedette:** cavalry scout.

**Volunteers:** (1) part-time 'home guard'; (2) aspirant officers serving in the ranks until a commission became vacant.

**Wadmiltilt:** waterproof tarpaulin made of wool, retaining the natural oils of the sheep.

**Wall-piece:** large-calibre musket mounted on a fortress-wall.

**Waterdeck:** waterproof, painted canvas saddle-cover.

**Water fascine:** fascine weighted with stone to make it sink into marshy ground.

**Watering cap:** cylindrical shako worn by cavalry in undress uniform, orig when watering horses.

**Watchcoat:** greatcoat.

**White light:** see 'Chinese light'.

**Wing:** (1) half an infantry battalion (or more loosely any element of a battalion); (2) shell-like epaulette worn by flank companies.

**Whiskers:** facial hair, moustaches, etc; also used as colloquialism for grenadiers, who at times wore moustaches.

**Wolf-pit:** cone-shaped pit used as anti-personnel trap; also *trou de loup*.

**Worm:** corkscrew-device for extracting an unfired charge from a gun-barrel.

**Yeomanry:** volunteer cavalry.

**Zigzag:** approach-trench in siege warfare.

---

## Territorial designations of British Regiments of Foot, of the 104 existing in 1815

| | |
|---|---|
| 1st | (Royal) Regt (1812, Royal Scots) |
| 2nd | (Queen's Royal) |
| 3rd | (East Kent) (Buffs) |
| 4th | (King's Own) (Lancaster) |
| 5th | (Northumberland) |
| 6th | (1st Warwickshire) |
| 7th | (Royal Fuzileers) |
| 8th | (King's) |
| 9th | (East Norfolk) |
| 10th | (North Lincoln) |
| 11th | (North Devon) |
| 12th | (East Suffolk) |
| 13th | (1st Somersetshire) |
| 14th | (Bedfordshire) (1809, Buckinghamshire) |
| 15th | (York East Riding) |
| 16th | (Buckinghamshire) (1809, Bedfordshire) |
| 17th | (Leicestershire) |
| 18th | (Royal Irish) |
| 19th | (1st Yorkshire North Riding) |
| 20th | (East Devonshire) |
| 21st | (Royal North British Fuzileers) |
| 22nd | (Cheshire) |
| 23rd | (Royal Welch Fuzileers) |
| 24th | (2nd Warwickshire) |
| 25th | (Sussex; 1805, King's Own Borderers) |
| 26th | (Cameronians) |
| 27th | (Enniskillen) |
| 28th | (North Gloucestershire) |
| 29th | (Worcestershire) |
| 30th | (Cambridgeshire) |
| 31st | (Huntingdonshire) |
| 32nd | (Cornwall) |
| 33rd | (1st Yorkshire West Riding) |
| 34th | (Cumberland) |
| 35th | (Dorsetshire) (1805, Sussex) |
| 36th | (Herefordshire) |
| 37th | (North Hampshire) |
| 38th | (1st Staffordshire) |
| 39th | (East Middlesex) (1807, Dorsetshire) |
| 40th | (2nd Somersetshire) |
| 41st | |
| 42nd | (Royal Highland) |
| 43rd | (Monmouthshire) (1803, Monmouthshire Light Infantry) |
| 44th | (East Essex) |
| 45th | (Nottinghamshire) |
| 46th | (South Devonshire) |
| 47th | (Lancashire) |
| 48th | (Northamptonshire) |
| 49th | (Hertfordshire) |
| 50th | (West Kent) |
| 51st | (2nd Yorkshire West Riding) |

(1809, 2nd Yorkshire West Riding Light Infantry)
52nd (Oxfordshire) (1809, Oxfordshire Light Infantry)
53rd (Shropshire)
54th (West Norfolk)
55th (Westmoreland)
56th (West Essex)
57th (West Middlesex)
58th (Rutlandshire)
59th (2nd Nottinghamshire)
60th (Royal American)
61st (South Gloucestershire)
62nd (Wiltshire)
63rd (West Suffolk)
64th (2nd Staffordshire)
65th (2nd Yorkshire North Riding)
66th (Berkshire)
67th (South Hampshire)
68th (Durham) (1808, Durham Light Infantry)
69th (South Lincolnshire)
70th (Surrey) (1812, Glasgow Lowland)

71st (Highland), (1808, Glasgow Highland; 1809 Glasgow Highland Light Infantry; 1810, Highland Light Infantry)
72nd (Highland)
73rd (Highland pre-1809)
74th (Highland)
75th (Highland pre-1809)
76th (1807-12 'Hindoostan Regt')
77th (East Middlesex)
78th (Highland) (Ross-shire Buffs)
79th (Cameronian Volunteers) (1804, Cameron Highlanders)
80th (Staffordshire Volunteers)
81st (1793-4 Loyal Lincoln Volunteers)
82nd (Prince of Wales' Volunteers)
83rd
84th (1809, York and Lancaster)
85th (Bucks Volunteers) (1808, Bucks Volunteers Light Infantry)
86th (1809, Leinster; 1812, Royal County Down)
87th (Prince of Wales' Irish; 1811,

Prince of Wales' Own Irish)
88th (Connaught Rangers)
89th
90th (Perthshire Volunteers)
91st (Argyllshire Highlanders pre-1809)
92nd (Highland)
93rd (Highland)
94th (Scotch Brigade)
95th (Rifles)
96th
97th (Queen's Own Germans)
98th
99th (1811, Prince of Wales' Tipperary)
100th (1812, Prince Regent's County of Dublin)
101st (Duke of York's Irish)
102nd (New South Wales Corps taken into line 1808)
103rd (ex-9th Garrison Bn)
104th (New Brunswick Fencibles taken into line 1810)

# *Index*

# Bibliography

The literature on Wellington and his army is vast. The titles below are a selection of the most valuable or most accessible, primarily concerning various aspects of the British Army. The number of personal memoirs and autobiographies is vast and invaluable for any study of the period; though none are specified here for reasons of space, an important listing may be found as an appendix to Oman's *Wellington's Army*.

Adye, R.W., **The Bombardier and Pocket Gunner**, London 1802.

Chandler, D.G., **Campaigns of Napoleon**, London 1967.

Chandler, D.G., **Dictionary of the Napoleonic Wars**, London 1979.

Dundas, Sir D., **Rules & Regulations for the Formations, Field-Exercise and Movements of His Majesty's Forces**, London (new edn.) 1798.

Dupuy, R.E., & Dupuy, T.N., **Encyclopedia of Military History**, London 1974.

Emsley, C., **British Society and the French Wars**, London 1979.

Fortescue, Hon. Sir J., **History of the British Army**, London, from 1899.

Fosten, B., **Wellington's Heavy Cavalry**, London 1982.

Fosten, B., **Wellington's Infantry**, London 1981-82.

Fosten, B., **Wellington's Light Cavalry**, London 1982.

Fraser, Sir W., **Words on Wellington**, London 1889.

Glover, M., **The Peninsular War 1807-14**, Newton Abbot 1974.

Glover, M., **Warfare in the Age of Bonaparte**, London 1980.

Glover, M., **Wellington as Military Commander**, London 1968.

Glover, M., **Wellington's Army in the Peninsula**, Newton Abbot 1977.

Glover, R., **Britain at Bay**, London 1973.

Glover, R., **Peninsular Preparation**, Cambridge 1963.

Griffith, P. (ed.), **Wellington Commander: the Iron Duke's Generalship**, Chichester 1985.

Haythornthwaite, P.J., **British Infantry of the Napoleonic Wars**, London 1987.

Haythornthwaite, P.J., **Uniforms of the Peninsular War**, Poole 1978.

Haythornthwaite, P.J., **Uniforms of Waterloo**, Poole 1975.

Haythornthwaite, P.J., **Weapons and Equipment of the Napoleonic Wars**, Poole 1979.

Haythornthwaite, P.J., **Wellington's Specialist Troops**, London 1988.

Jones, J.T., **Journals of the Sieges undertaken by the Allies in Spain**, London 1814.

Katcher, P.R.N., **The American War 1812-14**, London 1974.

Longford, Elizabeth Countess of, **Wellington: The Years of the Sword**, London 1969.

Longford, Elizabeth Countess of, **Wellington: Pillar of State**, London 1972.

Napier, W.F.P., **History of the War in the Peninsula**, London 1832-36.

Oman, Sir C.W.C., **History of the Peninsular War**, Oxford 1902-30.

Oman, Sir C.W.C., **Wellington's Army**, London 1912.

Pivka, O. von, **Navies of the Napoleonic Wars**, Newton Abbot 1980.

Pope, D., **Life in Nelson's Navy**, London 1981.

Rogers, H.C.B., **Wellington's Army**, London 1979.

Rothenberg, G.E., **The Art of War in the Age of Napoleon**, London 1977.

Sutcliffe, S., **Martello Towers**, Newton Abbot 1972.

Verner, W., **History and Campaigns of the Rifle Brigade 1809-13**, London 1919.

Ward, S.G.P., **Wellington**, London 1963.

Weller, J., **Wellington at Waterloo**, London 1967.

Weller, J., **Wellington in India**, London 1972.

Weller, J., **Wellington in the Peninsula**, London 1962.

Wellington, Duke of, **Dispatches of Field-Marshal the Duke of Wellington** (ed. J. Gurwood), London 1834-39.

Wellington, Duke of, **Supplementary Despatches** (ed. 2nd Duke of Wellington), London 1858-72.

Periodicals: Much information may be found in the publications of various societies, most notably the **Journal of the Society for Army Historical Research** (London). The magazine **Empires, Eagles and Lions** (Cambridge, Ontario) is an important contemporary source of research into the tactics of the Napoleonic Wars.

Unless indicated below illustrations were supplied by the author:
**Apsley Museum**: p7, 125(b), 128. **A Harrison**: p20(t), 133. **MARS**: p11, 57, 62, 73, 79(t), 103, 131, 139, 142, 147, 155, 157, 161, 165, 186. **Mary Evans Picture Library**: p175. **National Army Museum**: p13, 25, 48, 50, 52, 68, 71, 88, 97, 105, 110, 113, 115, 122, 129, 134. **National Maritime Museum**: p163, 167, 169(b), 171, 172, 177, 181. **Royal Naval Museum**: p159.